MANAGEMENT DYNAMISM IN STATE-OWNED ENTERPRISES IN ASIA

MANAGEMENT DYNAMISM IN STATE-OWNED ENTERPRISES IN ASIA

Asian Productivity Organization
Tokyo, 1989

ISBN: 92-833-2068-9
© Asian Productivity Organization, 1989

FOREWORD

Universally, there is an increasing concern over the performance of State-Owned Enterprises (SOEs). Some of the major problems of SOEs lie in their rigidity, managerial limitation, inadequate autonomy, over staffing, erosion of commitment, inadequate competition, pricing and the like. In the present context of rapid technological changes, shifts in management concepts and pressures from an external environment, efficient performance and significant productivity growth are all the more vital in the management of SOEs.

The key factor determining the efficiency of an enterprise is not whether it is publicly or privately owned, but how it is managed. Most of the earlier studies on SOEs have focussed on macro-level issues. To explore the dynamic process of management improvement of SOEs at the enterprise level, and to identify ways and means of bring about changes, the Asian Productivity Organization (APO) launched a two-year survey in 1987 under the title of "Management of State-Owned Enterprises." This survey was conducted in nine member countries during 1987 and 1988, with an in-between coordination meeting of the researchers in Bangkok, Thailand in collaboration with the Thailand Management Development and Productivity Centre. While the survey took advantage of the findings from past studies, it attempted to avoid merely reidentifying well known problems of SOEs. Instead, its aim was to suggest "how to improve management of SOEs, their efficiency and productivity, given the hard reality," with a futuristic perspective on the dynamics of change.

Following the survey, a five-day symposium was organized in Colombo, Sri Lanka in October 1988, in collaboration with the Asian Development Bank as well as the National Institute of Business Management, Sri Lanka. The symposium provided an opportunity to share experiences gained and findings made during the survey among participants and observers from within and outside the region as well as to suggest to the member countries possible ways and means to improve management systems and practices in general and human resource development programmes to be followed by the APO in particular.

The present publication includes the integrated survey report of the Chief Expert, Dr. Vudhichai Chamnong and selected national suvey reports along with the report of the symposium.

The APO takes this opportunity to express its deep appreciation to all the national experts, Chief Expert, Dr. Vudhichai Chamnong, and resource persons for the symposium as well as other concerned people for making this publication possible, and hopes that the publication will stimulate further actions in all member countries.

NAGAO YOSHIDA
Secretary-General
October, 1989   Asian Productivity Organization

TABLE OF CONTENTS

APPENDICES

Part I.

Integrated Summary of the Survey

INTEGRATED SUMMARY OF THE SURVEY

by   Dr. Vudhichai Chamnong
Professor of Organizational Behaviour
School of Business Administration
National Institute of
Development Administration (NIDA)
Bangkok

State-Owned Enterprises (SOEs) in Asian countries have long contributed significantly to the nation's economic activities both in national products and employment terms. Studies and literature on SOEs, however, usually reflected the low productivity, inefficiency and mismanagement of the entities. The familiar reasons for those criticism fell into certain categories like the high degree of bureaucratization, political interferences and over-control by various controlling agencies. Unfortunately, the recommendations to cope with such problems have mostly been unrealistic. And, inefficiencies as well as mismanagement of SOEs still prevail in many cases.

The Survey on Management of State-Owned Enterprises in nine Asian countries under the auspices of the Asian Productivity Organization during 1988 — 1989 has revealed many favourable incidents of the SOEs. A few SOEs in each of nine countries were selected for the survey based on, intentionally or unintentionally, successfulness and/or better performance. In all favourable cases, the outcomes came from more appropriate government policies, adapted strategies as well as better management functions of the SOEs themselves. In other words, we have learned that the improvement and/or efficiency of any SOEs ought to be viewed in a total picture. Every bit of SOEs' contexts has to be treated in congruence with the others in order for it to yield the ultimate result. There may be problems in the process of improvement as we will see in the text; their solutions have to be strategically appropriate as well.

In order to understand the total picture of any SOE, at least three contexts, i.e., environmental, organizational and functional, must be considered. Although SOEs in Asian countries may be somewhat different in relation to types, sizes, culture, levels of development, etc., their contexts could reveal to certain extent the Asian experiences.

1. SOEs' Environmental Contexts

SOEs in their environmental contexts, may have to play different roles which in turn are dependent upon the demand characteristics of such contexts. The roles and/or functions of particular SOEs are therefore affected directly by those environmental contexts such as the establishment of the SOE, its controlling agencies and the public expectation.

1.1 Establishment

The reasons behind as well as the main objectives of the establishment of SOEs usually define the "path" of their operations and, of course, their constraints. In India, for instance, the public sector is being used as a vehicle for promotion of exports and earning foreign exchanges in addition to the production and supply of consumer goods and helping hands for ailing private companies. The government of India therefore totally owns the SOEs under the President's name. Indian SOEs, like SOEs in Sri Lanka, are in almost all sectors of the economy. While Singaporean SOEs are mostly in trading and manufacturing industries, SOEs in Japan concentrate on public utility and no other area such as manufacturing. Initially, Thai SOEs have been used as a tool for expansion and development of the national economy.

The span and objective for the establishment of SOEs in each country would trigger the concentration of their operations. Each SOE's development through history also seems to follow its establishing objectives, unless certain problems take place, then new developmental strategies would be employed.

Although most SOEs have been established by Parliament, quite a few were also promulgated by local governments as well as the ministries concerned. These practices usually lead to the high portion of shares owned by government. While in Thailand the enterprise is determined to be an SOE once the government owns over fifty percent of the shares; other types of SOEs like joint ventures and subcontractors exist in other countries. At any rate, SOEs frequently enjoy their monopolistic operations in the market. It was originally believed that all public utilities ought to be monopolized as services of the government. More and more public utility SOEs, however, are in the process of privatization. It seems also that, to a certain extent, the government establishes SOEs in order for them to perform "official functions business-like." But once they are set up it turns out to be that SOEs are performing "business functions official-like."

Once the SOEs are in full operation based upon the nature of their establishment, most of them become targets of criticism concerning their ineffectiveness, inefficiency and/or even failure. According to Asli, the failure of SOEs has been attributed to four main reasons:

- incompetent management,
- corruption,
- political interference and,
- lack of effective central coordination and monitoring mechanism.

At the micro-level, as in the case of Japan, SOEs faced problems like contradictory direct interest groups, i.e., the government and labour unions, unspecific target market, lack of proper strategies, limited marketing activities, financial plan not based on cost consciousness, lack of research and development, and formidable and strict structure.

These reasons which are considered to be the cause for failure of SOEs help to push the governments, at least in Malaysia and Japan, to look for new strategies to deal with such problems, then, privatization seems to be attractive and appropriate. Although the process of privatization may create certain problems along the line, the results are quite favourable. In fact, SOEs in other countries have tried one way or the other to be privatized, since privatization can take many forms, i.e., complete privatization, partial privatization, rental, subcontracting, franchising, and joint venture. Each of these forms may be selected according to the stage of privatization process and/or internal/external constraints.

Another alternative strategy taken to improve the performance and management of SOEs is that of China. The common problem shared by four SOEs is "insufficient size." They moved to formulate the merger strategy with the purposes to obtain:

- economy of scale,
- synergy,
- management betterment, and
- stability of demand and supply of petro-chemicals.

The operating results are satisfactory since SOEs moved to merge one by one while creating less friction.

1.2 Diversification

Diversification could be regarded as another strategy to enhance efficiency of SOEs as the Keppel Corporation of Singapore has tried. It could be eventually called "A National Company." Other SOEs in

Sri Lanka, India and Nepal, for example, take a straightforward strategy to improve their own management through the modification and/or development of business functions like production, marketing and transfer of technology.

It may not be conclusive, but the trend is that the government of each Asian country has tried to employ various policies and strategies in order for SOEs to be more efficient, and of course lessen the burden of the government itself. Strategic approaches in each country are relatively dependent upon the level of development of SOEs as well as the degree of national economic development.

1.3 Controlling Agencies

Another aspect of SOEs' environmental contexts is those controlling agencies that most of the time become a target of criticism. Controlling agencies are usually blamed for creating unfavourable causes that lead to ineffectiveness, inefficiency, low productivity, or even the failure of SOEs. In certain cases, nevertheless, it is controlling agencies that help rescue the SOE.

Since SOEs are the creatures of the government, owned wholly or partially by the government, there have to be some sorts of control, monitoring and coordination carried out by the so-called controlling agencies. In Sri Lanka, like some other Asian countries, while the Board of SOEs performs day-to-day management functions, the supervisory ministry "steers" SOE's direction. SOEs thus are controlled in terms of setting missions and policies, decision making as well as budgetary approval by supervisory ministries, inter-ministerial agencies like budget bureaus and national economic and social development boards, auditor generals, public accountant commissions, cabinets and eventually parliament. The direct effect on SOEs is that the taller the levels of controlling agencies the slower and the more conflicting the decision making process.

Thai SOEs experienced and suffered from inter agency communication conflicts, evaluation differences and political intervention. It is evident, however, that if the SOE could be managerially and technically effective like the case of the Electricity Generation Authority of Thailand (EGAT), there need less political intervention. This is true even when the board members are appointed by the cabinet, they consist of competent and qualified representatives.

Korea defines causes of SOEs' inefficiency to be government control on the one hand and insufficient systems of evaluation on the other. Evaluation has been based on financial ratio only. According to the new policy, the government set up an Evaluation Board and Evaluation Group to come up with a comprehensive evaluation scheme. In addition, SOEs are provided with autonomy on organizing, adjusting the budget, executing procurement and construction contracts as well as the personnel functions. The new evaluation indices together with the new policy have greatly enhanced SOEs productivity.

In Japan, the Special Committee on Administrative Reform has gone so far as to recommend "privatization." The outcome is more than satisfactory. It is reported that Nippon Telegraph and Telephone Corporation (NTT) today (after privatization in 1985) has the highest stock market valuation of any company in the world. That is almost twice the combined worth of IBM, General Motors, and AT&T (*Fortune*, October 10, 1988).

Controlling agencies, therefore, ought not to be blamed for inefficiency, ineffectiveness, and/or failure. As mentioned earlier, they may be a big booster for ailing SOEs. All in all, it is up to the attitudes of controlling agencies regarding the existence, performance and growth of SOEs. If the controlling agencies play the world police role, most SOEs will begin to decay.

1.4 Public Expectations

Still another aspect of environmental contexts is public expectations that might create a self-fulfilling prophecy. It is not so obvious in the survey of management of SOEs in the nine Asian countries. Nevertheless, the degree to which different SOEs are successful could be partly derived from the attributes of public expectations as well as public recognitions. The monopolistic nature of many SOEs, as the public generally recognizes, could draw back creativity of management and operational alternatives. The public also takes it for granted that quality of SOEs' products and services are somewhat lower than desired. They therefore put less demand on them. This includes recognition and expectation of red-tape and bureaucratic behaviour of SOEs.

If the public is concerned with competitiveness and business-like operation, they can put pressure on and/or support improvements. SOEs in Japan, Singapore, India and Malaysia, for instance, benefit from and enjoy favourable public expectations and of course, they appropriately respond.

2. Organizational Contexts

A second set of SOEs' contexts which is equally significant is organizational contexts. It is the platform where actions, i.e., functional contexts, are going to take place. No matter how favourable environmental contexts are, if the organizational contexts are not conducive, SOEs' performance may never be fruitful.

Organizational contexts could be viewed from at least three different aspects: technological, social relationship and procedural aspects. All of these aspects ought to be in congruence in order to yield optimal organizational performance.

2.1 Technological Aspect

It is currently realized that high productivity and advancement of enterprises depend largely on high technology and qualified human resources. Those SOEs that are far behind in terms of effectiveness, resulting in a loss of efficiency, relied to certain extents on out-dated technology. They might not be able to afford new and high technology; but it is a must in order for them to gradually improve their methods.

In 1979, the government of Singapore announced a "Second Industrial Revolution." By then, according to Sikorski, Singapore's leaders had identified a coming Information Age, and the Telecommunication Authority of Singapore (TELECOMS) was seen to be the key institution in leading the way to this future age. It is the government's intention that TELECOMS should virtually skip the step of copying the advanced countries. Thus TELECOMS was said in 1986 to be the first to use optic fibres for high volume traffic. And, it also was as far ahead as any other country in developing an Integrated Systems Digital Network (ISDN). In fact, Nippon Telegraph and Telephone Corporation of Japan (NTT) is fiercely committed to developing this new generation of telecommunications equipment and service called ISDN, although NTT employees laughingly refer to it as standing for "I still don't know" (*Fortune*, October 10, 1988).

Following are two examples trying to achieve high technology. One, TELECOMS, is still a SOE while the other, NTT, was formerly an SOE but later became privatized. In this regard, SOEs do not have to always be privatized in order to develop their technology. Success is relevant to the strategies and industrial matters and that the government and SOEs themselves will take action.

Most SOEs however, seem to gradually develop software technology while still employing the originally established hardware. The emphasis is essentially based on foreign technology and know-how. Transfer of technology could hardly take place unless SOEs take the collaboration approach. Sri Lanka Tyre Corporation (SLTC) has recently entered into a technical collaboration agreement with B.F. Goodrich of the U.S. to harness advanced technology to produce a tyre up to internationally acceptable standards.

In order to produce small cars appropriate for the local Indian market, Maruti Udyog Limited (MUL) selected Suzuki Motor Company in 1982 to be its collaborator. The choice of Suzuki was influenced by their size, attitude toward production system and technology transfers and the cost effectiveness they had achieved in all their operations. Their production technology also seemed to be the right mix of automation and use of human labour for adoption in India.

The results of the collaboration both in terms of efficiency and transfer of technology have been favourable in SLTC and MUL cases. This approach may be the most essential means to improve SOEs' level of technological development from the base.

The Oil and Natural Gas Commission of India (ONGC) takes another route on its continuous search for excellence. It is claimed, according to Jain, that within a span of 30 years, ONGC has assimilated the world's best petroleum expertise which developed over the last 100 years. It has emerged as a multi disciplinary organization with complete in house expertise and capacity. It is one of the few companies of the world engaged in almost all aspects of oil exploration, drilling and production and is becoming increasingly self-reliant in related advanced and sophisticated technology.

2.2 Social Relationship Aspect

The working place in any organization is always interwoven by certain kinds of social relationships. This could promote or demote cooperation, coordination as well as motivational scheme. Proper relationships will lead to success and growth of the SOEs.

A positive organizational culture, for instance, will induce effective performance since it reflects the way people do things in the organization. Keppel Corporation in Singapore obviously maintains mutually supportive relations. In fact, SOEs in Singapore marked evidence of a network of cooperative relationships among people and institutions. That kind of organizational culture helps to facilitate growth and effectiveness of SOEs to a large extent.

At SLTC, Sri Lanka, there has been a high degree of managers' involvement in the corporate planning process which yields a high level of acceptance at the operational level. In contrast, the bureaucratic organizational culture at Sri Lanka's National Paper Corporation (NPC) and Ceylon Ceramics Corporation (CCC), as well as many other Asian SOEs, have led to low morale and, of course, performance. NTT of Japan has also changed after privatization from a conservative culture to a challenging and aggressive culture.

In relation to management and leadership styles, certain SOEs have been prosperous, mainly because of this aspect of social relationship. Many Thai SOEs suffered during mission and policy implementations because of the lack of top management continuity. It is obvious, in Thailand at least, that any implementation and/or operation depends to a large extent on the style of both the board and the chief executive officer. The EGAT and the Petroleum Authority of Thailand (PAT) have relatively enjoyed continuity of leadership and management styles.

NTT of Japan's management style has made it very successful. Initially, working groups of middle management were set up to survey problems for privatization. Later, four characteristics were identified to reflect management approaches during the privatization process:

- Quality control groups were employed in addition to management innovation.
- Top management has seriously identified with privatization.
- Discovery and utilization of vanguards.
- Utilization of middle management and involvement with external collaboration.

Keppel Corporation in Singapore is said to have a managing director who is "a man of vision." It is also backed up by the cooperative network in Singapore's SOE leadership team. This is somewhat similar to ONGC in India where there is "a strong foundation and illustrious, powerful founder chairman who is a distinguished petroleum geologist."

China Petroleum Development Corporation (CPDC) has solved merger problems with the other three petro-product SOEs via its management system and exchange of management experience. CPDC is also claimed to be the best in management calibre with the youngest group of managers.

2.3 Procedural Structure

In reality, the formal structure of SOEs may not tell the whole story. It is only a guide to see how formal the information flow should be and where the decisions should be made. As a matter of fact, management and leadership styles have much influence on the organization's procedural structure.

At CCC in Sri Lanka, for example, the corporate plan is merely a document to satisfy the requirement. Quite a number of Thai SOEs similarly practices routine management functions in order to satisfy controlling agencies. In such SOEs therefore, one can observe that there is not much flow of communication nor participation.

MUL of India has established a good communication system, which may be called an informal and personal system. They practice open office policy, have regular meetings with printed documents and displays. Also, through the use of proper communication, SLTC of Sri Lanka can obtain efficient and effective information for decision-making.

Participation has also been practiced by many SOEs. After privatization, Japan's SOEs welcomed participation by middle along with top managers. It is observed that people from the bottom to the top ranks gather at one time, not just every two weeks as the former hierarchical chain suggests. ONGC of India also seeks involvement of employees in decision making, whereas only merger problems in China are solved by participative decision making.

Where participation and involvement of lower echelon people with top managers takes place, commitment, cooperation, and eager operation and performance by organizational members at all levels will be high, as is true in many SOEs.

3. Functional Context

The last set of contexts is functional. It reflects, to a large extent, the impact or consequence of the environmental and organizational contexts. Each set of contexts therefore may not be mutually exclusive. It is also recommended to look into individual SOEs in relation to those contexts in order to see the real and total picture of functional management performance.

It might be because of the intentional selection by the nine national experts of better SOEs to be surveyed in this endeavor, that almost all of them are quite favourable and/or successful cases. In order to be able to give any recommendations to the management of SOEs in the future, there ought to be another side of the coin, that is, the survey of failed and/or unsuccessful SOEs which are finding no way out. Some may, of course, learn from those successful cases; but others will have to find new and innovative strategies to deal with their own problems. There should be, after all, some commonalities of strategies.

Functional contexts of SOEs' management can be evaluated in

general business functions like financial performance, marketing, production, and human resource management.

3.1 Financial Performance

Most of the time, the management of SOEs has been evaluated based upon financial return or their profitability only. By so doing, many SOEs are in bad shape. And that is why the Korean government has spent tremendous efforts trying to come up with a variety of evaluation indices for its SOEs. Even so, SOEs selected to be in the current survey are more or less successful cases where most of them are making their financial ratios look good. As in the case of CPDC of China, it is reported that the merger resulted in satisfactory financial performance.

The capital structures of SOEs usually consist of subsidies and guaranteed loans by the government, from both domestic and foreign sources. Some Thai SOEs and Keppel Corporation in Singapore have issued bonds. SOEs in Sri Lanka even received financial back-up from contributions and grants. Whenever the SOEs could make a profit, their retained earning would be another source of the coffers of states.

In that regards, there may be some hidden or latent objectives in establishing SOEs. No matter what the manifest objectives of SOEs spelt out, SOEs in Thailand have to supply parts of their earning to the government. In other words, the Thai government regards and counts on SOEs as additional sources of income. Public utility SOEs are trying to minimize loss, while those SOEs in other areas were dissolved and/or sold out when they made big losses.

Cost saving is another aspect many SOEs have taken a look at. Nepal Electricity Authority (NEA), for example, succeeded in a cost reduction scheme. ONGC of India demonstrates very good cost consciousness. In its main office, there is no luxurious furniture and it goes into "nuts and bolts" for saving.

All in all, most SOEs under this survey have shown financial performance results, more than were strategies formulated for financial management.

3.2 Marketing Management

Most SOEs originally enjoyed their monopolistic operation to the extent that they tended to ignore the significance of the marketing function. Just recently SOEs are more aware of the usefulness of the marketing management concept in order, to improve their performance. It is noticeable that private business' marketing aggressiveness has caused SOEs to pay more attention to the marketing aspect of enterprise.

It is obvious that privatization of SOEs, once successful, will accelerate the degree of emphasis on marketing management. This is because, after all, they have to really do the job business-like. Even if they still are SOEs, competition could play an important role in formulating their marketing strategies. The case of Janakpur Cigarette Factory (JCF) of Nepal is a good example. Not until JCF realized that there were other brands of cigarettes in the market did it begin to differentiate its products, manipulate prices and reach more and specific target customers.

MUL of India even did a market survey to determine its product range. Once they found out a specific model of small car suitable to the locals, they concluded agreements to collaborate with Suzuki Motor Company. Petrochemical Corporation of Singapore Pte., Ltd. (PCS) has claimed that it has been successful in marketing due to the strong marketing function of the government. Still another example is that the marketing concepts tend to be stronger after the merger, as in the case of Chung Tai Chemical Industrial Corporation (CTCC) of China.

3.3 Production Management

Needless to say production management of any SOE is closely related to the technological aspect of organizational context. This can be observed in the cases of TELECOMS of Singapore, ONGC of India and NTT of Japan, for instance.

Through a merger that creates economies of scale, the result in production management terms is the reduction of:
- management expenses,
- maintenance costs,
- material costs,
- waste in utilization of vehicles and facilities.

It is also concluded that as the result of the merger, production efficiency has been enhanced and research and development rendered possible. Unfortunately, there is no trace of production processes illustrated in the survey of SOEs in the nine Asian countries.

3.4 Human Resource Management

While it has long been excused by many SOEs that the environmental contexts, particularly the controlling agencies, have much influence on personnel and human resource management, the current survey reveals that organizational contexts and SOEs' improvement strategies have played a great role in human resource management. Essentially, practical human resource management depends to a large extent upon SOEs' management and leadership styles. All the SOEs in the nine Asian countries reported good human resource management as responsible for their successful and improved operation. Some highlights of them are as follows:

In the privatization processes of STM of Malaysia and NTT of Japan, for example, there must be certain conflicts among those who are "for" and "against" privatization. SOEs tried their best to have a lot of meetings in order to "unify" opinions and thinking. Once the channel of communication was opened, the difficulties tended to be much easier. In the process, they also made a very small reshuffle so that they would not stir up dissatisfaction. Also, certain modifications of allocation of human resource were carried out, such as changing positions on an ability based not on length of service but moving the most able men to districts. They also moved to unite several labour unions into one, so that they could easily deal with authoritative representatives at one time. It has been observed that the attitudes of employees changed as a result of cooperation with management. Thus NTT of Japan could claim that they changed human resource management from "subtractionism" to "additionism."

Keppel Corporation and FELS of Singapore enjoyed very good industrial relations. They maintained very close cooperation between employees and management. While FELS emphasized staff development, Keppel has gone so far as having annual wage pact negotiations. TELECOMS of Singapore is called "a good employer." In 1985, TELECOMS got the Plaque of Commendation from the National Trade Union Congress (NTUC) for industrial health, safety, good union-management relations, staff welfare and training.

CPDC of China, after the merger, realized certain benefits in relation to human resource management such as:

- centralized recruiting which saves much time and energy,
- better economy of scale in both in house and outside training,
- welfare activities, which can reach more people,
- transfer of idle personnel, and
- absorption of acquired personnel in solving merger problems.

Also, ONGC and MUL of India have taken very appropriate human resource strategies to improve their productivity and efficiency.

Examples are:
- entrepreneurial development,
- selection of best personnel as main resource,
- limited but competent work-force,
- human resource as key element,
- realization that motivation, skill and efficiency determine productivity,
- conveying a sense of equality, and
- establishing credibility of management.

4. Conclusion

The management of SOEs could be understood better through the scrutinization of their contexts, i.e., environmental, organizational and functional contexts. In addition, the strategies implemented by certain SOEs to improve their performance like privatization, merger, and diversification could also determine their efficiency and productivity. As for the successful SOEs, they seem to have similar contexts, although they may take different strategies. All in all, technological development, human resource utilization and development, and management and leadership styles are among the most significant determinants of SOEs' excellence. Efforts should therefore be put more into these aspects of contexts for many yet to be successful SOEs.

Annex

State-Owned Enterprises Surveyed

Asli, Musalmiah. *Survey on Management of State-Owned Enterprises in Malaysia*
- Klang Container Terminal Ltd. (KCT)
- Telecommunication Company Ltd. (STM)

Chandrasiri, K.S. *Survey on Management of State-Owned Enterprises: Sri Lankan Experience*
- Sri Lanka Tyre Corporation (SLTC)
- National Paper Corporation (NPC)
- Ceylon Ceramics Corporation (CCC)

Jain, S.B. *Factors of Excellence in State-Owned Enterprises, Indian Experience*
- Oil and Natural Gas Commission (ONGC)
- Maruti Udyog Limited (MUL)

Kanda, Makoto. *Survey on Management of State-Owned Enterprises in Japan: Privatization and Its Implications*
- Nippon Telegraph and Telephone (NTT)
- Nippon Tobacco Industry Corporation (NTI)
- Japan Railways Corporation (JR)

Lim, Jong Soo. *New Policy and Performance of Korean SOEs.*
- The Korea Telecommunications Authority (KTA)

Public Enterprise Institute, Chulalongkorn University. *Survey on Management of State-Owned Enterprises in Thailand*
- Metropolitan Electricity Authority (MEA)
- Telephone Organization of Thailand (TOT)

Seetoo, Dah Hsian. *The Strategy and Implementation of China Petrochemical Development Corporation's Merger: A Case Study*
- China Petrochemical Development Corporation (CPDC)
- Chung Tai Chemical Industrial Corporation (CTCC)
- China Phosphate Industrial Corporation (CPIC)
- Taiwan Alkali Corporation (TAC)

Sikorski, Douglas. *State-Owned Enterprises in Singapore*
- Keppel Corporation, A national Company
- Far East Levingston Shipbuilding (FELS)
- Promet Private Limited, A private Company
- Petrochemical Corporation of Singapore Pte., Ltd. (PCS)
- Singapore Aircraft Industries Pte., Ltd. (SAI)
- Telecommunication Authority of Singapore (TELECOMS)

Thapa, Deepek B. *The Agricultural Tools Factory Ltd. (ATF):* An Example of Result Process of Management and Technology Innovation

Thapa, Deepek B. *New Issues in Marketing Management: Janakpur Cigarette Factory (JCF) Losing Monopoly*

Thapa, Deepek B. *Tariff Policy: Nepal Electricity Authority (NEA)*

Part II.

The National Case Studies

CASE STUDIES: REPUBLIC OF CHINA

by   Dr. Dah-Hsian Seetoo
Dean & Professor
Graduate School of Business Administration
National Chengchi University

This study is about the merger among four state-owned enterprises in the Republic of China. The series of mergers took place in 1982 and 1983. The companies involved included:
- China Petrochemical Development Corporation (CPDC)
- Chung Tai Chemical Industrial Corporation (CTCC)
- China Phosphate Industrial Corporation (CPIC)
- Taiwan Alkali Corporation (TAC)

Before the merger, almost all of these companies shared the problem of insufficient size, and some of them faced very serious operational obstacles. However, several years after the merger, the performance of the firm became quite satisfactory. Many of the problems encountered during the merger process have been solved, providing excellent model experiences for future merger management.

In this report, several topics will be dwelled upon: the background and purposes of the merger, the process the merger, the economies of scale and synergies created by the merger, the problems encountered during the earlier stages, how they were solved and the performance of CPCD after the merger. And finally, some lessons for management from this merger experience will be discussed.

1. Background of the Merger

The government of the Republic of China have quite actively participated in the petrochemical and chemical industries because of the following reasons:
- these industries play a critical role in the national industrial structure,
- a minimum economy of scale is often required in these industries and sometimes it takes a long time to pay back the investment.

Therefore the government owns and operates several important firms in such industries, including China Petroleum Corporation (CPC), the largest business enterprise in the Republic of China.

The four firms to merge used to be owned and operated as state-owned enterprises under this industry policy.

1) China Petrochemical Development Corporation (CPDC) was formed in 1969. Its main investor, China Petroleum Corporation, had a very close tie with CPDC. In comparison with the other three companies, CPDC was probably the best in management calibre, with the youngest group of managers of them all.

Prior to merger (around 1981), CPDC's production was centered on three items, namely, ethylene, AN, and DMT. Among them, ethylene took up only 6% of the total sales volume. Since this part of production was contracted by China Petroleum Corp., there was no problem about its profitability.

AN constituted 71% of the annual sales and was considered quite monopolistic in the business, so great profit was generated there. DMT, whose downstream industry was polyester fiber plants, occupied the rest of the sales, about 23%. As its production efficiency and quality were not satisfactory, coupled by the fact that it had vastly been substituted by PTA, the production of DMT was doomed to be terminated. With the understanding of this inevitable trend, CPDC was seeking new opportunities to keep its operation scale in case the DMT plant was to be closed. (In 1982, after the merger, the production of DMT was terminated.)

2) Chung Tai Chemical Industrial Corporation (CTCC) was formed in 1970, and produced CPL as its sole product, which was the material for nilonfiber. Until 1980, the company enjoyed a short period in a partially — monopolistic position, because of a limited amount of importation. Competition increased over time under the policy of liberalization of international trade. Production problems leading to a lack of guarantee in supply to customers, plus the drop in price of foreign products, had both contributed to a demand for lifting the ban on importation.

The major weakness of Chung Tai lies in its marketing concept, thinking only of reflecting its own costs without making any attempt to reduce the cost to compete with foreign products. Improvement in production started about eight months before merger, and the pro-duction volume has boosted drastically since then.

The management of CTCC consisted of and was influenced by several groups: China Petroleum Corporation, Taiwan Provincial Government, and the military. Different styles of management and value systems existed simultaneously among the top management of this company before the merger.

3) China Phosphate Industrial Corporation(CPIC) was formed in 1972 as a reinvested company by Taiwan Fertilizer Corporation, which is another state-owned enterprise with a long historical background. Many among the CPIC management team had work experience in Taiwan Fertilizer Corporation and inherited the management system and method of that company. CPIC's main products were DCP and STPP.

STPP is an additive for detergents, and its substitute, zerolite, can be imported. DCP is an additive for feed, sold to feedmakers. Despite the monopoly of the product, other substitutes such as the imported low quality DCP were often used in place of the company's product. The problems encountered by China Phosphate Industrial Corp. before the merger were:

- new products had been mass produced before they were accepted by the market, so the effects of research and development were not materialized.
- the building of a second CPL plant as part of the expansion project had brought about idle capacity and heavy financial burden.

4) Taiwan Alkali Corporation (TAC) was a company with a history of more than half a century. Staff in the lower echelon of the hierarchy consisted of those promoted gradually from the first line, while most of the management team were transferred from CPC to their new assigned posts. No wonder the company lacked a concensus between the two.

The major products of TAC were chloroalkali and hydrochloric acid, with satisfactory sales and profits. Starting from 1972, TAC began to expand its production lines to include that of Titanium. However, the expansion was a failure due to the following reasons:

- In addition to the obstacles encountered in production and the failure to obtain the required quality, there was the problem of high cost.
- The investment, being insufficient to manufacture the ultimate product, Titanium, could only produce an intermediate product — synthesis rutile, which lacked a high added value.
- The rapid shrinking of the space industry in the U.S. resulted in the decrease in the demand for the expensive, artificial Titanium.

From the brief account of the companies, we sensed the problematic environment in which they survived, and the potential challenges facing the merger.

In addition to the weaknesses manifested in the nature of the organization, the business side of these companies was not optimistic either. Since the product lines of these companies were not broad enough to meet the demands of market fluctuation, the production run was seriously affected, resulting in a diminishing of profit.

By this time, the industrial policy of our government underwent changes somehow. Existance of private firms in related industries were encouraged. Apart from the competition from the private sector, imported goods took away part of their market as well. Having lost their monopolistic positions, CTCC, CPIC, and TAC began to go under water. Losses from operation brought debts and eventually financial crisis.

Each of these three companies was compelled to take prompt actions to correct deficiencies and improve its performance, however, the effects were limited.

It was under this situation, that the proposal for a merger was made and seriously considered by the Ministry of Economic Affairs.

2.   The Purposes of the Merger

The merger (or more precisely, this series of mergers) was proposed with the following purposes in mind:

1)   To obtain better economies of scale. It was hoped that the broadening of product lines after the merger will not only strengthen the companies' capability of meeting market fluctuation, but also bring economies of scale in the salesforce and production. Meanwhile if the material procurement, R&D activities, and administrative organizations could be combined, a certain degree of EOS could be created.

2)   To obtain synergy through the merger. Since there was a relatively high degree of similarity among these companies, many of the functional capabilities could be transferred from one company to the other. Some planned benefits included the synergy in market risk diversification, transaction cost reduction, and certain kinds of financial synergy.

3)   To achieve management betterment. The management systems and caliber in China Petrochemical Development Corporation were obviously better than those of the other three companies, there-

fore a merger could be an effective method to transfer its total management system to other companies and at the same time remove ineffective management from the less successful firms.

4)   Finally, to stabilize the demand/supply relationship in the petrochemical industry; probably the ultimate purpose of this merger. The closed upstream/downstream relationship within the petrochemical industry prohibits any operational failure along the "chain", therefore smooth and balanced operations of the industry have become synonomous with primarily state-owned companies. This merger, in a sense, was considered instrumental in bringing about the desired effect.

3.   The Merger Process

There were three stages during the series of mergers, in which, administrative as well as business operations had been combined or eliminated in accordance with need. The following is a detailed account of the merger process:

1)   The merger of China Petrochemical Development Corp. and Chung Tai Chemical Industrial Corp. (the first wave):

During this stage, General Management, Accounting, Personnel, and the Planning Departments of both companies were consolidated after the merger. At the same time, a new information center was established in China Petrochemical Development Corp. As for the plant operations, the Tou Feng plants of both companies, next door to each other, were consolidated. After the consolidation, part of the staff were transferred and some of the temporary employees were laid off. For instance, the plant manager of China Petrochemical Development Corp. Tou Feng plant was assigned to be the head of the new information center, and about 35 people (including engineers, operators, and maintenance people) were transferred to Da She plant, the newly established acetic acid plant near Kao Hsiung. As regards the sales operations, revisions were made starting from 1986 by setting up a Sales Administration Department, in charge of taking orders and collecting accounts, etc.. Whereas the former sales department was able to be more specialized in pricing and after services. Through this kind of reshuffling, the economy of scale was gradually achieved in sales operations.

2)   The merger of China Petrochemical Development Corp. and Taiwan Alkali Corp.:

This was the second wave of the entire merger case. In July 1982, China Petrochemical Development Corp. started to act on behalf of

Taiwan Alkali Corp., and then formally took over in April 1983, thus completing the merger process.

Personnel problems were solved during the transitional period, with CPDC absorbing 237 chloroalkali plant employees, and China Petroleum Corp. absorbing 200 mostly young employees from the Titanium plant as well as same older people who were unwilling to retire. Around 700 people were laid off, each receiving six months pay, which eventually brought about a loss on the 1983 income statement of CPDC.

3)   The merger of China Petrochemical Development Corp. and China Phosphate Industrial Corporation:

This was the third wave of the merger. Starting from January 1983, China Phosphate Industrial Corporation became the Hsiao Kang plant of CPDC. Of the 485 employees, 402 remained in service, 65 people were laid-off, while the rest were transferred to the sales department. The R&D department was relegated to a lower level section within the plant.

To sum up, the operations that were eliminated are as follows:

Chung Tai Chemical: Administration, Tou Feng plant, and the Sales Department.

China Phosphate: R&D, Administration, and Sales Departments.

Taiwan Alkali: all except the 237 people in its Kao Hsiung plant, which was also transformed into the Chian Chen plant of CPDC.

4.   Economies of Scale Created by the Merger

The economies of scale created by the merger could be found in various functional areas.

4.1 Production

1)   The reduction of management expenses, as for example, the administrative and overhead expenses of the plant.

2)   The reduction of maintenance costs. For each plant, there used to be 50 to 60 people in charge of maintenance. The annual overhaul took at least 2 weeks and it was done mostly by outside contractors. After the merger, the company had only to schedule each plant's maintenance period properly to make the best use of personnel and facilities, since four out of the five plants were located in the Great Kao Hsiung area.

3)   The reduction of material costs. After the merger, the acquisition and distribution of raw materials, information on common

and indirect materials such as equipment parts, wires and cables could be stored on computer by the material section of the administration department. Prior to any purchase, the personnel in charge should check the computer printout to see whether the specific item is available (in any of the plants). This kind of economy of scale could be obtained only after the material coding system had been unified in all the plants.

4) Full utilization of vehicles and facilities through reciprocal borrowing.

5) Because of the merger, CPDC had a cessation of production of DMT without seriously affecting its own survival.

4.2 Sales

1) The economy of distribution was found to be limited. Products such as acetic-acid, AN, and CPL were sold directly to downstream plants, while such products as DCP and chloroalkali were distributed through agents. As there were differences in the methods of distribution, the nature of products, and the after-sale services, it was not justifiable to make any attempt to consolidate the operation.

2) However, in view of the growing scale of operation, it was feasible to enhance the level of specialization by setting up a Sales Administration Department to facilitate sales representatives to become more specialized in service.

4.3 Research and Development

1) Direct economies of scale in R&D were limited, traditionally, in all these companies, R&D work is commissioned. Since different plants had different interests in topic selection, the economies of scale were limited in this area. Nevertheless, there were still advantages of centralizing the use of the R&D fund and setting the priority.

2) There were indirect benefits such as the sharing of R&D administrative personnel and expenses. An R&D meeting took place once every three months and the group discussions and exchanges of view benefited and encouraged all the participants.

3) Job rotation of technical people helps individual's personal growth and stimulates an exchange of technical know-how among staff of the plants.

4.4 Finance

The company possessed a greater attraction to banks after the merger.

4.5 Personnel Management

1) The Centralized Recruiting Process saved much time and energy.

2) The company could enjoy better economy of scale either in the in-service training programme or outside-commissioned training programme. And the orientation programmes could be so arranged that employees could pay a visit to each and every plant and by so doing obtain a better picture of the relationship between the individual job and the whole operation of the company. It would also be much easier to send people abroad for training since the resources of the company have been enlarged.

3) Idle personnel could be transferred to where they have more potential contribution. Middle managers and engineers could also have rotations in jobs, so that, on the one hand, the bottlenecks of personnel management in state-owned enterprises could be broken, while on the other hand, the pursuit of personal growth as well as the exchange of views in management and know-how among fellow plant staff would also be rendered possible.

4) Welfare activities (such as sightseeing trips or parties) became better endorsed since there were more people and better participation.

5) In view of the growing number of plants, it was possible to hold various kinds of competition among plants to improve managerial performance and productivity.

5. The Synergies Created by the Merger

Synergy refers to the '2+2=5' effect, especially in a merger or diversification case. It implies a certain kind of benefit/capability exchange between different organizational units. Synergies derived from this merger could be observed in the following.

5.1 Production

1) Taking better advantage of the garbages. The waste oil bicyclic ketones of the Kao Hsiung plant could be piped to serve as fuel in the Da She plant.

2) Chloroalkali produced by the Chian Chen plant could be transported to other plants for use. In comparison with the former procedure of having to make bids in securing purchases from Taiwan Alkali Corp. or other suppliers, this was much more convenient.

5.2 Sales

1) AN (the material for manufacturing synthesic fiber), and CPL (the material for making nylons), have the advantage of being complementary to each other in facing the fluctuations of the international prices. Hence, the merger of China Petrochemical Development Corp. and Chung Tai Chemical would result in the reduction of risks assumed by each. However, it was later proved that both AN and CPL enjoyed a picking-up of business worldwide.

2) STPP (for use in making detergents), DCP (used primarily in feed), and Chloroalkali products are faced with different market environments. The risks, being relatively greater when they belonged to a single line company, were shared and thus drastically reduced after the merger.

5.3 Finance

1) AN and CPL are highly lucrative (the latter had already brought in a profit); whereas STPP and DCP were not as profitable. Therefore, the former ones helped to make up for the latter ones.

2) One of CPDC's strengths was its finance, which could be of great help to the newly merged units. The reasons why CPDC was strong in finance were: (a) A high return on investment had won a good reputation in its dealings with banks, (b) As China Petroleum Corp. is a major stockowner in CPDC, it was possible to buy raw materials on credit, which had once been for a record period of twelve months. At present, approximately 60% to 70% of the dollar amount of procurement goes to CPC.

5.4 Personnel

The merger was most conducive to the enhancement of morale among employees, and this seems to be a very special type of synergy in merger cases.

As CPDC was a SOE with excellent performance, to merge with such a company was instrumental in boosting the moral of the employees. For instance, employees got more bonuses than before, because of a better method of evaluation under the new system. And it became easier to get requests granted such as more office supplies, more business trips abroad, since the merged company was financially better-to-do. In one of the acquired plants, a new cafeteria was built which was also encouraging to the employees.

6. Problems Encountered During the Early Stage

During the early stages of the merger, many expected and un-expected problems occurred. Some more important ones are reported as follows.

6.1 Organizational Adjustment

In order to realize the potential economies of scale, many units in these companies were to be consolidated and reshuffled. Many managers lost their administrative positions or even the whole unit, and the power structure transformed drastically. Economical and political considerations interwove because of this consolidation and organization change process.

6.2 Personnel Problems

In order to turn the poor performance around, lay-offs and forced retirement became inevitable. Thie created a psychological imbalance and resistance among many employees, especially, those in Taiwan Alkali Corporation, where people were older and less qualified on the average.

6.3 Financial Arrangements

Although China Petroleum Corporation was the major investor in all four companies, several other investors, each with different pro-portions of shares in each company, were also concerned about finan-cial arrangements. The ratio of stock exchange, the reassessment of assets, and debt management, etc., all presented certain types of difficulties.

6.4 Restructuring of the Management System

A company, after merger, should have a unified management system, but for companies with many years of history and tradition, to rebuild a total management system is extremely difficult. Even the management system of CPDC had to adapt somehow to the operation of each acquired company, and people had to be trained to become familiar with the new system. As a matter of course, a certain degree of resistance was observed during the transitional period.

7. Management of the Merger Process How the Problems were Solved

Basically, the whole merger process was quite well planned. The following are some of the more significant methods or principles through which the problems were tackled and the merger process put under good control.

7.1 Decision Making by Participation

In the very beginning, the top management of CPDC took into account the fact that 1) many stakeholders would disagree on how important decisions were going to be made, and 2) only the first line would know how their operations should be arranged. As a result, many planned meetings were conducted to gather the opinions of various parties. Related government agencies were consulted for decisions near the strategic end, while decisions concerning operations were decided with the help of the very persons in charge. As the series of meetings were properly arranged, decisions were reached systematically based on the preconceived framework. And before a decision was made, the premises of that particular decision must have been determined.

7.2 Management System Setup

Since the acquired companies badly needed modern management style, several management systems were transplanted from CPDC.

1) "Management by Objectives" was set up in the three companies to provide a better planning and control environment for marketing and production operations.

2) A group incentive system was adopted to create healthy competition among plants, which, after the merger, were similar in size and accounting procedures.

3) A performance evaluation was conducted in order to strengthen the control function.

4) Many task forces were organized to implement the reassessment of properties and the revision of accounting and inventory systems.

7.3 Exchange of Management Experience

In order to speed up the organizational change process, CPDC held a series of seminars and conferences to share their experience in management. Various kinds of topics, such as QCC, managerial accounting systems, etc., were included in these seminars and conferences, where people not only learned from others' experiences, but also exchanged views and opinions. Potential problems in implementing these management systems in various plants were also discussed.

7.4 Absorption of Acquired Personnel

In order to solve the personnel problem, the management tried its best to make the new organization absorb, as many employees as possible. At the same time, despite the abolition of many managerial positions, people uttered no complaints in regard to organization change, for the past performance had been far from satisfactory. Also CPDC tried to let China Petroleum Corp. absorb some of the employees.

Though most people were transferred to a position below their former rank, they were otherwise rewarded. For instance, they were entitled to a larger amount of bonus, enjoyed better opportunities for promotion and job rotation.

7.5 An Attractive Retirement Plan

The company guarantees the laid-off people a very attractive retirement plan, in order to reduce the resistance to early retirement.

8. Performance after the merger

The performance of the merged company is considered to be quite satisfactory. It can be described from several angles.

8.1 Enhancement of Production Efficiency

With the implementation of the QCC and the continued modification of production procedures, the production efficiency in almost all the plants has been improved considerably since the merger. For instance, in 1986, AN production was 148,561 tons, constituting a growth of 17% since 1985. Some other annual growth rates in 1986 were: CPL, 8%; DCP, 24%.

8.2 The Possibility of More Research and Development

Because of the limited size and low profitability, almost no R&D projects were conducted before the merger. With the expansion of both scale and profitability, R&D expenses increased to a large extent. In

1986, R&D expenses accounted for 8.2% of total company sales.

8.3 Management Improvement

Many modern management systems have been implemented since the merger. Undoubtedly the top management of CPDC nowadays has much better control over the operation of the company.

8.4 The Accumulation of Merger Experience

There have been a limited number of mergers and acquisitions in the Republic of China in the past. Therefore the experience accumulated in the merger projects would be most valuable both to other state-owned enterprises and private companies.

8.5 Satisfactory Financial Performance

The following financial indicators give a clear picture of CPDC's good financial performance:

1) Sales volume grew with a better profit rate. (Sales and profit are in million NT; 30NT$=1US$)

	1984	1985	1986
Sales	11,597	12,179	14,145
Sales Growth	75%	5%	16%
Profit	469	730	1,429
Profit Rate	4.87%	6.80%	9.13%

2) Administrative expenses were used more efficiently.

*Administrative Expenses (in Millions of NT$)				
	1982	1983	1984	1985	1986
CPDC	34.4	66	78	81	98
CTCC	34.5	—	—	—	—
CPIC	11.1	—	—	—	—
TAC	64.5	—	—	—	—
Total	144.5	66	78	81	98

* For several years after the 1982 merger, the average savings in administrative expenses were about 63.75 million NT dollars.

3) Equity capital increased to 65.5% by 1986.

4) The debt ratio decreased so that interest payments decreased drastically.

9. Conclusion

This experience attests that merger is a possible solution to management problems, however, the prerequisites to success are detailed planning in advance and prolonged efforts in implementation.

There had been few cases of mergers and acquisitions in Taiwan in the past. A great number of business firms lack the sufficient size, and they lack the dynamics and flexibility usually found in small businesses. The reason they hadn't adopted the merger strategy is simply that there was no previous successful model/example to follow. This present case serves to exemplify the advantages of merger.

The present case analysis describes separately various kinds of economies of scale and synergy, such as in the fields of production, distribution, personnel and R&D, etc. Their performance provides excellent reference points for future mergers. The organization and personnel problems encountered during the merger and their solutions also serve as future references.

Many state-owned enterprises in our country are operated poorly, so merger provides a feasible solution. Some of the state-owned enterprises are similar in many ways to the CPDC case:

1) Many SOEs produce very similar products, with plants adjacent to each other, just like the situation in the case.

2) Many of them are doing business with each other, so a merger could simplify transaction procedures.

3) Many matured or saturated industries can obtain new life by conducting mergers, as in the case of CPDC.

4) Superfluous employees can be laid off by means of a merger.

If the merger of state-owned enterprises is conceived, some preliminary work can be performed at the outset. For instance, the coding of materials must be unified, and business areas of each SOE to be merged should be divided through strategic planning.

CASE STUDIES: INDIA

by Mr. Suraj Bhan Jain
Adviser
Standing Conference of Public Enterprises
(SCOPE)

1. Policy Behind the Public Sector

1.1 Weak but Independent India

Independent India inherited an agrarian economy with a weak industrial base. The basic infrastructure necessary for any worthwhile industrialization was almost non existent. The level of savings and investment was low, the vast majority of the population was extremely poor, there were considerable inequalities in income, employment opportunities were very few, serious regional imbalances in economic attainments were noticeable and there was a considerable lack of trained manpower in administrative, managerial, scientific and technical fields. In this situation it became necessary for the State to play a progressively active role in the development of industry. In the first five- year plan, the basic objective behind the creation of the public sector was to help in building up the economy by setting up enterprises which were basic from the point of economic growth, and which either by virtue of the size of the capital involved or other reasons were not likely to be taken up by the private sector. The public sector would include government companies either in the city centre or in the provinces as well as government departments engaged in both industrial and commercial activities. However, the second five year plan went a little further and stated "the public sector has to expand rapidly. It has to initiate not only development, which the private sector is either unwilling or unable to undertake; it has to play the dominant role in shaping the entire pattern of investment in the economy, whether it makes investments directly or whether these are made by the private sector."

1.2 Socialist Society

India through its Constitution adopted a socialist pattern of society, and this social objective was also assigned to the public sector. It was in this context that the second five-year plan stressed the importance of using the public sector as an instrument to check the concentration of economic power. The third plan emphasized this aspect by the statement that, "Increased profits which in the private sector would create inequalities and possible conspicuous and wasteful consumption, in the public sector can be directly used for capital accumulation."

1.3 The Role of SOEs

As and when the economy faced different problems, the roles assigned to SOEs were extended. For instance, when the country faced the problem of food-grain shortages and there was a need for procuring and maintaining the food stocks, it was stated in the fourth five-year plan, "The matter of crucial significance will be the emergence of the public sector as a whole as the dominant and effective area of the economy. This will enable it to take charge more and more of the commanding heights in the production and distribution of basic and consumer goods ..." Thus, the public sector was also assigned the role of producer and supplier of consumer goods. This role was emphasized in later plans also. The public sector is being used also as a vehicle for promotion of exports and earnings of foreign exchange. Apart from promoting their own State-Owned Enterprises, in India a large number of companies in the private sector, after they became "sick," were taken over by the State for rehabilitation purposes and as a welfare measure to protect the workers from retrenchment.

2. Present Status

2.1 State Sector Only

It will be seen that in India, the roles and activities of State-Owned Enterprises are being extended not by accident, but as a result of deliberate policies. Under the Industrial Policy Resolution of 1956, all new units in the following fields were exclusively reserved for the State Sector:

- Arms and ammunition and allied items of defence equipment.
- Atomic energy.
- Iron and steel.
- Heavy castings and forgings of iron and steel.
- Heavy plant and machinery required for iron and steel production, for mining, for machine tool manufacture and for such other basic industries as may be specified by the Central Government.

- Heavy electrical plants including large hydraulic and steam turbines.
- Coal and lignite.
- Mineral oils.
- Mining of iron ore, manganese ore, chrome-ore, gypsum, sulphur, gold and diamonds.
- Mining and processing of copper, lead zinc, tin, molybdenum and wolfram.
- Minerals specified in the Schedule to the Atomic Energy (Control of Production and Use) Order, 1953.
- Aircraft.
- Air transport.
- Railway transport.
- Shipbuilding.
- Telephones and telephone cables, telegraph and wireless apparatus (excluding radio receiving sets).
- Generating and distribution of electriciy.

2.2 Private and State Run Enterprises

While keeping the field open for private enterprise also, the state decided to increasingly set up new undertakings in the following fields:

- Other minerals except "minor minerals."
- Aluminium and other non-ferrous metals.
- Machine tools.
- Ferro-alloys and tool steels.
- Basic and intermediate products required by chemical industries such as the manufacture of drugs, dyes and plastics.
- Antibiotics and other essential drugs.
- Fertilizers.
- Synthetic rubber.
- Carbonization of coal.
- Chemical pulp.
- Road transport.
- Sea transport.

2.3 Types of Production

With the extension of the public sector's role from time to time, SOEs in India are now producing defence equipment, steel, minerals and metals, coal, power, petroleum, chemicals, fertilizers, pharmaceuticals, heavy engineering equipment, medium and light weight engineering equipment, transportation, consumer goods, agro based products, textiles, bread, family planning aids etc. Many of the enterprises are operating in the service sector eg. trading and marketing, transportation services (rails, roads, waterways and airways) contracts and constructions, industrial development and technical consultancy development of small industries, tourist services, including hotels financial services, banking, insurance and telecommunication services. Starting with an investment of Rs.29 crores in five enterprises in 1951, the total investment in central SOEs alone as of March 31, 1987 stood at Rs.61,603 crores (roughly 48,000 million US dollars). The total industrial employment in the public sector including governments, quasi-governments and local bodies in 1986 was about 17.67 million as against only 7.35 million industrial employees in the private sector.

3.   Unity in Diversity

3.1 Similar Roots

Even though central SOEs in India operate in diverse areas and regions, have diverse activities and are controlled by different ministries, the external environment and rules and regulations under which they operate are more or less similar. Barring a few SOEs which were set up under Acts of Parliament, almost all of them were incorporated as companies under the Companies Act, having their own Memorandum and Articles of Association. Central enterprises, like private sector enterprises, are required to pay taxes, and are subject to all the industrial and commercial laws of the country. While the shares in private sector businesses are owned by different persons, the shares of SOEs are held by the President and his nominee. Various powers have been delegated by the President of India to various ministries and departments under the Allocation of Business Rules and the powers of the President are generally exercised by the administrative Ministry to which a particular enterprise is attached. The mimistries in turn are required to consult other ministries to whom different subjects are allocated and in a case of difference of opinion and in very important matters the decisions are taken by the Cabinet. Appointment of the Chairman and the Board of Directors requires the approval of the Appointment Committee of the Cabinet which is headed by the Prime Minister. The government has the power to appoint or dismiss the directors and also to fix the number of directors from time to time. The remuneration i.e. salary, fees and allowances of the Chairman or Directors are fixed on the basis of uniform policy, though the basic grades of pay vary, depending on the comparative importance of the post — namely the schedule in which the particular post is categorized.

The Board of Directors is entrusted with management but in the following matters Government approval is necessary:

- Transfer of shares.
- Increase, reduction and alteration of share capital.
- Long term borrowing on capital accounts. Borrowings for meeting working capital requirements from banks and financial institutions do not require government approval.
- Issuance of bonds and debentures.
- Large investments can be made only after the project reports are approved by the Central Government. The Public Investment Board (PIB) consisting of several secretaries to Government and headed by the Secretary of Expenditures examines such proposals and only if this PIB approves, the proposals are placed before the Cabinet for orders.
- Central Government appoints the auditors on the advice of the Comptroller and Auditor General of India.
- The accounts are also liable to a supplementary or test audit by the officers of the Comptroller and Auditor General of India.

3.2 Overriding Provision

In every Memorandum and Article of Association there is an overriding provision that the President has the power to issue any directives or instructions in regard to the affairs and conduct of the business. In particular the President has the powers to:

- give directions to a company as to the exercise and performance of its functions in matters involving national security or substantial public interest.
- call for any information
- approve the plans of development and capital budgeting.
- approve foreign collaboration agreements.

3.3 Impact on Other Enterprises

As all the enterprises are owned by the Central Government and as most of them operate in a monopoly situation, any unilateral action by one enterprise does have serious repercussions elsewhere. They enjoy many advantages which are not available to the private sector, such as allocation of scarce and or national resources at very concessional rates, and absence of competition. As there is no alternative source of supply, it is always possible for a State monopoly to raise its prices and yet be able to sell its products as before, but this seriously affects the economic viability of other producers, including other SOEs as about 62% of output by SOEs is input for them. Similarly, enterprises, which because of fortunate situations in which they are placed have high profitability, can afford to be very lavish in payment of wages and allowances to their employees. But any such unilateral payment by one, generates demand from the employees of losing units also, and the government cannot afford to close such loss making units which are supplying essential services or products. Then, there are several other social objectives to which the nation is committed, such as development of less developed regions, uplift of less developed communities etc. Placed in such a situation and with a view to maintain harmony, the government issues directives from time to time on such matters as:

- Investment or project approvals.
- Clearance for import of capital goods.
- Releases of foreign exchange.
- Release of rupee funds from the central budget for projects.
- Fixation of prices especially in key and infrastructure sectors — such as coal, steel, petrol, electricity, fertilizers etc.
- Setting by Government of broad parameters for wages, salaries and allowances to to workers.
- Reservation in the matter of less developed communities.
- Need for austerity.
- Price preference for other SOEs and small sector units.

As the ministries are accountable to the Parliament for the performance of the enterprises, the overall performance indicators are monitored from time to time. The ministries also nominate one of their senior officers as Director to keep in touch with the enterprises.

3.4 Ministerial Override

Even though enterprises with or without autonomy are clearly demarcated there are several instances when the ministries interfere with the discretion of the management, as well as cases where the Chairman and Managing Director, ignore the directions and guidelines of the government with impunity. Much depends on the relation of the Chairman with the Minister and the Prime Minister etc.

3.5 Unequal Performance

It can be seen that in India, almost all central enterprises are subject to more or less the same rules, regulations and constraints, yet some of the enterprises have done very well in the areas of profitability, productivity and development, while many others continue to be a burden on the National Exchequer. Many of the external reasons for poor performance have been already identified in several studies in such criteria as obsolete technology, over employment, heavy interest burden, lack of adequate finances etc. Apart from these external constraints, there is something in the organization itself which makes it progressive and successful. We shall look into two enterprises from India. Oil and Natural Gas Commission and Maruti Udyog Ltd. Both of them are headed by two distinguished Chairmen Col. S.P. Wahi and Mr. V. Krishnamurthy, who have been decorated with the award of Padma Bhushan by the Government, which in recent years has been the highest award to which any civil servant can aspire. Higher awards of Padma Vibhushan and Bharat Ratna are given to other celebrities in the arts, sciences or politics.

4. Oil & Natural Gas Commission (ONGC)

4.1 Oil Scene in India before ONGC

In India systematic exploration and production of oil began in 1869 with the formation of Assam Oil Company. In 1947, when India became independent, the indigenous crude production was only 0.25 MMT mainly from Assam. Realizing the importance of oil for the economic and industrial progress of the country, oil exploration was made an exclusive prerogative of the State. As a first step for achieving a wider oil base, Geological Surveyors of India undertook a large scale reconnaisant and detailed mapping between 1947 and 1953 in parts of Punjab, Himachal Pradesh, Cambay, Kutch, Andaman and Nicobar Islands to locate the oil bearing areas. A petroleum division was created within the Geological Survey of India in 1955 exclusively for oil exploration work. In 1956 this division was converted into the Oil & Natural Gas Commission. In 1959, the Oil & Natural Gas Commission was set up as a statutory body under an Act of Parliament.

4.2 Objectives and Goals of ONGC

The main objective of ONGC was "to plan, promote, organize, and implement programmes for the development of petroleum resources and the production and sale of petroleum and its products." The ONGC was assigned the task of taking necessary steps:
- for conducting geological and geophysical surveys for the exploration of petroleum.

- for drilling and other prospecting operations to prove and estimate the reserves.
- to undertake, assist, encourage and promote the production of petroleum from such reserves and its refining.
- for the transport and disposal of natural gas and refinery gases.
- to undertake, encourage and promote geological, chemical and other scientific investigations.
- to undertake, assist or encourage the collection, maintenance and publicizing of statistics, bulletins and monographs.

4.3 Achievements

1) Within a span of 30 years, ONGC has assimilated the world's best petroleum expertise developed in the last 100 years. It has now emerged as a multidisciplinary organization with complete inhouse expertise and capacity. It is one of the few companies of the world engaged in almost all aspects of oil exploration, drilling and production and is becoming increasingly self reliant in well advanced and sophisticated oil exploration and production technology. Of late, it has started providing technical know-how even to highly developed countries. The phenomenal growth of ONGC in size and stature has enabled India to be on the international oil map. ONGC is today recognized as the 12th largest profit making company among the giants of the world.

2) It has shown tremendous progress in the matter of exploration, production, profits and the development of technology.

India has a sedimentary basin covering 1,720,000 square kilometers (1,400,000 onshore and 320,000 off-shore) containing 16.6 billion tonnes of prognosticated resources, out of which 4,062 billion tonnes have been converted into geological reserves by ONGC. The total accretion to geological reserves in the Sixth Plan was 694.07 MMt. of oil and oil equivalent gas, while in the first two years of the Seventh Plan itself ONGC has added another 411.17 MMt. to its geological reserves.

3) The following comparisons in the last 7 years alone are indicative of ONGC's continuous progress.

Of the overall profits earned by all enterprises together, ONGC has a lion's share. In 1986—87, 109 central enterprises earned pretax profits of Rs.4803 crores, while 100 enterprises incurred losses totalling Rs.1708.38 crores. Thus the net pretax profits of all central enterprises were Rs.3095.34, out of which 68% was accounted for by ONGC alone.

Drilling (in 000 meters)

Year	Exploration	Development	Total
1980—81	117.70	94.50	212.20
1981—82	151.80	170.00	321.80
1982—83	176.60	209.10	385.70
1983—84	192.40	275.60	468.00
1984—85	299.40	232.10	441.50
1985—86	296.49	293.59	590.08
1986—87	333.48	399.35	732.83

Production

Year	Crude (Million tonnes)	Natural gas (Million cubic meters)	L.P.G (000 tonnes)
1980—81	9.21	972.1	—
1981—82	13.18	1230.41	73.05
1982—83	18.23	1856.72	161.22
1983—84	23.15	2222.51	195.51
1984—85	26.26	2789.94	241.72
1985—86	27.51	3315.00	320.36
1986—87	27.86	5039.56	450.40

Profitability (in Rs. crores)

Year	Gross revenue (Before depreciation, interest and taxes)	Pretax profits
1980—81	451.83	—
1981—82	1,348.49	573.04
1982—83	2,401.63	1,182.87
1983—84	3,472.82	1,607.66
1984—85	4,034.98	1,627.41
1985—86	4,387.90	1,898.21
1986—87	5,627.39	2,104.96

4) Contribution to state coffers

Substantial amounts have been contributed to the Central Government by way of excise, cess and corporate taxes, customs royalties, dividends. And to State Governments by way of sales tax, royalties and octroi.

Year	to Central Government (in Rs. crores)	to State Government	Total
1981—82	433	109	542
1982—83	909	113	1,022
1983—84	1,743	110	1,854
1984—85	1,847	139	1,987
1985—86	1,867	348	2,215
1986—87	2,785	328	3,113

5) Outflow of foreign exchange

ONGC has been significantly successful in reducing the outflow of foreign exchange through incremental production, which has grown from a level of 9.21 million tonnes in the beginning of the Sixth Plan (1980—81) to 27.86 million tonnes in 1986—87. The cumulative production in the Sixth Plan (1980—85) and the first two years of the Seventh Plan (1985—87) has been 145.4 MMt valued domestically at Rs.21,999.02 crores. In international price terms this production level is equivalent to Rs.31139 crores, which the country would have had to spend during this period (1980—87) in foreign exchange.

6) Comparison of prices

It is to be noted that the domestic price paid to ONGC has been well below the international average price. The domestic administrative price has been about 10 U.S. dollars a barrel, whereas the prevailing international market price has peaked well above 35 U.S. dollars a barrel.

7) Indigenization

ONGC has been promoting indigenization of oil field equipment, materials and services in a systematic manner through active collaboration of indigenous industries. In 1986—87 alone it saved over RS.2900 crores in foreign exchange. The foreign exchange outflow in relation to the planned expenditure has been brought down from 69% in 1981—82, to 41% in 1986—87. A large number of capital items like platforms, jack-up rigs, supply vessels, compressors, MSVs, well heads, Christmas trees and oil field chemicals are now being manufactured by Indian companies, both in the private and public sector. In Services the major sectors which have been indigenized include: charter hire and management of OSV's NDT vessels and MSVS, diving services, coating/wrapping and laying of pipeline, engineering and soil investigation surveys, tidal observation, radio positioning equipment and satellite navigation systems as well as engineering consultancy and certification. Service contracts worth Rs.309.51 crores were awarded during the period 1986–87.

8) Entrepreneurial development

In addition to the regular employment needs a lot more employment is generated as a result of the multiplier effect of the economy. In addition, ONGC is promoting entrepreneurship by farming out low technology areas like maintenance, transportation and shot hole drilling. Already, ancillary units in shot hole drilling have been started in the Western Region. An ancillary development cell has been formed within ONGC in the Eastern Region for this purpose. ONGC has also started vocational training centres at Dehradun and in various regions/ working centres for the dependents of deceased employees to develop skills in such areas as sewing, knitting, printing and sample making etc. This has been done with a view to their independence in starting their own vocations.

4.4 Factors of Excellence

1) Investments by themselves not sufficient

Undoubtedly ONGC is the best performing enterprise in India, in the matters of productivity, technological advancement and profitability. It has been always on the march. One has therefore to inquire and analyze why it is so. Is it because of the investment made by the Government? No, it is not just that – ONGC ranks fifth in the matter of investments as can be seen from the following information as of March 31, 1987.

If one goes by the share capital only, which is a good indicator as interest on loans is deducted before arriving at the pretax profit, ONGC will rank 19th. The big investments by themselves therefore do not contribite to success.

Name of enterprise	Total investment (Rs. in crores)	Paid up share capital	Loans
Steel Authority of India Ltd.	6,415.76	3,937.56	2,478.20
Coal India Ltd.	6,275.12	3,559.50	2,715.62
National Thermal Power Corporation	6,147.79	3,358.41	406.40
Rashtriya Ispat Nigam Ltd.	3,116.23	2,885.78	230.44
Oil & Natural Gas Commission	3,078.41	342.85	2,735.58

2)   Strong foundations illustrious and powerful Chairman

The reasons for continuous growth and success, in spite of the fact that the Chairman and the Members have changed, speak highly of the intrinsic strength and traditions of the organization. The credit for success goes mainly to Mr. K.D. Malviya, who as the first Chairman laid solid foundations for the ONGC. Mr. K.D. Malviya the Founder Chairman started with several advantages which are not available to many. He was the son of Late Pandit Madan Mohan Malviya, one of the most eminent personalities of pre-independent India, who also founded Banaras Hindu, University. Mr. K.D. Malviya himself was a distinguished petroleum geologist, a voracious reader who had kept abreast of the latest technological advancements in the petroleum sector. He was also a Minister for Petroleum in the Central Government and was close to Pandit Jawaharlal Nehru. In the earlier stages, ONGC sought technological assistance from oil giants in the western countries, but for their own commercial reasons, they advised that India's reserves were not rich and would not be commercially viable. They were, however, prepared to acquire oil concessions. Mr. Malviya studied hard and observed that geological data in certain areas like Cambay had a lot of similarity to the Saudi Arabian region. He therefore felt convinced about the existence of large reserves of oil. Having failed to get any assistance from the world's oil giants, except on very unfair terms, Mr. Malviya approached Russia. He invited the top Russian geologist, Mr. Kalinin, who after spending about one year, identified several areas in Gujarat, Bay of Bengal, Cavery Basin where rich reserves could be found. Based on the report of Mr. Kalinin, Mr. Malviya asked for funds for drilling etc. In spite of opposition from the Finance Ministry, which felt that such an investment would be a waste of funds, he had his way and got the funds. Even after the funds were available, ONGC could not get drilling equipment from western countries and again Mr. Malviya got the equipment from Russia, with whom he had developed an excellent rapport. Luckily for him and ONGC, the very first well drilled produced oil which boosted up the morale of ONGC.

This was followed by many other successful strikes, and ONGC went ahead, with the result that even those giants and countries which were reluctant to assist India, now vie with each other for providing technology, equipment and securing contracts. Had Mr. Malviya hesitated in the early years, the oil scenario in India could have been altogether different.

3)   Selection of the best personnel as reason for success

When a new organization is set up, the rules for recruitment are not framed, considerable discretion vests in the management in the matter of the number of posts created and recruitment for such posts. It has been the experience of India, that in such a situation the Chief Executives are ready to oblige the politicians, by having a very large labour force and by employing the supporters from their constituency. Powerful bureaucrats also push in their sons and nephews who are unable to join the civil services on the basis of fair competition. As recruitment to regular civil services, so far, have been free from such influences credit goes to Mr. K.D. Malviya, the first Chairman, for not creating a large number of unnecessary jobs. He also insisted that only the best people join ONGC, on merit and merit alone. He could afford to ignore other politicians and bureaucrats because of his personal status as a Central Cabinet Minister and his closeness to Prime Minister Jawaharlal Nehru. Persons who join on the basis of merit and not as a result of favouritism are generally much more efficient and dedicated, and also are fair when dealing with their juniors. This is one of the key factors why ONGC since its inception made considerable progress.

The Government also considered ONGC very important to the national economy, and therefore appointed only persons of proven merit as Chairmen and Members of the Board, and such persons do not generally allow interference from outsiders in their internal management. The initial recruitment of bright and competent personnel has been the most important factor for ONGC's continuous growth and progress.

4) Limited but competent work force

The second important factor was that ONGC did not create a work force larger than what was required for operational reasons. It is important to note that even though the operations of ONGC are spread throughout the country and its rank is 11 in terms of number of employees with 43,349 and in terms of profit ONGC rank as number one. Steel Authority of India employs as many as 202,419 employees, a very large work force. Apart from causing a drain on the profits it is also detrimental to discipline and productivity — idle workmen disturb others and efficiency goes down.

5) Involvement of employees in decision making

ONGC has always had a system of active employee participation and involvement. ONGC has frequent brain storming sessions. All concerned employees and executives express their viewpoints freely and frankly and give suggestions to improve efficiency. Their suggestions and views are taken due note of when taking decisions. Once a decision has been taken, after considering the pros and cons, everybody tries to implement it. This process which is not very common in India, has also contributed to the progress of ONGC.

6) Cost-consciousness

ONGC is a highly profitable organization with an excellent cash flow position. Normally, such organizations are not very cost-conscious and become lavish in their expenditures. However, ONGC unlike other profit earning state enterprises does not indulge in lavish expenditures. The management controls expenditures at the micro level, no luxurious furnishings are bought, even the Chairman in his Delhi office sits in a small room with functional, fairly old, though well maintained furnishings.

ONGC continuously goes to the nuts and bolts to find cost savings areas. Management and operational studies are regularly carried out to ensure optimal use of human and material resources. ONGC believes that, "improvements in productivity will automatically lower costs." For effective energy management an energy audit cell has been constituted which monitors the energy consumption at macro and micro levels. To reduce the cost of carrying large inventories, task forces occasionally identify surplus inventory of stores, spares and capital items. This cost consciousness, even when flush with funds, is rarely seen in Government departments or State enterprises.

7) Training and retraining

ONGC operates in a high tech, high risk area. Any error on the part of an employee can cause devastation and heavy damages. In the initial year ONGC did not have much expertise. By the force of necessity, it had to provide extensive and intensive training to the employees who were engaged in exploration, drilling and production of oil. In the initial stages when new technology is introduced, ONGC engages foreign technicians, but very soon the foreigners are replaced by ONGC employees, on whom nothing is spared to train and retrain both in Indian and foreign theory and practice. Employees are always encouraged to acquire higher education and to develop expertise in multiple occupations. Now ONGC is providing technology and technical skills to other countries as well.

In several enterprises, agreements are reached with trade unions whereby employees recruited for a particular job would not be asked to attend to other jobs. But ONGC's position is different. Its employees are given multitrade training, so that in case of need employees from one job can be diverted to other jobs. ONGC provides accelerated career opportunities to those who are research oriented. This policy helps in technological assimilation and advancement at various levels.

Even though ONGC is expanding its activities, it has decided to freeze its work force at the level maintained during the Seventh Five-Year Plan 1985–1990. This is proposed to be achieved by farming out jobs which involve low or medium technical skills to outsiders especially to cooperative societies. This, while checking the proliferation of regular employees, will provide self employment and good income to the people in the neighbourhood. It will also result in greater efficiency.

8) Technological advances

ONGC operates in a high tech area so must keep abreast of the latest in the fields such as exploration and drilling. It carried out geological and geophysical surveys, and has now adopted the latest technology of 3-D seismic surveys. In this survey data is collected which shows a complete sub-surface, seismic picture in its initial stages of development. This enables understanding of complex, sub-surface geology – both structural and stratigraphic – resulting in overall reduction in the development costs of a production field. ONGC has been conducting gravity combined with magnetic surveys off shore for quite some time. ONGC has been constantly upgrading its drilling technology through: directional drilling, introducing mobile rigs, use of sophisticated mud logging units and computer control, and the introduction of desert and heli-rigs. Through the improvements in 1985–86 alone rig month input increased by 13% and cycle speed by 13%.

9) Research

Taking into account the continuously increasing domestic demand for oil, ONGC is extending exploration in hostile, highly risky and hitherto unlikely areas, by acquiring specialized equipment and advanced scientific knowledge. Emphasis is being given to basic research in the ONGC's Institutes for Petroleum Exploration and Drilling Technology in Dehradun, as well as reservoir studies in Ahmedabad and production technology, engineering and ocean technology in Bombay. ONGC has launched a pilot project to gasify huge coal reserves in Gujarat. ONGC is also undertaking studies to prognosticate resources in water depths of more than 200 metres. ONGC has turned to advanced computer application for Management Information and Control Systems, Financial and Personnel Information Systems, Project Monitoring Equipment and Inventory Management Systems. It is responsible for the modernization and advancement of the Indian communication system, which had been neglected so far.

4.5 Focus of Excellence

In its continuous search for excellence, ONGC has the following areas under focus:

1) Inventory
   - Use task force for inventory management and disposal of surplus at corporate as well as regional level, in business groups and in every unit of operation.
   - Distribute or trade spare inventory.
   - Manage inventory via computer.
   - Train staff to deal with inventory.

2) Manpower
   - Sub-contract low/medium level technical activities.
   - Develop skills.
   - Review R&D regulations to make them pertinent to the needs of the job.

3) Optimal utilization of equipment
   - Undertake a systematic technical audit by management.
   - Set up an independent department for equipment management to ensure effective maintenance and technical support.
   - Plan a maintenance system.
   - Set up task forces at corporate and regional levels for disposal of surplus/condemned equipment.
   - Implement computerized maintenance management system.

4) Exploration
   - Enhance oil recovery.

5) Production and development
   - Use deep water technology and production.
   - Increase oil recovery.
     Development and Production from marginal/isolated fields.
   - Set up pilot schemes.
   - Utilize sub-sea production as R&D project.
   - Insitu-combustion.
   - Associate with international companies.

6) Cost control
   - Continuously review cost of operation through optimization studies — management and technical audits.

4.6 Strategy to Meet Growing Petroleum Demand

1) Short-term strategy

Maximizing recovery from the existing production fields through close monitoring, supervision, productivity improvements and the introduction of innovative methods for improving cycle speeds and work-over indices have substantially contributed towards enhancing production. A one percent increase in recovery can give an additional 30.58 MT recoverable reserves. Therefore ONGC put emphasis on additional enhanced oil recovery and infill drilling.

2) Maximizing recovery through work-over operations

A special emphasis has been given to workover operations thereby reducing the number of sick wells and consequently enhancing output from the wells. The number of sick wells has already been brought down from 446 in April 1980 to 243 in April 1987, in spite of an increase in the number of wells to 3121 from 1718 in April 1980.

3) Long term strategy

A situation audit 'SWOT' analysis, conducted in 1981—82 brought to focus the availability of an adequate hydrocarbon reasource base, a strong human resource base and sound infrastructure support. A deliberately planned approach, for training and development, modernization, information management, upgradation of technology, focus on costs as well as a participative and aggressive commercial culture have contributed to manifold growth with stability and continuous improvement in productivity.

4) Steps taken

For the first time in the oil industry, a long-term conceptual plan was drawn up by ONGC bringing out three strategies to meet the demand for approximately 100 million tonnes of oil and the equivalent of gas by the year 2004—2005.

ONGC is aware that the growth rate of demand for oil related products in the industrial and transportation sectors is fast outstripping the stock for expected demand. It has therefore started policy initiatives on a national level for the management of energy demand in the industrial sector through improvement in fuel efficiency, by shifting to less energy intensive technologies and by substituting other tyes of fuel.

4.7 Future Thrust Areas

ONGC has also identified the following future thrust areas:
- Deep water exploration and production.

- Horizontal drilling.
- Enhanced oil recovery.
- Early production system.
- Sub-sea completion technology.
- Insitu gasification of coal.
- Considerable oil recovery.
- Increasing complexities of drilling.
- Multiple completion technology.
- Development and utilization of isolated pools.
- Production from tight reservoir.
- Natural gas utilization, including use of compressed natural gas.
- Energy conservation increases the availability of energy.
- Reduction in costs of running offshore structures.
- Environments and safety consciousness.

4.8 Advantages ONGC Enjoys

ONGC as an enterprise has several advantages which are not available to others. Apart from the fact that it is operating as a monopoly it is in a field which is profitable all the world over. Oil companies, but for the recent fall in prices, have been making huge profits. In India, petroleum prices did not go down at any stage. Further, ONGC has at its disposal the territory of the entire country, which has rich oil reserves onshore and offshore. It has the power and authority to start drilling in any area and the royalties paid are quite modest. It is only since January 4, 1984 that the rate of royalty has been raised to Rs.192 per metric tonne from Rs.61 per metric tonne. Setting of higher prices along with trifling royalties does result in considerable financial advantage for ONGC, which makes it possible for them to expand and go in for new projects. That to some extent may account for its high profitability, yet ONGC has also been making great strides in the matter of increased productivity.

The ONGC is a dynamic organization, it has already drawn up strategic plans for the future and has identified the areas where future thrust will be given. It is a vibrant organization which is financially and internally strong enough to meet new challenges and developments.

4.9 The Automobile Industry in India Before Maruti

Automobile manufacture in India started in early 1950s when Hindustan Motors and Premier Automobiles commenced operation, soon followed by Standard Motors, Mahindra and Mahindra, Telco and Ashok Leyland. Each of these companies started with a foreign collabo-

ration for assembly and a subsequent phased manufacturing programme. Production gradually built up to a level between 30,000 to
40,000 automobiles a year, but stagnated at that level until the 1980s
without any worthwhile innovation or upgradation of technology.
Before Maruti came on the scene, the automobile models had minor
variations from the original models. Compared with the standard world
production level of 40—60 vehicles per man per year, Indian automobile manufacturers were operating at about 2 to 2½ vehicles per
man per year.

4.10 Maruti Udyog Limited (MUL)

1) Objectives and goals

It was with this background that the Government of India decided
to set up an automobile company in the public sector with the following objectives:

- to modernize the Indian automobile industry;
- to effect a more economic utilization of scarce fuel by
  introducting fuel efficient vehicles;
- to ensure higher production of motor vehicles.

2) Achievements

Maruti manufactures a small, 800 cc, four door, passenger car,
800 cc van and a 1000 cc vehicle called the 'Gypsy.' It has production
capacity for 100,000 units per year, which could go up to 120,000
units worth of production. A total investment of US$200 million has
been made on plants and equipment in a phased manner, since 1982.
The project was within the originally planned time and cost estimates.
The optimal phased usage of facility has resulted in no idle plant
capacity at any stage. The plant reached its capacity two years ahead of
schedule. The yearly production always exceeded the projected target,
as can be seen from the following:

Period	Target	Actual production
1983—84	Nil	852
1984—85	20,000	22,372
1985—86	40,000	51,580
1986—87	60,000	80,150
1987—88	100,000	Already exceeded

The following figures also show that even during the gestation
period Maruti started earning profits: (Figures in millions)

Year	Share capital	Net profit
1983—84	283.3	17.0
1984—85	315.3	6.9
1985—86	567.3	31.9
1986—87	740.6	104.3

3) Reputation

Maruti Udyog, today is considered an example of excellence in the engineering industry. It has the largest and modernest automobile plant in India. It started production within record time of about 1½ years after signing a collaboration agreement. It has exceeded production targets from the beginning, has set new Indian standards for productivity in automobile manufacturing of roughly 10 times the previous norm. It has been a leader in the establishment of a different organizational and work culture, which lays emphasis on quality and innovation. Its main emphasis has been on quality — quality of products, quality of operation and quality of customer service. Maruti has been a catalytic agent and has affected not only the automobile industry but other industries as well. Now, more and more manufacturers in different fields are improving the quality of their products, as they can take the Indian customer for granted no more.

4) Commitment at highest political level leads to success

One may ask why Maruti alone has brought about this different work culture. It is recommended to examine its background, as this will show that things are likely to go well if there is a political will.

The late Mr. Sanjay Gandhi, son of the late former Prime Minister Indira Gandhi, had a dream for a small car which would be cheap and fuel efficient. He set up a company — Maruti Ltd. and he tried to produce a small, fuel efficient car, but because of financial and other constraints he could not succeed. Many allegations were made by the opposition parties against Mrs. Indira Gandhi, thus between 1977 and 1980 when she was out of power she along with her son and many other officials who had dealt with Maruti Ltd. were harassed and resented. She later returned to power with a majority, but soon thereafter Mr. Sanjay Gandhi died in an air crash. Mrs. Indira Gandhi, who loved Sanjay very deeply, decided to cherish his memory by setting up an automobile company with the same name and at the same place to produce a small car which should be remembered for quality. A trusted, eminent and distinguished professional Mr. V. Krishnamurthy, who had been Secretary to the Government of India, and had the drive and the clout to get things done, was designated as the Chairman with complete authority. Signals were given to all Government Departments that all help be extended to Maruti and its proposals be cleared swiftly, without any bureaucratic delay or objections. The best available persons were selected. And all those who joined Maruti were quite conscious of the fact that unless they showed results they would have no place in the organization or elsewhere.

5) Initial care and planning

The hand picked team of professional managers at Maruti Udyog Ltd., were of the view that careful selection of the right products and technology, equipment and plant layout, technology transfer arrangements, cost control strategy and timely project implementation were necessary prerequisites for future excellent performance. If these aspects were not ensured, then regardless of subsequent company effort, the result would be sub-optimal. Taking the right decisions has contributed a great deal to Maruti's success story.

6) Choice of product range

Even before the establishment of Maruti Udyog Ltd., the Government had started the process of locating a product and a collaborator for the project. They had discussions with automobile manufacturers in Europe and had selected an 1800 cc model of Renault as suitable for launching in India.

The Maruti team felt that this choice was not correct. In order to arrive systematically at a better suited vehicle for the Indian market, the team commissioned a market survey and studied the world automobile industry. The market survey made an enquiry into the spending capacity, pattern of car usage, buying considerations, etc. of potential customers. The results of the market survey indicated that Indian customers gave the highest priority to the initial price and running cost in their decision to buy a car. Further, the study established certain facts about the usage pattern of cars in India, which demolished the myth that since a large number of passengers would be carried a large car was required. The survey found that almost 90 percent of the time a car is used, less than 6 passengers travel in it and similarly almost 90 percent of the time no luggage is carried.

A study of the world automobile market also established that the Japanese automobile industry had a clear edge over others, as Japanese cars offered a high level of quality at a lower price. The search, therefore, narrowed down to selecting among the models offered by Japanese automakers.

7)   Selection of collaborator

The choice of Suzuki Motor Company was influenced by their size, approach to production systems and technology transfer, and the cost effectiveness they had achieved in all their operations. Typically, Japanese international competitiveness is based on having, through a series of innovations in the production function, reduced the cost of operations while improving upon the quality of production; and this was demonstrated in Suzuki also. Suzuki had certain other strong points which made them most attractive as a partner in our project. They were the leader in Japan for small cars — they had the largest share of the small car domestic and export market cars. Their production technology also seemed to have the right mix of automation and use of human labour for adoption in India. Their commercial terms were also the most competitive. The agreements with Suzuki Motor Company were finalized in October, 1982.

8)   Maruti's project decisions

Maruti decided on its project size and product-mix after a careful study of optimal project size considerations and the Indian market requirements. At that time the combined production of the Indian car industry amounted to just over 40,000 vehicles per year. However, Government forecasts predicted a demand of 150,000 cars per year by 1989—90. Modern automobile plants in Japan and elsewhere are built for capacities ranging from 100,000 to 500,000 and up. The volume in this industry is highly sensitive and a high production level is necessary to enjoy low costs possible through economies of scale. Keeping these considerations in mind, Maruti decided on a project size of 100,000 vehicles per year.

Further, the company decided to launch several models built around the same power pack. This was a strategy already adopted by many manufacturers. Through this means, the company could offer several models to attract different segments of the market and thus enlarge its overall market size. The company would also have greater flexibility to change its product-mix in response to any market preference fluctuation.

9)   Step by step approach to project implementation

The project was implemented in two phases. The first phase created a capacity of 40,000 vehicles a year, and was completed by July, 1984, and the second phase which raised capacity to 100,000 vehicles a year was completed in April, 1986. An important feature of the project implementation was the adoption of a stage by stage approach to capital investment. The installation of various facilities was done progressively, starting from the downstream end. Thus the assembly shop was the first facility to be commissioned. Then came the welding shop and the paint shop, followed by engine assembly. The press shop and the machine shop which supply input for the welding shop and engine assembly shop respectively, were commissioned last. This approach has ensured that idle capital was minimized, as most facilities were fully utilized within six months of commissioning. It has also helped Maruti to absorb and understand the technology in stages, to fully master one activity before proceeding to the next, to recruit and train technical and managerial manpower gradually, and to minimize problems arising from the grouping of new activities together at any one time. This step-by-step approach is typical of the Japanese system of project implementation, and has shown that it has great advantages in minimising cost and ensuring that facilities installed are commissioned smoothly, and reach full utilization in much shorter periods of time than is the general average in the country.

10) Transfer of technology

Maruti wanted to make sure that they would have a successful collaboration and their products would be comparable in quality, cost and productivity with that of their collaborator. A major priority, therefore, was to ensure the effective transfer of technology. In planning the project, and in the selection of equipment, they were guided by Suzuki engineers, but their own engineers were involved in every stage so that they would be fully familiar with all the details of the project right from the planning stage.

Apart from sending their managers and supervisors to Japan for training at Suzuki's factories, Maruti also got Suzuki supervisors to work together with their supervisors and workers on the shop-floor so that technology transfer could take place on the line itself. These methods contributed a great deal to the speed and effectiveness of learning the Japanese methods.

11) Human resources — the key elements

From the exposure to the functioning of their Japanese collaborator, Maruti learned that while engineering know-how and the knowledge of the techniques of production are important, one of the most critical functions of an organization is the management of its human resource.

a. The motivation, skill and efficiency of the people working in an organization eventually determine the productivity of the whole organization including the output and quality of the machines. The Japanese organizations were keenly aware of this fact and had for many years been consciously involved in the development of their people.

b. Japanese organizations seemed to work like one large group. Everyone worked with coordination and commitment towards common, shared goals. It was important to bring that feeling into the organization.

c. At Maruti Udyog Ltd., conscious steps were taken to achieve the following two goals in respect to employees:
   - motivate every employee to contribute his/her best to the work;
   - promote a work-culture in which everyone works in a systematic and concerted manner to achieve the goals of the company.

d. The steps they took can be classified into four groups:
   - Conveying to every employee, the sense that he/she is equally important to the company.
   - Eestablishing a system for good communication.
   - Education and training.
   - Establishing the credibility of the management.

e. Conveying a sense of equality
   They attempted to make every employee feel special especially those at lower levels and that they were equally important to the company. The first step was to treat everyone as equal human beings, Maruti adopted systems which would be symbolic of this egalitarian culture and tried to avoid any measure which tended to widen disparities. Some of the measures they adopted were:
   - Identical uniforms, including the fabric and tailoring, for all Maruti employees starting from the Chairman downwards.
   - A common canteen with the same food and same sitting area for all employees up to the Chairman.
   - Common toilets.
   - Common transport facilities.
   - Open offices with no separate rooms for anyone except the Chief Executive.
   - Equal facilities for all in offices, including air-conditioning, furniture etc.

12) Establishing good communications
   Communication informs, educates and motivates. Maruti took several steps to create an open culture in which there was sharing of useful and relevant information across departmental boundaries and across hierarchical levels. Some of the measures implemented include:
   - Open offices, with managers and staff sitting together in a large hall. There are no closed cabins for managers. Every manager

and subordinate is visible and approachable which not only
makes for easy communication, but also good supervision.

- Practise of regularly scheduled meetings such as morning
  meetings consisting of all persons from one section or department;
  Inter-departmental problem solving meetings such as Production
  Planning and Control Meetings, Quality Coordination Committee meetings, Product Committee meetings etc.
  Management Committee meetings — a weekly meeting on a
  fixed day and time attended by all members of the top management team.
- Printed monthly news and policy bulletins such as a company
  newsletter and managing directors letter.
- Display of production results and quality performance on the
  shop floor.
- Maruti Sahyog Samiti, a forum constituted by employee representatives of all departments and hierarchical levels, to discuss
  issues of common interest to all employees including personnel
  policies.
- Establishment of detailed systems for smooth work in all
  areas, and the progressive computerization of these systems to
  improve their efficiency.

13) Education and training

A new work culture based on different value systems required
an intensive re-orientation and education programme. Many of Maruti's
employees had joined from other organizations and had brought with
them different ideas about the way of working in a company. They had
to be persuaded to Maruti's point of view. There were also a number
of recruits who were either fresh from educational or training institutes
or had very little previous experience; they had to be inducted into a
new way of life.

The education process was carried out by internal seminars, discussions, training in Japan and associated exposure to Japanese
methods, through various policy statements by the Chief Executive in
letters to employees, through orientation programmes and through the
use of posters. A sustained effort had to be put in over many years and
is still continuing.

Another Japanese idea which has been gainfully employed in
Maruti is that of the Quality Circle (QC). Each QC is a training forum
in which workers and supervisors voluntarily participate. Through the
QC a large number of employees spend time thinking about how to

improve productivity in his or her work area. It changes their attitude toward work.

In Maruti, there are over 300 Quality Circles. In 1986—87 over 15,000 suggestions were generated, of which 27 percent were implemented, leading to a recurring saving of Rs.6 lakhs/month. Every month between 1000—2000 fresh suggestions are generated.

14) Establishing the credibility of management

Since management was acting in the position of teachers it was all the more necessary first to establish their credibility. Practising what was being preached seemed to be the most effective way of communicating and impressing the new ideas on the others.

It was, therefore, important that all managers set a visible example by wearing the same uniform, eating together in the canteen, making efforts to become familiar with subordinates, and in learning about the work etc. All rules and practices were made equally applicable to managers.

Similarly, on the shop floor Maruti emphasized that the managers and supervisors be knowledgeable of the work being done and where required, for example's sake, do the work of an assembly line worker or welder as the case may be. Engineer Trainees are required to work on the shop floor for 6 months as part of their induction training, before they are absorbed in their respective departments.

In Maruti, if employees are being exhorted to work hard, then managers must actually work the hardest in order to set an example. Once that is so, the message gets home.

4.11 Conclusions

It can be seen from the above that a very major factor for success was the selection of the right products, technology and equipment plant lay out, technology transfer arrangements, cost control strategy and project implementation without any time and cost overruns. Maruti management was strong enough to convince the Government to modify its investment decisions. This was possible because of the stature of Mr. V. Krishnamurthy, who apart from having been secretary to the Government of India, had direct access to the late Prime Minister, Mrs. Indira Gandhi, and later on to Mr. Rajiv Gandhi. No politician or bureaucrat, even at the level of Minister or Secretary to the Government, could interfere with the management of Maruti. Mr. Krishnamurthy had a free hand in the selection of personnel and technology collaborator and got the finances which he asked for. Even

Government policies have been modified from time to time, eg. regarding industrial licencing, importation policy, custom and excise duties etc. In order to provide flexibility in the product mix, the Government permitted many industries to change the product mix within the licenced capacity this is called broad-banding. Formerly imports of equipments and parts were not permitted but the Government relaxed import restrictions and reduced excise duty on fuel efficient cars.

The parallel with ONGC makes it apparent that enterprises will do well if great care is taken in the selection of technology and personnel and if the management is given a free hand. Regarding human resources, training and retraining, multitrade expertise, and active participation are sina quo non for quality and technological efficiency. If the people are bright, dedicated and motivated and adequate care has been taken in the initial stages of selecting the product and technology, any organization can meet future challenges on the basis of their internal strength alone.

CASE STUDIES: JAPAN

by   Professor Makoto Kanda
Associate Professor
Meiji-Gakuin University

1. Introduction

Current Status of State-Owned Enterprises in Japan

In Japan there are four kinds of State-Owned Enterprises (SOEs), in terms of ownership.

1) Completely owned SOE:
The State has a 100% ownership.

2) Partly owned SOE:
The State has less than 100% ownership. Of course, those enterprises can be classified into smaller groups, based on the degree of ownership and on the partner.

3) Indirectly owned SOE:
The SOE (completely or partly) has an owner.

4) Locally owned SOE:
The local government has its own enterprise.

The working area of SOEs concentrates on public utilities, social capital, finance and insurance, and social services. There is no such area as manufacturing.

In comparision with other countries' SOEs, Japanese SOEs are said to have three characteristics.

1) The role that SOEs take in the national economy is not very important on a quantitative basis. The ratio of SOEs' net assets to national net assets is less than 10%, and the proportion of their labor forces is about 5%.

2) Japanese SOEs are limited to so called infrastructure sectors such as transportation, communication, and so on. They don't expand their activities into basic industrial sectors such as steel, oil, aircraft, etc., which can be seen in some European and Asian countries.

3) However, SOEs in the finance sector have played an important role in the post-war economy. They invest in and finance economic

61

areas which are important to the national economy but overlooked by private enterprises. Thus they complement private accumulation of capital, and assist the national economy to realize a high rate growth.

The post-war history of Japanese SOEs is summed up as follows:

1945—1955: Dissolution and reorganization of prewar SOEs and establishment of new SOEs
1955—1965: Establishment of SOEs in the finance sector
1965—1975: Emergence of management crisis
1975—1984: Simultaneous progress of the management crisis and the financial crisis of State Government
1985—   : Privatization and division

So, Japanese SOEs are at a historical turning point, the movement towards privatization.

Three public corporations were cited as typical SOEs in Japan. They were Japan National Railways Corporation (JNR), Nippon Telegraph and Telephone Public Corporation (NTT), and Japan Monopoly Corporation (JMC). All of these have already been privatized. On April 1, 1985, NTT and JMC were privatized and changed their names to Nippon Telegraph and Telephone Corporation (NTT) and Nippon Tobacco Industry Corporation (NTI). On April 1, 1987, JNR was privatized and changed its name to Japan Railways Corporation (JR). So they are all in the on-going process of revolution.

2.   Survey Objective and Framework

Considering the situation in Japan as mentioned above, it was most promising to make a survey on the process of privatization. The current main task of Japanese SOEs' management is how to overcome the deficiencies of state owned enterprises while maintaining the quality of their services, by transforming them into private corporations.

2.1 Survey Objective

Our main survey objective is to discover and overcome the problems of SOEs' management, by researching the transition processes of privatization of typical SOEs; Nippon Telegraph and Telephone Corporation (NTT) and Japan Railways Corporation (JR).

The objective was broken down into the following questions:

- Why did they have to proceed to the privatization, or what was their management crisis and how did it emerge?
  - The answers to these questions will bring the management

problems and the mechanism of their emergence into relief.
- How did they achieve the privatization?
    - The answer to this question will clarify the way to introduce big change such as the privatization into SOEs, that is the management of transition.
- What has changed and is changing after the privatization, or what kinds of management problems in the pre-privatization period did they resolve and how?
    - The answers will make clear the meaning of privatization and the way to improve the management of SOEs.

2.2 Survey Framework

Based on an organization theory and strategic management theory, our theoretical framework of the survey is contrived as in Figure 1. An SOE is a corporation which provides products or services to a competitive market under the restrictions given by direct interest groups — controlling bodies (the Government, controlling agents) and labor unions.

The performance quality of an SOE increases or decreases according to the extent it adapts to its market passively or proactively (external fitness) and to the extent that strategy, organizational structure, management system, and organizational culture adapt to one another (internal fitness). Therefore, a task imposed on the management of an SOE is to achieve external and internal fitness at one time.

Detailed explanations of these variables are as follows.

2.3 Direct Interest Groups

Those organizations which directly limit the behaviour of an SOE. The Government (the Diet) regulates the scope of its activities by means of laws and controlling agents (the Ministries concerned) and guides the behaviour both formally and informally. The labor union also restricts them through its bargaining power.

2.4 Market

A market gives important information about the action that an SOE should take. The characteristics of its customers, the life stage of the market, the degree and nature of competition, etc. all influence its strategic behaviour, and vice versa.

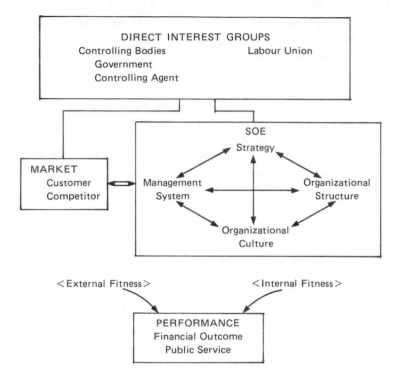

Fig. 1   Framework of Survey

2.5 SOE

This indicates those factors that show the behavior of an SOE, which are the object of its management. They consist of four sub-categories;

— strategy: mission (goal), scope of business and service, functional strategies such as finance, marketing, R&D, and so on.

— organizational structure: the features of the hierarchy, formal structure of authority, pattern of division of labour.

— management system: communication and management information system, decision making system, incentive system, promotion system, recruiting system, education and training system, and so on.

— organizational culture: value system relating to the mission, management style, individual action, etc.

2.6 Performance

This indicates the results of SOEs' behaviour, that is, the degree of
of both external and internal fitness.

3. Problems Faced: What Makes an SOE So Inefficient?

Privatization is a solution to the management crisis of an SOE.
Therefore it is indispensable to know why and how an SOE became
problematic. The blame cannot be laid on only one cause. There were
many causes, and these interacted with one another to make a vicious
circle. Based on our framework, this vicious circle can be analyzed as
follows.

3.1 Direct Interest Group

After the Second World War, Japanese transportation, telephone
and telegraph systems started from a zero base. Because the systems
were in the public utility sector, government and controlling agencies
regulated the activities of JNR and NTT strictly.

By the laws concerned, the business areas were constrained to railway transportation and telegraph and telephone, and the most critical
decisions, such as business plans, budgets, personnel management of top
management, fare or charges, equipment investments, etc. had to be
approved by the National Diet. Retired government officials of the
Ministries of Transportation and Posts and Telecommunications
(controlling agents) joined their top management.

This meant that SOEs were inclined to be affected by political
movements; an inclination to produce inefficient services under the
name of a public utility, disregarding cost. It also meant that the top
management of SOEs had little free hand to manage; they had low
morale and little responsibility.

The management had no authority to decide major working conditions such as wages. The wage was decided by a third body disregarding each SOE's financial outcome so that employees of all public
enterprises had an equal wage level. This meant that the management
and the labour unions of an SOE could not open normal bargaining; the
labour union could not trust the management as a bargaining partner,
which gave rise to antagonism between them; it would rather negotiate
mainly with the Government (which had substantial decision making
authority), which implied that its activities became a sort of political
struggle taking no account of the financial performance. The labour
union of JNR broke itself up into several unions according to different

political creeds. They supported different political parties and fought against one another.

3.2 Market

The market was rapidly changing. An SOE as a public utility had had the ultimate goal to deliver universal service all over Japan. Given that the transportation market was in the birth or growth stage and there were no other transportation systems, and telegraph and telephone markets were not in the mature stage and there were no competitors, it still might be an ultimate goal. However, on one hand, transportation structures (or transportation needs) had changed and other transportation systems became strong competitors. On the other hand, the advent of an information era evoked many kinds of needs for telecommunication and new competitors entered into the market. An SOE had to respond to a variety of customers' needs and had to struggle against competitors.

Immediately after the Second World War and until the 1960's, railway transportation was taking a leading role. However, short and middle distance transportation was shouldered by car and private railway companies, and long distance, by airplane.

Until the 1970's, the demand for telephones had excelled the supply. But after that, the frequency of new telephone installations decreased, and the revenue of telephone services, which formed about 90% of NTT's income dropped drastically. Also, a variety of needs for telephone services such as facsimile, car telephone, etc. gradually appeared.

3.3 Strategy

Because of the legal regulations and the comparably stable environment of the above mentioned — uniform needs and little competition — the strategy of SOEs focussed on a narrow scope of business and uniform service for all customers in that business area.

JNR made it a central objective to provide equal transportation service all over Japan, and restricted its business to transportation on rails.

NTT promoted 'no waiting' for installation of telephones and perfect transfer from non-automatic hand connection systems to automatic dial connection as two main goals until 1980.

The marketing strategies of SOEs were extremely limited, and little effort was devoted to responding to customers' needs. JNR and NTT barely listened to customers' grievances in order to improve their services. They had no need to show what kind of enterprises they were, through public relations activities. They had little knowledge of customer relations.

Finance strategy was not based on cost consciousness. JNR continued to borrow money not only from the Government but also banks, insurance companies, etc., to invest in construction of the super express train and other equipment. The total funded debt accumulated to more than 23 trillion yen in 1985. Under the strict budget system and huge volume of necessary investment for a telecommunication infrastructure, NTT also had more than 5 trillion yen of accumulated funded debt in 1980.

R&D strategy focussed on basic research and sometimes excess investment was undertaken.

These strategies adapted to the past environment. But since then the environment changed, and they should have evolved.

3.4 Organizational Structure

Structure follows strategy. Under the monopoly, functional organizational structure is the most rational approach to realize unity of technology and universal service all over the national network.

JNR had a hierarchy with three major layers; at the top was the head office with its 25 departments; then the 28 railway management bureaus; and at the bottom were 23 operating organizations. Each level was divided by its function into general affairs, accounting, operations, sales, equipment, and electricity. Decision making and communication routes were also divided by their functions from the top to the bottom.

NTT had a functional organization with three product divisions. It had a four-layer hierarchy; the head office; 11 telecommunication bureaus; 69 city or district telecommunication departments; and at the bottom, telephone exchange offices. Each level was also divided by function into sales, operations, maintenance, etc., and decisions and communication were made by these functional routes.

According to this functional organizational structure, the decision making structure was highly centralized at the Head Office. The hierarchy was tall and strict. This organizational structure could have been effective, if the environment continued to be stable.

3.5 Management System

Because the business area and the core technology (aggregate knowledge to do the business) was stable, decision making systems were centralized. The Head Office set an operation object and budget, and controlled operation departments based on it. Information flowed up and down the functional communication loops, and conflicts among operation departments were solved by the upper sections.

The Human Resource Management System is an important management system. It consists of recruiting, education and training, merit rating, reward (incentive), and a promotion system. The recruiting and promotion systems are linked tightly together. A small number of university graduates were recruited by the Head Office as candidates for the top management. Other university graduates were recruited by local offices as candidates for middle and lower management. High school graduates rarely became managers. There was a rigid three-track recruiting and promotion system. This caste system spoiled employees' aspirations and bore social disunion, the feeling of "us and them." Furthermore, since quick promotion of univeristy graduates deprived them of their opportunities to relate with customers directly, top management were becoming more and more out of touch with customer orientation.

Merit rating systems were characterized as so called "subtractionism": if you didn't commit any faults, and did nothing to challenge the system, you received an average score, and climbed up your career ladder step by step. This planted a non-challenging attitude among all management.

Management positions were closely linked with a qualification system which had 13 ranks. A Head Office position was ranked higher than that of the same in the local offices. Wages of management were also linked with the location. So to climb up the career ladder, they had to change their position/location. Actually they changed the career ladder. Thus, management changed every two or three years, and under this situation, they were trained and developed as generalists, not specialists.

On one hand because SOEs were owned by the State, there was no fear of bankruptcy or dismissal. On the other hand, only enough authority to run the enterprise was given to management. Both management and employees lacked a seriousness towards business, sensitivity to competition, and customer orientation. The organizational structure and management system made the organizational members very conservative. Therefore, most members thought it was right to do only things which were ordered from the higher ranks.

4. Triggers for Privatization

There are two objectives in proceeding with privatization; one is to improve an SOE's efficiency, and the other is to make it able to adapt to its changing environment. Of course these two interact with each other, and each privatization attached more importance to one than the other. The privatization of NTT laid more emphasis on the former, and that of JR on the latter.

NTT was the only enterprise which showed no red figures, and a good financial performance. But with the coming era of an intense telecommunication network it required global competitiveness.

JNR subsided into red figures in 1964, when the "Shinkansen," the super express line opened between Tokyo and Osaka. It had been producing a deficit since then. Seven rebuilding programs were tried, and failed. There came about a kind of consensus that no efforts within an existing framework would succeed. Some drastic reform programmes were eventually sought.

The pressure of imbalanced finances of the Government made it an urgent task to reform public administration. In 1981, the Government organized a Special Committee on Administrative Reform which discussed and made a report on how to improve the administration. Problems of SOEs were also discussed and privatization was the answer. The answer appeared in 1982, and the law concerning the transition towards NTT's privatization was passed in 1984, and that of JNR in 1986.

The direct kickoff of NTT's revolution happened in 1981, when Hisashi Shinto was appointed President. In the previous year, the fact came out that NTT had manipulated its accounts illegally — as if there had been a lot of overtime work and business trips etc., so as to provide more pay than determined by the Diet. He had been President of Ishikawajima-Harima Heavy Industry and had rebuilt it successfully. So he was expected to reform NTT satisfactorily.

He felt at first the necessity to change NTT's way of thinking. Because of the monopoly, state ownership and long term scarcity of telephones, there was no customer consciousness. So he introduced a lot of changes as listed below.

4.1 Public Relations System

Of course there had been a public relations system, but it had been a one-way communication system, from NTT to the customer; that is, no efforts had been made to listen to the customer. In 1981, the so called PONTIACS (Project Of NTT's Total Information And Communication Strategy) was introduced. Its slogan was "Public Heart to NTT, NTT's Heart to the Public," and its main purpose was to listen to the public and to build up a two-way communication system with the customers. In other words, it was to implant in all the members the needs of the customer first, instead of NTT's. To realize this purpose, three mechanisms were made: a customer representative council, an orange committee, and an orange counter.

The customer representatives council consisted of people with leadership in a community around each telephone office. It was held quarterly, and customers revealed the needs in their own area. Orange was the color which was selected to symbolize the PONTIACS. The orange committee was an organization in NTT whose task was to respond as quickly as possible to opinions and grievances from customers. Customers were also able to voice their opinions at an orange counter in a telephone office.

4.2 Working Group

Among the SOE members, especially management, they were apt to do only the things which were ordered by a superior. The main reason for this was that subordinates had little authority to decide, and the division of labour made it difficult to do the things which required cooperation among departments. In 1982, the President organized working groups consisting of middle management throughout the departments. They were divided into eight groups, which surveyed the problems (those which NTT faced at that time and those it would face in the near future) and provided remedies.

Although almost all managers were very conservative, a few talented young middle managers were dubious that NTT could get along without drastic changes, and eagerly wanted to do something new. They were key members for the revolution, because they could influence not only upper management but also front line workers. They were gathered from every department, and given responsibility and authority. The President attended the meetings as often as possible. He injected his management policy into them through discussion and questioning.

4.3 Rationalization of Work

NTT moved only by existing rules. However, a variety of needs could not be satisfied by out-of-date working rules. In 1981, a committee was established to improve ways to work. The rationalization was realized by introducing quality control groups in every workshop. Quality control activities in blue collar workshops were named the ASK movement, which stood for Anzen (safety of work), Sokuou (quick response to customer), and Kouritsu (efficiency of investment).

Rationalization in white collar workshops was called MI (management innovation) movement. The first step was aimed at questioning the way work had been done, and to eliminate waste. Paper reduction, rearrangement and cut down on survey reports, and readjustment of documents and files was conducted. The second step was to check the remaining materials and to put some of them into a computer data base. The final object of the MI movement was to realize office automation.

These efforts of course were effective in achieving rationalization of work. But they also had more important effects. Workers in the bottom echelons participated in the process of revolution; they began to doubt their own past behavior, and decided to change.

4.4 Accounting System

As in the budget decided by the Diet, NTT settled an account only once a year. This made members less cost conscious. So the system was changed to provide a balance sheet every month. By this accounting alteration, cost consciousness was awoken, and cost was reduced.

By making these changes, a spontaneous reaction appeared at the management level. In Chugoku area, the top management decided to move towards privatization. In the beginning he put up seven emphases on action; all employees participate in sales activity to maintain and increase share; to open a circuit and to speed up repair on customers' base; to give good service; to build up a reliable sales system; to increase efficient investment; rationalization of work; and to realize reasonable arrangement of personnel. This spontaneous movement spread out to other areas.

All these changes meant that NTT had taken a step toward privatization by itself before the Diet decided to transfer its ownership to the public.

The Committee for the Rebuilding of the Japan National Railway was established in 1983 by order of the Diet, and it started to make plans for the division and privatization. But resistance by the parties concerned was strong. Management of JNR split in two. One was a group against privatization, and the other for it. The former consisted of many more members than the latter. Initially the "against" group won, and the members of the "for" group were expelled from the Head Office to district offices. The "against" group made its own reform plan supporting non-privatization and non-division, and was confronted by the Committee. At that time the trend lay towards the non-privatization of JNR.

During this against trend, "for," or reformer groups, tried everything they could. One person who was expelled to Hokkaido made a lot of experiments for the reformation. His experiments were related to discovering a way to respond to customers' needs, which could not be achieved through the standards at the Head Office. Through these successful experiments the seeds of reform were sewn.

The reformer group, though small in number, also tried to approach statesmen and the Committee for the Rebuilding of Japan National Railways. They met the Chairman of the Committee, and stressed the necessity of changing the top management of JNR to take a step towards rebuilding.

The trend changed when the President and chief executive officers were reshuffled in 1985. The inside revolution process began then. Main changes were established as follows.

4.5 Decision Making

The new President Sugiura set up the Headquarters Committee for Promotion of Rebuilding which had 22 project teams to investigate a variety of problems in transformation towards privatization and division, and a Headquarters Committee on Surplus Workers.

He also changed decision rules; the decision making process proceeded from first line management meetings to top management meetings step by step along the management hierarchy. This had taken about two weeks. The framework of decision making was changed but the existing bureaucratic hierarchy remained. People concerned with the theme being discussed were gathered from bottom to top one at a time, and a conclusion was made. Through this change, not only was decision making accelerated, but also all necessary information was flowed through the President.

4.6 Personnel Administration

Personnel administration was one of the critical factors in the transition. The President did not reshuffle management personnel drastically at first, because drastic changes from "against" group members to "for" would produce another big split among management, which would make it more difficult to introduce a smooth transition. Only small amounts of reshuffling took place, and a lot of meetings were held to unify both groups.

In 1986 when the law concerning division and privatization began to be passed by the National Diet, a big reshuffle of management was undertaken. This was a kind of preparation for division and privatization in the coming year. Almost 20,000 management personnel were moved to new positions. There were two aims for this reshuffle. One was to change positions on an ability basis, not on length of service as before. This meant a change in the reward system, and was intended to change management's attitude toward work. The other was to move able men to district areas. Men of ability had been moved from district areas to the Head Office, which had bred the attitude of ignoring district activities and their different individual needs. So this change meant that JNR changed its stance regarding districts and expected management to change their attitude from Head Office orientation to district orientation.

In short, some spontaneous movement towards privatization had already begun both inside NTT and JNR according to the movement outside.

4.6.1 Changes in Relation With External Interest Groups

The spontaneous movement inside evoked changes in relationships with external interest groups.

NTT already had a good labour relationship between management and unions. Comparing with unions of JNR, its stance toward privatization was more moderate. The main interest of the union was to improve their members' working conditions. Although NTT achieved good performance, wage and other working conditions they kept equal with other public corporations in red figures. So privatization, which meant that workers could get better wages and other working conditions when they achieved better performance, was positively accepted at last.

Of course agreements among them were not automatically realized. A bargaining system was required to reach the agreement. It had a four-level bargaining system; Head Office, district, area, and shop level. Each level had its own bargaining function. By thoroughly discussing matters, both management and union leaders understood each other completely. Though it took much time, it was a better way to represent workers' opinions than when only Head Office level bargaining was held and professional leaders had an inclination to leave workers far behind while searching for an ideological goal.

JNR had a different situation. It had many trade unions. However, the bigger ones were Kokurou, Tetsurou, Dourou, and Zenshirou. The biggest one being Kokurou was most militant. In 1984, surplus work forces reached 24,500, and management proposed to unions a reduction plan consisting of three measures; revision of the retirement system, calling for layoff at request, and temporary transference. Tetsurou, Dourou and Zenshirou agreed, seeing that it was unavoidable to maintain employment. Though Kokurou refused at first, they finally came to an agreement the following year.

In 1986, management asked them to cooperate to solve the problems faced and to receive cooperation from the government and other outside groups concerned. Again the same reactions occurred. The three moderate unions came to an agreement but Kokurou did not.

The three unions which changed their way to collaborating for reformation towards privatization as mentioned above, began to move hand in hand to get leadership in unions without Kokurou. The workers also began to show their change in attitude. A lot of workers withdrew from Kokurou and joined one of the three others. The three unions organized a conference on the revolution of JNR, and began to take the first steps to become one union.

JNR also tried to change their relationship with politicians. Occasionally public corporations were sources of concessions. At first constructions of new lines and other facilities were targets, then came rights to open a shop in a station. The decision to permit shops in stations was transferred to a chief area officer. Because he had a close relationship with the area and the local politician in charge, who rarely refused an application. This was one of the reasons for inefficient investments. So JNR decided to change the application system by checking all applications at the Head Office, which made it easier to refuse.

Another change was with so called related companies. JNR and NTT had a lot of related companies, and they were called "NTT family" or "JNR family." These companies made continuous transactions based on personnel and other ties. Usually they imposed more cost than in competitive transactions. So they began to try to introduce competition in transactions. They opened all material obtainable to non-related companies.

4.7 Privatization and Division

With all these changes both inside and outside of the SOEs, privatization was decided by the Diet. Though NTT was not divided at that moment, the dispute concerning division still existed, and it was included in the laws concerning the privatization of NTT to discuss the matter again three years after the privatization. And in 1988, the Ministry of Posts and Telecommunication began to investigate the necessity of the division.

For JNR, on the contrary, it was decided to be divided. The passengers department was divided into six district bases; Hokkaido, Higashi Nippon, Tokai, Nishi Nippon, Shikoku, and Kyushu Passengers Company. Luggage transportation department became an independent company. JNR Liquidation Company was established to liquidate the accumulated deficit of JNR.

The distribution of the accumulated deficit and work force were the most important matters. Almost all of the deficit was taken over by JNR Liquidation Company, and other new companies distributed the rest based on their expected profits. It was planned to transfer nearly all of the work force to new passenger and luggage companies. When a surplus work force was produced, JNR Liquidation Company would take care of it. There were about 260,000 workers at JNR, and 200,000 transferred to new companies. More than 50,000 workers were retired and about 6,000 surplus workers were under the protection of JNR Liquidation Co.. However, they would have to find alternative employment in three years.

4.7.1   Key Factors for Success of Transformation

Though many different factors for success were found between NTT and JNR, there were some important key factors common to both, which are shown as follows.

1)   Top management personnel

The change of top management does not always mean that the movement towards privatization will be led to success. But top management who have had some experience with privatization or who have had a lot of experience within private enterprise are necessary, because they are executors as well as symbols of necessity for privatization.

2)   Discovery and utilization of vanguards

Although small in numbers like the "for" group in JNR, there were some people who felt the necessity for change and did something for the change spontaneously. The first step was to discover who and place them in core positions as change executors. It was they who had more commitment to the change than anyone else.

3)   Utilization of middle management

Middle management is a critical layer in an organization, not only because they understand top management policy completely, but because they know about what goes on shop floors in detail. Meaning, they are in the right position to link changed policies to reality. Of course to make it reality, some system must be devised. An important one is a decision making system. Like working groups in NTT, middle management have to participate in top decision making. This makes it possible to let necessary information flow both upward and downward without distortion, which is indispensable to bring about big changes in unions. Another important one is to transfer not only responsibility but authority.

Utilization of middle management has another meaning. It is unavoidable to include all workers in a change process to make it successful. Involving middle management is the first step to extend the change movement to shop floor workers.

4)   Reform within an established framework as a first step

Transformation from state-owned enterprise to private enterprise is a big change, and is not completed in a day. It also means a sort of paradigm change, a change in organizational culture. The very first step has to be defreezing the established paradigm or established way of behaviour. This can be done by questioning all of the established behaviour patterns. ASK movement and MI movement in NTT for example.

Although there is no big change in strategy, organizational structure, management system, and organizational culture, all members become distrustful of behaviour and prepare to accept a big change. This defreezing process is a pre-requisite to bring in such reforms as privatization.

5)   Involving external collaborators

An enterprise can not exist by itself. So, if it has any intentions to change, it needs someone outside to help. As trade unions have a strong influence on behaviour, collaborators must be found. In the JNR's case, there were three unions which agreed to transfer to a private enterprise. Though the biggest union resisted, privatization was completed by the assistance of the agreeable three.

As it is very difficult to find an external collaborator, it is necessary to build good communication routes on a daily basis like the one found in NTT's bargaining system.

5.   Changes in Privatized SOEs: A Search for New Fitness

As mentioned above, there was internal and external fitness in the SOEs. However the pressure from direct interest groups and the conditions of markets have changed. Therefore, it must discover a new fitness both internally and externally. To know how to realize this fitness, it is required to understand how the direct groups and the market has changed.

5.1 Direct Interest Groups

The changes in laws concerning the privatization have slackened the interventions of politics. There are still regulations on the behaviour of these SOEs on behalf of public welfare. For example, NTT has regulations on telephone charges, personnel of top management, sale of important assets, and so on. However, the degree of intervention from politics has weakened.

The attitude of trade unions has also changed. The change can be seen especially in JR trade unions. They reorganized themselves. According to the transition to private enterprises, the biggest and most militant Kokurou has decreased its members, and divided itself into two unions, Kokurou and Tessan Souren. The three moderate unions have unified themselves into Tetsudo Rouren, and become the largest. Kokurou had more than 140,000 members before the privatization, and has shrunk to 40,000. Tessan Souren has 30,000 members and Tetsudo Rouren, 130,000.

Tetsudo Rouren has a campaign policy which is the most critical goal to make JR get on the right track, and that it is, the most desirable way to acquire better working conditions is by co-operating with the management. Harmonious and stable labour relations are being built gradually, using these methods.

5.2 Market

As mentioned above, the market of JNR was very competitive. The customers had already been given a basic transportation service. The quality rather than quantity of the service became a key point of competition. JR had to satisfy various needs much more quickly.

NTT's market has drastically changed since privatization. It enjoyed the monopoly before, but after privatization it faced a free market. Basically any private enterprise can enter the telecommunication business. The market is divided into three by the law concerned. Enterprises in the first grade telecommunication business are those which have a telecommunication network facility of their own and provide telecommunication services. As this business has characteristics of a public service, the entrant is required to get a license from the Minister of Posts and Telecommunication. The second grade telecommunication business is to provide many kinds of services by renting telecommunication facilities from a first grade enterprise. It consists of two kinds of businesses. The special second grade enterprise provides its service nation wide or internationally, and the general second grade, within a district. The former has to register when it starts its business.

NTT is a first grade business, and seven new entrants called as new common carrier (NCC) have received licenses. NCCs are backed up by giant companies such as Toyota, Tokyo Electric Power, JR, and so on. Special second grades number 17, and the general second grade, more than 500. The competition in the market is becoming more and more intense.

These changes in the environment make it necessary to introduce changes in the SOE.

5.3 Strategy

Since both transportation and telecommunication markets have become more mature, uniform service does not satisfy the customers' needs. So, not only providing service at lower prices but also quick response to various kinds of needs has become the main strategy in the core business.

Telecommunication business is still the core business in NTT, for it produces more than 80 per cent of its revenue. Making proposals for new usages of telephones and increasing conveniences of facilities are raised as main objects.

Main revenues of JR Higashi Nippon comes from innermetropolis transportation and middle distance interurban transportation. It changes its diagram to strengthen services in these areas.

Maturity of the market also requires diversification of businesses. However, these privatized enterprises have only a little experience in undertaking other businesses. They utilize external resources to develop their know-how. They establish as many subsidiary companies as possible with private enterprises. Of course in those business areas where they can transfer their own accumulated know-how, they establish companies of their own ownership. According to the degree that they can not use their own skill, they decrease their share of ownership.

NTT has established more than 100 subsidiary companies since privatization. Enlarged business areas are classified into four categories;

1) Information network industries where the technology of NTT can be utilized

2) Telecommunication service industries which assist the core business

of NTT

3) Telecommunication related industries where human resources and facilities of NTT can utilized

4) Community service industries where NTT can assist the development of the community

JR has the intention of becoming like other private railway enterprises. They have already diversified their businesses and more than 30 percent of revenue comes from outside railway transportation, such as real estate agencies, retail, fast food, and so on. Revenue of JR from other businesses is only 3 per cent, so many more subsidiary companies in other business areas are needed.

The marketing strategy of NTT changed gradually after the alteration of top management, as mentioned above. It not only devoted itself to gathering customers' needs, but also displayed commercial messages on its corporate image and products positively. The same happened with JR after privatization.

Without governmental control on finance, NTT and JR were able to plan flexible finance, according to the change in the money market. They can change creditors freely from high rate to lower. Actually NTT cut the average rate of interest from 8 per cent to 7 through this change. Furthermore, it raises funds abroad because of lower costs.

Change in R&D strategy can be seen in NTT more clearly. Before privatization most efforts were devoted to basic research. However after it, not only basic but also applied research and product development were equally pursued. Research laboratories increased from four to eleven, and they specialized in different technology areas. This change was to set up a system to create more original technologies. Product development is delegated to a division which is nearer to the potential and real users of the technology. Therefore, a lot of reserchers moved to divisions.

All these changes in strategy were suitable for a more competitive and stable environment.

5.4 Organizational Structure

Functional organization had its demerits. It took too long to respond to customer needs. It blurred responsibility. To overcome this, organizational structure was changed.

NTT introduced divisionalization. Service related works were divided into departments by the kind of service; telephone, telecommunication network system for companies, high grade telecommunication service, data processing department, and so on. They act on a self-supporting basis so that they are cost and profit conscious.

JR simplified its organization as a first step. JR Higashi Nippon, for example, reduced its departments and sections from 550 to 150, which made the delegation of decision making easier and quicker.

5.5 Management System

According to changes in organizational structure, decision making systems shifted from centralized to decentralized. This made it easier to respond to customers' needs in different districts in different ways.

A new human resource management policy was announced in NTT in 1986. It was called "Basic policy in personnel management from now on," and consisted of five items.

- Develop and appoint those who have plenty of initiative and a challenging spirit
- Build up professional human resource groups
- Grade work force only on its performance and competence
- Make the management layer thinner and attach importance on the front line where customers touch directly
- Get rid of "subtractionism" and the principle of safety first, and put proper merit rating into practice

Big changes were introduced in the human resource management system according to this policy. The first steps taken in the change were to abolish the rigid three-track recruiting system. Discrimination among university graduates was abandoned by recruiting at the Head Office from a wide range of universities.

The merit rating system changed from subtractionism to additionism. In the new system, those who challenged new jobs got higher points;

challenge new job and make it a great success . . . . 3 points
challenge new job and make it a moderate success . . . . . . 2 points
challenge new job and make it a little success . . . . 1 point
challenge new job and fail . . . . 0 point
challenge none of the new jobs at all . . . . minus point

This new system was expected to plant a challenging spirit in all management and actually some outcome is appearing.

First, close linkage with qualifications was abolished. Now workers with the same qualifications as others could reach a higher position and receive a higher salary. Therefore, reshuffling of personnel can be done without considering qualifications.

Both changes are totally different compared to that of before privatization. Now promotion is done on a competence basis rather than on length of service. Some people even skip two or three ranks.

Also, importance is attached to front-line business, i.e. telephone offices. Then those who are able are moved from the Head Office to telephone office branches. Therefore, Head Office personnel decreases and front line workers increase.

The basic policy in training and development system also changed from breeding generalists to specialists. On the job training and development by career shifts is stressed more than off the job training.

All these changes in human resource management are much more flexible and quicker, and therefore more effective in responding to customers' needs.

5.6 Organizational Culture

Because of drastic changes in organizational structure and management system, the attitude of organizational members is gradually changing from very conservative to challenging and aggressive.

5.7 Performance

Though it is too hasty to judge performance of privatized enterprises, some promosing outcomes are appearing. Concerning public services, the attitude toward customers is changing remarkably. Now we can receive a lot of new services more quickly. The financial outcome also shows good results. NTT is still achieving high scores, and JR has achieved more profits than expected in the first year after the privatization.

6. Concluding Remarks

The privatization has just begun. It is too hasty to say if it is successful or not. But so far, results tell us it is promising.

The analysis here shows two important implications. The first is that the change of ownership is not a satisfactory condition for the vitalization of SOEs. According to the change, strategy, organizational structure, management system and organizational culture all have to change together.

The first implication implies a more important one. That is, revitalization itself can be realized without the shift of the ownership, or the privatization. If we give an SOE a much freer hand and make it more flexible so that it becomes able to adapt itself to its environment more dynamically by changing its strategy, organizational structure, management system, and organizational culture, then it can achieve better performance.

CASE STUDIES: SINGAPORE

by   Dr. Douglas Joel Sikorski
Senior Lecturer
School of Management
National University of Singapore

1. Current Status of State-Owned Enteprises in Singapore: Perspective for Privatization

How can the transfer of state-owned enterprises (SOEs) to private ownership be justified in Singapore? The answer to this question is the same as if we were to ask, 'How was the creation of state-owned enterprises justified in Singapore?' Either question can be investigated through an examination of the origins of SOEs in Singapore and their role in the economy to date. Part I surveys this historical context, and then reviews some of the initial privatization efforts. The discussion will reveal the underlying consistency in the government's reasoning throughout, that is, the original rationale for the establishment of SOEs in Singapore is consonant with the logic behind the present privatization policy.

1.1 Overview of the Political-Economic Context

The rationale for the government becoming involved directly in business enterprise ranges from ideological reasons, to rescue takeovers, to a pragmatic design for development. It is no coincidence that those governments which are guided by the latter line of thought have spawned business institutions that are now in many cases keenly competitive in the international arena. Development policies have not only been directed at domestic modernization and progress but also — especially with the wide acceptance of export-oriented (as opposed to import substitution) strategies — at increasing competitiveness in international markets.

The Singapore Government originally became involved in business enterprise to eliminate unemployment and improve the housing situation, which were the major issues in 1959 when the Peoples Action Party (PAP) took office. This purpose soon evolved into a broader motif, as government initiative seemed the most efficient means to rapid industrialization. The Housing Development Board was established in 1960, the Economic Development Board in 1961; and the pace of government formation of new enterprises continued to accelerate throughout the decade. By the 1980s the government's initiatives were more sophisticated, including for example an overseas investment company to manage external reserves and an industrial science park to promote research intensive activities.

One lesson that Singapore seemed to provide to the Third World was that government participation could evolve from two different extremes, only one of which seems advisable for development. First, there is the strategy of nationalizing existing firms, a policy that was disclaimed long ago by Goh Keng Swee.* Second, which is Singapore's stated policy, is public investment in new ventures. In this way the government starts a new operation, creating new wealth. Success then finances more enterprises through internal growth and diversification; and confidence in the government encourages further private invest- ment, often in joint venture with the government. The Jurong Industrial Estates, which in 1963 had only two factories, by 1979 had 902, and by 1988 had 1800.

By 1979, one worker in ten was a government employee. Although this figure is the same as for West Germany, it does not tell the whole story. The dominance of multinational corporations (MNCs) in Singapore would suggest that local participation is indeed mostly governmental. While "the general view is that public enterprise may probably contribute about 14—16% of gross output of total manu- facturing" (in the private sector) (Lee, 1978:150), net investment commitments in manufacturing in Singapore have throughout the 1970s and 1980s generally been more than three-quarters foreign. Thus, concerning domestic response, "The Government is the most important entrepreneur." (Tan Chwee Huat, 9/8/74 Far Eastern Economic Review (FEER))

The greatest concern of policy-makers is that SOEs will be in- efficient and will act as a drag on national development instead of providing the expected impetus which inspired the government to undertake the enterprise in the first place. This is indeed the usual cir- cumstance. However, it will be apparent (from the case studies later) that Singapore's SOEs have performed very well, contrary to the general prediction of mainstream political and academic thinkers. Most problems of SOEs essentially stem from the influence of politics and the imposition of noneconomic goals on management. But Singapore

---

* Goh Keng Swee, a Deputy Prime Minister during the 1960s and 1970s, is generally credited as being the architect of Singaporean economic policy, including the SOE system.

seems to be an exception to the general rule, where it has been observed that "political leaders look upon government and politics as an exercise of state management ... " (Chan, 1981), Chan goes so far as to say that the "style of government looks for the elimination of politics."

The greatest concern of private enterprise, both multinational and domestic, in Singapore as elsewhere, is that the public sector gets privileged treatment. The Singapore government is at least philosophically opposed to favouritism. Per Goh Keng Swee, SOEs should "receive no special privileges." However, there are countless instances to the contrary, certainly in Statutory Boards, for example, the Post Office Savings Bank's (POSB) tax-free savings accounts. In 1979 the Association of Banks in Singapore submitted a written appeal for fairer treatment vis-a-vis the POSB. The government took no action on the appeal. Even so, the attitude of the Singapore Government to protectionism is so derogatory that its SOEs generally seem to staunchly avoid and denigrate this means of competition.

SOEs in Singapore are indeeed subject to the rigours of the market. Goh Keng Swee argued that SOEs should be run like private business. Unsuccessful enterprises have been allowed to fail. Ideologically, Singapore is strongly committed to the free trade movement, hence to free enterprise. Goh Keng Swee has said that "We do not own and run enterprise on ideological grounds." This is tempered by the statement of Prime Minister Lee Kuan Yew (1965) that Singapore is "half socialist, half capitalist, and let the future be decided by the next generation."

One test of the government's ultimate designs is whether its involvement ever reverses itself. In 1979, Goh Chok Tong, then Minister of Trade and Industry, said that "once ... companies succeed, we should in fact divest ourselves of their shares." (FEER, 10/8/79:44) This philosophy portended the privatization policy announced in 1985.

1.2 Historical Development of the Singapore SOE System

Ow (1976:162) presents early data from the Department of Statistics on the relative share of gross fixed capital formation by sector of the economy:

Million S$ by	1960	1965	1973
Public sector	67	216	824
Private sector	75	260	1793

By 1987 the figures were: public sector $5,275.2, private sector $9,907.3. The public sector consistently represented between one-quarter and one-third of total capital from 1974 through 1987 (increasing to over 40% in 1986). (Source: Department of Statistics)

The public sector was indeed extensive: and this sector includes only the government itself and statutory boards, that is, does not include SOEs in the private sector, which we now discuss.

Most private sector companies were owned by the government through holding companies. "Prior to 1973, only the Development Bank of Singapore and the Intraco (International Trading Company) were de facto holding companies for the Government." (Low, 1984: 268) DBS was a spin-off from the Economic Development Board (EDB) in 1968 and became the national development financing institution, later to be licensed as a full-fledged commercial bank. Intraco was also formed in 1968 and expanded and diversified rapidly in subsequent years. The continued growth and success of government enterprise was leading to a complex network of major companies.

The government's main holding company, Temasek, was also Singapore's largest company in terms of net worth. "The Temasek Holdings Pte. Ltd. (THL) formed on 25 June 1974, took over ... shares previously held by the Minister for Finance Incorporated." (Low:Ibid) The Ministry of Finance, directly or indirectly, in fact initiated many new enterprises throughout Singapore's history, and may even be regarded as the nation's original holding company. In addition, the Ministry of Defence "has a holding company, Sheng-Li Holding Company Pte. Ltd. formed in January 1974 which has since 1 December 1975 taken over all equity investments in those companies which were formerly under the Ministry of Finance ... The Ministry of National Development has also incorporated its own Ministry of National Development Holdings Pte. Ltd. on 26 March 1976." (Seah, 1983:136)

In 1979 Temasek was given a full-time secretariat to become more active in project development. From a staff of only two in 1979, by 1986 Temasek had more than 30 people, some of whom were formerly in the Ministry of Finance (but no longer civil servants after joining Temasek).

Although Temasek generally did not interfere in the decisions of its subsidiaries, decisions concerning shareholder matters were monitored. The means of control was primarily through appointment of company directors. There was also periodic review of past performance and future plans of selective companies, through meetings and reports. Equity capital or shareholder loans were provided where required for the development of approved projects.

The news on 11 November 1985 said, "The 450 companies* owned or backed by the government are held by three holding companies, Temasek Holdings Pte. Ltd., Sheng Li Holdings Co. Pte. Ltd. and MND Holdings Pte. Ltd. All in all, the government has fixed assets worth S$10 billion in these companies which employ some 58,000 workers (1984 figures)." The figure of 58,000 workers represented 5% of the total labour force employed and was less than half the total employment in the public sector in 1984 (using manpower statistics from the Economic Survey of Singapore).

The same news article also listed "some companies" with government ownership, as follows:

Industry:Company	S$Mil profit	Number of staff	Government's share %
Aviation-transportation:			
Singapore Airlines	113.4	10,177	80.9
Singapore Aircarft Industries	19.4	2,000	100.0
Farming:			
Primary Industries Enterprises	3.1	392	100.0
Financial services:			
DBS Bank	57.7	1,876	47.9
Export Credit Insurance Corp.	−7.1	55	50.0
Government Investment Corp.	0.5	45	100.0
Housing and construction:			
Construction Technology	13.8	535	100.0
Development and Construction Co.	3.4	18	100.0
Int'l Development & Consultancy	4.0	na	100.0
Resources Dev. & Consultancy	8.4	850	100.0
Urban Development and Management	12.1	186	100.0

* The figure of 450 is far from exact, representing what the media or other outside researchers have been able to ascertain. The Public Sector Divestment Committee (mentioned later) identified 634 such "government linked companies" in early 1986.

Industry:Company	S$Mil profit	Number of staff	Government's share %
Manufacturing:			
Acma Electrical Industries	-0.3	620	12.2
Allied Ordnance Co.	2.3	89	60.0
Cerebos	0.5	130	45.0
Chemical Industries	0.6	100	22.9
Hitachi Electronic Devices	0.6	1,000	15.0
National Iron & Steel Mills	3.6	906	19.7
Singapore Biotech	0.2	7	55.0
Singapore Technology Corporation	49.8	5,300	100.0
Sugar Industry of Singapore	1.4	230	40.0
Tata Elxsi	-0.3	19	15.0
United Industrial Corporation	5.8	300	16.5
Petrochemicals:			
Denka Singapore	-0.1	30	20.0
Petrochemicals Corp of Singapore	16.0	500	47.5
Phillips Petroleum S'pore Chemical	-8.5	117	25.0
Polyolefin Company Singapore	-9.8	260	25.0
Printing:			
Singapore National Printers	1.0	353	100.0
Shipping-marine services:			
Neptune Orient Lines	6.6	400	62.3
Ship repair and shipbuilding:			
Jurong Shipyard	1.2	1300	43.0
Keppel Shipyard	-118.2	1700	68.0
Mitsubishi S'pore Heavy Industries	-4.7	148	44.0
S'pore Shipbuilding & Engineering	1.7	550	86.8
Trading:			
Intraco	0.0	200	26.7
National grain elevator	0.6	39	37.0
Paktank Singapore Terminal	-0.2	7	12.0
SAF Enterprise	1.5	50	100.0
S'pore Airport Dupty Free Emporium	1.7	2	20.0
Singapore Food Industries	1.8	140	100.0
Singapore National Oil Company	0.2	1	100.0
S'pore Offshore Petroleum Services	1.8	150	33.3
Singapore Pools	18.8	310	100.0
Van Ommeren Terminal	0.0	45	8.0
Yaohan Singapore	0.0	1323	12.6
Tourism-leisure:			
Hotel Premier	0.2	16	100.0
Jurong Bird Park	-0.1	100	100.0
Singapore Zoological Gardens	-0.5	140	100.0

Source: Valerie Lee and Loong Swee Yin, "The Government's Giant Hand in Business," *Straits Times*, 11 November 1985, p. 21.

The Temasek portfolio was constantly changing in rather complex ways. For example, on 30 May, 1986 United Industrial Corporation announced a bid to takeover Intraco. (The Prime Minister's brother was Chairman of UIC and a board member of Intraco.) "The Singapore Government's response to the move is likely to be the determining factor. Temasek ... which owns 41.36% of Intraco and 11.4% of UIC, is expected to be predisposed to accept the offer in view of the government's desire to divest its stakes in local firms. But the government is not noted for giving away assets on the cheap ..." (FEER, 12/6/86:147) (A final outcome of all this was that Temasek divested UIC itself.) Temasek was continually adding to and pruning its portfolio. The Far Eastern Economic Review reported, "The Singapore Government investment company Temasek Holdings, along with Sembawang Shipyard [partially owend by Temasek], is buying 22 vessels of the Selco marine group, part of the failed Pan-Electric conglomerate. [Pan-Electric was one of Singapore's major private companies, which went bankrupt in 1985.] ... Temasek deputy chairman PY Hwang said the decision to buy the vessels was made 'to save the salvage business for Singapore'." (FEER, 10/4/86:10) Based on this quote the acquisition may be regarded as a 'rescue takeover,' but more likely it was simply a cheap investment opportunity.

Besides equity investment, the government also participated in its enterprises' debt capital, through the Development Fund. Loans outstanding as of 31/3/85 are listed as follows.

Borrower	Outstanding (S$mil)	Interest rate	Purpose
Applied Research Corp.	0.4		
DBS	2,132.1	9—11%	Line of credit
Housing Development Board	8,880.0	6%	Low cost housing
Jurong Shipyard	5.0		
Jurong Town Corp.	1,570.1	8—10%	Industry development
Neptune Orient Lines	0.2		
Ngee Ann Polytechnic	6.1		
Phillips Petrol. (S) Chem	28.0		
PSA	3.7		
PUB	265.2		
Science Centre Board	1.7	8%	Planetarium project
Sentosa Dev. Corp.	12.0		
SIA	144.2		
Singapore Polytechnic	1.7		
Singapore Sports Council	16.6		
Singha Shipping	20.8		

Borrower	Outstanding (S$mil)	Interest rate	Purpose
Telecomm. Authority	3.1		
Temasek	146.9		
Polyolefin Co.	51.2		
DBS Finance	0.3		Mechanisation of
DBS	3.0		construction industry
Hong Leong Finance	2.3		
Overseas-Chinese Bank	0.4		''
Overseas Union Bank	0.1		''
United Overseas Bank	0.1		''
Total	13,295.2		

Source: Accountant-General reports

Note: Where interest rate and purpose are not given, the loan was carried forward from prior years. Examining records back to 1972, the only loans given to private companies included the construction financing listed above (the last four financial institutions are private).

The growth of the Singapore SOE system may have finally started to down as a result of the 'privatization' policy announced in March 1985. One piece of evidence on this divestment drive was the number of companies on the list submitted to Parliament by the Finance Minister, which declined between 1983 and 1985: "... the lineage of public enterprises is complex and the count of public enterprises varies depending on whether only first-level companies, namely only those of the three main holding companies and their direct subsidiaries, or companies beyond this level are considered. For only first-level companies, the number given for 1985 was only 56 companies compared to 70 in 1983, while the number for 1983 increases to 450 if all companies in which the government has direct or indirect ownership, are included, (excluding another 40 subsidiaries of statutory boards)." (Low, 1986:3)

1.3 Privatization

From the mid-1980s, it has finally become fashionable among Singapore policy-makers to decry the role of government in enterprise. "Singapore's current perspective is that private entrepreneurship should be the engine of growth in the 1980s ... The Singapore Government believes that government enterprises are approaching the limits of their growth and private entrepreneurs are needed to seek out new areas of investments for Singapore's maturing economy." (Pang, 1987) This quote was originally taken from a 1984 conference paper by Pang, which was about as early as any academic was recording what then seemed the government's attitudinal turnabout.

The word 'privatize' did not become part of the local vernacular until the initial plan was announced in Parliament on 8 March 1985, but a form of privatization had been proceeding in Singapore from the outset, as a number of major SOEs invited market investment in their equity. For example, Keppel Shipyard and Neptune Orient Lines, both of which had been wholly-owned by Temasek, issued shares to the public in 1980 and 1981 respectively. Indeed, DBS had obtained its listing on the Stock Exchange of Singapore at its initial formation in 1968. The overriding objective of the exercise then, as now, was to channel funds to industry. Brigadier-General Lee, Minister for Trade and Industry, put the privatization policies in perspective by explaining on 15/10/86 that the government still intended to be intimately involved in managing the economy.

The first official announcement of the privatization policy (in March 1985) was by Dr. Tony Tan in his last budget speech as Finance Minister. On 2, February 1986 the government announced the forma-tion of a Public Sector Divestment Committee, described in the news as "another big step in the march toward privatization." The committee was charged with deciding which companies to privatize, to what degree ownership should be reduced in each case, and a schedule for imple-mentation.

In February 1987 the Committee Report was submitted to the Ministry of Finance. It recommended a potentially massive sale of government assets, emphasizing that "as many" enterprises and "as much" government equity should be transferred as could be effectively absorbed by the market, within a timeframe of "say, ten years." Statutory boards with commercial operations were also considered eligible for limited privatisation. The rationale of the exercise was stated, as to "withdraw from commercial activities ..., broaden and deepen the Singapore stock market ..., and avoid or reduce competition with the private sector." This rationale was contrasted with "common objectives in other countries": to raise cash or eliminate cash drain, and to eliminate political interference and bureaucratic rigidities, which were considered inapplicable to Singapore.

From the evidence of the first twenty-two full or partial divestitures, the government seems to be emphasizing the privatization of firms to augment their own and also Singapore's financial flexibility and development. The most profitable government companies and and statutory boards such as Telecoms are most frequently mentioned for future privatization. Enterprises not likely candidates for divestment include those that are mandated with carrying out social policies such as the Housing Development Board (HDB), industries involved in activities of strategic importance such as Singapore Aircraft Industries, or enterprises where other stakeholders have to be consulted such as with Petrochemical Corporation of Singapore. Another recommendation in the Report was that local companies or foreign companies "substantially established" in Singapore be tapped for the required financial services for privatization. DBS, which had underwritten many SOE securities issues in the past, was particularly well placed to benefit.

Dr. Richard Hu, who followed Tony Tan as Finance Minister, told Business Times at the beginning of 1986 that privatization means giving up not just ownership but also management of the companies. A local economist and Member of Parliament Dr. Augustine Tan argued in Parliament on 27, February 1986 that this change in ownership and control might destroy some of the companies. However, the impact of privatization still remains to be seen. Responsibilities undertaken on behalf of the government by its companies, for example Intraco's rice stockpiles, may have to be turned back to other government agencies. Some responsibilities could still be contractual, such as National Iron and Steel Mill's obligation to be an assured supplier to HDB. Other obligations, such as Intraco's position as the country's trading link with the Communist Bloc, might still be performed because the practice had been well established and would not necessarily be abandoned.

Furthermore, simply because the government was divesting some enterprises, there was nothing to prevent new government enterprises from being formed. For example, a recent joint venture between the government and an Australian enterprise, Cahners Exhibition Group, was defended on the basis that the land concerned belonged to the Civil Aviation Authority of Singapore, the initial investments were substantial, and Cahners had requested for commitment from such agencies as the airport and aircraft industries.

1.4 Privatization of Singapore Airlines

After the announcement of the privatization policy the first major divestment was of Singapore Airlines (SIA). Two differences were apparent between this privatization and other public issues of shares by Singapore SOEs. First was in terms of the scale and magnitude of the flotation. The second distinguishing feature was that part of the issue was provided by Temasek, so that there was an actual government divestiture.

On 18, December 1985 SIA obtained its long-awaited listing on the Stock Exchange of Singapore. Malaysia's national carrier, MAS, had preceded SIA by one month, and Thailand announced in March 1986 that its airline would also float shares. However, the impact of these Southeast Asian 'privatizations' was less dramatic than the privatization of a Nationalized Industry in Britain. After privatization the Board of Directors of SIA was still government-appointed, as had been the case with Neptune Orient Lines, Keppel Shipyard and other Temasek companies which had floated shares on the stock market some years earlier. Temasek had its proportional ownership in SIA reduced to 63% but was disallowed in the underwriting agreement to sell any more of its shares for one year after the flotation.* (On 5, February 1986 the newspapers reported that DBS Nominees, a DBS subsidiary which in turn was partially owned by Temasek, had been acquiring SIA shares as part of its market trading operations, thus causing Temasek's stake to increase 1% at that point.)

There were, nevertheless, certain effects on SIA of privatization. The news on 3, March 1986 noted that SIA had increased its market value by S$1.5 billion to S$4.2 billion, based on the 28 February closing price of S$6.70. (SIA's share price continued to climb, reaching an all-time high of S$15 just before the world stock market crash in October 1987.) As far as company behaviour was concerned, the Chairman in his New Year message to staff pointed out that, to satisfy investors, more emphasis must be given to profits. Another effect was the publication of a prospectus, as required by law, which revealed information the company had heretofore never been required to disclose — a new generation of openness was heralded, as may be necessary to gain the confidence of the market.

The flotation exercise itself was one of the grand events in SIA's history, and indeed the entire nation took an interest in what was to become the local exchange's premier blue chip stock. Citibank and DBS offered share financing schemes.

DBS was the managing underwriter, and foreign banks underwrote the international portion of the issue. Of the 100 million shares floated, DBS acquired 48.4 million from Temasek and 1.6 million from

---

* In March 1987 a government-appointed advisory group, the Public Sector Divestment Committee, recommended the government's shareholding be further reduced, in stages, to 30%. In contrast, the privatization of British Airways in 1987 constituted total divestment by the British government of its shareholding.

employees at S$4.875 per share. Details of SIA's equity financing from inception are shown below.

Equity Financing

Date	Instrument	NBVPS* S$	Shares (mil.)	Price S$	Amount (mil. S$)
1972	Capitalization of net worth	1.00	61.0	1.00	61.0
1974/5	Share issued	1.35	30.0	1.00	30.0
	Share dividend		24.4	1.00	
1981/2	Rights issue	4.12	103.86	3.89	400.0
1985/12	Share dividend		284.8	1.00	
	Non-rights public offering	3.66	50.0	5.00	250.0

Note*: NBVPS means 'net book value per share' based on year end figures. SIA announced 'net tangible assets per share' for the privatization issue of S$3.27, based on internal calculations.

None of SIA's share issues to Temasek suggest any government subsidy, in fact quite the opposite. The 1974/5 issue gave Temasek an investment with a 'book value' more than double their investment cost (because of the benefit of the share dividend). In contrast, the price to both SIA and Temasek of the public issue seemed more generous, in terms of book value purchased, than any prior flotation.

Temasek had not only been very conservative in providing funds to SIA, it had been slow in its deliberations. A study of debt/equity ratios indicates a 'stickiness' in the ability of SIA to raise equity capital from its government owners.

Debt/Equity Ratios

Years	1973	1974	1975	1976	1977	1978	1979	1980	1981	1982	1983	1984	1985
Ratio	3.59	3.57	2.29	1.92	1.59	1.91	3.91	5.17	4.92	2.93	2.45	2.48	2.45

1.5 Conclusion

Privatization was the vogue of the 1980's, heralded by the advocation of Prime Minister Thatcher's government in the United Kingdom. The concept was hardly mentioned in Singapore until late 1985, when almost every government official took up the cry in unison. Before then, few would have disagreed with Philip N Pillai's prediction that "the case for privatization of the public sector has not and is unlikely to find expression in Singapore in the near future." (Pillai, 1983:107)

Well in advance of the privatization policy, however, and even before Goh Chok Tong's 1979 suggestion of the possibility of divestment of government ownership, some SOEs had already floated shares publicly. (Significantly, the government invariably retained some equity.)

Notwithstanding the past and present participation by private investors, state enterprise remains relatively dominant. This fact is never doubted — as one Singapore commentator asserted, "There are not many countries, with the obvious exception of the centrally-planned economies, where the government has itself been such a major player in the economy. In most free-market economies, the government is content to restrict itself to the more conventional role of managing the overall economy. In Singapore's case, the government plans strategy, draws up and implements rules, and competes in the game as well." (ST 22/10/86) It is significant that this perspective (by Patrick Daniel) was written well after the privatization policy became the order of the day.

SOEs have played the key role in modernization and development of the economy, for example in promoting the 'Second Industrial Revolution' in the country. They have been efficient, largely because they have not been burdened with pursuing socio-political objectives. They are expected to behave like private enterprises and set the standard in a highly competitive open economy, with no sympathy for weak performance. Political interest has generally coincided with enterprise (SOE) interests. The fact that many SOE managers have been recruited from the civil service has not hampered their independence and entrepreneurship, because they have been key members of the national leadership team. (For example, the Chairman of SIA was also Chairman of Temasek and DBS.) Anyway, the Prime Minister puts a fire under his administrators — who needs profit incentive?

The government has been the chief venture capitalist in Singapore, but evidently now feels that local private investors are ready to play a bigger role. In the past local capital was more attracted by the property market and other non-industrial, speculative ventures (Lee, 1978), and if the Singapore public's 5% participation in the SIA privatization is any indication, the government may still be disappointed.

So why is it appropriate to privatize, for the government to divest itself of its good investments? Is it a response to private sector complaints about special SOE privileges? This rationale was indeed 'officially' stated by the Divestment Committee (see earlier). Nevertheless, it would be very uncharacteristic of the Singapore Government to initiate policy change due to pressures from such quarters, as the government has generally been proactive, anticipating rather than re-acting to pressures for change. (However, it is likely that overseas attitudes to SOE were more influential.)

The answer to this question has not changed since the 1968 public share issue by DBS. The core of their reasoning is the same as ever: to position the economy for more success, that is, to facilitate and promote the channeling of funds to Singapore enterprise.

There may also be a real concern for the future prospects of the old system. To date, the Singapore SOE system has been entrepre-neurial and avant garde. What of the long term — can past success continue? The factors which have led to the past success of the SOE system included a fortuitous circumstance in terms of the particular stage of development — the Singapore formula of decentralization of operations and centralization of control worked well, whereas problems of control and the emergence of a bureaucracy might well arise in the future. Also important have been political stability and rationality, with limited powers for pressure groups and less vociferous participation of the masses and opposition political groups in national decision-making. It seems to be true that only in this environment were SOEs allowed to be profit-seeking, without political interference or other political orien-tation. But environmental factors are invariably dynamic.

If the December 1984 election can be taken as a precipitant for the privatization policy announced in 1985, the government may have reasoned that the population would inevitably demand more politics at the expense of economic rationality. Social pressures for more liberalism in the style of Western advanced countries may be irresisti-ble, regardless of the implications for economics. Prime Minister Lee is in the process of passing power to the next generation of political leaders, who seem able and united and who share his philosophies. Lee's famous quote, that Singapore is "half socialist, half capitalist, and let the future be decided by the next generation" (1965) is appro-priate to recall now, for the future has arrived. The new leaders seem intent on retaining the same Fabian socialism; but there is only one Lee Kuan Yew, and his passing may cause some disruption to the old ways, which seem to have depended to a large extent on his personal style and intellect. It is widely predicted, especially in the Western press, that "the days of Mr. Lee's steamroller style seem to be ending ... What is happening is that Singapore is becoming middle-class, with increasingly middle-class values." (AWSJ, 19/6/86)

Therefore, despite past success, it is surely well adivsed to privatize, to turn over ownership to private investors (and make a profit on the transaction) before the inefficiencies of SOE that plague the Western mixed economies manifest themselves in Singapore.

References

1. Chan Heng Chee, "The Emerging Administrative State," in *Singapore Towards The Year 2000*, Saw Swee Hock and RS Bhathal (eds), Singapore University Press, 1981.

2. Lee Sheng Yi, *Public Finance and Public Investment in Singapore*, Singapore: Institute of Banking and Finance, 1978 (chs 7&8)

3. Low, Linda, "Public Enterprises in Singapore" in *Singapore: Twenty-Five Years of Development*, You Poh Seng and Lim Chong Yah (eds), NanYangXingZhouLianheZaobao (Singapore), 1984

4. Low, Linda, "Privatisation in Less Developed Countries: The Singapore Experience," Conference on Privatisation in LDCs, International Development Centre, University of Manchester, 16–17 December 1986

5. Ow Chin Hock, "The Role of Public Enterprises in National Development in Singapore: Problems and Prospects" in *The Role of Public Enterprises in National Development in Asia: Problems and Prospects'* Nguyen Troung (ed), Singapore Regional Institute of Higher Education and Development, 1976

6. Pang Eng Fong, "Foreign Investment and the State in Singapore" in Vincent Lafre (ed), *Foreign Investment in Developing Countries*, Croom Helm, 1987

7. Pillai, Philip N, *State Enterprise in Singapore: Legal Importation and Development*, Singapore University Press, 1983

8. Seah, Linda, "Pubic Enterprise and Economic Development" in *Singapore Development Policies and Trends*, Peter SJ Chen (ed), Singapore: Oxford University Press, 1983

9. Sikorski, Douglas, "Public Enterprise in International Competition: The Case of Singapore", Bradford University (unpublished thesis), 1987

10. Tan Chwee Huat, "State Enterprise System and Economic Development in Singapore," Wisconsin University (unpublished thesis), 1974

2. Case Studies of National and Private Shipyards in Singapore

Sections 2.1 — 2.3 are case studies of two state-owned and one privately owned shipyard in Singapore, while Section 2.4 is a comparative analysis of the cases. The objective, to see how the state enterprises differ in behaviour and performance from the private enterprise, is the major theme of the following case studies.

2.1 Keppel Corporation, a National Company

Incorporated in 1968, Keppel Shipyard dated its origins from when Singapore's first drydock was built in 1859 by a private colonial company at Keppel's modern location. In 1914 the colonial government took over all commercial shipyards. By 1968 the dockyard was operated by the Dockyard Department of the Port of Singapore Authority (PSA), "and performed a service function in support of the main activities of the port which were operating the wharves. In 1968 the Singapore Government decided to reorganize the docks as a commercial undertaking. A five-year management contract was signed with the Swan Hunter Group from the United Kingdom. Their task was to modernize and upgrade the facilities, and train and develop local management to run what was then to be Keppel Shipyard on a fully commercial basis. Local management responded enthusiastically, and by June 1972, when the Swan Hunter Management Contract expired, it was not renewed and Keppel Shipyard came entirely under local management." (Chung, 1981:2)

PSA transferred dockyard plant, machinery and equipment to Keppel on 1, September 1968. Keppel's liability was established in a "vendor's account" payable to the Ministry of Finance, for which a S$40 million 7% debenture was planned. The instrument was not issued by Keppel until 1978. Costs were minimized as the Ministry functioned as underwriters for the debenture.

2.1.1   Growth and Diversification

Records were not sufficiently available to examine performance and behaviour until 1975; but a case study on Keppel's major investment in shiprepair, S$200 million for the Tuas Yard, examined the company's early growth. "By the early 1970s, in spite of worldwide uncertainties, investment in shiprepair facilities in Singapore continued to be made." (Chung, 1981:8) Keppel began to contemplate expansion beyond the confines of the Dockyard. The Tuas project "was evaluated over a 22-year life ... An ROI of about 14.3% was expected." (Ibid:18) From 1974—1984, however, Keppel's net profit before tax actually declined, while the group's profit grew at an average annual rate of only 0.8% (not to mention the loss in 1985). In contrast, total assets grew at 20% and net fixed assets at 16%. (See Table 1)

The PSA was also expanding. In 1981 Keppel "management had been informed by the PSA that the Tanjong Pagar Yard would be in the way of the future expansion of the Container Port. Consequently, a special agreement has now been finalized for Keppel to give up the Yard in exchange for the development of a comparable Yard on Pulau Hantu. The Agreement will insure that the Company will be adequately compensated, without it incurring any loss to its shiprepair facilities." (AR (Annual Report), 1981:5) "An agreement in principle was reached with the PSA whereby the Company will transfer subject to government approval its Tanjong Pagar Yard to the PSA in return for an equivalent yard to be developed in Pulau Hantu by the PSA at a construction cost estimated to be considerably higher than the NBV of the Tanjong Pagar Yard which at year end was about S$64 million." (Ibid:33)

In late 1985 an executive explained that an earlier emphasis on growth had been displaced by a priority for ROI (return on investment). Until that time Keppel had been expanding and diversifying aggressively. In an interview with Chairman George Bogaars, published in Business Times (BT) on 20/7/83 the newspaper reported, "Keppel's top decision-makers have stated in no uncertain terms their aim to turn the already diversified group into a world renowned conglomerate"; and that policy seemed to have been in effect from the start. Bogaars himself was quoted as saying, "it has been steady progress with us, eroding the conservatism of our main shareholder [Temasek] who has been generally taking the line that a 'cobbler should stick to his last' ... The government has been very reticent about what the Temasek-controlled companies should do. Of course, they monitor the operations of the respective companies. But, there hasn't been much policy guidance. The companies themselves have been going to Temasek and suggesting various investment opportunities ... [Keppel's] major effort has been to persuade Temasek and the Ministry of Finance that we should be diversifying into marine-related industires, shipowning and other activities ... It was the same with diversification into financial services. We spent a lot of time, energy and effort to get the major shareholders to understand that finance is another branch worth putting their investments in." (in Lim, 1985:151)

Initially, Keppel and its few subsidiaries concentrated on shiprepair activities, including some shipbuilding locally and in the Philippines. Keppel did not pursue shipbuilding actively because, as a company executive explained in 1985, Singapore's comparative advantage was in shiprepair along the main oil tanker route between Japan and the Middle East because of a locational convenience; and major shipbuilding efforts would encounter stiff competition from Japan and South Korea.

In 1974 Keppel formed their own ship management company, which was a portend of a late 1970s expansion into shipping. Shipping may be seen as competition with Neptune Orient Lines, the national shipping company, but rather was complementary as NOL operated ships of different sizes and purpose and along different routes. (Tong, 1985)

Kepmount, Keppel's wholly owned holding company, was formed in 1976, and by 1981 held 10 shipowning companies. Shipping capacity increased from 15 million dwt in 1975, to 210 million dwt in 1977, to 410 million dwt in 1981 which was Keppel's highest profit year, and to 544 million dwt in 1984. Returns on investment in shipping reflected a small operating profit in 1984, but an operating loss of $11 million was reported in 1985. During that year Keppel announced it was engaged in a major sell-off of ships, and they confirmed early in 1986 that eight ships had been sold.

Keppel worked closely with Sembawang Shipyard, a major national shiprepair firm (74% government owned), on a contract in China, first mentioned in the 1984 annual report. Keppel and its subidiary Far East Levingston (FELS) also joined in a nine-member consortium of Singapore companies to operate an offshore supply base in China. The consortium, led by Intraco, the partially government-owned trading company, was a 30% equity investor with the Chinese partner owning 70%. Operations began in October 1984, although it was officially opened on 23 November 1985 at a dinner on site, attended by Minister for Trade and Industry and Minister for Defence Brigadier-General (Reserves) Lee Hsien Loong. In his speech he said that the base should show the way for many more cooperation projects between the two countries. It was certainly a showcase in cooperation — "Chinese Premier Zhao Ziyang has been there. So has Dr. Goh Keng Swee." (Straits Times (ST) 3/12/85) This base led to further opportunities.

The Keppel Group indeed regarded China an important source of new business opportunities, and was even exploring property investment and development through its Straits Steamship Property Division.

In response to a question concerning any advantage of state-owned enterprise in working with socialist countries such as China, a company executive said that the Trade Development Board office in Beijing had a good relationship with government companies, and helped in "arranging meetings and bringing to our attention Chinese opportunities." The chairman of the TDB was also chairman of Intraco. That chairman and Sim Kee Boon, who was Chairman of FELS and Keppel (and the first chairman of Intraco), were among the entourage accompanying Singapore's Second Deputy Prime Minister on a trip to China in May 1986.

George Bogaar's Chairmanship of National Iron & Steel would have provided helpful contacts in Keppel's acquisition reported in BT 29/6/83. "Keppel Shipyard is to buy a 10 percent stake in National Oxygen Pte. Ltd. Yesterday, National Iron & Steel Mills, the majority shareholder (51%) announced that it had sold 10% ... to Keppel."

On 26/4/85 the BT described Keppel as the "biggest steel fabricator in Singapore." This development was initiated several years earlier — the 26/10/83 BT reported, "Keppel Shipyard's industrial engineering division is investing a further $2 million to upgrade its steel fabricating plant in Tuas, making it the biggest steel fabricator in Singapore." Then on 7/1/86 the ST reported "Keppel Shipyard has entered into a joint venture with an Australian company to do steel structure drawings and consultancy in Singapore. The venture, BDS Technical Services (S) Ltd., will be one of the few companies in Singapore that can make such drawings ... Previously, most of the steel structure drawings had to be done in Australia ... Staff of the BDS Technical Services will be trained at the joint-venture partner's Brisbane head office ... The company hopes to service local and overseas companies ... Use of steel structures was growing ... Jobs that BDS has handled include the Mass Rapid Transit projects and commercial buildings for Singapore and the United States." The 1985 annual report noted, "1985 was a significant year as we succeeded in penetrating the United States steel fabrication market after many months of marketing effort."

This capacity coincided with a national need which had emerged simultaneously. "There has been a steady trend in Singapore towards the use of steel as a structural material for high rise buildings. Three major government buildings now under construction, namely the MAS [Monetary Authority of Singapore] Building, the Treasury Building and the Ministry of Environment Building, are using this system." (BT 18/11/83)

Keppel's venture into the field of finance began with Shing Loong

Finance in 1978. Originally a factoring company, it was given a license by the Monetary Authority of Singapore in 1981 to operate as a finance company. Another venture was announced in BT 25/4/83, that "Keppel Shipyard Ltd. has acquired a 9.17% stake in Asia Commercial Bank." A moneybroking firm, KT Forex, had been acquired in joint venture with a Japanese company in 1981. In 1984 "KT Forex merged with Degani, Tullet & Riley to form the largest broking firm in Singapore" (ST 21/4/84); but Keppel disposed of its share the same year. The ST 8/11/84 quoted a company representative, "'It is more proper for banks and other financial institutions to get involved in these foreign exchange activities. Furthermore, it did not fit into the scheme of things.' However, he emphasized that the move does not signal a shift away from the financial activities of the group." Bogaar's policy, last stated in a BT 9/3/83 article, was still intact, that financial operations will become "the second leg of Keppel's corporate existence."

In 1984 Keppel entered the insurance business with the acquisition of Malayan Motor and General Underwriters (MMGU). This was a joint venture with Post Office Savings Bank (POSB, a government-owned bank) for $24 million, but Keppel later bought POSB's interest for $13.25 million. Then on 22 September 1986 the ST announced "Keppel enters the life insurance business." This had been a result of selling 40% of MMGU (for a $5.5 million gain) to a Netherlands-based international insurance and financial services group. MMGU's life insurance license was the first to be granted by the Monetary Authority of Singapore since NTUC Comfort, a company affiliated to the National Trades Union Congress, was given one in 1970.

Keppel's largest acquisition at S$400 million was Straits Steamship (SS), a British company involved in not only shipping and engineering, in which Keppel had experience, but also property, leisure, and data processing. Although this acquisition was not consummated until 1983, Keppel was already contemplating expansion into property in the 1980 annual report. "The Keppel Group's involvement in property development is still small. There are plans to expand further and a major project is now in the pipeline." Keppel's adviser on the takeover bid was DBS (Development Bank of Singapore), but Keppel originally asked the international merchant bank Jardine Fleming Singapore for advice on valuation of SS. The final deal was discussed in the ST 18/6/83: "The Keppel Group Managing Director had led a top secret trip to Britain to negotiate the purchase of 58 percent of Steamer's equity shares from Ocean Transport and Trading. Mr. Chua was accompanied by ... Tay Kim Kah ... and Ng Tee Geok ... It is considered a coup of the first magnitude in business circles, and followed a tentative approach by OTT to Keppel ... When the deal is finished ... Keppel will rank as the biggest company in Singapore (not including banks)." After all was said and done, however, there was considerable controversy as to whether Jardine Fleming had given competent advice. It was argued by the Far Eastern Economic Review (based on hindsight since SS soon reported major losses) that the deal was way overpriced. Jardine Fleming had its Singapore banking license revoked on 4/10/83 by the Monetary Authority of Singapore.

On 8 May 1986 Keppel Shipyard Limited changed its name to Keppel Corporation to reflect the fact that it was a conglomerate rather than only a shipyard. However, even though shiprepair had by then been significantly rationalized, it was still the company's main line of business. The Chairman's Statement in 1985 said, "For as long as Singapore remains a major port there is a need for the shiprepair industry."

2.1.2 Financing

Keppel's initial capital financing was either provided or backed by the government. In 1975 and 1976 government guaranteed bonds were issued, but a 1977 bond issue signaled the end of that practice. A Keppel executive explained that Temasek did not generally guarantee funding once its enterprise was well established.

The 1979 annual report noted, "The critical factor in the competition for contracts, however, still is the availability of government financing." Similarly, Keppel's subsidiary FELS' 1981 annual report expressed a hope for "the continued support of the Government through ECICS which provides the financing to the industry ..." These comments were apparently in reference to the two financial support schemes in Singapore, the DBS-Government Ship Financing Scheme (which in November 1979 was extended to rig building) and the Export Credit Insurance Corporation of Singapore (ECICS). The purpose of these government programmes was to provide ship and rig-building financing (and from 1980 capital goods export financing from ECICS) at subsidized rates for buyer and supplier credits. These subsidies were also available to private shipyards in Singapore, and similar schemes were utilized in most countries. According to a Keppel executive, the Singapore schemes provided less support in terms of amount, interest cost and term of financing than generally allowed by the International Union of Credit Insurers, which organization included most major shipbuilding countries. Singapore joined the union in 1978.

Singapore's state-owned enterprises were often in the vanguard of national business developments, as Keppel's financial initiatives illustrate. Many debt issues were the first of their kind in Singapore. In November 1986 Keppel anounced an issue of $75 million in bonds with attached warrants. The warrants gave holders the right to buy up to 30% of Straits Steamship from Keppel's shareholding. The news called the instrument "the first of its kind in Singapore and Malaysia." (ST, 3/11/86) Two years earlier the annual report noted, "In April 1984, the Group received considerable publicity when it became the first company in ASEAN to issue commercial papers in the United States' capital markets." The 28/11/84 BT said, "The first Singapore dollar revolving underwriting facility (RUF), an instrument popularized in international capital markets only four years ago, has been put together for Keppel Shipyard. The $100 million notes to be issued by Keppel under the five-year facility will be underwritten by ... DBS [lead underwirter and manager] , OCBC, OUB, and Tat Lee. [The latter three were private banks.]" On 26/8/83 the BT reported, "Keppel Shipyard is making an interest rate swap [its floating rate notes to a third party] which will leave it paying [11.5%] on US$50 million ... The transaction is believed to be the largest of its kind and one of the first to be arranged with a Singapore company. At the signing of the swap agreement yesterday, Citicorp said the transaction was possible because of the 'forward looking and sophisticated management' of the Keppel Group ... the only other known arrangement of this kind in Singapore was an ... issue by DBS ... " In 1977 the annual report also announced a Singapore first: "During the year, Keppel consolidated its credit ranking in the international money market with two bond issues ... The first was a Singapore Dollar unguaranteed issue of $35 million. The second was an issue in October which gave Keppel the distinction of being the first ever Singapore company to float in the Asian Dollar Bond Market an unguaranteed bond."

Keppel turned to DBS for most investment banking services. DBS was lead underwriter for the 1984 share issue, the 1986 bonds with warrants, and the revolving underwriting facility, and Keppel's adviser on the takeover offer on Straits Steamship. (DBS at that time owned 769,500 shares in SS.)

2.1.3 Management

Training was emphasized in the company. "The company's reputation for the training and development of its employees is evident in the expenditure of more than $1 million annually in this area." (AR, 1979:6) The 1976 annual report had noted a particular achievement: "Keppel's Training Centre [set up in 1967], acknowledged as one of the best training institutions of its kind in this region, turns out 200 apprentices annually." There was national support for Keppel's training efforts. "The various schemes of training offered culminates in the award of a nationally recognized certificate." (AR, 1979:8)

Although Keppel's top management had a stable membership from inception, major changes occurred in 1984 and 1985. The finance director resigned in 1985, after 16 years with Keppel, and was followed out by another longstanding board member. They had been part of a three-member team (along with Chua Chor Teck), "who went to London in June last year to negotiate [the Straits Steamship acquisition]." (ST, 1/11/84) The newspaper noted the coincidence that the resignations occurred "about six months after [Mr. Bogaars] ... observers were quick to link the ... resignations to the widely publicized Keppel-Steamers deal." However, Bogaars retirement was more likely an indication of two needs: a need for a new leader to speed rationalization of shiprepair, and a need for retirement of Singapore's first generation of leaders. (Also, Mr. Bogaars was in ill-health.)

Chua Chor Teck stayed as Managing Director, but he died of cancer in January 1986. His eulogy was delivered by the Minister of State (Education), who described him as a "man of vision."

2.1.4 Rationalization

During 1985 and 1986 major retrenchment programmes were implemented by all Singapore shipyards. The total workforce in ship repair was reduced from 25,000 to 18,000.

On December 17, 1985 it was revealed in the headlines of the Straits Times that Keppel would move from its original facilities at the old Singapore Harbour Board site (now called Keppel Harbour) to Tuas Yard. This move had been broached many years earlier in the Harvard case study: "in about 15 or 20 years, major policy-makers would have to decide whether Keppel Shipyard or the port should remain at Keppel Harbour ... the obvious decision would be to resite Keppel." (Chung, 1981:19) Tuas Yard was suggested in the case as one of the strategic alternatives for Singapore to resolve the problem.

In April 1985 Keppel and Sembawang Shipyards had commissioned an American management consultant group to recommend alternative rationalization strategies for the two companies. On 26/9/85 the Far Eastern Economic Review reported that Keppel was resisting recommendations by the consultants to close both the Main and Tuas Yard at Keppel, rationalizing Singapore ship repair to Sembawang's facilities. "Not surprisingly, Keppel's management is understood to have rejected the recommendation outright. The need for capacity reduction was not disputed but Keppel is believed to have argued for across-the-board reductions by all yards in Singapore." On 3/12/85 Keppel and Sembawang announced that they would not follow the consultant's recommendation to merge. In a joint statement the companies gave as their reasons that minority (non-government) shareholders would suffer. (It had been mooted in the Business Times on 16/4/85 that Neptune Orient Lines, the national shipping company, was also a merger candidate.)

The chairman's Message in the 1984 annual report had anticipated these events: "It appears that the long-term solution lies in some rationalization and reduction of overall capacity in the ship-repair industry in Singapore." In the 3/12/84 ST Sim Kee Boon was reported to be currently "mapping out the future direction of the group in consultation with the majority shareholders ... Temasek ... Details of this plan are not known but can be summed up in three words – consolidation, rationalization and optimization." In BT 13/4/85 a Keppel source was quoted: "A recovery in the industry in the short-term will only be possible if the overall capacity in the ship repair industry is reduced and rationalized. Similar sentiments from others in the industry have been conveyed to the Government." The Prime Minister himself spoke about the matter in his National Day speech in August 1985, and other comments at the same time. Mr. Lee said, "They have taken about three years [sic] to reach an agreement in principle between all major shipyards to reduce capacity by one third. More time should not be wasted – the agreement should be implemented quickly."

On 11/10/85 Keppel agreed with four other yards to reduce dock use by 20% by adopting a 24-working-day month. The agreement was concluded by Keppel, Sembawang Shipyard, Jurong Shipyard, Hitachi Zosen Ribon Dockyard, and Malaysia Shipyard and Engineering, which together accounted for 90% of Singapore's ship repair capacity. Sembawang and Jurong Shipyards were part of the Temasek portfolio of companies, and the other two were private shipyards.

The Tuas move announced two months later would cut Keppel's capacity by 45%, and total Singapore capacity by 20%. Now Keppel was being optimistic. The move would "trim costs and improve our operational efficiency and competitive position." The company was planning to convert its old yard into a marina-condominium development, an idea which was well outside the company's original mission. The 1987 AR reported that this plan "was approved in principle by the relevant authorities, but without the residential and commercial components so that future use of the natural deep-water frontage would be safeguarded." Coincidentally, the move to Tuas was deferred.

2.1.5 Industrial Relations

Keppel's 1984 annual report exemplified the ongoing favourable relationship with all unions in the Group: "Management-Unions relationship in the Group remained harmonious. That Keppel has so far successfully implemented numerous ... productivity improvement measures is due in large part to the support and close co-operation it has received from the Union."

Keppel was the second company in Singapore to agree with its union to negotiate annual wage pacts, following the pronouncement in 1985 by the Minister of State (Defence, and Trade and Industry) Lee Hsien Loong (who was also the Prime Minister's son) that the National Wages Council annual increments should be discontinued. The first company was General Electric. "But one difference is that Keppel's union had earlier pledged to forgo salary increments or NWC wage increase [sic] for 1986" (ST 19/10/85). Keppel's agreement confirmed a wage freeze earlier announced by the Prime Minister. (The freeze was to last two years. On 16/12/87 Tay Eng Soon, Minister of State (Education) and advisor to the Union of Keppel Shipyard Employees, announced the signing of an agreement with the management to begin restoring benefits in phases.)

2.1.6 Conclusion

As one of Singapore's largest companies, Keppel was at the vanguard of national development efforts. No backwater shipyard, the company had an exemplary record of achievement in technology, finance, and manpower development. The leaders of Keppel were key members of the national leadership team. From 1968, Keppel proceeded on an aggressive course of expansion and diversification, and the modern group was a sophisticated conglomerate. A major member of the Group was Far East Levingston Shipbuilders, which case study follows in Section 2.2.

Table 1   Keppel Corporation Performance (million S$)

Year group	Total revenue	Net profit	Total assets	Net worth	Total loans	Dividend %
1987	670.7	22.4	1764.9	930.8	435.0	5.0
1986	576.3	5.1	1563.8	740.0	481.8	2.5
1985	616.1	−129.6	1750.6	727.4	667.7	1.5
1984	808.0	−173.9	1966.5	865.0	679.1	7.0
1983	666.9	80.0	2222.4	906.6	845.0	15.3
1982	645.8	86.0	1414.5	595.2	354.7	25.0
1981	723.3	87.2	995.3	501.5	230.6	25.0
1980	535.9	74.2	883.5	407.4	269.6	20.0
1979	368.6	25.9	722.2	215.3	347.2	15.0
1978	na	1.8	684.3	197.6	361.3	15.0
1977		27.6	727.8	205.2	394.2	15.0
1976		22.1	488.8	182.2	186.5	15.0
1975		28.4	321.6	159.2	76.3	12.5
1974		32.1	238.2	123.1	32.9	10.0

Year company	Operating revenue	Net profit	Net fixed assets	Capacity '000 dwt	Drydock	Shipping
1987	225.8	4.9	244.5			
1986	213.0	4.3	250.3			
1985	164.3	−164.7	263.6			
1984	224.7	−94.3	282.0			544.400
1983	219.7	100.5	297.7			
1982	225.2	46.4	254.6		570.000	470.990
1981	286.1	56.4	217.7			410.000
1980	na	44.0	202.6			270.000
1979		23.3	154.0			240.000
1978		16.6	149.1			
1977		24.2	203.7		190.000	210.000
1976		17.3	169.9			
1975		24.3	105.5		40.000	15.000
1974		29.2	76.7			

Table 2   Keppel Corporation: Board of Directors @ 5/1/88

Name	Position	From/to	Other positions held
Hon Sui Sen	Chairman (former)	1968/70	Former Minister of Finance; First Chairman Economic Development Board (1961); First Chairman & President Development Bank of Singapore (1968);
George Bogaars	Chairman (former)	1970/84	Chairman Far East Levingston Shipbuilding, National Iron & Steel, Guinness Mahon, Straits Steamship; Director Acma, International Trust & Finance, United Industrial Corporation; before Keppel: Head Civil Service, Permanent Secretary Ministry of Defence
Sim Kee Boon	Chairman	1984	Head Civil Service (1979–84); Permanent Secretary Commerce Ministry and Finance Ministry; Founder Chairman Intraco; Chairman SS, FELS, Insurance Corp of Singapore, National Grain Elevator, National Grain Elevator Enterprises, Civil Aviation Authorities Enterprises
Chua Chor Teck	Mg. Dir. (former)	1969/86	Before Keppel: Singapore Harbour Bd; Other positions na
Low Wing Siew	Mg. Dir.	1974 na/1987	Chairman or Director 47 Keppel companies
Billie Cheng			Chairman Sentosa Transport Services, Singapore Cable Car; Director MAP Services, Port of Singapore Authority, Paktank Tank Storage/Terminal
Choo Chiau Beng	Mg. Dir. (FELS)	1983	Chairman or Director 20 Keppel companies
Moses Lim Kim Poo		1985	Director Personnel, Education Ministry
Kung Yew Hock	General Mgr.	1983	Director 7 Keppel companies
Dr. Bernard Tan		1982	Assistant Professor & Member of Council, National University of Singapore; Director Singapore Symphonia Co.

Name	Position	From/to	Other positions held
Hwang Peng Yuan		1986	Chairman PCS, Sembawang Salvage, Intraco (1987); Deputy Chairman Temasek; Vice Chairman Hitachi Electric Service; Board member of PT ASEAN Aceh Fertilizer (Indonesia); Director Development Bank of Singapore, FELS
Lim Chee Onn	Mg. Dir. (SS)	1983	Member of Parliament: Secretary General National Trades Union Congress (1979—83); Minister w/o Portfolio (1980—83); Director National Iron & Steel; Director of 45 Keppel or SS companies
Dr. Cham Tao Soon		1982	President Nanyang Technology Institute; Dean of Engineering at NUS; Chairman Singapore Automotive Eng; Director Applied Research Corp, Wearne Brothers; Member Jurong Town Corp
Teo Soon Hoe	Finance Director	1985	Director Asia Commercial Bank

2.2 Far East Levingston Shipbuilding (FELS), a Keppel Subsidiary

Keppel became majority owner of Far East Levingston Ship-building (FELS) in December 1971, two years after FELS had entered the rig-builder industry and four years after original incorporation in 1967. The 31 May 1970 FELS annual report tells the story: "Your Company had a modest beginning, and during its first two years in business its operations were confined to the construction and repair of unsophisticated vessels, like small barges and tugs. It became increasingly apparent to the Management during the 1969/70 fiscal year that an explosive expansion in drilling activities for oil and gas in the coastal and offshore waters of South East Asia was imminent ... Ours was the first shipyard in South East Asia to undertake and successfully complete such drilling rigs. While this work was in process, your Management became increasingly cognizant of the need for [a US partner. The company] negotiated agreements with Levingston [Shipbuilding Company of Orange, Texas, and their] ... wholly owned Singapore subsidiary, which agreement came into force in July, 1970. Under these agreements the Levingston Companies provide us sales, purchasing and engineering services, a General Manager, and numerous additional skilled personnel... The Levingston Organisations have fulfilled our greatest expectations. The scope of customers interest in doing business with us has been broadened immeasurably. The Levingston's way of engineering, planning and building ... is fast permeating our operations." The stage was also set for Keppel to buy in: "During the past year your Company had suffered from a shortage of funds for working capital as well as for capital additions. We have incurred bank carrying charges and prices from our vendors have been higher than normal because of our limited funds." – and the following year's annual report went on," ... your Company has continued to suffer from a shortage of funds ... Therefore your Company has increased its paid-up capital by alloting 3,500,000 shares of $1.00 each to Keppel Shipyard ...," which was a controlling interest. The 1972 annual report noted, "Prior to the participation in the Company by Keppel ... the Company was clearly under-capitalized."

1970 annual report also set the stage for companies like Promet to enter the field. "The opportunities available in our chosen field of marine oil field work have attracted respected competition ..."

2.2.1 Management

FELS was by the 1980s undoubtedly an industry leader. "FELS is the only yard in this region to have built the whole range of mobile offshore drilling units ... This wide construction experience placed FELS in the forefront of the offshore industry." (AR, 1982:6, 7) The 1982 annual report also heralded the start of a move to diversify. "FELS has also diversified into other business. Two subsidiaries and two associated companies were formed, all of which were engaged in activities complementary to FELS' main core of business."

During the period when the major shipyards in Singapore (including Keppel – see section 2.1 were immersed in rationalization exercises, FELS was acquiring subsidiary enterprises more aggressively than its parent. There was some concern expressed about a need to diversify out of rigs.

FELS, like Keppel, expanded its asset base steadily. Some of the expenditure was explained in the 1983 annual report. "Internally, FELS is also continuing to strive to further improve productivity by putting more investments in well-planned facilities and manpower development. A total of S$20 million had been spent between 1981 and 1983 on new cranes, sea-front improvements, administrative office, workshop improvement, computer systems and others. Another S$40 million programme to further improve the yard ... is in progress. By the end of 1984, FELS will have [greatly expanded facilities] ." The 1981 annual report noted a "plan to build a new yard which will be the biggest single rig-building facility in Singapore ... Marketing efforts have also been intensified to sell the yard's facilities for rig-builder after 1983. It is hoped that with the continued support of the Government through ECICS [Export Credit Insurance Corporation of Singapore] which provides the financing to the industry, and with the Company's reputation for quality ..." the company's success would continue.

On 1 September 1986 FELS released a statement to the press that the company would take over the facilities abandoned by Mitsubishi Singapore Heavy Industries, which had withdrawn from the ship repair business during 1985. Mitsubishi, which had been a 50% joint venture with the government, was the industry's major casualty of that era. The yard contained a 400,000 dwt dock, the largest in Singapore. The Managing Director of FELS observed, "the prohibitively high cost of dock construction had prevented FELS ..." from building a new yard despite the company's growth in business. During the 1970s and until now they had been able to make use of the facilities at Keppel, Singmarine (a Keppel subsidiary), Jurong Shipyard (a partially government-owned company), and Mitsubishi.

FELS also enjoyed good industrial relations. The 1983 annual report announced the "formation of FELLO, our house union." The national movement toward house unions, spearheaded by the National Trades Union Congress (NTUC), was just beginning. The 1981 annual report had said, "Management-Union understanding is also at an all time high. As a result, productivity has been raised appreciably ..."

Staff development was emphasized. The 1983 annual report mentioned "the implementation of the nation-wide BEST [Basic Education and Skills Training] programme." "To complement the facilities improvement, FELS has embarked on a comprehensive manpower-development programme ... The BEST programmes are drawing good response ... Skills-development programmes are continuing ..."

FELS 'reputation for quality' seemed to be substantiated by the construction performance on two rigs in 1981. "The rigs were also of such quality as to be commended by the owners for the workmanship on them ... In appreciation of this fine performance, the Company was awarded bonuses on both the rigs by the respective owners."

The source of client companies for FELS' rigs seemed to change over time. FELS' first client was a US company, and most contracts through the 1970s followed that pattern. During the 1980s major deals were announced with the Soviet Union, Indian government companies, and a US government agency (in addition to other non-government contracts). US clients still featured prominently in the 1988 order book.

A major potential market for the future was China, which contracts are mentioned in the Keppel case.

The data in the following tables was selected for the same period as was available for Promet (see next section 2.3). It also marks the period during which a civil servant was chairman.

2.2.2 Conclusion

FELS' star began to rise when they joined forces with a US multi-national company, and skyrocketed after their acquisition by Keppel. FELS grew to be the premier local rig-builder, and like its parent Keppel had an exemplary record of achievement, notably in technology and manpower development.

Another local rig-builder was not destined for such good fortune, which case study (Promet) follows now.

Table 3   Far East Levingston Shipbuilding Performance (million S$)

Year	Production revenue	Net profit	Total assets	Net worth	Term loans	Dividend %
1986	110.0	13.3	306.4	221.7	—	12
1985	137.8	6.6	277.3	212.2	—	10
1984	150.6	23.3	301.0	207.7	0.1	12
1983	193.3	17.9	268.6	188.0	3.4	10
1982	214.7	41.8	313.4	172.8	3.1	25
1981	259.1	31.4	249.9	95.5	3.6	20
1980	121.1	0.5	93.1	26.9	—	12

Table 4   FELS Board of Directors @ 5/1/88

Name	Appointed	Other positions held
Sim Kee Boon (Chairman)	26/4/84	(See Table 2)
Choo Chiau Beng (Mg. Dir.)	3/80	(See Table 2)
Loh Wing Siew	1/80	(See Table 2)
Hwang Peng Yuan	8/86	(See Table 2)
Lim Chee Onn	1/85	(See Table 2)
Chang Yun Chung	3/81	Director of numerous private companies
Tong Chong Heong (Gen. Mgr.)	4/83	nil
Goon Kok Loon	5/86	Deputy Exec Director Port of Singapore Authority; Chairman Suzue-PSA Cold Storage; Deputy Chairman Specs Consultants, Map Services

2.3 Promet Private Limited

Headlines in Singapore and Kuala Lumpur newspapers on 27 September 1986 announced the sad news: "Promet goes under receivers" (Straits Times [ST]). Now commentators, referring to past dreams, speak of "once-proud Promet", the "bluest of blue chips." What had happened?

2.3.1   Growth and Diversification

"In 1971, a 28-year-old Brian Chang started the business in Singapore reputedly because he was unable to get a job. The one-secretary company provided offshore services to the booming oil exploration activities in the Asian region. In July 1981, the Singapore-based Promet Private Limited was absorbed into Bovis South East Asia Berhad after Brian Chang purchased the whole stock equity of P&O Asia of Hong Kong, whose main asset was an 80% stake in Bovis. Bovis was then renamed as Promet Berhad." (Lim, 1985:125-6) Little information is available on Promet prior to 1981 as it was a "family-run business" (Ibid). The 1981 manuever changed Bovis' public Listing on the Kuala Lumpur and Singapore Stock Exchanges to Promet on 11 July 1981. The Singapore-based Promet thus became a Kuala Lumpur-headquartered company, much touted by investment analysts.

After its public listing, growth and diversification proceeded rapidly, through 1984. "According to Brian Chang, 'At present (1982) rig building represents more than 70% of the estimated M$350 million turnover ... rig-building revenue will represent no more than 10% or 15% of our total business (in six years' time')." (Lim, 1985:131) The pattern of expansion was of course affected by the judgment and investment interests of the company's leadership, and the four key directors were Brian Chang and his brother Benety, and until 1986 the Mohamed brothers Ibrahim and Abdullah (the Chairman and the Joint Managing Director respectively). Brian Chang's expertise was as a rig-builder, but from 1981 Promet's growth emphasis shifted slightly, notably to include property development.

Promet Berhad could also take advantage of its favoured position in a country whose government, openly and actively, promoted Bumiputra participation in the economy to reduce the dominant role of Chinese Malaysians and foreigners. Companies with 30% Bumiputra ownership were put first in line in bidding for government contracts, and Promet had Bumiputra status through the Mohamed brothers. It seemed likely that the Bumiputra status greatly enhanced Promet's participation in the Langkawi resort development project, in partnership with the Malaysian government. "Langkawi Resort City will be Malaysia's biggest tourist and holiday resort. Promet is the developer, co-ordinator and owner of this integrated holiday city." (company pamphlet) Government bodies worked closely with Promet for planning, implementation, and marketing. A M$70 million international airport was built. However, on 30 May 1986 Brian Chang stated that work in Langkawi had stopped since April because "the necessary approval and investment incentives from the necessary authorities have not been received"; but on 7 July 1986 the Government granted an incentives package for the resort including duty-free status. The newspapers connected this good news with the addition to Promet's board of Syed Ibrahim, a wealthy Bumiputra. (The Mohamed brothers left Promet in early 1986.)

Oil and gas exploration was a likely activity for a rig-builder, and Promet entered into a number of concession agreements in the early 1980s in Southeast Asia and China. However, these were to result in major write-offs by 1985.

Promet was also "one of the largest steel fabrication companies in the region." (company pamphlet) Contracts included "transtainers for the Port of Singapore Authority, ... and the first and only floating transhipment plant in the world for Thailand." (Ibid)

Promet had far-flung international operations, not all confined to Southeast Asia. Activities were frequently cited in the Middle East, South America, and worldwide. The company was also involved in numerous joint ventures with major multinational corporations. Promet and Baker Marine Corporation, a US company, entered into a joint venture to develop an offshore service port in Texas. These relationships potentially could provide technology transfer back to Singapore. For example, "SEPM Pte. Ltd., a joint venture between Promet Pte. Ltd. and Baker Marine Pte. Ltd. is the first offshore design engineering company to be set up in Singapore." (Ibid)

This growth and diversification proceeded through 1984, but Promet suffered severely from the general downturn in the marine industry beginning about that time. The first mention of rationalization was in the 1984 annual report: "As part of a rationalization exercise your Group has disposed of its fleet of tugs and barges to Chuan Hup Marine Limited in exchange for shares ..." On 30 May 1986 the newspapers reported that the Singapore office had been reduced from a peak staff level of 3000 to "a nominal staff of 50." The Singapore yard was rumoured to be up for sale.

The 1985 annual report indicated that in view of substantial losses incurred that year due to a "collapse in both oil prices and the Malaysian property market," it would be necessary to achieve "a disposal of non-performing assets." This intention was re-emphasized in an announcement on 1 August 1986, where the company did not detail the assets nor the businesses it would discard, but suggested the stake in Bakers Port would go, among other investments. On 10 September it was reported that Promet had sold its interest in Chuan Hup Marine, and during 1985 Promet had substantially written down some oil and property assets. The news on 2 August 1986 quoted Brian Chang's statement, "the company needs to return to the business it knows best — contracting."

One significant success in Promet's 'return to contracting' was the signing of a memorandum of understanding on 21 July 1986 with two major enterprises, one alleged to be the world's largest mining conglomerate. The 'big 3' claimed to have clinched three large-scale engineering and construction projects already.

2.3.2 Management

In early 1986 Promet was the object of media attention, for the first time since its reformation in 1981. However, this time the news coverage was less auspicious — a proxy battle was impending. On 2 January 1986, two shareholders called for an Extraordinary General Meeting, with the intent to oust Chairman Tan Sri Ibrahim. The shareholders were Miss Sim Cheng Huay, a Singaporean, and Morgan

Grenfell Nominees representing major western investors (15% owners). The meeting was scheduled for 23 January 1986 but had to be adjourned and rescheduled because of a legal hitch. "Okay, we screwed it up," admitted Brian Chang, the Chief Executive. The 23/1/86 ST had predicted, "The EGM will be the culmination of more than two months of controversy starting from last November's whispers of a falling out between Tan Sri Ibrahim and Mr. Chang over differences in the running of Promet and Tan Sri Ibrahim's bid to shift part of his personal debt burden to Promet via his Selangor Properties shares." The truth of these rumours was not established, but the 14/12/85 ST speculated, "Tan Sri Ibrahim planned to inject his stake of some 15 per cent in Selangor Properties Berhad and other property interests into Promet to enlarge his stake in Promet."

It was also rumoured in the press that the Malaysian Prime Minister wanted Brian Chang out.

Both men repeatedly denied any rift, but in a 2 January 1986 Board meeting "Tan Sri Datuk Ibrahim tried to close ranks with Mr. Chang by naming him Chief Executive and Managing Director. [Until then he had been Joint Managing Director with Datuk Abdullah, Datuk Ibrahim's brother.] Tan Sri Datuk Ibrahim's title came out without the 'executive' before the word chairman ... The following day, Mr. Chang edged further away from the troubled brothers by resigning from his directorship in Tan Sri Datuk Ibrahim's listed Amalgamated Properties and Industries Berhad." (ST 20/1/86) "Mr. Chang was appointed a director of API in 1981. A year later ... a joint-venture company, Promet-API Property Development Services Sdn Bhd, was formed to undertake property projects for the two companies." (ST 10/1/86)

Three days before the aborted meeting Datuk Abdullah resigned, objecting "to the employment policy, awarding of sub-contracts and procurement policies [all of] which favoured Singaporeans; the way the development of Pulau Langkawi was being carried out and the availability of management information ... Matters were later complicated by an Overseas Union Bank suit against Datuk Abdullah who stood as a co-guarantor for non-payment of loans and interest amounting to US$25.7 million." (ST 23/1/86) The 9/1/86 ST reported that Promet, "in a statement to the Kuala Lumpur Stock Exchange, said Datuk Abdullah's involvement in the loan was in no way related to any activities or borrowings of Promet ... The loan was given to a private company [United Securities Sdn Bhd] of which he is a director."

The proxy battle was finally settled by Tan Sri Ibrahim's resignation announced in the news on 13 February 1986, taking effect 7 February. He would continue in Promet as Group Adviser. The brothers reduced their shareholdings in Promet significantly, and the company lost its Bumiputra status. For Promet to regain the Bumiputra status, it was necessary for other indigenous investors to take up a 30% stake. However, this seemed unlikely as Promet shares continued to slide.

Another allegation in the news in March 1986 was that Brian Chang in September 1985 had tried to get then Chairman Datuk Ibrahim to join him in a scheme to borrow $42 million which would be used to support Promet's share price. Datuk Abdullah claimed Brian Chang had confided this in him, to which he had expressed the opinion, "I felt that the scheme could well be construed as an impropriety as it was a form of share manipulation and I told him I was not interested." Datuk Abdullah claimed that Brian Chang had already been speculating in Promet shares and if the scheme failed he would have to dispose of a large block to cover costs. He said in November he himself was approached by a broker representing Chang to buy 10% of Promet. In partnership with a Malaysian businessman named Mak Kok, he claimed to have verbal agreement to buy 100 million shares from Brian Chang who later reneged. The case was taken to court, but later dropped.

The Datuks, Abdullah and Mak Kok also operated together after the former's resignation from Promet. On 13 May 1986 they took up directorships in Supreme Corporation, one of the major casualties of the infamous Pan Electric failure in Singapore in December 1985. In a joint press conference they said they had new plans and would bring in more funds to the company. However, "despite these public declarations, Supreme had told the Kuala Lumpur Stock Exchange that it had yet to receive either details of the two directors's shareholdings in Supreme or concrete proposals of their plans." (ST 7/8/86)

2.3.3 Financing

Promet's major financiers were comprised of foreign and Malaysian institutions and did not include Singapore-headquartered banks.

During 1986 Promet was negotiating with its banks to restructure its total debt of M$320 million. The asset write-offs had reduced net worth below the level which had been agreed with the bankers, requiring re-negotiation of repayment terms. In September 1986 the deliberations reached a crisis, which was first manifested in the suspension of trading of Promet shares on the stock exchanges in Singapore and Malaysia at the request of the company (after a pre-cipitous drop in price). Of the company's 33 creditor banks, initially three and later seven more had sent letters demanding liquidation of loans. The ST of 16/9/86 said, "According to a creditor, the banks took a tough stand because Mr. Chang had not complied with certain conditions of 'an informal agreement'." The banks wanted to manage the asset disposals being undertaken by the company, and bankers were unhappy with what they regarded as Brian Chang's uncooperativeness in this and other matters. The 16/9/86 ST continued, "According to Mr. Chang, if any of the banks start legal proceedings, the others would follow suit in breach of their representations, which would result in irreparable harm which cannot be compensated for in damages as the companies would be wound up." Promet obtained a temporary injunction preventing legal action by the banks, on the grounds that they were still negotiating. However, in the last week of September the banks took action to freeze Promet's assets, and a banker observed, "Promet has just lost its year-long battle to stave off its creditors." On October 1st Promet and its banks went to court. The judge's decision announced the following week turned management of the company over to the receivers.

(A restructuring agreement was reached in late 1987. Brian Chang's management team was reinstated, and trading of Promet shares resumed on the Stock Exchange of Singapore in early 1988.)

Table 5   Promet Pte. Ltd. Performance (million MS$)

Year	Turnover	Net profit	Total assets
1986	3.7	−2.6	76.0
1985	2.3	−64.3	387.8
1984	13.3	10.8	445.7
1983	12.3	11.1	406.9
1982	30.2	8.4	196.0
1981	45.1	−0.3	190.7
1980	19.5	−3.4	26.6

Table 6   Promet Berhad: Performance (million M$)

Year	Turnover	Net profit	Total assets	Net worth	Total loans	Dividend (%)
1986	105.1	1.4	254.0	267.9	266.0	—
1985	292.8	−113.6	744.8	297.0	295.3	—
1984	327.2	33.1	871.6	361.3	253.3	5
1983	373.5	63.9	715.0	360.7	165.1	5
1982	307.2	46.5	508.9	181.0	165.7	4
1981	369.8	28.7	315.9	177.6	19.7	—
1980	261.7	8.1	176.3	11.6	35.5	—

Table 7   Promet Berhad: Board of Directors @ 11/11/87

Name	From/To	Other positions held
Datuk Ibrahim Mohamed (former Executive Chairman)	1984/86	Chairman Genting Highlands Holdings Bhd, Genting High Hotels Bhd, General Ceramics Bhd, Public Textiles; Deputy Chairman Associated Plastics Industries Bhd (renamed API Amalgamated Properties and Ind); Director for approximately 20 other companies
Dato' Brian Chang	1974	Founder and 30% owner; Director API (1981–6)
Dato' Abdullah Mohamed (former Joint Managing Director)	1984/86	Managing Director API; Director United Securities Sdn Bhd, Idris Hydraulic Bhd, Pub Textiles Bhd,
Moehamad Izat Emir	1986	Chairman Malay Chamber of Commerce and Industry, Federal Territory branch; (was Deputy Chairman until receivership)
Dr. Benety Chang	1975	na
Nik Din Sulaiman	1985	na
Dr. Paul Yong Min Hian	1986	Managing Director Promet Consultancy, Director Holian Holdings Bhd.
Dato' Syed Ibrahim	1986/87	Deputy Chairman Construction and Supplies Bhd.
LEC Letts	na	Director, Austral Amalgamated Tin Bhd, seven other Malaysian companies

---

* The case narrative covers company history until commencement of receivership in October 1986.

2.4 Comparative Analysis of Shipyard Companies

2.4.1 Origins and Objectives

Keppel was originally a colonial company, then a government-owned enterprise. Keppel's original plant was given to it by the government in exchange for an open-dated promise to pay. It learned from multinational companies (MNCs) in its early eyars as an SOE, while Promet was started by an entrepreneur and did not turn to the MNCs until it was already well established. FELS* started much the same as Promet but used MNC help to move into more sophisticated operations, then availed itself to government capital through its acquisition by Keppel. The combination of government capital and MNC technology and markets was a competitive advantage. As to whether SOEs have better access to MNCs, the evidence was not conclusive; but at least it seems likely that size and maturity of an enterprise are an advantage in making contact, and in Singapore state backing is also helpful. At Promet initial success largely depended on one businessman (Brian Chang), and further diversification strategy was constrained by the expertise of particular individuals.

The original capitalization of Keppel is evidence of a cooperative arrangement among parties with a mutual interest in the overall, national result. It is reasonable to suppose that private parties would have more difficulty in agreeing to deferred payment for a future amount at a future interest rate — especially when the future date was left open.

2.4.2 Management and Control

Controlling agencies were at least 'once removed' from government in all SOEs studied. The standard mechanism was the use of holding companies, and FELS was further separated by being a subsidiary of a Temasek-held company. Temasek Holdings provided a buffer for Keppel, whereby the company was more free to conduct its operations and investments without direct interference by the government. This represents one step towards decentralization, but where goals and

---

* The following acronyms are used throughout this section:

FELS	Far East Levingston Shipbuilding
POSB	Post Office Savings Bank
PSA	Port of Singapore Authority
SOE	State Owned Enterprise
SS	Straits Steamship

constraints can still be established at a political level. " ... there is a conceptual virtue in decentralizing the control system. It makes necessary a rigorous determination of the criteria by which the de-centralizing agencies are expected to work. While preserving for the government, under the parliamentary checks, the right to determine the broad goals ... this lends clarity to the way in which these goals are formulated. What society gains is ... they are controlled in terms of the 'socially' best ... options of behaviour and decision." (Ramanadham, 1984:194–6)

Keppel was led by a team of directors who were primarily senior civil servants, and an executive management group who were primarily from the private sector. However, even the private sector leaders of SOEs showed a public spiritedness, which was either nurtured over time or a personal quality that might be prerequisite to their selection. Indeed, Keppel, and hence FELS, had the talents of an entire nation to tap. The case studies in both Parts II and III illustrate that in Singapore the best people, even from the private sector, are tapped for service in the nation's enterprises. Promet's Mohamed brothers, in contrast, did not evince the same solid character and ability as Keppel's and FELS' leaders.

Another characteristic of the leadership is the strong evidence of a network of mutually supportive relationships, including cross-directorships. This seems to be true of Singapore in general, and the limited evidence of cross-directorships in Promet demonstrates that it is not entirely confined to the public sector. However, in the public sector this collusive capacity impinges on national decision-making, not just cooperation in business opportunities.

Both George Bogaars and Sim Kee Boon were moved to Keppel from their post as Head of the Civil Service, which suggests an intimate prior knowledge of important people and positions in Singapore. Many instances of opportunities for collaboration were possible, all of which demonstrate a cooperative network in the best interests of 'Singapore Inc..' Mr. Krishnapillay, for example, could use his experience as Commissioner of the Bases Economic Conversion Department in the conversion of Sembawang Shipyard from a British base to a commercial facility, which experience would in turn be valuable for Keppel in its startup. He also could help coordinate the acquisition of 50 hectares of reclaimed land (from the ocean) for Tuas Yard, the Gul Yard, 50 acres of land for FELS, and the acquisition of Pulau Hantu in exchange for Tanjong Pagar to PSA, because he had been Commissioner of Lands. (All property was leased from Jurong Town Corporation.)

Billie Cheng was a PSA director, which institution worked closely with Keppel. Ng Tee Geok was a POSB man, whose expertise would be helpful for financial ventures, especially the joint POSB-Keppel acquisition of Malayan Motor and General Underwriters.

The move to Tuas Yard illustrates Keppel's close working relationship with PSA and Sembawang Shipyard, both government enterprises. With PSA, Keppel had also coordinated many important decisions in the past, since its initial startup agreement negotiated through the Ministry of Finance. On the transfer of Tanjong Pagar Yard to PSA, the "subject to government approval" phrase indicates that the Ministry of Finance was not required to be directly involved in negotiations as it had been in 1968. The Pulau Hantu development costs to be footed by PSA seem much more generous than might usually be expected of an 'eminent domain' type of land acquisition. Of course, PSA might have anticipated that even the new facilities would be theirs again someday, as it nearly turned out.

Another intricate network of cooperative relationships was evident in the Keppel group's business in China. Keppel (and FELS), the Trade Development Board and Intraco were an effective team of enterprises whose leaders were very close. Sim Kee Boon had once been Intraco's chairman. Partly through Sim's chairmanship of the Civil Aviation Authority of Singapore the 'China connection' overlapped with other key Singapore government enterprise interests.

There were many more indications of a cooperative network in Singapore's SOE leadership team, apart from the obvious fact that they were colleagues in a small Civil Service Corps. For example, Keppel's development of a steel fabrication capacity seemed to reflect an uncanny ability to see emerging national (and notably government) needs.

One clear advantage of the SOE over the private shipyard was in the power of SOE management. This partly was a result of SOEs often being large, dominant companies on the local scene, but also top managers were part of the national leadership team. Perhaps the most telling instance to show management 'clout' was the expulsion from Singapore of Jardine Fleming, for giving bad advice to Keppel (and other reasons). Promet sorely missed such influence in their negotiations on debt restructuring!

2.4.3 Growth and Diversification

Neither Keppel nor Promet were content to rely on the marine industry for the long term, and both began major diversification programmes earlier than the major downturn in their traditional activities. Keppel at one time seemed ready even to become a financial services company, and the government has not publicly dissuaded them from such plans. However, it would appear that the company's ambition to be a conglomerate had a tenous connection with the origins and initial objectives of the company when set up by the government. Once Keppel was no longer needed to provide leadership in an industry of national importance (such as ship repair was and, according to Sim Kee Boon, always will be), the government seemed content to simply let their investment look after itself. Privately owned companies would be lucky to have such autonomy. (Privatization was also under consideration.)

In the past the government did not restrain Keppel from a rather free-wheeling diversification strategy, and the proven consistency of government policy would indicate that nothing has changed. The Straits Steamship (SS) deal did evidently have adverse repercussions at high government levels, though this is not public information. Concerning any need for advance approval of diversification moves, The Far Eastern Economic Review asserted, "As of 1983, plans for expansion and diversification of state companies appear to require the approval of the First Deputy Prime Minister." (FEER, 22/9/83:13) However, the SS decision did not reflect any evidence of such high level scrutiny in advance. A confidential memorandum was circulated by the government in 1984 or 1985 (exact date unknown) advising SOEs to exercise caution in diversification outside their main line of business. This may have been in reaction to Keppel's own expansion policy, which by that time had included what the local newspaper termed the "ill-fated" acquisition of SS. (It should be noted that SS profitability did recover by 1985 to vindicate the company's acquisition decision.)

Most of Keppel's diversification could be considered as being development-oriented. Even SS activities were of national interest. SS property development was in line with activities of the old Housing and Urban Development Corporation and other major government building projects, and SS leisure interests were connected with travel, that is, tourism which was a major government concern.

There was some support for the notion that government companies have an advantage in obtaining contracts with other governments' enterprises, in particular in socialist countries, especially illustrated by FELS' contracts. Particularly business in China was clearly promoted at top governmental levels.

Keppel's innovation in finance and its excellent labour relations were indicative of its position of national leadership in business management. These are examples of the many fields where SOEs, especially major SOEs like Keppel, played a role in the 'state entrepreneurialism' that characterizes the Singapore SOE system.

Keppel also, in conjunction with Sembawang, implemented the national rationalization of the shipyards. Though Promet was evidently not consulted, it was not a major shipyard. In any case, Promet too was cutting back its marine business. Not being part of the national team effort in planning for cutbacks, Promet may have acted less decisively. Indeed, the company was paralyzed for a time with its boardroom battle to remove the chairman. (However, the financial data does not show Promet to be any more hesitant than Keppel itself, which also had to suffer before accepting the need for drastic action.)

A Keppel executive, in response to a question concerning rationalization, had responded that the Managing Director is the decision-maker, and the decision is made by the enterprise alone, that is, not in consultation with the government. So we must distinguish between company-wide and country-wide rationalization. A national need to rationalize the ship repair industry seems to have been seen as long as three years earlier, according to the Prime Minister — though it is difficult to see evidence of such advance notice or indeed any real adjustment in planning so long ago. Perhaps the PM meant three months, not years. But the point is, the decision was initiated outside the company, and then left to the various enterprises to work out details.

Keppel's record reflects a history of optimism through 1983, with a marked change in mood from 1984. Total assets, gross fixed assets, net fixed assets and net worth all expanded steadily, at average rates of 20%, 17%, 16%, and 19% respectively through 1984. Return often seemed to justify this investment buildup until at least 1984, even though return was declining and turned to loss in 1985.

FELS, like its parent, was expanding rapidly and efficiently. Financing was readily available. Promet also expanded, though erratically. Returns were not as impressive as at FELS and Keppel. Use of the so-called Dupont analysis (described in most business finance texts) may indicate for Promet that the lower returns were due to inefficient use of assets, that is, the Dupont formula ROA=Operating margin x Asset turnover. Profit margin was certainly high, but assets were not producing high enough sales. Therefore, not all Promet investment was paying off.

By 1986 Promet was severely constrained from Singapore operations, while its direct competitor in rig building, FELS, was success-

fully pursuing oppourtunities, notably as part of the Singapore government's business team in China. The financial analysis of FELS reveals a
much more solid enterprise. Growth was largely financed from shareholders' funds, as indicated by the low level of liabilities. In addition,
the high liquidity indicates further that the company was able to fund
asset expansion. (The explanation for the low level of borrowing seems
to be that FELS could rely on its parent company Keppel for obtaining
most bank financing.) Since the rig-building industry had a doubtful
future, FELS' asset expansion could be questioned, but the case information implied that the expenditure was largely for upgrading facilities.
One expansion plan was cancelled. FELS managed to endure the
business downturn with ample working capital and was poised to take
advantage of a future turnaround.

    FELS and Promet were both at the vanguard of their industry,
though FELS was the first in Southeast Asia to build a rig. FELS' initial
entrepreneurialism preceded Keppel's involvement in the company.
Keppel's influence on events in FELS seemed to be, first and foremost,
through financial backing, and also Keppel directed the diversification
of the early 1980s since the two companies had the same chairman. It
seems likely also that FELS' efforts in human resources development
were inspired by Keppel. Keppel, in turn, followed national priorities,
for example, the move to house unions and the utilization of national
educational programmes.

    The major lesson of the FELS case is that the company's acquisi-
tion by Keppel solved their capital shortage problem. This acquisition
was very different in character from the 'nationalization' of industries
elsewhere because FELS was 'nationalized' by a government enterprise
as part of that enterprise's development strategy, rather than by a
government ministry for sociopolitical reasons. FELS' share price rose
substantially after the takeover. Other financing had not been forthcoming for FELS, even though business opportunities were in the
offing. Banks and investors in Singapore had a reputation at that time
for being more inclined to put their money in property or other non-
industrial investments, while the government was Singapore's major
venture capitalist.

    There is also a need to analyze non-financial factors in govern-
ment companies, such as product quality, marketing effort, and human
resource development. The case studies of both Keppel and FELS
indicate good performance in these areas. For example, in 1981 two
rigs had been built by FELS which were heralded in the annual report:
"The rigs were also of such quality as to be commended by the owners

for the workmanship on them ... In appreciation of this fine performance, the Company was awarded bonuses on both the rigs by the respective owners ... Marketing efforts have also been intensified to sell the yard's facilities for rig-building after 1983." "FELS ... intensified its manpower development programme. Company personnel were sent for courses ... and in-house courses conducted ... "

As illustrated above by the FELS case, training was a factor. Training was less notable in the private company Promet. Of course, Promet's relatively small size (compared to Keppel Group) would limit the scope and intensity of training programmes.

2.4.4 Recapitulation

The case studies of Part 2 compared state-owned with privately owned enterprise in the domestic ship repair industry in Singapore. The governnent role in Keppel and FELS did not hamper business activities, and in fact seemed to have the opposite effect, as the SOEs entrepreneurial abilities were enhanced, rather than encumbered by bureaucracy or other predicted difficulties. Civil servants behaved much like ordinary businessmen, except they were more than that; the civil servants were Singapore's professional elite and key members of the national leadership team. The government invariably played a proactive role.

Other differences between the state-owned and private enterprises seemed also to be to the advantage of the SOEs. Promet had been in the hands of receivers, and we might suspect that Keppel would probably not have been subjected to that fate. Keppel's bankers would more likely have trusted the government to liquidate the company's obligations.

A resource advantage for SOE is suggested by the original provision of assets and financing for Keppel, and the quality of their personnel resources (especially the civil servants). Most important was their position on the 'cooperative' government team.

There was ample evidence to support the argument that there is a network of cooperative relationships and institutions in the Singapore SOE system. The major rationalization of shipyards, opportunities in China, acquisitions of facilities, and other internal dealings within the system manifested a nation-wide team effort. Without doubt, the system as a whole benefitted. It was also apparent that the government role in its enterprises can be characterized as 'promotional' and oriented on national economic development (as opposed to distributional and regulatory in approach). This was evident from start-up, through hard times, and in all business relationships. Primary government attention was to long-term viability, manpower development, and international competitiveness, rather than such concerns as provision of jobs, subsidies, or other services to voters.

References

1. Chung Chee Kit, "Keppel Shipyard," Harvard Business School, 1981
2. Dong Sung Cho, "Global Competition and Global Strategy: A Case of the Shipbuilding Industry," Academy of International Business conference paper, Singapore, June 1984
3. Kaye, Lincoln, "Hazardous Straits," *Feer.* 6/12/84, pp. 75-82
4. Lasserre, Philippe, "Promet Berhad," National University of Singapore School of Management, June 1982
5. Leong Cheng Chit, "Singapore's Shipyard Sector: Present Status and Future Direction," forum on Stable Employment, *Shipbuilding & Marine Employees' Union*, Hyatt Hotel Singapore, 22 August 1986
6. Lim Chai Boon, "The Present and Future Status of Shipyards in Singapore," forum on Stable Employment, *Shipbuilding & Marine Employees' Union*, Hyatt Hotel Singapore, 22 August 1986
7. Lim Ghee Soon, "State-owned Enterprises in Competitive Environment: A Comparative Study into the Marine Industry in Singapore," Academic Exercise, National University of Singapore School of Management, 1984/5
8. Ramanadham, *VV, The Nature of Public Enterprise*, Croom Helm, 1984
9. Tong Lai Han, "Government Controlled Enterprises: A Case Study of Neptune Orient Lines and the Shipping Industry," Academic Exercise, National University of Singapore School of Management, 1984/5

3.   Case Studies of Three State-Owned Enterprises in Singapore

Sections 3.1 and 3.2 are studies of enterprises created by the Singapore Government for purposes of international competition. These cases illustrate the tactics and strategies employed by government to bring about the development of new industries and improve national competitive strength. Section 3.3 is a case study of a statutory board, which provides an example of how the government operates in the development of infrastructure and provision of utilities to its citizens while simultaneously enhancing the national ability to compete in world markets. The final Section 3.4 of this Part III analyzes the case studies to ascertain the nature of behaviour and performance of state-owned enterprises (SOEs) in Singapore.

3.1 Petrochemical Corporation of Singapore Pte. Ltd. (PCS)

Incorporated in August 1977, PCS commenced production in February 1984. PCS was the upstream company in a complex which, at the official opening in March 1985, included four downstream companies and constituted Singapore's largest industrial undertaking. The complex was located on an island 3.5 km offshore which had formerly been a fishing village.

The petrochemical complex was a joint project of the Singapore and Japanese Governments and a consortium of multinational enterprises (MNEs). The development of a strong oil-processing industry had long been a Singapore Government objective, the first refinery being established in 1961. Singapore was currently the world's third largest refining centre and Asia's largest, at a capacity of over one million barrels per day. Negotiations on the petrochemical complex were initiated in 1971 with exploratory meetings between the Singapore Government and various MNEs. The lead was taken by Sumitomo Chemical Company of Japan, whose President Hasegawa met with Singapore Minister of Finance Hon Sui Sen and the Japanese Ambassador in December 1971 and afterward announced plans for a petrochemical plant in Singapore. (Hasegawa was to be a key figure throughout, noting on several future occasions that his company's participation was strongly influenced by his respect for Mr. Hon and Prime Minister Lee Kuan Yew and their commitment to free enterprise. On this occasion he described Singapore as "the best place to invest in Asia.") Mitsubishi Corporation had also discussed the prospective project with Prime Minister Lee in September, and Shell had earlier expressed an interest. The major private participant was to be Sumitomo, and letters of intent were exchanged between Sumitomo and the Singapore Government in 1973. The oil crisis intervened, but Sumitomo started a feasibility study in April 1974 (costing S$1.2 million) which was favourable. On January, 1, 1975 Hon Sui Sen announced the signing of the basic agreement with Sumitomo, and indicated that the project would be on stream by 1979.

However, by early 1976 the two partners agreed to seek wider participation. By May 1977 Sumitomo had gained the support of the 11 major petrochemical companies in Japan. Then in June, 1977 during a visit to Japan by Singapore Prime Minister Lee, Japanese Prime Minister Takeo Fukuda announced official backing for the project. A 3 billion yen investment was committed through a Japanese Government agency, Overseas Economic Cooperation Fund (OECF). This represented 30% of Japanese equity (15% of the total equity), with the other 70% from a Sumitomo-led consortium of the 11 cooperating Japanese companies, plus 12 other Japanese firms including banks, trading companies and others. The Japan Singapore Petrochemical Company was set up by this group of 23 Japanese companies and OECF in July to hold Japan's 50% share in the upstream company, PCS. Singapore's half of the 50—50 deal was held by the Ministry of Finance (95%) and Development Bank of Singapore (DBS) (5%). Later Temasek Holdings took over 35%, leaving 60% with "Ministry of Finance Inc."

A final round of talks was held July 8—14 between two Sumitomo executives and officials of Singapore's Finance Ministry and Economic Development Board. The Board of Directors was selected, comprised of four Singapore civil servants led by JY Pillay as Chairman, and four Sumitomo representatives. The Managing Director was appointed from Sumitomo, but it was agreed that Singapore could appoint a qualified local Managing Director ten years after start-up. The other Singaporeans on the board included S Dhanabalan who was then Executive Vice President at DBS and was to become Minister of Foreign Affairs, Ngiam Tong Dow who was Chairman of the Economic Development Board, and Deputy Director of the Public Works Department Francis Mak. (The current, somewhat larger Board of Directors is shown in Table 8. — Singapore contingent only.)

The Prime Ministers of both countries attended PCS's incorporation ceremonies in August. The ongoing personal interest of the national leaders was continued by then cabinet minister Yasuhiro Nakasone's visit to Singapore in September, when he and Lee Kuan Yew discussed the problems of marketing and pollution control. Nakasone told reporters that Japan would help Singapore successfully complete the project.

This personal commitment was honoured in 1983 when the Japanese Government increased its participation from 3 to 7.58 billion yen, as the total investment in the project nearly quadrupled from 10 to 37.9 billion yen. (There was some reluctance according to the Far Eastern Economic Review (FEER) because of doubts about future prospects. It was reported to be "a political rather than an economic decision ... instigated in talks earlier this year between Japanese Prime

Table 8 PCS Board of Directors @ 17/11/87 (Singapore)

Name	Date	Civil service	Other positions held
Hwang Peng Yuan (Chairman Since)	13/7/82 22/4/86)	x	Deputy Chairman Temasek; Former Chairman Economical Development Board; Chairman Sembawang Salvage, Intraco; Director Keppel, DBS; Vice Chairman Hitachi Electric Service
Han Cheng Fong (Deputy Managing Director)	1/9/84		Chairman Sembawang Projects Engineering; Director Tetra Chemicals, Sembawang Construction
Tan See Jay	22/4/86	x	Director National Grain Elevator
Lum Choong Wah	15/10/82	x	GM Temasek; Chairman Singapore National Printers; Director MRT, NOL, Singmanex, Loyang Valley
Patrick Yeoh Khwai Hoh	1/7/78	x	Chairman DBS Land, Raffles City, NDC Merchant Bank; Director DBS, ASEAN Finance Corp, Asfinco
Cheong Kwee Wah	25/1/85	x	nil
Daniel Selvaretnam	20/4/87	x	Director Economical Development Board, Sugar Ind. of Singapore
Foo Siang Tien	18/10/82	x	nil
Gan Kim Kok (Alt)	21/3/83		Director Orient Leasing Singapore, Yeo Hiap Seng

Minister Yasuhiro Nakasone and Lee." (FEER, 13/10/80:80))

The second oil crisis slowed further commitments until 1980, when construction work began on PCS. (Site formation had been completed in 1977.) Three of the four downstream companies were incorporated in 1980, and the fourth in 1982. Further downward integration was planned. The Singapore Government held between 20—50% of the equity in each of the companies.

The complex was heralded as the commencement of Singapore's Second Industrial Revolution which had been declared in 1979. In 1980 Hon Sui Sen observed, "The petrochemical complex is a fitting start for the Eighties when Singapore will be striving to upgrade the economy and the technological level of our manufacturing industries."

3.1.1 Performance

During the early 1980s there was a marked pessimism about the future of the complex reflected in articles in the foreign media. Two oil crises and a recession had plagued the world economy since the idea of setting up the complex was first put forward, and by the 1980s other Southeast Asian and Middle Eastern countries were considering or had already built their own complexes. The Far Eastern Economic Review alleged that only prestige considerations had compelled the Singapore Government to continue with the project, predicting that "losses could run up to S$100 million a year" (FEER, 24/9/82). PCS itself predicted a loss of S$50—60 in the first year, but contracts from China and elsewhere were to significantly improve on early dire expectations. (See Table 9) The company cited a "turnaround" by mid-1986, pro-

Table 9   PCS: Performance and Financing (Million S$)

	1984	1985	1986
Turnover	318.2	555.7	441.0
Net loss	33.6	66.2	18.3
Capital employed	975.4	888.2	963.8
Long term debt	322.3	301.3	395.2

Details of individual loans:		
Creditors	Date	Amount
DBS Morgan Guarantee Bank of Tokyo Sumitomo Bank Industrial Bank of Japan Exim Bank of Japan Nippon Credit Bank	30/1/81 (paid 2/4/85)	¥42.6 billion
DBS Sumitomo Bank Other Japanese banks	26/2/85	S$40 million
DBS Bank of Tokyo Industrial Bank of Japan Sumitomo Bank	27/2/87	S$111.648 million ¥2.5 billion
DBS Industrial Bank of Japan Bank of Tokyo	27/2/87 (paid 28/8/87)	¥14 billion
DBS Industrial Bank of Japan Bank of Tokyo	28/8/87	¥12.6 billion

jecting a profit for the coming year, 1987. Losses in the first three years were attributed to very high debt payments and depreciation writeoffs, and were expected to turn to profit as more downstream plants came onstream. DBS and other shareholders took measures to alleviate anticipated cash flow problems by converting loans to equity in the form of straight grants, thereby eliminating the need for debt repayments.

In the Prime Minster's National Day address of August 1985 the petrochemical industry was singled out as one of the sectors that should be restructured because of excess capacity. Nevertheless, the entire complex had been operating at nearly full capacity (87—90%) even before the Prime Minister's speech, and on 17/5/86 Han Cheng Fong said the entire complex was "running flat out." In response to an inquiry about whether PCS planned any capacity reduction, a company spokesman replied that the problem now was rather how too overcome constraints to increased output.

3.1.2 Marketing

Marketing turned out to be one of PCS's successes. Managing Director Kosai noted in August 1985 that demand for the complex's products was holding up effectively against new Saudi Arabian plants "because we have succeeded in our marketing." At the commencement of production in February 1984 Mr. Hasegawa also noted that the trading companies in the group had helped solve the marketing problem.

There were some instances of Prime Minster Lee acting as marketing agent. In September 1985 he visited China, at which time China promised to buy more petrochemicals from Singapore if the price was right. That same month China established a representative office in Singapore of China National Chemicals Import and Export Corporation(Sinochem). A month later Polyolefin, one of the downstream companies, secured a 2-year contract with option for renewal, assuring China 30% of its output. The Trade Development Board Chairman in Singapore Mr. Chandra Das announced in July 1986 that exports to China had doubled since Sinochem's arrival, now constituting 25% of the petrochemical total.

3.1.3 The Future

In August 1987, one decade after incorporation of PCS, Shell submitted an offer to buy overall Singapore Government interests in the entire complex. The offer was unexpected, and there was no precedent for policy considerations. The Report of the Public Sector Divestment Committee had categorized PCS as an "exception" to the privatization policy because of "foreign government participation." Such enterprises were "long term projects and changes in shareholding would only be effected after due consultations." By early 1988 no decision had been announced. The complex by then included two new plants, with another joint venture proposed in January 1988 and awaiting shareholder approval. The first of the two new projects was a joint venture between PCS (60%) and a Japanese trading company (40%), the second between American and Indonesian interests, and the last proposal involved one of the downstream companies. Each new plant took the complex one more step towards full integration, which would mean that there would be maximum value added to end products.

3.2 Singapore Aircraft Industries Pte. Ltd. (SAI)

On 25 February 1982, headlines in the Straits Times proclaimed, "Aerospace — new thrust by government." The newspaper was announcing the formation of SAI, an investment holding company for the Defence Ministry's aerospace companies. SAI in turn belonged to Sheng Li Holdings, which held the Ministry's two commercial enterprises. (The other Sheng Li company was a light arms manufacturer, Singapore Technology Corporation.) Within SAI, initially there were only two subsidiaries (SAMCO and SEEL), but by 1987 there were six subsidiaries and one associated company — see Table 12.

The Economic Development Board had established the goal of making Singapore "a regional integrated centre for aircraft repair and overhaul services and a base for the manufacture of aircraft equipment and components." Specifically, in declaring aerospace as a priority industry for the 1980s, the government stated objectives:

1) to further develop Singapore into the most comprehensive aviation repair and overhaul base, and

2) to develop Singapore into a major aircraft component manufacturing base for worldwide exports.

The government, through Jurong Town Corporation, had also reserved prepared industrial land. Ready-built factory premises for immediate start-up were available, or simply prepared land sites where companies could construct their own factory buildings. Near the airport, the Loyang Industrial Estate was reserved; and an ex-military base, Seletar Air Base, was being redeveloped into a general aviation complex.

Aerospace had been earmarked as a priority industry even by the early 1970s. News accounts of the 1980s put the birthdate of the industry in Singapore at about 1977. Certainly by then it was clear that aerospace was an excellent prospect. In 1975, the national carrier Singapore Airlines (SIA) carried 12.7% of the world's airline passengers, and was growing dramatically. This grand airline was probably the government's finest enterprise and indeed kept pace in the aerospace industry itself. Also in 1975, SAMCO was incorporated (see Table 12) to be the principal contractor to maintain the Singapore Air Force's fixed and rotary wing aircraft, replacing Lockheed.

Unlike the Engineering Division of SIA, SAI was formed expressly to bid for overseas contracts. During the period 1980 to 1985, export sales increased proportionally from less than 3 times domestic sales to nearly 10 times. By late 1983 it was announced that SAI was looking into the feasibility of co-producing helicopters with major international manufacturers. In early 1984 Samaero announced an Aerospatiale offer to be the foreign partner. Similarly in 1983, SAI was also studying options for entering the field of aircraft manufacturing, as a made-in-Singapore plane was planned for as early as the 1990s. However, the Chairman emphasized that any deal would take time to deliberate. "We must get the right partner first, and the product must be able to sell," he said, "then we can go into our first aircraft manufacture ... It is our long term goal to see at least one aircraft come out of Singapore, but whether it is done in five years, ten years or twenty years, we still are not sure." Minister of Communications and Information and Second Minister for Defence Tay Eng Soon observed on 11 May 1985, "The only thing they have yet to do is to build a new aircraft." By 1988 no announcement had been made.

3.2.1 The Aerospace Exhibition

Since technical and strategic information on SAI was not publicly available, the instance of the Asian Aerospace Exhibition will provide us with a glimpse of the way things were done, and especially the cooperative relationship between SAI and its government. The Economic Development Board (EDB) regularly sent a contingent to the two top world exhibitions in London (Farnborough) and Paris (Le Bourget), and aspired to make Singapore the third most important air show. Singapore hosted the first four Asian Aerospace shows in 1981, 1984, 1986, and the most recent show in January 1988 at its permanent site at Changi Airport. A decision had been reached on 10

January 1986 between Singapore Government officials and the Cahners Exhibition Group of Australia to make Singapore the permanent host for the Asian Aerospace Exhibition. In August 1986, Asian Aerospace Pte. Ltd. was formed, a joint venture between Cahners and SAI. The joint venture partners would share equally the estimated S$12 million development costs. The land for the site was owned by Civil Aviation Authority of Singapore (CAAS). CAAS had participated in the 10 January 1986 meeting, and its Chairman was an SAI director.

Data on SAI performance was secret, but the EDB periodically published figures on the industry as a whole. (See Table 10)

Table 10   Performance of Aerospace Industry in Singapore*

Year	Cumulative investment (S$mil.)	Employment	Output (S$mil.)	Increase (%)
1977	28.84	1,400	47.0	—
1978	40.20	1,900	121.2	157.8
1979	74.04	2,340	168.0	38.6
1980	98.90	2,761	203.5	21.1
1981	144.00	3,124	233.2	14.6
1982	244.87	3,547	262.8	12.7
1983	253.93	3,945	382.0	45.4
1984	303.84	4,276	457.3	19.7
1985	334.00	5,065	767.2	67.8

* 28 Companies surveyed by the Economic Development Board, not including the Engineering Division of Singapore Airlines.

Table 11 SAI Board of Directors @ 17/11/87

Name	Appointed	Other positions held
Quek Poh Huat (Managing Director)	23/6/83	
Su Guaning	1/9/84	
Col George Yeo	3/12/85	
Low Puk Yeong	1/6/82	
Col Lai Seck Khui	23/6/83	
Jimmy Poo Aun Neow	10/7/85	Professor (Engr.) National University of Singapore
Lim Hock San	17/6/85	Chairman Civil Aviation Authority of Singapore
Lim Ming Seong	24/12/81	
Col Lui Pao Chuen	24/12/81	
Chew Leng Seng	17/6/85	Singapore Airlines executive
Col Michael Teo Eng Cheng	1/6/82	
Chua Soo Tian	22/6/82	

Table 12 SAI Subsidiaries and Associated Companies

Name	Start-up	Owned (%)	Paid in capital
Singapore Aerospace Maintenance Company (SAMCO)	1975	100	$20 mil
Singapore Aero-Components Overhaul (SACO)	1982	60 (1)	$ 5 mil
Singapore Aerospace Manufacturing (SAM)	1981	60 (2)	$10 mil
Singapore Aero-Engine Overhaul (SAEOL)	1977 (3)	100	$15 mil
Singapore Electronic and Engineering (SEEL)	1969	100 (4)	$15 mil
Singapore Aerospace Warehousing (SAWS)	1982	60 (5)	$ 5 mil
Samaero Company (6)	1977	20	$ 4 mil

Notes:

1) Owned 20% by SAMCO and 20% by SEEL.
2) Owned 20% by SAMCO and 20% by a local private company.
3) Operations started in 1974 as part of Singapore Airlines, and SAEOL became a separate subsidiary in 1977, with 1/3 owned by the Defence Ministry. SAI acquired total ownership on 1 February 1985.
4) One share each held by JY Pillay and Estate of Hon Sui Sen.
5) 40% owned jointly by SAI's subsidiaries.
6) Joint venture between SAMCO and Aerospatiale of France.

3.3 Telecommunications Authority of Singapore (TELECOMS)

The modern enterprise traced its origins back to the first telephone service in Singapore in 1879. The national telephone network was taken over by the colonial government from the Oriental Telephone and Electric Company in 1954, forming the Singapore Telephone Board; and at independence in 1965 the other half of the telecommunications function, external services, was also taken over from a colonial company, Cable and Wireless Ltd., by the Telecommunications Department in the Ministry of Communications. The department was converted into a statutory board in 1972, and the two boards merged to form the modern corporation in 1974. The 1972 and 1974 reorganizations resulted from recommendations by the International Telecommunication Union which was commissioned by the Singapore Government to survey the administration of telecommunications. In 1982 the Postal Service Department also merged with Telecoms to prevent unwanted competition between government agencies in the provision of electronic mail services anticipated in the future. Two years later Telecoms initiated a 5-year S$75 million programme to provide more post offices offering more services opened for longer hours (and a complete refurbishing of the old colonial post office building), and the Minister for Communications and Information pledged that fully computerized services would be available by 1988—89.

Milestones in the development of telecommunications infrastructures and services in Singapore include:

1965 — First voice grade submarine cable in South East Asia; by 1988 an eighth cable was being planned, the first digital submarine cable.

1971 — Satellite communications introduced; by 1988 there were five satellite antennas.

1972—1988 — Nearly 5-fold increase in number of telephones per capita, which rate of provision ranks among the best in the world.

1975 — Opening of Telecommunication Training Centre (Telecentre)

1977 — First to use optic fibres to carry live traffic.

1979 — Computer based telephone exchanges installed.

1979—1983 — Replacement of all rotary dial telephones with push-button sets, making Singapore one of the first and few nations in the world to have 100% pushbutton sets.

1988 — Field trial of Teleview, a "world first".

1988 — Commence ISDN commercial service ("Telecoms believes that the ISDN is the network infrastructure for the Information Age." (Sung, 1987))

3.3.1 Management

The first Chairman of the Authority was Ngiam Tong Dow, who retired in 1972. A Permanent Secretary in the Ministry of Finance, Mr. Ngiam was a key member on the boards of several state-owned enterprises and was later to become the Chairman of the Economic Development Board. The next Chairman at Telecoms, from 1972–74, was Herman R. Hochstadt. He was then a Permanent Secretary in the Ministry of Communications and also served on the boards of state-owned enterprises including Singapore Airlines, Central Provident Fund, and the Economic Development Board.

The third chairman was to stay on for twelve years. Frank Yung-Cheng Yung came from the private, formerly colonial company Inchcape and was thus the first non-civil servant Chairman of Telecoms. However, in Mr. Yung's own assessment (at retirement from Telecoms) there was little effective difference in abilities or attitudes from the civil service: "The civil servants represented on the Telecoms board are as open-minded and liberal in their thinking as anyone else. Members from the private sector are generally well briefed on national policy issues." He was seconded by the government to join Telecoms and also serve as a board member of Development Bank of Singapore. He had been a board member of Singapore Telephone Board since 1972, becoming Deputy Chairman in 1973. Frank Yung served until 1986 when he was named to be Chief Executive of Singapore Press Holdings (SPH), the country's dominant newspaper group. He had been named to the SPH board in 1984 after the government-directed merger of the three major newspapers into SPH. SPH's 1985 annual report expressed the objective of "becoming a worldwide communications and information technology group," similar to Telecoms' own corporate purpose. Telecoms was a major shareholder of SPH, owning over 8%.

Mr. Yung's temporary replacement at Telecoms was Tan Chin Nam, a civil servant on the Telecoms board since 1983 who was also General Manager of the National Computer Board and a director of the Economic Development Board. Mr. Tan was replaced the same year by Koh Boon Hwee. Mr. Koh was also the second Chairman to be seconded by the government from private business, as Managing Director of the local subsidiary of Hewlett Packard. The youngest Telecoms chairman at 35, he had already served on the Economic

Table 13 Telecoms Performance Data

(Million S$)

Year	Operating		Net Surplus	Capital Expend.	Total Assets	Productivity* (%)	Staff Strength
	Revenue	Expense					
1986/7	980.5	687.7	365.0	281.5	3483.4	3.48	12497
1985/6	953.0	710.3	314.7	412.1	3551.5	3.03	12751
1984/5	942.3	677.7	366.2	433.0	3264.4	2.95	12920
1983/4	842.4	621.5	298.3	333.0	2774.0	2.94	12922
1982/3	803.1	505.2	368.5	288.3	na	3.48	11698
1981/2	666.1	380.7	396.0	243.5	1921.8	na	10552
1980/1	555.6	333.8	301.9	220.9	1593.2		10281
1979/80	458.1	283.2	227.5	213.8	1324.2		9862
1978/9	400.1	245.4	190.8	166.0	1114.2		9572
1977/8	316.6	186.1	161.7	178.1	900.8		9069
1976/7	272.5	149.2	155.1	185.3	780.9		8479
1975/6	228.8	110.7	152.9	149.6	642.2		7478
1974/5	195.4	97.9	128.8	65.4	512.2		6390
1973/4	107.4	42.3	88.3	47.8	190.5		5434

* Value added per S$ employment costs.

Committee and the advisory panel of the National Productivity Board. A banker was quoted as commenting on Koh's appointment: "I'm not surprised, he is regarded as a hot commodity."

The General Manager at Telecoms since incorporation was Goh Kim Seng, who started as a technician in 1952 with the Telecommunications Department. Retired in 1986, he was replaced by a Permanent Secretary in the Ministry of Communications, Lam Chuan Leong. Soon Mr. Lam was replaced by Wong Hung Khim, a civil servant who was also General Manager of Port of Singapore Authority.

The current board of directors had four members from the private sector. The board is listed in Table 14.

Table 14   Telecoms Board of Directors @31/3/87

Name	Other positions held
Koh Boon Hwee (Chairman)	Managing Director, Hewlett Packard (S)
Wong Hung Khim (GM)	Former GM, Port of Singapore Authority
Dr. Hong Hai	GM, Wearne Brothers
Colonel Lai Seck Khui	Chief Signal Officer, Ministry of Defence
Lew Syn Pau	Assistant Director, National Trade Union Congress
Lim Ho Kee	Senior VP, Union Bank of Switzerland
Pek Hok Thiam	Director (Comm.), Ministry of Communications
Tan Chin Nam	GM, Economic Development Board
Keith A. K. Tay	Managing Partner, Peat Marwick & Co.

3.3.2   Technology Policy

According to a newspaper interview of retiring Chairman Frank Yung in 1986, the prevailing technology policy at Telecoms was attributed to a mid-1970s decision by the board of directors that the corporation should be at the forefront of technology. By then Telecoms had freed itself from "the nitty gritties" of simply catching up with the backlog of telephone applications and could concentrate on technological advancement. The newspaper said, "It was a bold decision, Mr. Yung admitted." However, it was no chance coincidence that the same decision was being made on a national basis at about the same time. The government announced a "Second Industrial Revolution" in 1979. By then, Singapore leaders had identified a coming information age, and Telecoms was seen to be the key institution to lead the way to this future age.

An example of how Telecoms acquired new technology was Teleview. A closed tender was called at the turn of the decade for a joint venture partner to develop a system which met Telecoms' particular requirements. General Manager Goh Seng Kim observed, "The problem was people (telecommunications companies) didn't have the same vision as us. They thought we were on cloud nine." Finally a British company was selected, and field trials were expected by 1988. It was projected to be the world's first picture quality graphics with telephone and television technologies.

Mr. Yung was paraphrased in the 1986 interview also as saying that Telecoms now "should virtually skip the step of copying the advanced countries." His replacement Koh Boon Hwee observed a year later (1987) that "Telecoms will keep abreast of new and emerging technologies and introduce them whenever possible." On 9 May, 1987 the Minister of Communications and Information stated, "We aspire to position Telecoms at the very top of the league of international tele-communications centres." Numerous innovations have been announced by Telecoms, but of course no purely new technology actually preceeded equivalent developments in one or more advanced country. An example of where Telecoms achieved a novel application of existing knowledge was in February 1987 when Telecoms was said to be the first to use optic fibres for live traffic. Singapore (Telecoms) also was, according to Frank Yung, "as far ahead as any other country in developing ISDN."

In February 1986 Frank Yung said, "We have seen rapid changes in technology and kept to the forefront. As a result, it has become traditional for Telecoms to offer the highest grade of service at the lowest cost." Telecoms periodically reduced charges for various services, which was possible, the company claimed, because of cost savings derived from the investment in technology. Telecoms' technology policy, Mr. Yung said, had enabled the corporation to be highly "efficient, dynamic and progressive." The corporation boasted utility rates that were among the cheapest in the world.

Telecoms policy was consistent with national policies. General Manager Goh Seng Kim observed at his retirement from Telecoms: "My role was to try to interpret national policy and convert it into Telecoms policy."

3.3.3   Competition Policy

In March 1987 the Public Sector Divestment Committee published its Report which "recommends that further study be made with the view to privatise ... Telecoms." No timetable had been determined, but in preparation for this eventuality Koh Boon Hwee's first Chairman's Statement (in the 1986/87 annual report) announced a liberalization policy to make Telecoms more "market-driven." (In November 1985 the Minister of Communications & Information announced in Parliament that customers could now own and maintain their own terminal equipment, and this was cited by the newspaper as marking the start of the liberalization policy.) Liberalization, as recommended by the Economic Committee, meant allowing private sector competition in equipment provision and service. For example, from March 1987 Telecoms opened the sale and maintenance of its business telephones to private competitors.

3.3.4 Financing and Investment

Telecoms debt since 1972 was provided from three sources. In 1973/4 the government arranged a yen loan equivalent to S$7 million from the Overseas Economic Cooperation Fund of Japan to finance an antenna at the Sentosa satellite station. Telecoms paid the government 6% interest.

The World Bank loaned approximately S$40 million in 1974/5 for expansion of telephone facilities.

From 1978/9 Telecoms carried various liabilities to "deferred creditors," reported at S$63.7 million in 1979, increasing to S$265.5 million by 1986, but declining to S$64.3 million in 1987 as Telecoms was attempting to depend more on market financing by that time. The creditors were Export Credit Agencies from various countries financing Singapore's share in the construction of submarine cables, and the loans were at preferential rates.

Telecoms' investments since 1972 included memberships in various global satellite organizations, a single subsidiary named Integrated Information (originally General Telephone Directory Company), and until 1987 a small holding of Singapore Government stocks. From 1982 Telecoms reported "quoted investments," which by 1987 represented 2/3 of the total investments on the balance sheet.

A consultancy subsidiary was formed in March 1988.

3.3.5 Human Resource Management

According to outgoing Chairman Yung in 1986, Telecoms was well known as a good employer — one of the best in the government service and as good as the best in the private sector. Training and career development were high priorities. Recent annual reports described over several pages the in-house and other training offered, and the Chairman's Statement repeatedly pledged, "We shall continue our commitment on human resources management."

From 1984 there was a change in manpower policy evident, as for the first time total staff employment began to decline, despite continuing growth in operating volume. The Chairman's Statement in the 1982/84 annual report said, "Following the merger (with the post office), it is now the intention of the Authority to progressively introduce a series of measures that will counter the traditionally labour intensive nature of the postal services." The 1986 annual report announced, "Over the next five years, management will aim at reducing manpower in line with the exercise for a trimmer Civil Service." It was also stressed that this policy corresponded with the Second Industrial Revolution concept.

Many instances of the government's own human resources priorities were evident in Telecoms' programmes. In conjunction with the National Courtesy Campaign, Telecoms conducted its own exercise annually, and a similar effort was made in keeping with the National Productivity Campaign.

On 1 May, 1985 Telecoms was awarded the Plaque of Commendation by the National Trades Union Congress (NTUC) for contributions to industrial health and safety, union-management relations, and staff welfare and training. There was consistently one official from the NTUC on the Telecoms board.

3.3.6 Intra-Government Cooperative Arrangements

Telecoms provided ongoing agency and consultancy services to various government boards and departments. For example, hardware and software maintenance and consultancy were provided for various systems of the Civil Aviation Authority of Singapore.

In 1985 Telecoms collaborated with the Economic Development Board, National Computer Board and National University of Singapore to formulate a National Information Technology Plan.

Telecentre was jointly utilized by Telecoms and Singapore Broadcasting Corporation (SBC).

Telecoms was working with other government agencies to develop Tradenet, a data interchange system for agencies and participating businesses. Sung (1987) noted, "Telecoms also provides facilities management services for multinational corporations ... This is a proactive approach towards supporting the Economic Development Board's emphasis in encouraging large corporations to set up regional operational headquarters in Singapore ... It has always been Telecoms' strategy to align itself with the national economic policy ... Besides supporting economic policy, Telecoms also has the role of being a national catalyst to promote economic development. Since the mid-1970s Telecoms has taken on a more enlightened policy in recognition of this dual role."

3.4 Case Analysis of PCS, SAI, Telecoms

3.4.1 Origins and Objectives

The incorporation of PCS* and SAI* was a result of deliberate government initiative, in partnership with foreign multinational corporations (MNCs). Government capital and risk-bearing were essential ingredients to their creation, and it therefore seems likely that, if left to the private sector, no such enterprises would exist in Singapore today. In PCS's case, the Japanese MNCs' participation was strongly influenced by the positive stand made by Singapore's Prime Minister and Finance Minister, as stated by the central character in the negotiations. As was true of the shipyards (see Part 2), for both PCS and SAI, MNC technology and government support were an essential combination. For PCS and SAI, clearly the government provided an effective matchmaking, venture capitalist service. PCS's working relationship with Japanese trading companies and others, SAMCO's joint venture with Aerospatiale of Europe, and Telecoms' Teleview project all indicate the ability of state-owned enterprises (SOEs) to establish effective partnership arrangements with foreign MNCs.

The government also provided important access to domestic assets, for example, land. It is not easy to imagine how else the Seletar Military Base could have been so readily turned over to the aerospace industry. Indeed, the base was even renovated for that purpose. Similarly, CAAS made space for a permanent aerospace exhibition, and Jurong Town Corporation reserved an estate at an ideal location near the airport. Nor could the consortium of Japanese MNCs ever have even located an island to build PCS, let alone taken it over and displaced local inhabitants. Direct involvement of a network of government agencies, and even the top government leaders, was essential.

Telecoms' origin was the usual case of monopoly government provision of utilities, but the government was interested in more than merely satisfying their constituency with services, as the international

---

* Note: The following acronyms are used throughout this section:
   CAAS   Civil Aviation Authority of Singapore
   MNC   Multinational Corporation
   NTUC   National Trades Union Congress
   PCS   Petrochemical Corporation of Singapore
   SAI   Singapore Aircraft Industries
   SAMCO   Singapore Aerospace Maintenance Company
   SOE   State Owned Enterprise
   Telecoms Telecommunications Authority of Singapore

commercial value of a strong telecommunications and information industry was perceived very early.

In all cases, therefore, it is evident that SOEs' origins and objectives were couched in national development priorities. Goals were non-political and concerned with long term strategic economic prospects. SAI explicitly, but all three SOEs were part of the broader policy of export oriented development; and PCS and Telecoms explicitly, but all three SOEs were part of the government's Second Industrial Revolution.

3.4.2   Management

Since PCS and SAI did not publish annual reports or avail them-selves to public scrutiny of internal operational procedures, the calibre of their management teams was not easily judged. Certainly top level personalities were put in charge, recruited from the nation's leading enterprises, as was the case for example at Telecoms where the Managing Director came from Hewlett Packard, a premier American MNC, Telecoms and SAI performance was exemplary, in terms of product quality, revenues generated, marketing and the like; which may also be assumed to be true at PCS if we believe that initial losses were inevitable.

Although we know little about general management issues such as industrial relations at PCS and SAI, we do know that Telecoms received the NTUC award, indicating a very outstanding effort in industrial relations. The Chairman claimed the corporation was an ex-cellent employer, and there certainly was a strong training programme, which especially emphasized national priorities in human resources development. Telecoms also was not hesitant to reduce staff numbers, though they never had to retrench employees against their will.

One of the most crucial advantages in the leadership of Singapore's SOEs was the marked evidence of a network of cooperative relation-ships among people and institutions. JY Pillay, PCS's first Chairman, headed Singapore's most important financial institutions in addition to the national airline and other organizations. Financing was indeed one of the keys to PCS viability. Pillay's successor, PY Hwang, was also in the inner circles of national leadership. His name also appears on the list of Keppel directors, illustrating that the coterie of top leaders in Singapore's SOE system was closely knit. Telecoms' chairmen were similarly prominent members of this small elite corps, and almost all of them had excellent track records (because Singapore's SOE system had always performed well almost without exception). Cross-directorships and other mutually supportive relationships among government enterprises, as directly alluded to in the case studies, linked Telecoms with NPB, SPH, PSA, NTUC, CAAS, NCB, NUS, SBC, and EDB; SAI with EDB, CAAS, SIA, and JTC; and PCS with EDB, PWD, DBS, and the Finance Ministry. And these links obviously provide an incomplete list.

3.4.3 Growth and Diversification

All SOEs seemed free to invest into traditional and new ventures, although in Telecoms' case it is not evident when such enterprise autonomy became allowable — perhaps from the outset. Evidently, however, none of the three SOEs was free to diversify out of its main line of business, in contrast to the case of Keppel. As they grew, ample opportunities to invest in traditional business existed. And all investment was in strategic, national competitive interests to create industries with long term viability.

The joint venture of SAMCO with Aerospatiale, a European SOE, suggests a possibility that SOEs may establish contact readily with SOEs from other countries, perhaps more readily than do MNCs. Even the Japanese MNCs which joined the petrochemical complex were contacted by the Singapore Government, indicating that there may be an important role for intra-government relationships in establishing international business arrangements.

Telecoms' move into new high information-technology fields was, according to retiring Chairman Yung, its own idea. Such autonomy, and such initiative, may be in contrast to the degree of control traditinally exercised in most national SOE systems. Telecoms' expressed intent to move to the forefront of new technological developments, rather than copy the leaders, suggests more strongly than any other evidence in the case studies a dynamic, forward-looking enterprise.

3.4.4 Recapitulation

These three enterprises also, like Keppel and its subsidiary FELS (Part 2), were part of the Singapore cooperative system, which was an exemplary model of national competition. The formation and progress of PCS and SAI illustrate the competence of the Singapore team. Telecoms' sophistication and futurist orientation further underlines the value of the promotional, supportive role of the Singapore Government in its enterprises. Organizational 'culture' in all these enterprises was enhanced by the government's presence.

References

1. Chua Swee Kiat, "Good Grounding," *Singapore Business,* September 1981
2. Editor, "A Petrochemical Giant is Born," *Asian Finance,* 15/9/80.
3. Elson, Benjamin M., "Singapore Firm Seeks Aircraft Projects," *Aviation Week and Space Technology,* 21/11/83
4. Kerns, Hikaru, "Betting on a Loser," *Far Eastern Economic Review,* 13/11/83
5. "Singapore Petrochem Complex Faces Uncertain Future," *Petromin,* 5/85
6. Sung Sio Ma, "Telecommunications Development and Evolution of Manufacturing and Service Industries," *Telecom 87,* 22/10/87
7. Tan, Diana, "All the Right Connections," *Mirror,* 15/11/87
8. Telecommunication Authority of Singapore, "A Hundred Years of Dedicated Service in Singapore, 1879—1979," 1979

4. Conclusions

Sections 2.4 and 3.4 have argued that the Singapore SOEs* performed exceptionally well, which is contrary to the usual case. This final Part 4 addresses the questions why and how the Singapore SOEs are different, by contrasting the mainstream evidence and predictions in the literature about SOE behaviour with the case evidence here.

The focus of the following analysis is on evaluation of the government's role in its enterprises. Space does not permit an extensive review of the literature on this topic, but the nature of the government role evolves essentially around the influence of politics and the bureaucracy, such as the prevalence of non-economic corporate goals.

---

* The followng acronyms are used throughout this Part 4:

BT	Business Times
FEER	Far Eastern Economic Review
FELS	Far East Levingston Shipbuilding
PAP	People's Action Party
PCS	Petroleum Corporation of Singapore
SAI	Singapore Aircraft Industries
SOE	State-Owned Enterprise
UK	United Kingdom
US	United States

4.1 Goal Conflict

In the general case, SOEs may have a proclivity to diverse, unstable, confusing goals, depending on the importance of politics to the enterprise and depending on the extent to which political pressures are inconsistent. This is the prediction in the literature on SOEs, and conceptually that notion seems irrefutable. However, this typical SOE problem seemed less applicable to the SOE system of Singapore. If politics and social priorities are added to the enterprise's business objectives, surely some confusion must result. Alternatively, if public service and profit motives can be considered intertwined, this may be an important distinction because traditionally we have considered social and profit motives to be conflicting. "If the political factor is operating in such a way as to make profitability the principal desideratum in public enterprises, a management fixation on profitability will serve the public interest." (Garner, 1983:7)

Jones and Vogelsang (1983:12) characterized this 'multiple objectives' situation as one of 'plural principals,' who included managers and workers within the enterprise, a multitude of government overseers, and outside interest groups. Concerning the first mentioned 'principal,' Keppel's management team underwent one major revamping, coinciding with the retirement of Bogaars and some top executives, which also signaled a major policy shift in the character of the diversification and growth strategy. Promet had a similar change in leadership and strategy, but their's was a much more turbulent experience for the company — it seems unlikely that the Singapore Government as owner would have permitted such infighting. Thus, the major management difference between Keppel and Promet was in stability and longevity of leadership, with a significant advantage in this respect for the SOEs.

There was little indication of 'multiple objectives' in the management of the SOEs as might be manifested in stated corporate goals. Keppel did not reveal its corporate objectives, only noting they were in process of being formulated. There were no formally stated corporate objectives in earlier years. One major policy shift occurred, in the pace of their growth and diversification strategy, but this was an economic necessity. In fact, the evidence seemed to indicate that SOEs in Singapore enjoyed more policy stability than the private sector. Promet experienced proxy battles and shifting investment strategies, with management unwilling or unable to state clear goals for long term development. At least two factors may have created some doubts in the national industries, too, especially at Keppel — which circumstance relates to the problem of 'multiple objectives' in that future goals were uncertain. There were doubts concerning Keppel's future during the rationalization exercise of 1985, but by 1986 it was clear that Keppel would stay in the ship repair industry, as verified by the chairman. The privatization schemes beginning in 1985 also may have raised some doubts as to whether Keppel would remain a national company, but further privatization apparently would not make too much difference in Keppel's* case since it was already publicly traded. The government could probably maintain control over Keppel, even with less than majority ownership.

The stability of corporate objectives may be related to the stability of the political environment. "East Asia political systems are inherently stable and work to maintain stability ... (Hofheinz and Caldor, 1982: 249) In Singapore one leadership and one ideology prevailed since 1959.

The political economy was also less influenced by diverse, fractious special interest gorups (which groups are the third "multiple principal' as per Jones — see above). Numerous top government leaders made it clear that special interests were not going to have much power in Singapore. Foreign Minister Dhanabalan stated on 29/7/86. "We have kept our politics free of the pressures of organized business and special interests ... We have never allowed ourselves to be hostage to any vested group or interest." The government's ability to be free of such pressures implies that its enterprises might be even less bothered by outside groups than private enterprises in Singapore, and in either case actual interference with companies' operations would be less likely than in the more pluralist societies of the West. In Singapore, business reigned supreme over every other domestic power centre but the government.

Of course, the government itself constitutes a major pressure group, but the government-enterprise relationship was laissez-faire. The Singapore SOEs were less burdened with political missions, such as to solve unemployment problems. There was no doubt that business goals transcended all social goals; or, to look at it another way, an overriding social/political goal in Singapore was to be competitive in international markets.

There also seemed to be a more unified governmental supervision (which relates to Jones' second 'multiple principal', the government overseers). Although Singapore SOEs coordinated with a multitude of

---

* The Public Sector Divestment Report published in Singapore on 13 March 1987 recommended that government ownership in Keppel be reduced eventually to 30%.

governmental bodies, the holding companies could act as a buffer against outside interference in the management functions of finance, marketing, and other operations. Also, there was never any public evidence of significant policy splits within government, in contrast to the recurrent squabbles in the political arenas of the US and UK.

4.2 Growth Orientation

SOE diversification strategies are predicted in the literature to be relatively conservative, that is, they expand productive capacity but tend to remain in their original industry. Resistance to divestment is also typical of SOEs — 'barriers to exit,' per Jones and Vogelsang (1983).

Until the mid-1980s, there was a very distinct tendency to a growth orientation in Singapore firms generally speaking. The fast growth trend was modified to some extent by the new national policy direction which became evident in 1985. The new policy was reflected at Keppel, where an executive explained that earlier priorities, for growth, had been displaced by the priority for ROI (return on investment). Until that change, however, funds were available for expansion — from both public and private sources — as long as opportunities were evident. This was clearly demonstrated in all cases: FELS had a capital shortage until it was acquired by Keppel; and when Bogaars took the helm at FELS a dramatic expansion programme was undertaken. Keppel itself was growing aggressively, and some decisions taken by both headquarters (Keppel) and subsidiary (FELS) were shown to be ill-conceived. However, the critical point is that growth seemed generally to result in commensurate return. The private company, Promet, expanded less dramatically but also less successfully.

In the go-go years, diversification strategies were not relatively conservative as predicted in the literature. For example, Keppel moved just as quickly as Promet into diverse fields, even property development and travel which seem hardly appropriate for national industry. The government presence was felt, for example, Keppel did not find it easy to impress the government that financial operations were an appropriate activity for them; but obviously the company's arguments prevailed in that case. FELS was less affected by the government's presence, for example, they did not slow down their diversification moves even while their parent Keppel was in the throes of national rationalization in coordination with the government. (PCS, SAI and Telecoms have not attempted any diversification out of their main business, of course.)

The old adage that government companies generally are immune to takeover (Vernon and Aharoni, 1981:16) has to be reconsidered in light of the Shell bid to acquire the Singapore Government's share of PCS, and the United Industrial Corporation (UIC) attempted takeover bid for Intraco. Of course, this latter bid was only possible because the government owned its shares through holding enterprises rather than ministries. Even so, "UIC sounded out the Public Sector Divestment Committee on the government's response" prior to making its bid. (FEER, 24/7/86:84) The hypothesis should thus be qualified, to suggest that mergers of SOEs are actually quite feasible, but may be inhibited in certain circumstances, that is, if shares are not tradeable or if the government does not condone the deal. (In fact, acquisitions of private companies in Singapore are relatively difficult because shares of even the most active counters are often held by only a few share-holders. This point was made by Paul Ma of Peat Marwick Management Consultants on 19/11/86 who argued that mergers are generally difficult in Singapore, citing a statistic that 75.2% of the shares of listed companies in Singapore were owned by the top 20% of investors.)

Also, the idea that SOEs may operate in "imperfect markets" leading to "barriers to exit" (Jones and Vogelsand, 1983) was not applicable to the Singapore SOEs examined since they were eventually subjected to the discipline of debt and equity markets. Keppel, like Promet, found itself in a geriatric industry, but both the national and the private companies took stringent measures to divest. Keppel was aided in its rationalization by government insistence on a coordinated industry-wide effort.

4.3 Protectionism and Subsidy

We hypothesize a tendency to favour local interests over foreign, but that tendency in Singapore is deliberately spurned.

SOEs do, however, have special access to foreign business established through government relationships. The PCS case illustrates how governments arrange major business opportunities or package deals which often involve cooperation among various SOEs. The fact that the international business opportunity may be initially mooted — or even arranged in detail — at high levels enhances SOE bargaining power in the foreign country. In any case SOEs have superior bargaining power to private companies because of the implicit presence of government leadership, and business contacts established directly through the political actors gives even more legitimacy and power to the SOE. SOEs are seen to represent the nation and have an implicit government 'guarantee' for their commitments. The SOE can also be expected to have a different attitude towards its commercial interests if national loyalty becomes an issue, that is, it would place relatively more emphasis on loyalty to country over loyalty to commercial commitments, at least compared to MNCs. The classic case of divided loyalties in international companies was the oil industry, some of which historically have had conflicts of interests with their headquarter's country. This was why Winston Churchill argued for a national oil company for the UK, British Petroleum.

Unfair competition has been alleged within Singapore. "The Federation of Chinese Chambers of Commerce and Industry and other groups made strong representations to the government in 1978 on the respective roles of the public and private sectors and complained of unfair competition by the former." (Milne, 1983:178) A report on the Chamber's observations eight years later said, "It pointed to the Government's allocation of choice sites at relatively low cost and concessions such as high plot ratios, quick planning and building plan approvals to the then Housing and Urban Development Company to build flats at lower costs. The HUDC was thus able to sell them more competitively. Through the National Trades Union Congress the government operated supermarkets in housing estates at concessionary rentals. Private provision shops in the same estates had to pay 200 percent of NTUC's rates in rentals. The NTUC supermarkets bought in bulk from Intraco at special rates and were permitted to import, for example, rice, without being required to carry a stockpile ... As (the Post Office Savings Bank) was free of constraints such as the need to maintain costly liquidity ratios, the POSB was able to offer higher interest on deposits which were tax-free. It was also given preferential treatment to initiate savings schemes, for example, to national servicemen, army personnel and school children." (ST, 1/1/86:9)

Concerning protectionism in general, all Singapore SOEs were very careful not to mention any advantage they enjoyed from the government so information was scarce, and generally no strong attempt could be made to follow up any clues at the risk of alienating company interviewees. There was limited evidence to support the argument that SOEs tend to get help from the government, but also some evidence to indicate even private local companies are favoured — that is, Promet was regarded with some favour by the Malaysian Government as a Bumiputra success story, and the company was able to obtain fiscal concessions for its Langkawi project.

Subsidy which applies only to SOE exists in the form of cost of capital advantages, which probably cannot be proved. The value of shares in companies partially owned by the government would be boosted in market trading if there is faith in the government. For example, Keppel might have an advantage over Promet in the price of its shares. Also, development funds are available from the government for particular national priorities. These funds might also be available to private companies, but usually only SOEs would be called upon to undertake projects for which development money has been set aside. In fact, SOE management may have 'lobbied' for the funds.

A financial advantage was implicit in the fact that the government stood behind its companies, but evidently no subsidy was granted in finance charges. The ship financing schemes provided credit for some Keppel group operations, but such subsidy was available to Promet also. Furthermore, "Almost all of the major shipbuilding countries try to help their (shipyards) compete on the international market; for example, the United Kingdom, Sweden, France, West Germany, Japan, and South Korea." (Lim, 1985:106) The national development fund was made available to Telecoms, joint ventures in the petrochemical complex (Polyolefin), and to other enterprises based on development priorities. Evidently, it is common practice worldwide to support 'infant industries,' but the crucial question is whether government funds were offered at below market rates. Keppel's deferred payable to the Ministry of Finance at startup was a much more favourable deal than normal mortgage-type financing as it allowed them to build up initial working capital. This was one clear instance of important government support for its 'infant industry' SOE.

There was even some indication that the opposite to subsidy was true in Singapore SOEs for the provision of equity capital, in that it was no cheaper from Temasek and was difficult to obtain. The D/E ratios for Keppel reveal a stickiness in the expansion of equity, indicating government reluctance to provide further investment.

It especially seems a natural tendency for government owners to assist or subsidize their industries. SOEs may be more likely to attract subsidy than private local firms, because of their original objectives to pursue a particular national development strategy, and because they were part of the government team. Only SOEs were known to have received Development Fund allocations, except for privately-owned institutions which were acting as instruments of national development policy, that is, the private banks which were financing a national upgrading/rationalization of the construction industry. The instances of subsidy noted by the Federation of Chinese Chambers of Commerce and Industry more concerned domestic rather than international competition, and this may be a result of Singapore's adherence to the principles of the Free Trade Movement on a national basis.

The Singapore SOE system avoids cross-subsidization through the use of profit centres. There was little apparent cross-subsidization in the Singapore SOE system for redistribution purposes, alleged by Jones and Vogelsang (1983:25) to be an insidious cause of subsidy. However, Singapore was not immune to this common ailment of government enterprise: "The CAAS [Civil Aviation Authority of Singapore], for one, spends little of its own on airport development. The Public Works Department (PWD) pays for building airport terminals and other structures. So CAAS, Singapore's newest statutory board, has $50 million in reserves after just seven months of operations." (Seah, 1986:45)

Finally, concerning a question raised by Vernon, there were instances of 'international cartel arrangements.' Singapore SOEs seemed able to get business through state-to-state negotiations, notably with socialist nations (especially China) and with other SOEs, locally and in Asia. There was also an indicated advantage for SOEs in labour relations.

4.4 Performance and Personnel

'Follower' societies have the advantage that they can emulate the multinational corporations (MNCs) and advanced country management technology generally. A private sector management culture had been developed in Singapore SOEs, acquired largely as a result of exposure to international competition and MNC management and technology. Singapore SOEs in turn act as leaders in domestic corporate behaviour, and themselves adopt some aspects of the character of their teachers, the government and the MNCs. Subsidiaries or joint-ventures of SOEs, by virtue of having distanced themselves more from their government owners and the bureaucracy generally, follow MNC behaviour examples more closely than they do government behaviour and generally act more independently of national policy. Access to MNCs is enhanced by the government's power, its role as joint venture partner and generally its pervasive role in the economy. Level of development of business acumen can often be expected to be higher for the government sector than for private enterprise in less developed countries (LDCs). In many advanced societies the private sector is well-developed so a government role may be counterproductive, but in LDCs the government role can be essential. Private entrepreneurs, expertise, institutions and organization are lacking. The best people gravitate to government because that is where they find authority, responsibility and money. In fact, this may contribute to a 'crowding out' effect of indigenous private enterprise because management resources are scarce in developing countries. The government can become legitimized in a big role. Government initiative is well supported and succeeds where private enterprise is left behind. The nation becomes the responsive, proactive initiators for new direction, ideas, risks. Success breeds success. In Singapore, as a follower society, new initiatives come from the government, which itself is a model in effectiveness among world governments. It is frequently alleged in Singapore that the private sector is reluctant to take risks until encouraged by the government (see for example Lee (1978)), and innovation almost always seems to come from the government, which has the most competent people and best organizations. The state is a leading entrepreneur in Singapore, and SOE's — as compared with the domestic private sector — are relatively innovative, risk-takers, et al. This is "the Gerchenkron hypothesis ... that there is a greater potential for a state role in late-coming nations where the task is imitation rather than innovation." (Jones, 1982:233)

All companies studied, both national and private, were industry leaders and seemed to perform exceptionally well. Keppel and Promet, as premier local enterprises, were close followers of world leaders (such as European and Japanese shipyards for Keppel and Promet). Flexibility and productivity seem to be key secrets of success. Flexibility was clearly an institutional strength in Singapore, as all companies looked to the future unimpaired by political or other traditions. There were not many productivity measures available, except Telecoms' impressive statistics.

All SOEs studied were obviously very well managed and there did not appear to be any conservative tendencies (although the limited perspective afforded an outside researcher may not reveal actual internal behavioural differences caused by a government presence). Sophisticated management teams were in charge at all Singapore SOEs, and indeed the calibre of the leadership team seemed superior in the SOEs compared with Promet. All companies also seemed to have profitted from the example and technology transfer of leading multinational corporations (MNCs). PCS, as a joint venture with Japanese MNCs, obviously had complete exposure to MNC technology and management. SAI depended on MNCs for technological progress. Keppel could trace its startup to an MNC — the Swan Hunter Group. (Sembawang Shipyard also employed Swan Hunter for their initial years of operation, indicating a common contact for the government-owned shipyards.) PCS, SAI and Keppel utilized the joint venture tool to share the expertise of the MNCs. Promet did seem to have the same advantage in relationships with leading MNCs. The fact remains that SOEs could learn from both government and MNCs, and if the government had a valuable contribution to pass on, as the network of development agencies in Singapore had, then this augmented the development of SOE management.

An example of a management activity in which SOEs from less-developed countries (LDCs) may be surprisingly competent is the planning function, which is a matter of mimicking the models of leading corporations and/or learning from textbooks. LDC SOEs seemed to have an additional advantage in being able to coordinate with national planning, though only minor instances were evident. For example, Keppel's move into life insurance was said to be in anticipation of a government scheme to guarantee income for pensioners, planned for 1987. Another example: Keppel's steel fabrication capacity was developed just in time to benefit from major government building contracts. "There has been a steady trend in Singapore towards the use of steel as a structural material for high rise buildings. Three major government buildings now under construction ... are using this system." (BT, 18/11/83) One study (MacDonald, undated) found that in Singapore corporate planning is more prevalent in SOEs than in domestic private enterprise. All SOEs seemed to have well developed planning functions, and indeed, all were corporate leaders in Singapore in adopting sophisticated management techniques and advanced technology. It may be true that SOEs stress training more, if they accept the social objective of national manpower development. National priorities also will be more manifest rather than simply narrow company training needs. This social objective need not detract from profitability.

Telecoms and Keppel placed great emphasis on training, and the Singapore SOEs actively catered to national training priorities. A minister said on 7/2/87 that he would like to see firms take on a greater role in training, but the message evidently had been heard much earlier, at least by SOEs. FELS' training efforts seemed to intensify after its acquisition by Keppel. Promet, in contrast, did not manifest much of a training function, but they were a small company and had more pressing priorities in the 1980s. The SOE's attention to training can be considered an important national advantage in using SOEs as a development strategy.

An important explanatory variable for the quality of management was suggested by Millward and Parker: " ... does the management labour market operate so as to transfer the costs of any management inefficiency from shareholders to managers' own salaries, thereby creating incentives for management to pursue efficiency? In a perfect labour market, with perfect information, we would predict this outcome ..." (Millward and Parker, 1983:258) There was no reason to doubt that such leading enterprises would pay well. Also, civil servants in Singapore were well compensated.

Top management is also part of the national leadership team, more noticeably in a small nation like Singapore. They are nationalistic and act as statesmen. It may follow that management becomes politicized, which could be divisive in a politically contentious nation; but in Singapore they simply join the ruling elite. They are an effective bridge between the political world and business world. Government enterprises are instruments of foreign policy. In Singapore, where foreign policy is dominated by commercial considerations, the national interest generally coincides with enterprise (SOE) interests.

Top civil servants were more than just administrators, especially in Singapore; they were statesmen. JY Pillay, "the Prime Minister's favourite mandarin" (FEER, 23/10/86), made public pronouncements which were carefully monitored by markets and competitors. Sim Kee Boon and board members of Keppel, SAI and PCS accompanied the Prime Minister on state visits. Nor did any of the top business leaders ever make any political stand of any kind. They were capitalist statesmen — proponents of economic policy and the establishment.

In summary, all SOEs performed very well. The current calls for privatization notwithstanding, Singapore has no reason to regret — so far — its particular development strategy and the active government participation entailed.

References

1. Garner, Maurice R, "The Relationship Between Government and Public Enterprise," in G. Ram Reddy, *Government and Public Enterprise*, Frank Cass Publishers, 1983
2. Hofheinz, R. and KE Caldor, *The Eastasia Edge*, Basic Books, 1982
3. Jones, Leroy P. and Ingo Vogelsang, *Effects of Markets on Public Enterprise Conduct; and Vice Versa*, International Centre for Public Enterprise in Developing Countries (Ljubljana), 1983
4. Jones, Leroy P. (ed), *Public Enterprises in Less-developed Countries*, Cambridge University Press, 1982

5. Lee (op cit, 1978)
6. Lim (op cit, 1978)
7. MacDonald, Ian, "The Development of Corporate Planning in Singapore"
8. Millward, Robert and David M. Parker, "Public and Private Enterprise: Comparative Behaviour and Relative Efficiency," in Millward and Parker et al., *Public Sector Economics*, Longman, 1983
9. Milne, Steven, "Corporatism in the ASEAN Countries," *Contemporary Southeast Asia*, September 1983
10. Seah (op cit, 1986)
11. Vernon, Raymond and Yair Aharoni (eds), *State-owned Enterprise in Western Economies*, Croom Helm, 1981

CASE STUDIES: MALAYSIA

by Mrs. Musalmiah Asli
Director
Work Systems Division
Malaysian Adminstrative Modernization
& Management Planning Unite (MAMPU)
Prime Minister's Department

1. Objective of Survey

The objective of the survey is to present the current situation of the operation/management of State-Owned Enterprises (SOEs) or Public Enterprises (PEs) in Malaysia through the review of recent studies/publications and in-depth studies of selected SOEs. The broad definition of an SOE or PE is an enterprise which is either wholly or partially owned or controlled by the Government. The survey attempts to highlight the micro-level management features, potentials and constraints in the management of these enterprises and to explore ways to bring about managerial improvement.

Universally, there is an increasing concern over the performance of SOEs, and Malaysia is no exception. SOEs have been said to be facing problems of rigidity, inadequate competition, pricing and the like. In the present era of rapid technological changes, shifts in management concepts and pressures from an internal environment, efficient performance and significant productivity growth poses a more vital concern in the management of SOEs.

The present survey on SOEs as presented in this paper will involve looking at the SOEs within the context of their environment, organization and function that will determine their efficiency, effectiveness and potential growth and development. Within these contexts, the SOEs managerial problems will be reflected and ways and means of addressing these problems may be suggested. An in-depth study of two SOEs will be carried out for the purpose of this survey. The in-depth studies will focus on the process of privatizing SOEs as a means of improving their management and performance. The areas covered within this context will be reasons for privatization, changes in management after privatization, achievements, problems and solutions and the future scenario envisaged as a further improvement to the management of SOEs.

2.   Overview of SOEs in Malaysia

2.1 Establishment and Role

SOEs in Malaysia are extensively established and generally set up as part of the government machinery to implement government policies and programmes. They are thus formed for such reasons as:

1) The new economic and social responsibilities
2) The need for comprehensive planning and regional development
3) The need for greater flexibility and to overcome the problems of bureaucratic constraints
4) For specific political considerations

The purpose of establishing SOEs in Malaysia can roughly be divided into two phases, namely before and after the New Economic Policy (NEP, 1970). Prior to NEP, SOEs were established for the reasons of narrowing down the urban and rural income disparity through productivity improvement in primary activities. They were also aimed at eliminating regional disparity in economic development between the East and West coasts of Peninsular Malaysia. SOEs were then more concerned with land and agricultural development in the rural areas.

However, driven by the ideology of the NEP and fuelled by good money from high commodity prices in the seventies and eighties, SOEs grew rapidly. Accordingly, the purpose of establishing SOEs during this second phase after NEP was to help solve the problem of racial economic imbalance and promote economic development of the indigenous people. SOEs were thus assigned a big role in correcting racial and regional economic imbalances, in order to help achieve the Government's objective of national unity. During this time, more SOEs were set up to be involved in the industrial and commercial activities.

The most important role of SOEs in Malaysia would be in restructuring the disparity in the ownership and control of economic wealth among the various ethnic groups. Thus, SOEs have become a powerful instrument for implementing public policies, particularly in helping the indigenous people to achieve at least 30% ownership of the country's corporate wealth by 1990. The roles of SOEs can be classified as follows:

1) as 'patrons' of the indigenous people: eg. National Council of Trust (MARA) with the given task of training and assisting the indigenous people to participate in the industrial and commercial sectors,
2) as 'trustees' for the indigenous people: eg. State Economic Development Corporation (SEDC) was set up to hold equities in

various ventures with the view to transferring them to the indigenous people,

3) as 'joint-venture' partners with the indigenous people.

SOEs are also given the role in development aimed at the promotion of the development of economically backward, underdeveloped and depressed regions of the country. The need for SOEs to assume the development role can be explained by the fact that private investors are reluctant to set up industries in rural and backward regions.

Basically there are four types of SOEs in Malaysia: Departmental Undertakings, Statutory Bodies, Government Companies and subsidiaries of Statutory Bodies. Since Malaysia is a Federation, the SOEs come under the control of either the Federal/Central Government, State Government or the Regional Development Authorities. The SOEs are created in several ways, namely:

1) by 'Act of Parliament,' eg. (MARA) for the Indigenous People.
2) by Enactment of State Legislatures, eg. SEDC
3) incorporated under the Companies Act, 1965, eg. PETRONAS (National Petroleum).

Generally SOEs in the form of statutory corporations are established under their respective incorporating statutes, both Federal and State, and in the form of companies, either wholly or partially owned by the Government. SOEs take the form of Statutory Bodies in situations where the Government wants to give these SOEs statutory powers to carry out regulatory functions for the Government. SOEs in the form of a company has no such power. Secondly, the Statutory Corporations are wholly owned by the Government and will continue with that status; whereas the companies which are either wholly or partially owned by the Government, will one day be transferred partially or wholly to the indigenous people, in line with the Government's objective of using SOEs as a means of redressing regional and economic imbalance.

The management of the SOEs consists of the Board of Directors and the Management. The Board of Directors is the policy making body with a membership ranging from three to sixteen (although usually less than 14). Appointments are made by the supervising organizations or Ministries for a period of 2–3 years. The composition of Board of Directors reflects a balance of control, competence and representation. To ensure control, representation of the supervising organizations (Ministries or State Government) and the Treasury were appointed.

The financing of SOEs may come from the following sources:

1) Share Equity for a company and initial allocation and operational budget given for statutory bodies
2) Share Equity of private companies
3) Long term loans from Government and international bodies
4) Short term loans from banks and credits from suppliers
5) Surplus business and profit
6) Special taxes

The budget of government companies need not be submitted to the Treasury. Statutory bodies/corporations are required by law to seek approval by the Ministers for their annual budget. Profitable corporations however, may finance their own projects without seeking the Treasury's approval. Government companies may follow business accounting procedures. Auditors are appointed by the Board of Directors. For corporations, the Act requires them to follow government accounting systems. In practice, government companies have more freedom than statutory corporations in their operations because their Board of Directors and Management are free to make policies considered necessary as long as they are within the Companies' Acts, 1965. As such, these public enterprises followed the practices adopted by the private companies and are not constrained by the government's policies. For statutory bodies, the Board of Directors has to obtain the approval of the responsible Ministers for any decisions they want to make which are not stipulated in the legislation.

Presently there are about 936 active public companies and 56 non-financial public enterprises (NFPEs) by the virtue of the fact that their allocations do not come under the ambit of the Finance Minister's annual budget. Among the activities carried out by the SOEs are utilities, agricultural, transportation, mining, trading, wholesaling, banking, insurance, finance, construction, manufacturing, engineering, housing, equity investment, property management and tourist development. The activities of SOEs are being co-ordinated and supervised by various numbers of Ministries, such as the Ministry of Agriculture, Ministry of Land and Regional Development, Ministry of Public Enterprise and several others.

2.2 Performance of SOEs

The criteria used by the community to measure performance of SOEs are often multiple, inter-linked and complex. In terms of profitability, SOEs in Malaysia in general are doing poorly. The downward trend in the economy in 1985, the slow pick-up in activity in 1986 and the depressed demand affected the profitability and viability of several SOEs, with some of these companies facing cash flow problems. Financial profitability alone is not a reliable indicator of SOEs performace for it may reflect market distortions, monopolistic prices or access to cheap funds. Some of the SOEs investments are made for national reasons. Having a vital role in fulfilling NEP objectives can also affect their financial performance.

In the urban areas the SOEs fulfilled the NEP objectives by providing employment, training managers and developing entrepreneurs in trade and industry (eg. MARA and UDA). SOEs have provided up to 1/3 of the total jobs offered by the country's public sector, where a large proportion of the jobs are held by the indigenous people.

In the rural areas, SOEs play an important role in alleviating rural poverty and helping to ensure better deals for farmers, small-holders and fishermen (eg. MADA, RISDA and MAJUIKAN). Successive development plans by regional bodies in the North and East coast states have boosted farmers' incomes by improving irrigation facilities, roads and other infrastructures and supplying farmers with agricultural inputs. New land was opened up by FELDA ensuring new opportunities for the people. Various public marketing agencies (eg. FAMA) have also ensured that the rural farmers' produce is not skimmed off by the middlemen.

In spite of this, there have been complaints regarding SOEs. Some private sector groups are bitter over the SOEs 'crowding out' effect on the business environment. Instead of helping to promote indigenous business communities, SOEs are accused of competing directly with some of the indigenous people already in business and displacing their participation in trading and manufacturing. SOEs are also being blamed for having easy access to cheap funds, therefore contributing to the decline in the manufacturing sector's growth by discouraging private investment, distorting the market, creating uncertainties and bringing about unfair competition.

The failure of SOEs has been attributed to 4 main reasons: incompetent management, corruption, political interference and lack of effective central coordination and monitoring mechanism. The Government must have the political will to improve the business environment and reform the organization structure of SOEs to foster greater competition, more financial independence and accountability, managerial autonomy and a clear separation of management and political roles.

An effective monitoring of the performance and financial position of SOEs was made possible by the setting up of a Central Information Collection Unit (CICU) in 1985, jointly undertaken by the Treasury and the National Equity Corporation (PNB). This information system was intended to form part of the 'Early Warning System', designed to identify weaknesses and problems faced by SOEs so that early remedial actions could be implemented. To supplement the effort of CICU, the Government Agencies and Companies Monitoring Unit was established in the Treasury. The aim was to take up problemed SOEs identified in the CICU analytical framework with the view to rationalising their debt-equity structure and pave the way for the privatisation of suitable ones.

A review of the SOEs was made in 1986. For the purpose of macro-economic analysis, a total of 141 agencies with 51% or more Government equity and an annual revenue turnover in excess of M$50 million each were identified for monitoring purposes. The number of the SOEs monitored will be reviewed periodically to allow for inclusion of new agencies undertaking substantial investment or large projects with a high foreign exchange in the Fifth Malaysia Plan period.

Preliminary estimates as indicated in Bank Negara and the Annual Economic Report 1986, showed a significant deterioration in the financial position of the SOEs in 1986. In the face of a decline in revenue and a moderate increase in total expenditure, the activities of SOEs continued to moderate in 1986, with total operating and development expenditure increasing more slowly by 8.2% as compared to 10.5% in 1985 and 23.9% in 1984. The slow-down reflects continued efforts by the Government to restrain expenditure of public agencies as well as the generally depressed business environment which has affected the profitability and viability of some of the SOEs.

Early investigations by CICU have also indicated that the majority of the SOEs are facing financial problems due to insufficient capital and a high liabilities/assets ratio. Besides the economic recession in 1985 and 1986, which affected the local and foreign markets, the poor planning and poor management among the SOEs also seeemed to aggravate the problems further.

To assist the SOEs in overcoming such problems, several actions were recommended in 1987 which were as follows:

- improving cash flow either through re-financing, selling of assets or increasing capital equity
- increased sales through larger export markets and buying components from other suppliers at cheaper prices

- improving management effectiveness by replacing ineffective top management
- reorganization of the company to ensure better utilization of assets and resources
- to sponsor co-operation among other firms of the same industry
- privatization or mergers between companies of the same industry

Several SOEs also reduced the salaries and allowances of their staff during that year and cut down on unnecessary spending as a measure to contain the growth of their operating expenditure.

3. Privatization of SOEs

SOEs are also involved in the Government's exercise in reducing the debt-servicing burden and maintaining the long-term stability of the economy by cutting down on their development expenditures. But there is a limit as to how many cut backs can be made without impairing growth and sacrificing social progress. An alternative would be to improve on the quality and efficiency of public investment therefore imposing stricter control over the management, operation and investment of SOEs.

It is generally felt that managerial improvement can be brought about through privatization. In Malaysia, the concept of privatization arose from the realization that there are services and ventures which can be carried out more efficiently by the private sector. The Government's policy on privatization presents a new approach to the development of the Malaysian economy. It will have far reaching implications on the role of the Government and the private sectors in the socio-economic development of the country.

Privatization in Malaysia has a number of major objectives, for example:

- reducing Government financial and administrative burdens in undertaking and maintaining and ever-increasing service and investment in infrastructure;
- encouraging competition, improving efficiency and increasing the roductivity of services;
- hastening the nation's rate of economic growth by stimulating private entrepreneurism and investment;
- helping to reduce the size and involvement of the public sector, with its monopolistic and bureaucratic characteristics, in the economy;

- contributing towards realising the objectives of the New Economy Policy (NEP), since a core of indigenous entrepreneurs has been developed and they are now capable of taking up their share of the rivatized services.

In accordance with its objectives, privatization is seen as one way of improving the management and performance of SOEs. Privatization can be understood to mean the transfer of ownership and control in an existing enterprise activity or service, to the private sector by government departments and institutional bodies whether by sale of part or all of government interests. Privatization in Malaysia can take many forms.

3.1 Complete Privatization

Privatization is 'complete' or is effected in full when the entire government ownership, control and management of the enterprise is transferred or sold-off to the private sector. In this case the Government is deemed to have completely divested itself of any interest in the enterprise.

3.2 Partial-privatization

The Government can also transfer part of its ownership of an enterprise to the private sector. In this case the Government's interest is only partially divested. Control of the enterprise will depend upon the percentage of ownership still retained by the Government. Nevertheless, the process of privatization would be considered as having taken place even though only a part of the Government ownership has been transferred to the private sector. There is a possibility that at a future date more equity and control will be transferred to the private sector.

3.3 Selective Privatization

This method enables Government agencies responsible for any service or utility to sell or rent out only a part of such service or utility. The rest will continue to be owned, controlled and managed by the agency on the Government's behalf. This type of privatization does not indicate the form of ownership, control or management of the service or utility that is proposed for privatization. By means of this arrangement the Government can either identify services that can be privatized, or the private sector can submit proposals for Government consideration.

3.4 Management and Privatization

Participation of the private sector need not be in the form of an equity stake in a company. In such circumstances, only management expertise and know-how can be obtained from the private sector.

3.5 Private-sector Participation in Ventures and the Provision of Contractual Services

This method basically involves the assignment of responsibility for the provision of a special service currently undertaken by the Government to a private firm. Alternatively, a private firm may be invited by the Government to provide the new service or facility.

3.6 Rental and Privatization

A situation may occur in which the concept of rental may be included in a privatization proposal. Rental basically implies the renting-out of certain facilities in order to realise a return of income over a certain period. This method does not affect the ownership status of the Government. There is, however, a possibility that at the end of the rental period the borrower may wish to buy over the facilities. The Government may consider the sale of the rented service on the condition that the public and national interest will continue to be served even though the service will be owned and run by the private sector.

4. SOEs Selected for In-depth Study

An in-depth study was carried out on two SOEs, Klang Container Terminal (KCT) and Malaysian Telecommunication Corporation Ltd. (STM), to get an insight into the reasons and process of privatization, changes, benefit and achievements after privatization, limitations of privatization and their solutions. The selection of these two enterprises were based on:

4.1 Type of Organization

Container Terminal operations were handled by a Port Authority before they were taken over by KCT. Telecommunication Department on the other hand, was a government department before its business was taken over by STM. Thus, the processes of privatization of both enterprises were different.

4.2 Size of Organization

KCT is a comparatively small business entity with a staff strength of 801 compared to STM which provides a nationwide public utility and has a staff strength of 28,571.

4.3 Approach to Privatization

Container Terminal was privatized through the selling and renting of assets. Its operation was rented to a newly formed company, KCT, in which the Klang Port Authority is still a major single share holder. Telecommunication Department was privatized by turning it into a 100% government owned corporation.

4.4 Level of Implementation

The two enterprises are at different levels of the privatization process. KCT started to be privatized in early 1986 and is now fully privatized. The process of privatizing STM was initiated in early 1987 but is still not yet fully completed.

Based on the above mentioned rationale the two enterprises were chosen for the purpose of preparing this report. Details on the enterprises and processes involved shall be further elaborated.

5. Privatization of Container Terminal, Port Klang

5.1 Background of Container Terminal

Prior to privatization, the Container Terminal was a unit of Klang Port Authority (KPA) where it formed the operating department for the port. The unit was headed by a manager who was directly responsible to the Deputy General Manager (Operation). Located midway along one of the world's busiest shipping routes in the Straits of Malacca and being an "all-weather port", the terminal offered shipowners, ocean carriers and terminal users unhindered access throughout the year. The terminal handled about 60% of the total bulk cargo in the form of containerization for KPA. It provided container handling services such as loading and unloading of containers from the calling ships, storing of containers in the container yards, container freight station for container packing and unpacking operations and other services such as handling dangerous cargo. There were 801 employees working in the terminal.

An overall study by individual groups on the ports of Malaysia came up with three problems faced by the ports which were:

- Insufficient development funds to improve port service (government's drive on cutting cost)

- Strong competition from local and neighbouring ports
- No proper co-ordination in port development within the country

With the above identified factors in mind and gloomy trade patterns, erratic volumes, general downward trends and the stagnation of the economy, the Government decided to begin its privatization programme as a new approach for stimulating the economic activity. The privatization of the KPA's container terminal operation was the country's first experience of a partial privatization. The objectives of the privatization of the terminal were in accordance with the main objectives of privatization and could be summarised as follows:

- To inject new levels of efficiency whereby ensuring greater productivity
- To improve the competitiveness of the port
- To lessen the Government's burden on operating expenditure

As a result, when the government announced the privatization policy with regards to agencies providing public utilities, including ports, they received overwhelming response, plus several proposals on the privatization of the operations in Port Klang from the public sector. In 1984, the Cabinet made a decision to privatize the operations and transactions of KPA's Container Terminal. The Economic Planning Unit (EPU) of the Prime Minister's Department was then appointed as Secretariat Management while a merchant bank was appointed consultant to carry out a study and offer suggestions towards privatizing the Container Terminal in Port Klang. The terms of reference of the study were as follows:

- To value the business
- How to sell the business

The appointed merchant bank was also requested to negotiate with the highest bidder regarding the tender to privatize the terminal. By privatizing the terminal, Memorandum of Understanding and the Agreement which included the Sales of Business, Lease of Assets and Lease of Services were also prepared by the consultant.

5.2 Privatization Process

On 17 March 1986 the transactions and operations of Container Terminal, Port Klang were taken over by a newly formed company, Klang Container Terminal Ltd. (KCT) which is a subsidiary of Klang Port Authority. KCT comprises Klang Port Authority and Konnas

Terminal Kontena Ltd. (a joint venture company between Kontena National Ltd. and P & O Australia Ltd.) In this new company Klang Port authority holds 49% and Konnas Terminal Container holds 51% of the shares.

Kontena National Ltd. (KN) is the largest container haulier in Malaysia. It has over thirteen years of experience in the container haulage field which is the company's main activity. KN is also involved in shipping agency, freight forwarding, inland container depot operations and container leasing. The company operates on a nationwide basis and maintains offices in the key centres of Penang, Ipoh, Kluang and Johore.

P & O Australia Limited (POAL) is a company which has over 50 years experience in stevedoring and materials handling in Australia and on a worldwide basis. The company pioneered the introduction of containerization into Australia beginning 1968. POAL is active in the operation of four major container terminals in Australia; it is also involved in container road haulage, warehousing, freight forwarding, repairs and maintenance, storage, general ship management and cold storage.

Under the management agreements reached between KN, POAL and Konnas Terminal Kontena Ltd. (KTK) and KCT which were signed prior to the commencement of KCT's operations, KTK was given the management rights to the terminal for five years. There was also an option to extend the management rights for a further two years if desired. It was under the latter agreement that the KTK currently provides the Australian management support team of three executive officers and three Task Force members.

The expertise from Australia together with over 800 local staff make up KCT's operating team. Such expatriate involvement and the substantial capital investment reflects KTK's and POAL's strong commitment to the privatization of KCT. Also POAL's worldwide market contacts enable the company to provide an extensive marketing reach for the benefit of the Port.

Preliminary studies done by the management of KTK just before privatization took place, has identified several factors that might impede the efficient operation of the terminal, such as:

1) The existing management structure of the terminal lacked clearly defined reporting lines.

2) Operating systems in respect of the loading and unloading of goods, terminal yard and planning of shipment were found to be inadequate to enable the terminal to operate at maximum effici-

ency levels.

3) Productivity levels were below world standards.

4) Equipment inactivity due to faults was high. There was no formalised maintenance programme and the expertise of engine room staff was limited.

5) There were no formalised training and safety programmes.

6) Yard capacity was under utilized in terms of optimum layout.

7) Clearance and collection of containers was very slow.

Hence to address the above factors, the company aims at operating along the following objectives:

1) To implement an aggressive marketing strategy which would attract importers and exporters to use the services of KCT.

2) Attract direct Main Line calls to reduce and/or eliminate transshipment costs.

3) Revise operating procedures to improve cargo and container flows.

4) Improve communications between the terminal operators and users.

5) Work in harmony with government agencies for the benefit of the Nation.

The tangible benefits which the Government expected would immediately be derived from the privatization of the container terminal were as follows:

1) All future capital investment would be provided by the private sector.

2) The transfer of existing employees to the new company would reduce the public sectors operating expenditure and administrative burden.

3) An initial influx of funds would become available to the Port Authority for use in either debt reduction or as a ready source of finance for existing approved capital expenditure programmes.

4) The ability for employees to participate in ownership of the company when floated on the Kuala Lumpur Stock Exchanges.

In addition to the objectives listed above was the requirement that the previous employees of KPA who joined KCT, would enjoy the conditions of employment no less favourable than that of the

Authority.

In privatizing KCT the following course of action was undertaken.

1) KCT appointed Konnas Terminal Kontena to serve as their management for a fee that would not exceed 1.7% of the operating revenue or $500,000 a year, whichever is less.

2) Klang Port Authority issues licences to KCT to manage and run the Container Terminal. KCT is required to pay a licence fee of $25,000 per annum.

3) Klang Port Authority sold to KCT the operating rights, plant, machinery and goodwill at an estimated cost of $1.1 million.

4) Konnas Terminal Kontena has to pay a sum of $56.9 million for 51% shares in KCT.

5) KCT leases land from Port Klang Authority for its container terminals (Wharf 8, 9, 10 and immediate back up area) for a period of 21 years. Rental to be paid for this purpose is as follows:
   - basic rent — $16.9 million on 10% incremental basis at the end of every 3 years.
   - supplementary rent — based on excess containers from the numbers fixed for a year, and calculated at the rate of $150 per TEU (20 foot equivalent).

6) Amendments had to be made to the Port Authority Act 1963 for the purpose of privatization. One of the amendments pertains to tariff, that is, as and when KCT puts up a proposal to amend container tariff to KPA and does not receive any answer in the period of six months, the amendment will be considered to be enforced at the end of the said period.

7) KCT will have to float its shares after a certain period of time to show equity participation as follows:
   - Klang Port Authority   — 20%
   - Konnas Terminal Kontena — 40%
   - Employees of KCT   — 5%
   - Public   — 35%

One of the conditions of privatization was that KCT was required to employ all the 801 employees from Container Terminal. All the employees except 6 accepted the offer to work for KCT. Out of this number, all except one agreed to accept the service scheme of KCT. Only one person opted to continue the service scheme of Klang Port Authority.

The employees of container terminal were given the following options:

1) if an employee refuses to serve the company (KCT) his service can be terminated and he will not be permitted to serve in or with any Government agency.

2) an employee can choose to continue enjoying the pay and service conditions of Klang Port Authority while working for KCT, but he will not be entitled to any new benefits offered by KCT such as aquisition of shares and bonus award. His pension rights (as a government servant) will continue.

3) an employee can opt for the pay and service conditions of KCT. His pension will be frozen at the date he joins KCT but he has to contribute to the Employees Provident Fund.

To-date, KCT's pay scheme has not been implemented. The staff were offered two increments plus bonus over and above their present KPA salary under the Interim Pay Scheme.

5.3 Changes in Management After Privatization

5.3.1 Organization Structure

KCT management is headed by a Chief Executive and he is assisted by a General Manager who is also the Chief of Operation, a Deputy General Manager (Operation) and five Division Managers. Chief Executive, Deputy General Manager (Operation) and Engineering Manager are expatriates who are appointed, based on an agreement between KCT and KTK. The General Manager, Finance, Terminal, Personnel and Commercial Managers are Malaysian.

Under the management agreements reached between KTK and KCT signed prior to the commencement of KCT's operations, POAL of KTK was given the management rights to the terminal for five years. They were also given an option to extend those rights for a further two years.

KCT is governed by a Board of Directors which consists of a Chairman and 4 representatives from KTK and 4 representatives from the Government.

When privatisation took place KCT was organized into Operation, Finance, Personnel and Commercial Units. The Operation Unit was further divided into the Terminal Section and the Engineering Section which are each headed by a manager. Under KPA, these 2 units were under one head. The change was made in order to emphasize the importance of the engineering function in the terminal operation. In line with this an Engineering Task Force was set-up to improve the technical skills and efficiency of the Unit. The depot function was upgraded to be equipped with better skilled and trained staff.

5.3.2 Decision Making and Planning

The decision making process has drastically improved KCT since privatization. This was achieved by setting up advisory committees at all levels of management. This became a very effective channel for the workers to voice their problems and requirements and also for the management to receive feed-back regarding the working conditions of the employees. That information assists top management to make effective decisions. All the decisions made by top management will be implemented immediately and the administrative and operation problems can be easily solved. These situations enhance the motivation of the workers. Decision making is made simpler through decentralisation of leave administration and daily operations. Managers have been made more responsible and forward planning has been introduced as an integral part of day to day management.

5.3.3 Corporate Culture

A new set of corporate culture was seen to be practiced. The culture includes:

1) Senser of belonging to the company

This is achieved through the practice of open door management policy whereby communication flow was improved and problems were solved as soon as they arose. Daily visits by top management to various operations was also aimed at fostering greater sense of loyalty to the company.

2) Closer management — staff relationship

This is done through participation of all personnel regardless of level in regularly held recreational and sports activities. Open Days are organized involving staff and their families. All these activities are aimed at strengthening the policy of 'work together — play together'.

3) Information sharing

The company also practised an open policy on information sharing through the publication of corporate magazines, frequent meetings and visits. This is done so that everyone involved understands what is going on in the company and are jointly responsible for all undertakings.

5.3.4 Marketing

There was no marketing/commercial division when container terminal was under KPA. A commercial division was newly set-up under KCT and its function was to improve the marketing strategy, to expand the market and to draw clients from neighbouring ports. In their efforts to expand the market, more active marketing activities were conducted, which included several overseas marketing trips to advanced industrialized countries. The marketing missions were aimed at enlightening potential clients on improved ship and cargo handling capabilities available at KCT. These efforts have made the terminal an increasingly attractive port of call to shipowners and shippers alike. It is just over a year since Port Klang's container terminal was handed over to private management. During this time KCT has fulfilled all its expectations and has even received a message of congratualations from the Government.

5.3.5 Operation

The licence issued by KPA gives KCT the rights to operate, manage and control the business of Container Terminal as below:
- Container Terminal comprises of three wharves namely wharf 8, and 10, a RORO Ramp, Container Freight Station, three unpacking sheds, 100 refer points and 2 weighbridge
- Operations at the wharves
- Operations at the Container Yard
- LCL activities
- Receiving and delivery of container activities
- Transportation to and from the container terminals
- Other activities at the terminal and all other areas under KCT

A number of improvements were introduced during the first year of operation, including a new procedure for receipt and delivery of containers at the gate, and the reduction of the free storage period from seven to five days (which reduced the average storage time of boxes from ten to four days).

KCT plans to improve the efficiency of operations at the container freight station (CFS), which now has a capacity of some 50,000 TEUs a year. Last year the CFS handled a total of 42,292 TEUs, comprising 26,580 TEUs of export cargo and 15,712 TUEs of import cargo.

A major feature of KCT's first year of operation was the introduction in April 1986 of the train service between Port Klang and Penang. This service, operated by the Malayan Railway, links the

Kelang Container Terminal with the Inland Clearance Depot (ICD) in Prai operated by Kontena National, and the scope of this service has been boosted with the establishment of an inland container depot in Ipoh. The concept of block train service or intermodal transport offers an overall reduction in transport time of containers within the peninsular, to and from KCT.

5.3.6   Management Information System (MIS)

An advanced computerised tracking system was established under KCT to offer port users a fast and reliable service. The computer system monitors the status of containers, especially in receival, delivery, discharging, loading and tracking of boxes in the terminal. The computer system enables better yard planning, reduction in documentation monitoring and control of operations as well as integrated application systems for fleet maintenance, accounting, payroll and utility.

5.4   The Achievement of Privatization

5.4.1   Improves Container Handling

One of the major requirements of the privatization agreement was that the new terminal operator would improve container handling performance. Back in March 1986 the gross container handling rate was approximately 18 containers per hour. In the first eighteen months of KCT's operation, performance had improved to an average in the range of 23 to 26 containers per gross operating hour. The reasons for improvements in performance are attributed to better planned job schedules and decision making processes. It must be emphasized that KCT is a team operation and the company's achievements to date are the results of the efforts of team work.

Computerised documentation that links directly with customs, reduces delays and facilitates swift clearance and examination of containers. By taking advantage of computerization, KCT has implemented a new import and export receipt and Delivery System for Containers. The new system has virtually eliminated unwarranted delays and has brought about dramatic savings to users. Several closed-circuit television cameras with immediate close-up access are installed at strategic points in the terminal and control tower to permit round the clock surveillance. An efficient radio network is utilised throughout the terminal which links all key operational areas and mobile equipment with central control points.

5.4.2 Staff Development

This improvement has been almost entirely obtained by management's insistence that the majority of its maintenance work is done by its own staff rather than by subcontractors. This change has brought with it the oppourtunity for staff to improve their operating and technical skills. Training programmes have been conducted for all levels of engine room staff. The company believes that on the job training is the most effective way for staff to learn their respective skills. A number of programmes for staff to attend training courses organized by local training centres, and in some cases overseas training centres, were also arranged.

5.4.3 Cost Savings by Users

The improvements in both staff skills and the consequential improvement in terminal performance has also meant that the shipping companies, transport operators and other users of the terminal have benefited in terms of cost savings. For example, twelve months ago it was not uncommon for containers to be resident in the terminal for an average of twelve days after dishcarge from a vessel. Now as a result of both improved operating performance and changes to documentation procedures import containers are resident for only 3 — 4 days. The latter represents an improvement in terms of making containers available for export and import packing sooner and thus reducing their operating overheads.

5.4.4 Awareness of Modern Cargo Handling

At this point it should be emphasized that the terminal is only one part of a long chain of service operators whose responsibility is to get containers and other cargo through the transport system. In providing the container stevedoring service, KCT is endeavouring to create an awareness in industry of modern cargo handling technology and techniques as well as the benefits of using them. It is not common for terminal operators to actively involve themselves in the cargo marketing areas. Responsibility for the latter usually rests with the shipping company or its agent. In the case of KCT's operation it is imperative for the terminal to do everything in its power to encourage as much support as possible for its terminal for the good of its own corporate objectives. By increasing user awareness of the improvements which have taken place at the port and supporting the other service organizations such as the railways, hauliers, forwarding agents etc., the company can play an important role in ensuring that the transport chain is as efficient as possible. Obviously the latter requires each operator to make its particular link of the chain as efficient as possible.

5.4.5   Container Throughput

The expected throughput for 1987 will be in the region of 270,000 TEU's which will be 5,000 TEU's or 1.9% above the projected figure of 265,000 TEU's for the year, and 12% or 28,818 TEU's above the totals achieved in 1986. It is significant to note that for the first time in the history of the terminal, the throughput figure is expected to pass the quarter million mark and also equally significant is that in October an all-time high was achieved when 25,350 TEU's were handled at the terminal. In the breakdown by vessels contributing to this throughput we noted that main line vessels were expected to account for 67%, feeder vessels 29% and conventional vessels contributing the remaining 4% of TEU's handled.

5.4.6   Vessels Calling

Twelve thousand fifty vessels were expected to call at the terminal in 1987 — 48 vessels or 4.0% more than the 1202 vessels in 1986 — comprising 760 main line vessels and 490 feeders. The vessel handling performance has been consistently high with the average productivity for the first 11 months in 1987 being 276 containers per hour. The best performance achieved in the year was in November when 30.1 containers were handled per hour. The average turn around time of vessels, due directly to the better handling performance, has been reduced to 9 hours.

5.4.7   KCT Depot

Due mainly to user confidence in KCT's ability of providing efficient service this sector is experiencing impressive growth in especially LCL exports handled. The depot is expected to handle 47,000 TEU's comprising 30,000 TEU's consolidated as LCL exports and 17,000 TEU's unpacked as LCL imports. Average staying time of LCL containers was about 1.4 days.

5.4.8   Receivals and Deliveries

Owing to the increased output, especially the increases in exports, the demand for empty containers has put pressure on the road hauliers to meet their demand. Equally important was the demand by consignees for imports to be delivered within the KCT 'free storage period' of 5 days. 137,076 TEU's were delivered to hauliers with 126,552 TEU's being received from them. This clearly indicates that with such volume, there is an urgent need for the overall industry i.e. KCT, shipping agents, forwarders, importers, exporters, hauliers, customs, etc. to work together to ensure all around efficiency and therefore growth for the industry.

5.4.9   Intermodel Traffic

The Block Train service to Penang is now moving efficiently with a monthly average haul of 200 laden TEU's and 50 empty TEU's. The number of shipping lines using the service has also increased. The service to Johor known popularly as the 'Kluang Interchange' has begun and will provide the alternative route for Johor shippers through KCT.

The company recognises the dynamic nature of the industry and therefore the continuing need to review and modify its method of operating. Indications show that there is no intention on the part of management or staff to sit back rather it will do its utmost to continue to be innovative and industrious in the best interests of its shareholders, the users of its facilities and the port.

With the improved confidence in KCT service standards, as well as active marketing both locally and internationally, 1987 proved to be a growth year, after the slight slump in 1986. The improving Malaysian economic condition is expected to boost KCT throughput levels. The unfailing efforts and dedication of KCT staff has also been reflected in handling productivity levels which are now in line with international standards. This level of service will have to be maintained and improved upon, keeping pace with changes in container management technology. This is necessary for KCT to be a force in the challenging years ahead. Given expected increases in international trade, not only will patronage at KCT rise, but so will the expectations of terminal users, for a more efficient service from KCT.

5.5 How Success Was Achieved

5.5.1   Management

KCT introduced a new style of management called 'open door system.' Under this system:
- management actively practised an open door policy
- staff were given the opportunity to meet top management personally

- top management frequently visited their staff at ground level and during these visits spoke together

KCT has also set up Advisory groups at all levels. At the management level the group is known as 'advisory committee'. The 'advisory committee' is chaired by the general managers and consists of a head from each section and the leaders from each worker's group. At the lower level, groups are comprised of workers from all operating areas. Each of these groups has an advisor selected from the top management and they meet once a week after the main committee's meeting which is held once every five weeks.

In addition, the senior executives and executives meet the day before and the day after the main committee meeting. The mechanism is aimed at having a two way communication between top management and staff and also to follow through and to prompt decision making.

5.5.2 Operation

KCT's multi-user facilities has the versatility and flexibility to respond to the varying requirements of its clients. Being an 'all-weather port,' KCT in Port Klang offers shipowners unhindered access throughout the year. KCT has an immediate capacity to handle half a million TEU's. The terminal is equipped with 5 ship side pantry cranes and a ro/ro berth to accommodate a wide range of container and ship handling requirements. Its additional features include rail and road interchanges to effect immediate transfers and a sophisticated computer inventory system to support these operations. Working round the clock, a disciplined and well-trained workforce, with modern terminal handling equipment, assures smooth operations with high productivity.

5.6 Limitations and Problems

5.6.1 Structure

At the time KCT took over the operations of the container terminal in March 1986 the organizational structure was incomplete. There was only an operation unit in their structure, without a supporting unit to run the administration and financial functions. KCT did not have a building in which to house its Head Quarters, Management and supporting units. These factors slowed KCT's full operation.

5.6.2 Staffing

One of the conditions of privatization was to absorb all the previous 801 employees of the container terminal. The company had to create a personal file for each of the employees based on very little information available at that time. KCT was required to absorb even those employees involved in case of disciplinary action. This might have a demoralizing effect on the other employees. In terms of salary, KCT has agreed not to give the employees any less than what they had been receiving under the previous management. Reorganization of functions is necessary in line with the responsibility of the operation. Several posts were regraded commensurate with years of working experience, skills and qualifications. KCT also had to come up with a new pay scale to satisfy the new salary scheme. This involved processing job descriptions, job evaluations and market surveys for salary comparisons.

5.6.3 Shared Value

Due to the employees long exposure in a governemnt working environment, they found it difficult to adapt themselves to the company's working culture and were not fully prepared to accept privatization. Furthermore, they were not involved in the actual preparation for privatization. Thus, there was a 'culture shock' among many of the employees, of all levels.

5.6.4 Skill

Before privatization the employees were over specialised in certain fields and were not exposed to other fields. They could not and were not willing to undertake other duties which were not in their job description. The duty list for each employee was very rigid and specific. Thus, this posed some problems when KCT needed to reorganize its staff.

5.7 Future Plan for Further Improvements

Under the terms of its licence with the Port Authority, KCT has the exclusive licence to operate, manage and control the business of the container terminal for the period of its lease which is for twenty one years or any mutually agreed extension thereof. Furthermore, the licence provides preferential rights to the company which means that for any expansion in the container trade, KCT will get first preference to operate the venture. With this provision KCT will have less to worry about regarding competition.

Based on the provisions of the licence the company has an obligation to ensure that not only its own commercial objectives are met but also those of the Government as regards privatization. Volume projections for the next five years have been estimated by the company to be as shown below:

1988	283,000 teus
1989	311,000 teus
1990	327,000 teus
1991	346,000 teus
1992	374,000 teus

These volumes have been based on past trends as well as on estimates of the likely transfer of conventional cargo into containers and the normal annual growth in the volume of already containerized cargo. On the basis that a wharf crane can efficiently handle some 100,000 teus per annum the five cranes at KCT could cope with a volume of 500,000 teus per annum. On the basis that average vessel volume will continue at around 250 teus per ship call and that each call will last an average of 10 hours then berth occupancy of about 77% will occur when the volume reaches 500,000 teus. The occupancy rate of 77% can be increased to a 100% occupancy rate. Using the same average figures as above, when a berth occupancy of 60% is reached representing an annual volume of 389,000 teus there will be a need to consider an expansion programme to other areas of the port. The ideal area for such future expansion has already been identified at berths 18 to 21.

In addition to the physical development of the terminal the company has already identified the need to totally upgrade and expand the scope of its computer operation. A team of senior company staffers has recently completed a worldwide tour of the major terminal operations to find which organization had the best computer operation from the point of view of introducing it into KCT. The team found that quite apart from the needs of the company to install a system that can cope with its own day to day operating needs the international trend lies towards computer networking and community systems. As time is limited a full description of what these systems represent cannot be given, but suffice it to say that not having them in the near future compares to running a business without a phone.

It is anticipated that a computer community system will be established in Malaysia which will provide all participants in the industry with an opportunity to have access to computer operations.

Such a system will virtually enable a paper free operation and bring with it even greater levels of efficiency and therefore cost savings to the industry. KCT is trying to play a major role in establishing this system.

KCT recognizes its need to operate its business to support the Klang valley and thereby the Malaysian economy. In this regard, the company is actively involved in marketing intermodel transport operations with Kontena National and KTM. This initiative has already established encouraging cargo movements between Port Kelang and such centres as Penang, Ipoh, Kluang and even international destinations such as Bangkok. There is still a lot of work to do to get this intermodel system operating smoothly but KCT is confident that the service will prove to be very attractive to shipping companies as well as shippers.

The terms of the privatization of the terminal require KCT to float its shares on the Kuala Lumpur Stock Exchange within a reasonable time of its commencement of business. The success of flotation will rely substantially on the company's ability to operate efficiently in both physical and financial terms. Based on its overall operating performance to date the company has met its obligations well. After flotation the distribution of shares will be as follows:

KTK	40%
General Public	35%
LPK	20%
KCT Staff	5%

The company's prime objective is to operate profitably. However as a service organization the company's next major objective is to provide the best possible service it can for its customers. The latter can only be achieved by the effective intergration of the range of activities performed by all the organizations involved in the industry. KCT is totally committed to its involvement in achieving the latter result.

6. Privatization of Telecommunication Department

6.1 Background of Telecommunication Department

Telecommunication Department (TD) was a department under the Ministry of Energy, Telecommunication and Posts before it became Malaysian Telecommunication Company Limited (STM). The function of this department was to provide nationwide telecommunication services and hence is considered to be a type of SOE. The department was headed by a Director General, 2 Deputy Director Generals and 9 divisional heads. There were 6 branches which operated at the regional level headed by Regional Directors, and there were 84 'telecom shops' which provided services to the public. STM had 28,884 in its employ.

Financial standing of TD in 1986 was satisfactory although the country was facing a recession. Gross income increased by 8.9% to $1,500 million as compared to $1,400 million in 1985. However this performance was far below the growth rate achieved in 1984 which was 16.3%. This situation was brought about by a number of factors:

1) Decline in revenue from telephone services due to drastic reductions in telephone lines

2) Decline in revenue from telex and telegraph services

3) Old stocks valued at $42.7 million were written off as other expenses (non-operational)

4) Payment of interest rates on loans increased by 39% compared to the previous year and

5) Losses due to exchange rate amounting to $50 million as a result of increase in the value of foreign exchange

Despite the above problems, in 1986 TD made a net profit of $159.9 million. However comparing this profit with that made in 1985 which amounted to $348.9 million, it was 49.9% lower. The decline in profit was mainly due to the decline in the rate of growth of telephone services. The increase in the number of total direct lines was only 8.9% compared with that of 1985 and 1984 when there was an increase of 17.9% and 21.3% respectively. The growth rate of telex services also declined to 4.6% compared to 11.3% in 1985.

Privatization was to be introduced as a means to overcome problems faced by TD with the veiw to:

1) speed up the progress of the telecommunication services to the public

2) allow development in the telecommunication industry by bringing in modern technology, equipment and expertise

6.2 Privatization Process

TD is the first government department to be privatized. In 1983 a merchant bank was asked to put up a proposal regarding the privatization of TD to the Government. The Terms of Reference were:

1) To undertake a reconciliation of the assets recorded in TD's books with the physical existence of these assets.

2) To determine TD's liabilities, including an assessment of the additional liabilities due to corporate, import, sales, and other taxes if TD were a company incorporated under the Companies Act.

3) Assess TD's net worth based on the findings in (a) and (b) as well as the potential earnings over the next ten years, if TD were a company.

4) Provide a set of recommendations on the best form of capital structure of the Company upon incorporation and over the next ten years to finance the expansion of telecommunications services in Malaysia.

5) Provide a set of recommendations of the financial objectives most appropriate for the company particularly in relation to the self-financing ratio necessary for financing growth without undue adverse impact on the tariffs for telecommunications services.

6) Provide a set of recommendations concerning the mechanisms necessary to implement the diverstature of the government's ownership in the new company as well as the most appropriate time scale.

7) Propose a corporate structure to ensure efficient operations of the new company.

In January 1987, the Telecommunication Company Ltd. (STM) was set up by the Government to take over the operation of TD. This company is fully owned by the Government and is run under the Company's Act. In order to convert TD to a company, the Telecommunication's Act 1950 was amended and replaced by a new act which gave the right to the company to take over all the assets and liabilities of TD with the exception of what was needed by the Government.

Following the government decision to privatize TD, 28,884 employees were offered placement within the company. From this number 102 were hand picked to continue serving TD which was reorganized to be the regulatory and supervisory body. The body was responsible to ensure that the company will continue to fulfill its social obligations and maintain control over tariff rates.

It is also mandatory that STM will inherit committed capital spending programmes which extend at least to 1988. This committment is to be enforced to ensure that the Government's policy decisions to implement rapid and extensive improvement in telecommunications are adhered to.

With conversion of TD to STM, the company expects to measure up as rapidly as possible to commercial standard including accounting, record keeping, financial management, cost control, manpower planning, improved productivity, corporate planning, coordinated investment and maximum revenue realization. The period of 1987 to 1988 will be set aside to allow these reforms to take effect and to closely monitor actual results.

STM must realize as early as possible sufficient profit to allow payment of a nominal trustee status qualifying dividend and thereafter to achieve a profit record which meets the standards set by the Credit Investment Committee and Kuala Lumpur Stock Exchange. Any divergence from STM's properly formulated medium term corporate plan should be analyzed, corrective measures taken and future targets adjusted accordingly.

To effect the privatization of STM the following terms were agreed upon:

1) The Government (as a shareholder) must issue a statement of intent that it will not interfere in the day to day running and commercial decisions of STM.

2) The Government will establish a new regulatory body charged with ensuring that STM operates within the terms of the licence. The terms of the license include obligations to provide services, the framework for competition and the basis for tariff regulation.

3) STM is required to employ all the 28,884 employees of TD. The employees of TD were given three options and 397 of them chose the first option:
   - if an employee refuses to serve the company (STM) his services can be terminated, the post will be abolished and he will not be permitted to serve in or with any Government agency
   - an employee can choose to continue enjoying the pay and service conditions of the Government while working for STM, but he will not be entitled to any new benefits offered by STM such as aquisition of shares and bonus awards. Pension rights will be continued (scheme A).
   - an employee can opt for the pay and service conditions of STM. His pension will be frozen at the date he joins STM but he has to contribute to the Employees Provident Fund (scheme B).

The Government, as the sole shareholder, is faced with the task of reviewing the compositions of the Board of Directors, and the corporate structure and organization. The Government also needs to immediately appoint the Board members, the Chief Executive, Finance Director, Technical Director, Personnel Manager and Company Secretary. Another important pressing task is to formulate employment offers to staff which would ensure against loss of high calibre personnel, unnecessary surplus staff on STM's payroll, prolonged dual employment schemes, and adverse effects on the profitability of STM.

STM assets and liabilities need to be verified in order to determine its net worth. A systematic review of the financial and management accounting and control systems is called for, to ensure accurate and up to date management information on TD's performance. STM also needs to review the recommendations on tariff restructure made by the merchant bank and the corporate planning requirements. The latter is done by the introduction of a system that generates relevant decision making by management, formulation of a medium term corporate plan which coordinates investment, manpower training, traffic policy, cost control, market and traffic analysis and funding availability.

6.3 Changes in Management after Privatization

6.3.1 Organizational Structure

STM is now headed by an Executive Chairman and assisted by an Executive Director, a General Manager of Corporate Planning and four Divisional Directors, which are, Director of Operation, Director of Technical Services, Director of General Administration and Director of Finance. The above with the exception of the Executive Chairman and the Executive Director are former TD staff. The Manager of STM is controlled by a Board of Directors. The Board is chaired by the Executive Chairman of STM. Its members are the Executive Director, a representative of the Ministry of Finance (representing the shareholders, the Government, which holds 100% equity) a representative of the Ministry of Energy, Telecommunication and Posts (representing the regulatory body) and two members of the public. It is observed that the former TD managers are now members of the board.

A commercial division which was set up under the Telecommunication Department was reorganized and renamed the Marketing Division. This Division was given the task of improving STM's marketing strategy and expanding the market.

STM also created a new unit known as the Industrial Relation Unit to handle problems related to industrial matters which are being faced by STM. Experienced personnel from the private sector are employed to operate some of the newly created units/divisions.

6.4 Achievement of Privatization

6.4.1 Marketing

A number of improvements in their marketing strategy were introduced during the first year of operations. One of the strategies adopted was to popularize STM through the programme 'Know STM.' The programme was launched in the Eastern and Northern Region and will be extended to the rest of the country before the end of 1988. The programme provides a two way communication between STM and its customers which helps STM to improve its services.

6.4.2 Operation

STM introduced a number of improvements in their day to day operations. Some of the major improvements were:

1) Simplification of procedures related to telecommunication services such as, processing time for applications for telephones and installation procedures which was reduced to twenty-four hours downtime.

2) A special unit was set up to remind subscribers by telephone of late payment. In the event of no payments being received within a stipulated period telephones will be disconnected immediately. This ensured a more up to date payment of bills and a faster cash flow.

3) Itemized billing for trunk (outstation) calls was introduced as an optional service to subscribers in areas where telephone lines are connected to the computerized exchanges. This system would assist STM in resolving complaints of inaccurate billing.

4) A review in job description and job specification particularly for technical staff was carried out. Staff were retrained to be competent in all fields related to their job. As a result the staff requirements were reduced drastically and there was a cut in overtime hours.

5) In its efforts to recover bad debts STM pursued the defaulter until payment was received.

6) STM also introduced the accounting procedures as adopted by private companies.

As a result of these efforts STM had a turnover exceeding the previous year by a substantial amount.

6.5 Limitations and Problems

6.5.1 Organizational Structure

In the new organizational structure of STM, the top management positions were filled by three people of commercial background (the Executive Chairman, the Executive Director and the Finance Director), whilst the two former JTM top executives assumed the positions of the Operational Director and the Technical Director. However, the Administration Director position is still vacant. The Executive Chairman and the Executive Director are the only two management representatives to the Board of Directors. There was no representations on the Board by any of the former JTM top Management Executives who could have shared the previous JTM experiences with the Board in making decisions for the future of STM. The absence of the Administration Director also hampered the smooth running of the organization, especially in matters concerning personnel, training and general administration.

6.5.2 System

The new organizational structure was followed by the decentralization in the decision making process down to the Regional levels. Prior to corporatization of STM, decision making, especially concerning personnel, finance and handling of tenders, was handled at the Headquarters or the Government Central Agencies such as the Public Service Department and the Treasury. The sudden change in the roles of decision making has created confusion and uncertainty among the Regional Managers and they insisted in communicating and referring to headquarters for confirmation and finalization over these matters which slowed down operations.

When listed as a Public Company under the Company Act, 1965, STM lost all priviledges granted to a Government department. This meant that STM had to pay for various services which previously had been free for TD, such as paying for postage, licences, stamp duties and taxes. In guarding the safety interest of its properties, STM had to purchase several types of insurance and pay taxes for the vehicles, equiment, building and other assets and this required a large sum of money and administration.

STM also has to pay interest on the soft loans acquired from the suppliers and other foreign funding bodies overseas. In taking over the staff housing loan schemes from the Government, STM had to pay 8% loan interest to the Government as charged while the staff only paid 4% loan interest back to STM (as agreed before the transfer of the staff in protection of their welfare). This meant that STM had to make up for the differences in the interest charged.

STM inherited from TD the prevailing problems of accumulating bad debts uncollected amounting to a large sum of money. Like TD, STM was unable to trace the clients either because they had moved to an unknown address or the companies had gone bankrupt, hence leaving the accounts unsettled.

As indicated in the feasibility study by the consultant, STM faced the problems in reconciliating the assets recorded in TD's book with the physical existence of these assets, i.e. the problems in identifying and putting the actual values to these assets (eg. cables laid underground which still have some value although they have exceeded the depreciation period). Therefore it is not possible to compute the actual values of the assets for accounting purposes.

Ever since TD, telecommunication stations have been set up in various strategic places in every state of Malaysia to provide telecommunication services to the public. However, STM is now faced with the problem of identifying the actual titles to these lands where such stations are still situated. This is necessary in purchasing insurance for the properties (i.e. for the stations and the equipment). Identification of titles of lands is also necessary for STM to request access through the land/estates to reach the stations for operational or maintenance purposes. STM however is unable to purchase the land because of the high commercial rate and large cost of the area's involved.

Due to the very nature of the telecommunication operations and unexpected breakdowns, operational and maintenance work could and would often be stretched outside normal working hours. STM, like TD is faced with the excessive occurrences of overtime work. During TD, these had often been rewarded with time off and monetary rewards were only given to certain groups of workers. STM in accordance with the Employment Act 1955 of Malaysia is required to grant rewards in the form of money at a specified rate which is very much higher than that given by TD. Thus, STM faced the problem of a large sum of overtime allowances. The overtime rate according to the Labour Law as compared to the TD rate is as follows:

	JIM	STM	
Weekday	1—3/8	1—1/2	
Weekend	1—1/2	3	of normal pay
Public holiday	1—5/8	4—1/2	

STM had to employ or mobilize more employees to cater for the new and extended organizational structure where several divisions had been enlarged to cope with the new responsibilities (eg. Finance, Technical and Administration divisions). Such intakes and reorganization were also made necessary to handle an increase in administration work which were formerly handled by the Government departments such as PSD (Public Service Department).

6.5.3 Staff

In absorbing almost 28,571 TD staff, offering employment schemes A or B and having to cope with the various alternatives with a two year period in which to make a decision, STM faced a number of administration problems such as the need to monitor reports for those on pensionable schemes who opted for scheme A.

STM also discovered that there were insufficient records/data on personnel available. Some of the records were outdated, thus posing problems regarding actual job descriptions, job evaluation and salary scales.

Prevailing problems which concerned discipline, confirmation of jobs, unregistered workers yet on the pay sheet, workers which had not obtained permanent citizenship yet were on the pension scheme, and those who should qualify for the pension schemes, which were not settled during TD time, had to be settled by STM. However, STM has very little authority or is in a difficult position to settle such cases like pensioning, confirmation or disciplinary action for which JTM was previously accountable.

In honouring the agreement for privatization, STM had to absorb all the 28,571 JTM staff. Out of this number, STM discovered a surplus of workers which STM could not reduce until the period of five years was over. The situation of surplus workers came about when the decision to contract out STM workers to the 'turnkey project' to private contractors. Hence, most of TD's staff are required to do only the supervising work. This also allowed employees to miss opportunities in gaining skill and experience while working on the projects.

The high overtime occurrences were contributed to by the poor labour management such as; too many unskilled workers; poor supervision; and insufficient coordination and communication.

STM is faced with a high proportion of unskilled labourers who are not flexible or versatile to do other technical work.

6.5.4 Style

Accustomed to the Government sector orientation, STM faced problems in changing the managerial styles from the procedural orientation to the situational orientation. Still a large number of the managerial levels are uncertain of their roles and new responsibilities.

Being made a Public Company with the Government as the sole shareowner, STM is still strongly bound by the Government policies and decision making. This was ensured through the components in the Board members where representatives of the Government were present.

6.5.5 Skill

STM has a surplus of unskilled labour which cannot be deployed elsewhere or be terminated. Training and upgrading of skills is not easily accomplished due to constraints of the large number of workers, demographic distribution and the high cost involved.

Since recently being made a public company, STM personnel are not well versed with technicalities in Personnel and Industrial Relations, Labour Laws and Industrial Acts. Previously, such technicalities were being handled by the Public Service Department of Malaysia.

STM is also lacking people who specialize in marketing to promote STM services. At the moment marketing is being handled at a very minimal rate by the 'Kedai Telekom' (Telekom Shop).

With the expansion and reorganization of several divisions to cater to R&D, Consultancy Services and Marketing, STM is also faced with providing skilled staff for these departments.

6.5.6 Shared Values

Corporatization of STM came as a cultural shock for all levels of staff. Very little awareness was created and no acclimatization period was provided for them to get used to the new roles.

Being used to the Government sector urgency and seriousness in running a Public Company created confusion and tension among them.

6.5.7 Strategy

In trying to formulate new personnel policies and furnishing the personnel records, STM faced problems in satisfying the necessary requirements for the recruitment of former TD staff. STM cannot formulate a specific employment scheme to suit the agreement because of the constraint posed by the stipulated requirements in the Labour Law. Being a Public Company STM has to observe and abide by these laws.

Being commercially monopolistic in nature, STM does not rely heavily on marketing which might underdevelop its marketing ability. Generally, STM is not really involved in being competitive.

7. Issues of Privatization of SOEs

KCT and STM are faced with various issues as a result of their privatization programme. The main issues faced by KCT are the demands of the Port Authority Staff Unions (PASU) the inability to reduce excess workers and the requirement to maintain the personnel records of staff who have opted to remain in the government scheme of service. PASU, an in-house trade union of Port Klang Authority staff, is posing a major problem to KCT. It has a strength of about 2,500 members out of which 575 are the staff of KCT, who were previously the staff of Container Terminal Port Klang. One KCT union member is presently occupying the post of Vice-President while three other committee members are also union members. When Container Terminal Port Klang was privatized to become KCT, the Government agreed that PASU shuld continue to act on behalf of KCT staff until an in-house union for KCT was established.

Since there is no in-house union yet, the management of KCT have to get the consent of PASU, an external Union, whenever they want to change any terms and conditions relating to the personnel services. Any decision made by PASU as a result of the situation outside KCT will affect the staff and hence the operation. By this, KCT is faced with a situation where an external Union will have influence on the management of KCT staff. It is observed that efforts to set up an in-house union has been slow and not being encouraged by PASU. At present KCT's staff are represented by two separate unions, namely PASU and the proposed KCT in-house trade Union. However, a decision was made recently that only one union will eventually act as staff representative. Since PASU has majority members over the in-house trade Union, PASU was given the right to represent KCT staff in all negotiations with KCT's management.

KCT is also posed with the issue of inability to reduce its excess staff and absorbing staff who already have disciplinary records when they were with Container Terminal Port Klang. The excess staff do not have the required skill and qualifications to be redeployed to positions that are most needed by KCT. The excess but unsuitable staff will have to be kept on the payroll for a period of five years after privatization. Staff with disciplinary records are taken in with fresh personnel records of service and given equal offers as the rest of the staff who have no such record. This created discontent among the co-workers.

Since not all the staff opted to join KCT salary schemes, KCT has to maintain their personnel and services records according to the requirements of the government scheme of service. This situation requires KCT to allocate one of its staff to do the job. Many of the staff that have not opted for the KCT salary scheme are still young which means maintaining their service records for many more years.

The main issues faced by STM are evaluation of assets (due to management and legal problems), substantial liabilities, absorption of excess workers and attitude change. TD was run on a non-commercial basis. Records of its assets were poorly maintained and this led to delays in compiling a register of assets at STM's disposal. To date, the process of transferring these assets is still not completed.

As a government entity, TD was given the right to make use of Federal or State Government Land Reserve for its purposes. This right was ensured under the land laws of Malaysia. However since STM is no longer a government entity it can no longer enjoy the same privileges as TD. STM will need to purchase land from federal or the state government at current market price. This would involve a big amount of expenditure for STM. In addition to that the process of purchasing land from the state government takes a very long time. There is also a possiblity that the state government may not want to sell the land to a private entity. The land problem is not yet resolved therefore the status of all STM buildings is at stake.

When TD was privatized, STM was obliged to take over all the liabilities of TD. One of the major liabilities which it had to shoulder was the enormous amount of bad debts held by TD at that point in time. Over and above that, STM had to forego some of the privileges enjoyed by TD, for example exemption of stamp duties, road taxes and insurance which have now become a new liability for the company. STM would have to finance medical expenses for its personnel unlike TD which enjoyed free medical benefits.

The terms of privatization is stipulate that employees should not be worse off than when they were employed by the Government. This condition places significant limitations on the freedom to alter the size and compositon of the workforce for five years. Consequently STM has to carry the burden of continuing with a workforce that is not only large but lacking in skill, especially in the latest technology. Apart from this issue, the subject of employees affected by privatization is complicated by their legal and constitutional rights. At the same time, employees will need to be encouraged to opt for the privatized enterprise. Also dissatisfaction has arisen among co-workers with clean records by absorbing and giving a fresh start to employees who previously had disciplinary records against them.

TD being a government body, could not be autonomous in exercising its role. After privatization it is expected to exercise autonomy. But since the majority of the workers at all levels are from TD, exercising autonomy is still foreign in STM. The managers upheld the inclination to practice procedural management rather than to opt for a situational decision making. Being 100% government owned also dilutes the autonomy of STM.

The issues that are faced by the privatized SOEs are attributed to incomplete guidelines on privatization and they, being the earlier enterprises to be privatized. However, these issues were anticipated but some of these required careful consideration before the appropriate measures could be introduced to overcome them.

8. Conclusions

As deliberated in this brief paper the performance of many of the SOEs in Malaysia has been unsatisfactory. Enterprises under the trust agencies, with some exceptions, have been incurring losses and some have already been closed down to avoid further loss. The performance of enterprise is largely responsible for the provision of services, especially to the public, it also been the subject of great concern. There have been recurring problems relating to poor maintenance of plant, equipment and premises, and to the promptness, quality and reliability of services. The reasons for the unsatisfactory performance of many of the SOEs are attributed to unclear objectives, overlapping functions, ambiguous criteria for selection of programmes and projects, management problems such as inexperienced managers and recruitment of manpower from the public sector, and problem of coordination and control, especially financial control.

Privatization is regarded as a remedial measure to spur increasing competition, efficiency and productivity as compared to government agencies that are constrained by restrictive rules and cumbersome procedures. Generally, privatization in Malaysia is still at a relatively early stage. The privatization of the container terminal of Port Klang (KCT), the most profitable part of the port, is an example of selective privatization. The privatization of the Telecommunications Department (STM) however, began with the Government initially owning the entire equity of the company.

The privatization of KCT as a move to improve its management and operations has achieved its objectives. The container terminal which was then under the management of the Port Klang Authority tended to develop a style of operation which was not threatened by the need to compete. But as a private company, KCT expects all its workers to be production oriented. Non-performers are made to understand that their jobs are not indispensable because private organizations which do not make profit do not survive. With these kinds of values being instilled into all levels of workers, peer group pressure tends to ensure that all staff make every effort to do their share of the work.

The formation of KCT involved negotiations with the Government, investors, Unions and employees. However, the strong support of its staff enabled the company to minimize the effects of the change in the employment style.

The privatization of STM has somehow been on a slower pace. The direct conversion from a department to a company demands more problems to be solved before a smooth privatization process can take place. As a 100% government owned company STM still has to handle the strong influences from government officers who act as the representatives of the 100% shareholder. Problems such as obtaining an accurate valuation of assets and the process of transferring these assets to STM have yet to be resolved. Bringing about attitude changes to a large number of previously public sector employees poses a great challenge to the management.

While privatization of SOEs in Malaysia is progressing, there is need to be cautious of the effects of privatizing SOEs which deals with the welfare of the lower income group. To a great extent, privatization is expected to meet the distributional restructuring objectives of the NEP, besides releasing the full potential of the assets and other wealth of the nation from the domain of the state. Nevertheless, SOEs solely performing socio-economic development functions and other services affecting the livelihood of the rural and poor populace should be retained. However, to ensure they play their role as the country's economic engine of growth, a regular review on their effectiveness is in order.

CASE STUDIES: SRI LANKA

by Mr. K.S. Chandrasiri
Senior Consultant
National Institute of Business Management

1. Introduction

1.1 Introduction

State-owned enterprises (SOEs) play a vital role in the process of economic development in practically every country in the present world. They constitute a large, rapidly growing and strategic sector in most mixed economies, particularly the less developed ones. In terms of objectives state enterprises should promote overall economic growth by increasing their productivity on one hand and providing the necessary conditions for the expansion of the other sectors of the economy on the other.

State enterprises in their present form and strength in Sri Lanka are a post-war phenomenon. Especially after the political and social changes of 1956, they have become more important in the economy and their number has increased very rapidly. Now public enterprises operate in almost all sectors of the economy. The heaviest concentration of public enterprises can be found in the manufacturing, trade, transport and finance sectors. In 1986 government transfers to public sectors was about Rs.265 million and 76 percent of them were given as capital transfers while the balance was given as current transfers.

State enterprises are expected to fulfill various social political and economic objectives. In the present context of Sri Lankan economy, confronted as it is with various difficulties in the form of low level per capita income and the rate of economic growth, weak balance of payments, high rate of unemployment and inflation etc., the development of healthy state sectors playing a leading role in the growth of a national economy is of prime importance.

1.2 State Sector vs. State-Owned Enterprises Sector

The state sector in the Sri Lanka economy could be defined to include the following organizational forms.

- Central Government
- Local Government

- Public Corporations and Statutory Boards
- Co-operative Institutions
- Joint Ventures with a majority of share capital and or powers of management control in the hands of the Government and
- Government Owned Business Undertakings (Acquisitions, Act. No. 35 of 1971)

However, the state enterprise sector comprises of organizations which are engaged in the business of marketing their output. Accordingly the productive entities which fall into the state enterprise category take any one of four basic organizational forms given below.

- The department form
- Public Corporation form
- Joint stock company form and
- Government Owned Business Undertakings

1.3 Growth of State Enterprises in Sri Lanka

State enterprises have a long history in Sri Lanka. Since the country achieved independence from colonial rule in 1948, there has been a substantial growth in SOEs, in terms of numbers, variety, value added, gross savings, capital formation and employment. Especially during the last ten years the state sector in the Sri Lanka economy has shown a progressive expansion.

The growth of SOEs in Sri Lanka was due to many reasons such as the Second World War, political ideology, emphasis on social welfare governments' import substitution policy and self sustained economic growth. The growth of SOEs in Sri Lanka could be divided into six broad parts as follows:

Part I — Early 1920's up to political independence (1948). The State as a factory owner.

Part II — After political independence up to 1956 — Promotion of private enterprise system and policy of small-scale industrialization.

Part III — The period from 1956 to 1965 — Expansion of State Enterprise sector.

Part IV — The period from 1965 to 1970 — Emphasis on private enterprise in industrial development.

Part V — The period from 1970 to 1977 — Straight-forward policy towards nationalization and the Government's involvement in economic activities.

Part VI   — The period from 1977 onwards — Open economic policy and promotion of private sector enterprises.

The growth and development of SOE sectors in Sri Lanka is a result of all these social political economic changes that took place over the last 65 years.[1]

1.4 Methodology

At present there is an increasing concern over the performance of SOEs in Sri Lanka. This is mainly due to their heavy involvement in certain economic sectors and the Government's financial commitments in SOEs in terms of capital investment and current transfers. In addition the efficiency or inefficiency of SOEs seem to have a direct impact over GNP, wage levels, employment and price levels.

Managerial aspects have been identified as key elements in determining efficiency and effectiveness of an enterprise. There is a substantial amount of literature and research work on problems of SOEs. However, the present study is not intended to reidentify well known problems of SOEs. It is an attempt to study and analyze the dynamic process of management improvement in SOEs. Hence the study would make an attempt to address micro-level management features in a futuristic perspective. The focus would be more on "effectiveness" rather than efficiency. More specifically the main objectives of the present study would be:

- to critically examine the present state of affairs of selected SOEs.
- to assess the dynamic process of management improvement of SOEs.
- to examine forward planning process of SOEs and
- to recommend possible action programmes to promote effective forward planning at enterprise level.

With a view to examining these matters in detail, three public corporations: — The Sri Lanka Tyre Corporation (SLTC) National Paper Corporations (NPC) and Ceylon Ceramics Corporation (CCC) — were selected for the present study. These three enterprises afford different examples in the management of SOEs in Sri lanka. For instance, the SLTC offers the managerial dynamics of an industry which is based on imported technology and has been in operation for the last 20 years. The NPC presents an example of an old SOE operating under different social political economic conditions over the last 30 years. The case of Ceylon Ceramics explains the growth and expansion of an SOE over a period of 30 years with a low return on investment. Moreover these three cases would enable us to examine the degree of dynamism within an organization in response to changes in the environment. It would also help us to understand the differences in style of management and their influence over the overall efficiency of SOEs.

Most of the data pertaining to the study has been collected from four main sources:

- Secondary data on key performance areas of the enterprise,
- Both structured and unstructured interviews with managers at shop floor level,
- Detailed interviews with top level and middle level managers and
- Detailed interviews with policy makers and controlling authorities at Supervising Ministry level and national level.

Of these four sources, the secondary data relating to key performance areas of the enterprise was collected from the official documents of the three enterprises covering a period of six years from 1982 to 1987. Basically this included profit and loss account statements, balance sheets, progress reports on sales and production, cost of investment and summary statements of inventories.

1.5 Sri Lanka Tyre Corporation: The Nature and Structure of the Organization

The SLTC is a manufacturing organization within the country's state sector. It belongs to the post — 1956 era of development. It was during this period that the Government believed that rapid industrialization was a sine qua non for the advancement of socialism. This was also the period in which diplomatic relations were opened with the "socialist block." The SLTC was established on 1st January, 1962 as a part of Economic and Technical co-operation between USSR and Sri Lanka.

It was planned that the factory would produce 250,000 tyres and tubes in stage I and 360,000 tyres and tubes in stage II. Work commenced on stage I of the project in 1963. Commercial production commenced in April 1967. The authorized capital of the project was Rs.67 million which comprised of credit contributed by the USSR, to the amount of Rs.31 million. When commercial production commenced in 1967, the corporation produced only four sizes of tyres and tubes of the same size. However, over a period of 20 years it was able to increase and diversify its production capacity and presently the corporation manufacturers and markets 32 sizes of tyres and 17 sizes of inner tubes.

The management process, comprising management of production, marketing, materials, finance and personnel, though within the limits and bounds specified by or required by the external environment, yet geared towards achievement of the goals and objectives assigned to the enterprise is based essentially on foreign technology and know-how. Recently the corporation entered into a technical collaboration agreement with M/s. B.F. Goodrich of U.S.A. to harness advanced technology to produce a tyre which matches up to internationally accepted standards.

The SLTC provided employment in its first year of operations for 760 people and in 1987 this number increased to 1802. This number includes employees of all categories from workers to managerial staff in the factory as well as the staff in the corporation office. The Chairman is the Chief Executive of the SLTC and is in charge of the overall administration of the Tyre Corporation. The organization chart of the SLTC is given in Annex 1.

1.6 National Paper Corporation (NPC): The Nature and Structure of the Organization

The NPC is a manufacturing organization which has been in operation since the 1940's. Originally this was started as a small factory under the Department of Industries to turn waste paper into paper boards. At present the NPC operates its production work with two manufacturing units. Valichchenai Paper Mill and Embilipitiya Paper Mill. This Corporation has been developed into its present form by several stages. The original mill was designed with a production capacity of 3810 MT of writing and printing paper of limited grammes. The total annual production capacity of NPC is now 37500 MT. Its present product mix includes a wide range of paper items such as Typing, Photocopy, Roneo, File Covers, Manifold, Fulls cap, Bristol Board, Graph Paper, Drawing Paper, Writing Paper, Case Covers and Wrapping Paper. In addition to its own production, the NPC imports and sells small quantities of tissue and high quality papers.

The total staff strength of NPC in 1987 was 3976. The Chairman is the Chief Executive of the organization and is assisted by a General Manager and two Mill Manager residing at Embilipitiya and Valachchenai. In addition the key functional areas are headed by four functional managers, the Finance Manager, Production Manager, Marketing Manager and Personnel Manager. The organization chart of the NPC is given in Annex 2.

1.7　Ceylon Ceramics Corporation (CCC): The Nature and Structure of the Organization

The Ceylon Ceramics Corporation is one of the State-owned business enterprises which has a long history in the manufacturing sector of Sri Lanka. Ceramics was one sector identified by the Bureau of Industry in 1934 for Government investment. The pilot plant at Negombo was commissioned in 1944. Over a period of 34 years this SOE has expanded into ceramics and allied fields and now it is comprised of 18 factories, 22 retail shops, and four subsidiaries. The product items manufactured by the CCC could be categorized into the following groups.

1) Earthen-ware
2) Sanitary-ware
3) Bricks and Tiles
4) Electrical Insulators
5) Hydrated Lime
6) Mining and Processing of Clay
7) Mining and Processing of Feldspar Quartz

The CCC has its equity share in four private companies.

1) Dankotuwa Porcelain (Pvt) Ltd.
2) Lanka Porcelain Ltd.
3) Lanka Wall Tiles (Pvt) Ltd. and
4) Lanka Refractories Ltd.

The total employment strength of CCC in 1987 was 4902. The Chairman is the administrative head of the organization and is assisted by one General Manager and two Assistant General Managers. The organization chart of the CCC is given in Annex 3.

2.　Analysis of External Environment

The purpose of this section of the study is to examine the external factors that affect the performance of SLTC, NPC and CCC. More specifically the analysis would focus on three main factors i.e. external control structure, factor market conditions and product market conditions.

2.1　External Control Structure

At the very outset, it is relevant to examine how Government control originated in the operation of state enterprises. It has been stated that SOEs are in a delegated choice situation.[2] It is the case where a decision maker is actually making decisions in the best interest of society. State-owned enterprise is a legal entity created by the State. The Board is given responsibility for the "day-to-day management" of the enterprise, subject to directions from the Minister, of a general nature as to the extent and performance of their functions in relation to matters appearing to the Minister as affecting the "National Interest."

As explained earlier state enterprises in Sri Lanka cover four types of organizations. The nature of Government control over these four types of enterprises vary from one type of enterprise to another. For example, public corporations enjoy greater freedom from political and bureaucratic control than state enterprises run as departments. State enterprises were granted a substantial degree of autonomy in matters relating to management and finance. But the public accountability of state enterprises were not liquidated since they were expected to fulfil certain economic and social objectives.

Government control over the three state enterprises under study could be identified as follows:

- Control by Supervising Ministry — Ministry of Industries and Scientific Affairs
- Control by Inter-Ministerial activities
- Control by Auditor — General, Public Accounts Committee and the Parliament.

2.1.1 Control by Supervising Ministry

Government Control exercised in the form of directions issued by the relevant Minister occupies a very important place at Ministry Level. In terms of the Acts of Incorporation, the Minister's responsibility is to give policy directives and appoint the Board. By and large the Minister has the power to lay down the policy of a state enterprise, the power to issue directives in the public interest, the power to call for and receive reports and information; the power to require submission of the enterprises budget for approval, the power to sanction expenditure where it exceeds a fixed ceiling, the power of prior approval in all matters pertaining to borrowings, investment and distribution of profits. These powers are to ensure that the SOEs are run according to the objectives and principles of state policy laid down for them.

In the actual operation of SOEs Ministerial direction could be seen not only formally but also informally and covertly.[3] This has occurred so frequently that, in certain instances the concept of "autonomy" has become a mere word. However, in actual practice what has happened is that, whether it is formal or informal, the "directive influence" of the Government on any public enterprise has varied with the "personality" of the Minister, the strength and status of the enterprise, the calibre of its top management personnel and the strength and dependence of the Board.[4]

Besides exercising direct control in the form of Ministerial directives, the Government also exercises its indirect control through the supervising Ministry with respect to corporations under its charge. The objective of this kind of control is to ensure that the policies followed by public enterprises are consistent with national economic policy. In accordance with this objective, in 1969 the Government decided that it would be necessary for the supervising Ministry of each public enterprise to formulate its policy framework taking into consideration the special features of the activities managed by the enterprise concerned. This had to be done in consultation with the Ministry of Planning and Economic Affairs and Ministry of Finance. Moreover any revision of the policy framework had to be approved by the Cabinet Planning Committee. Also it was the function of the Supervising Ministry to approve new proposals and development programmes of the enterprises under its supervision. In addition, the enterprises were expected to get the approval of the respective Ministries for their annual budgets prior to the commencement of the financial year. The supervising Ministry had also to undertake a review of current operations of each enterprise on the basis of a quarterly comparison of the enterprise's economic and technical performance with budget targets, indices of efficiency being worked out for each enterprise. According to the Treasury Circular (Finance) 71, the purpose of this kind of control is not to reduce the independence of the enterprise — but rather to assist them in the efficient operation of their activities and to improve their performance.

In reality however, the Government's control at Ministerial level had not fulfilled the expected objectives. At Ministry level the system of control had disturbed the smooth functioning of the organization rather than helped them to function efficiently. The appointment of Directors and Board Members was made on political grounds with hardly any regard to their managerial ability or any special knowledge of the industry or business in which the enterprise operates.

2.1.2   Control By Inter-Ministerial Level

This includes control of state enterprises at Finance and Planning Ministry and Ministry of Plan Implementation level. As mentioned

Ministry and Ministry of Plan Implementation level. As mentioned earlier the supervising Ministry is required to formulate its policy framework for each state enterprise in consultation with the Ministry of Finance and Planning. According to Treasury Circular (Finance) 71, the Ministry of Planning is responsible for the final approval of new proposals and development programmes. By this it examines the demand projections and production plans and other factors on which development programmes are formulated. In addition, the Ministry of Planning co-ordinates development plans and expansion schemes according to national priorities and targets. Besides this, the Planning Ministry is expected to assist state enterprises in improving their performance by providing the necessary guidelines for the economic and financial evaluation of their activities.

State enterprises depend upon the state for financial support and assistance. Therefore, in this sphere the rationale for control by the Ministry of Finance becomes very clear. The Treasury functions as the principal direct agency of Ministry of Finance, and it is empowered.

1) To examine the Annual Budget in association with the supervising Ministry.

2) To review the draft annual accounts and balance sheet which should be made available to the Treasury within four months of each financial year.

3) To examine proposals relating to the appropriation of profits in association with the Ministry.

4) To advise on measures to promote financial administration, budgeting, accounting and other information systems.

5) To analyze information given in the Annual Budget, Annual Accounts and Balance Sheets from the point of view of costs, prices and return on investments.

6) To keep a watch on investments on behalf of the Government in order to obtain a fair return as well as to ensure the repayment of loans and interest.

7) To examine the capital structure and other related questions and prepare changes, statutory or otherwise, to provide essential uniform conditions which enable comparison of the activities of various corporations.

8) To collect and build up any other essential financial and statistical data.

With the introduction of the Finance Act No. 38 of 1971 the control powers vested in the Ministry of Finance were further increased.

1)   Ministry of plan implementation

The Ministry of Plan Implementation performs the function of monitoring the progress of SOEs through periodic reviews and reports to the appropriate supervising Ministry. It receives all the information regarding the performance of SOEs and functions as a co-ordinating agency between the national economic policy and the operational targets of SOEs. Therefore its intervention in the activities of SOEs is purely in an advisory capacity.

2.1.3   Control by the Auditor General, Public Accounts Committee and the Parliament

This includes the control over public enterprises by the Auditor General, the Public Accounts Committee and the Parliament (National State Assembly).

1)   National audit — The role of the auditor general

The Auditor General is the agent of Parliament. The Finance Act No. 38 of 1971 makes the Auditor General the Auditor of all public corporations and invests on him wide powers of inspection and reviews of the financial obligations of such enterprise. But even if these reports point out any defects in the activities they serve no useful purpose, as nothing is done regarding the findings of the Auditor General.

2)   The public accounts committee

The function of the Public Accounts Committee of the Parliament is to review the performance of SOEs. The basis on which they review the activities of the enterprise is by the Auditor General's past audit reports. Therefore this analysis is essentially history. But the suggestions made in these reports to overcome the short-comings of SOEs are implemented through the appropriate Ministers.

3)   Parliament (National state assembly)

SOEs are the creation of Parliament. They are not controlled but they are accountable to Parliament, the reason being that public enterprises are expected to fulfil social and economic objectives. The success or failure in achieving those objectives is discussed in Parliament. For example the Acts of Incorporation ensure that copies of the annual report, accounts, balance sheets, audit reports, and budget are tabled before the House of Representatives. This could be considered as a good opportunity for the discussion and criticism of SOEs in Parliament. This also serves the purpose of conveying accurate and systematic information about SOEs to the public.

Government control over SOEs appears to have a number of undesirable features. In practice the system of control is relatively centralized. As observed in the survey there has been continual intervention in the decision making process by the supervising Ministry and other Ministries. This has disturbed the line of authority and responsibility, duplicated decision making, wasted scarce resources, delayed the implementing of decisions and created dissatisfaction among SOEs. Hence there should be a system of control which provides a certain degree of autonomy to enable state enterprise executives to use their discretion at least in administrative matters.

2.2 Factor Market Conditions

This is one area which indicates a direct government influence over the activities of SOEs. For instance the capital structure of SOEs in Sri Lanka consists of contributions, grants, subsidies and loans by the Government at their establishment stage and thereafter. In addition SOEs receive funds from foreign sources and also from domestic banking sectors at subsidized interest rates. These concessions are normally channelled through the supervising authorities of the Government.

The capital structure of the three case studies and the degree of government influence over them is explained in Table 1, 2 and 3. From that, it is seen the percentage contribution of government capital to SLTC, NPC and CCC in 1987 was 29.4%, 22.7% and 23.4% respectively. It is also important to notice the K.F.W. Loan of Rs.144.0 million shown in the capital structure of NPC. In settling this loan the loan annual repayment to the Treasury is Rs.94.0 million and interest is Rs.10.0 million. The amount of long-term loans taken by the CCC was Rs.54.8 million as at the end of 1987. Since the mid 1980s there has been a tendency to assess the efficiency of SOEs in terms of return on capital invested. In the past the return on capital invested in SOEs was less than one percent.[5] Hence the Government has been exercising more control over the activities of SOEs.

In addition, government control over activities of SOEs at factor market level could be seen in the procurement of machinery, spare parts, raw materials and other intermediate inputs. The existing procedure sets out three types of tender procedures as follows:

1) Below Rs.2.00 millions to be decided by the Corporation.

2) Between Rs.2.00 million and Rs.5.00 million to be decided by a Ministry appointed Tender Board.

3) Over Rs.5.00 million to be decided by the Cabinet on the recommendation of a Cabinet appointed Tender Board.

It is the opinion of the managers at enterprise level that these procedures cause enormous delays in the procurement of machinery, spare parts, raw material and other intermediate inputs. This problem was analyzed in many studies and currently the supervising ministry is in the process of making certain amendments to the existing tender procedure.[6]

Another significant factor which affects the performance of SOEs at factor market level is the prices of raw material and intermediate inputs. The SOEs are directly influenced by the cost escalations of these items. For example the NPC was forced to revise its prices in the 1st quarter of 1988 due to significant increases in the cost of raw material and intermediate inputs. Moreover, the raw material inputs of the three organizations under study include a sizeable proportion of imported raw materials.

In 1986 the percentage of imported raw materials (value wise) used by the SLTC, NPC and CCC was 39%, 80% and 31% respectively. Hence the cost of production is further influenced by price fluctuations of raw materials in the world market. These factor market conditions have forced SOEs to take every possible action to minimize the effects of cost increases by way of strict cost control measures and substitution of local raw material. In addition non-availability of local raw material has also affected the operational efficiency of NPC and CCC.

The capacity utilization rate of plant and machinery is another factor that deserves attention under factor market conditions. As explained in Annex 11, the scale of production of SLTC, NPC and CCC are relatively low. This could be identified as a contributory factor towards the high cost of production.

Table 1 SLTC Capital Structure (Rs.M)

	1983	1984	1985	1986	1987
Contributed Capital	67.5	67.5	67.5	67.5	67.5
Capital Reserve	3.7	3.7	6.7	6.7	6.7
Expansion and Renewal Reserve	82.0	87.9	87.9	87.8	87.9
Employee Housing Reserve	10.5	10.5	10.5	10.5	10.5
General Reserve	14.1	14.2	19.3	32.6	47.0
NDB Loan	—	—	5.3	7.3	9.6
	177.8	183.8	197.2	212.4	229.2

Source: SLTC Annual Accounts

Table 2 NPC Capital Structure (Rs.M)

Capital & Reserves	1983	1984	1985	1986	1987
Government Contribution	321.6	321.6	321.6	321.6	332.2
Development Reserve	0.4	0.4	0.4	0.4	
Capital Reserve	12.8	13.7	13.8	13.7	45.1
Loan Redemption Reserve	41.7	41.7	41.7	41.7	
Profit & Loss A/C	(84.8)	(82.6)	(83.8)	(79.1)	(256.0)
Long Term Liabilities					
K.F.W. Loan	255.2	219.8	181.9	144.0	341.4
K.F.W. Loan Instalments & Interest	368.8	429.9	—	—	
Treasury Loan	0.5	—	—	—	
Interest on Treasury Loan	0.3				
	916.5	944.5	475.6	442.3	462.7

Source: NPC Annual Accounts

Table 3 CCC Capital Structure (Rs.M)

	1983	1984	1985	1986	1987
Contributed Capital	82.5	82.5	82.5	82.5	82.5
Capital Reserves	187.9	374.0	174.7	178.7	178.7
Book Value of Assets	20.9	20.9	20.9	20.9	20.9
Ministry Grants	1.5	1.5	1.5	1.5	1.5
Fixed Assets Repl. Reserve	78.5	46.1	56.5	44.1	67.8
General Reserve	0.3	0.3	0.3	0.3	0.3
	371.6	525.3	336.4	328.0	351.7

Source: Ceylon Ceramics Corporation Annual Accounts

2.3 Product Market Conditions

The product market conditions in the present study would be analyzed considering two basic product market conditions i.e. monopoly and competition. However, the analysis would focus on specific market characteristics of each product category separately.

In terms of number of suppliers the SLTC, NPC and CCC fall into the category of monopoly. For example the SLTC is the only organization engaged in production of tyres. However, the total supply of tyres in the market is met by three main sources i.e. SLTC, imports and tyre rebuilding industry. The supply of paper depends on two main sources; NPC and imports. Same product market conditions could be observed with regard to CCC products too. The only difference is in addition to imports there is competition from close substitutes i.e. glass-ware and plastic-ware, etc. However, this is limited only to few product categories.

The demand for tyres mainly depends on the vehicle population of the country. The vehicle population includes the total number of vehicles in use and therefore the product market could be subdivided into many user categories. These users purchase different sizes of tyres and they seem to vary significantly in terms of their behaviours in product selection. Moreover, different behaviour patterns could be observed within in each sub category of users. For instance, among the car owners, there are many segments in terms of age, income, employment and life styles. These factors seem to indicate different behaviour patterns among customers in the tyre market. The specific characteristics of each user segment is very important in strengthening SLTS's position in the market. This type of market information could be used to work out product positioning strategies and promotion strategies to reach different target groups in the market. The SLTC markets its products through a network of registered dealers. It enjoys about 90% of the market share for truck tyres and agricultural tyres. Its market share for car tyres and sector & motor cycle tyres is about 50%. It also enjoys a 60% market share in the light truck tyres market.

The NPC is also operating in a highly competitive product market. As stated earlier it markets a wide range of product items and the degree of competition seems to vary between different categories of products. The competition is directly from imported products. Competition from imports is due to combination of many factors; price, quality, availability, customer service and credit terms.

The data on demand for paper indicates a continuous upward trend. This trend is also likely to continue in the future. The consumer of non-industrial paper is influenced by dealer/printer in the choice of product items. These buyers select products based on appearance and feel. However, the industrial consumers seem to be more educative in selecting better quality products as the quality and thickness of paper affects the final output.

The product distribution is done through a number of channels i.e. registered paper merchants, directly to industrial users, directly to bulk buyers and through NPC's own sales centre. The product promotion is done mainly through advertising. In the area of customer service better facilities are provided by private dealers of imported items in terms of speed of service, availability of product, and delivery. The customers are becoming more quality conscious after exposure of the market for imported products. The current trend in general is more for coated paper. In the printing industry the trend is for offset printing and therefore product selection would be based more on quality than on price.

The demand conditions for ceramic products are also on the upward trend. Both per head consumption data and sales data clearly indicate this pattern. The total market for CCC products could be classified into three main categories i.e.; tableware, sanitary ware and bricks & tiles. The CCC markets its products through 10 area Managers and 16 Retail outlets. However, no sales promotion is done at either wholesale level or retail level.

The CCC is operating in a monopolistic market in selling its tableware products. These products are marketed both in the rural sector and the urban sector of the Sri Lankan market. However, Dankotuwa Porcelain products and imported glassware products seem to be well positioned in the high income segment of the market. They also seem to offer high quality products with attractive designs and packaging. Hence the presence of competition is seen in the tableware market.

The sanitary ware market is shared by the CCC and imported products. The imported products offer the advantages of superior quality and attractive designs over CCC products. The product display and sales promotion work done by the private dealers is by far superior to CCC. As a result the imported products seem to have captured the high income segment of the market. Moreover one private firm has already started to manufacture cultured marble sanitary ware under the trade name "Kendall." However, the demand for sanitary ware products in the household sector and institution sector should continue to grow in the future. This growth is mainly due to future development programmes of the housing sector and other development programmes of the country.

The demand for bricks and tiles depends on the growth and expansion of the housing sector and other development programmes of the country. the market share enjoyed by the CCC in this product category is about 40% and the balance is shared by medium and small scale manufacturers in the private sector.

The influence of all these external environmental factors over the three SOEs under study are graphically represented in Fig. 1.

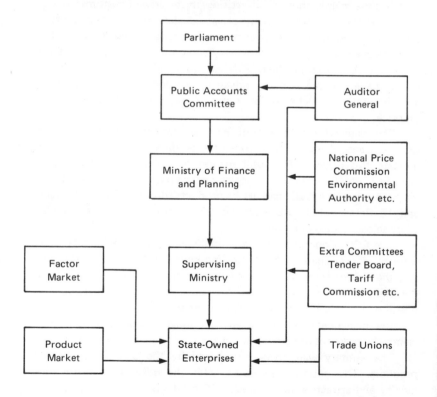

Fig. 1   Typical Components of a SOE System in Sri Lanka

3. Performance Analysis

The purpose of this section of the study is to analyse the performace of the three SOEs over a period of six years from 1982 to 1987.

The value added contribution of the SLTC is given in Table 4 at current prices and constant prices. Accordingly the value added of SLTC has increased by about 36 percent between 1982 and 1987. This increase is mainly due to inflation as value added at constant prices for the same period registered a decline. Moreover, a significant drop in value added of SLTC is recorded in 1983 and 1984.

Table 5 deals with value added of the NPC. It indicates an increase of value added at constant prices by about 48 percent between 1984 and 1986. The value added of CCC is given in Table 6. It also indicates a similar pattern of growth in value added as observed in SLTC. These value added contributions have been further analyzed as per head basis for 1986 and the results are given in Table 7. From this the highest value added contribution made by the SLTC as against the other two enterprises is clearly seen.

Table 4 SLTC Value Added at Current Prices and Constant Prices (Rs.M)

	1982	1983	1984	1985	1986	1987
Value added at Current Prices	100.0	60.6	81.1	107.3	132.7	136.4
Value added at Constant Prices	100.0	51.3	59.3	74.7	83.6	84.8

Table 5 NPC Value Added at Current Prices and Constant Prices (Rs.M)

	1984	1985	1986	1987
Value added at Current Prices	69.9	89.2	117.6	113.4
Value added at Constant Prices	51.1	62.1	74.1	70.5

Source: Annex 5

Table 6   CCC Value Added at Current Prices and Constant Prices (Rs.M)

	1982	1983	1984	1985	1986	1987
Value added at Current Prices	96.3	104.8	102.8	130.4	135.1	136.6
Value added at Constant Prices	96.3	88.9	75.1	90.7	85.1	85.0

Source: Annex 6

Table 7   Value Added Constributions of SLTC, NPC and CCC on Per Head Basis for 1986 (Rs.000)

	SLTC	NPC	CCC
Value added per employee (Current prices)	71.6	29.5	27.5
Value added per employee (Constant prices)	53.8	22.2	20.7

The return on capital employed for the three case studies is given in Table 8 below for the four years 1983 – 1987. This information has to be analyzed in line with prevailing market rates of interest with a view to assess alternative earning capacity's of capital employed in SOEs. Interest rates on fixed deposits of 12 to 24 months in the commercial banks were above 15 percent per annum during the period from 1983 to 1987. Lending rates of long-term credit institutions were generally between 10 and 16 percent annum. When considered the return on capital in comparison with above given interest rates the performance of CCC clearly appear to be extremely poor and unsatisfactory. The NPC seem to indicate satisfactory results only for 1986. The SLTC also indicates satisfactory results only for 1985, 1986 and 1987.

Table 8   Return on Capital Employed

	1983	1984	1985	1986	1987
Net profit before tax to capital employed (%) SLTC	0.16	8.9	16.4	21.78	19.7
Net profit before tax to capital employed (%) NPC	—	1.2	7.3	12.7	8.6
Net profit before tax to capital employed (%) CCC	0.1	Loss	1.2	0.4	1.4

The growth in the volume of sales, both in terms of quantity and value has been analyzed in respect of three case studies. The total value of sales of SLTC increased from Rs.285.0 million in 1982 to Rs.455.1 million in 1987. The SLTC achieved its highest sales both quantity-wise and value-wise in 1987. The index of total sales value-wise and quantity-wise is given in Table 9, taking 1982 as the base year = 100. It shows that the value-wise sales index of SLTC has increased from 100 in 1982 to 160 in 1987, showing a significant increase. However, quantity-wise sales index do not indicate such a rapid increase.

Table 9 Index Number of Total Sales (1982 — 100)

Year	SLTC		NPC		CCC	
	Qty-wise Index	Value-wise Index	Qty-wise Index	Value-wise Index	Qty-wise Index	Value-wise Index
1982	100	100	100	100	—	100
1983	90	95	101	106	—	103
1984	100	122	99	113	—	97
1985	94	126	97	133	—	110
1986	105	144	121	148	—	115
1987	120	160		160		113

The total value of sales of NPC increased from Rs.422 million in 1982 to Rs.674 million in 1987. The NPC has also achieved its highest sales both value-wise and quantity-wise in 1986. The sales index given in Table 9 further explains these increases in quantity-wise and value-wise. As observed in the case of SLTC, the quantity-wise sales index of NPC indicates a slow growth rate as against increases in value-wise sales. It is also important to notice the negative growth of sales of NPC for 1984 and 1985.

The total sales turnover of CCC increased from Rs.240.5 million in 1982 to Rs.271.5 million in 1987. As shown in Table 9, the CCC indicates a marginal increase in its sales from 1982 to 1987 except for 1984 which records a negative growth in sales. In the final analysis it appears that all the three enterprises have not been successful in achieving a continuous growth of sales in real terms.

4. Analysis of Future Scenario

4.1 Future Vision and Dynamism of SOEs

The main purpose of this section of the study is to examine future vision and dynamism of SOEs which are now operating in a world of change. To do this an attempt would be made to study the style of management and process of forward planning at enterprise level. The future vision and dynamism in managing SOEs at surpervising ministry level and national level would be studied separately to examine the readiness of controlling agencies to face challenges in the future.

4.2 Emphasis on Corporate Planning at Supervising Ministry Level

As stated earlier SOEs are creations of the Government. They are expected to plan their programme of activity in line with the development policies at national level. To do this it is necessary for the controlling agencies to assist SOEs both in operational planning and long term planning. A recent study carried out by the ILO on SOEs in the manufacturing sector of Sri Lanka states strategic planning as an area in which the Government not only has a right to intervene but an obligation. It has further identified this as one of the areas of supervisory control which requires strengthening.[6]

In line with these recommendations a separate division was created by the Ministry of Industries and Scientific Affairs in 1985 to introduce and promote corporate planning at enterprise level. This unit was assisted by a consultant from the World Bank.[7] This programme was continued in 1986 and 1987, and necessary guidelines were given to all corporations on objective setting, identification of business objectives, assigning responsibilities and preparing action programmes.

4.3 Corporate Planning in Practice at Enterprise Level

Application of Corporate Planning as a planning tool at enterprise level was examined in the present study. This included a detailed study of corporate plans prepared by the three SOEs and its influence over the operational activities of the enterprise. The views of supervising authorities on corporate planning at enterprise level were also examined as a part of the study. The rest of the paper would be devoted to presenting these findings.

The practice of corporate planning exercises at enterprise level was observed in the cases of three SOEs studied in the present survey. Of the three enterprises, the corporate plan prepared by the SLTC seemed to be well in line with the accepted corporate planning methodology.

The corporate plan of SLTC consists of three volumes and each volume covers the following specific details.

Volume I — Deals with mission, objectives both in quantitative and quantitative terms, threats, opportunities, strengths, and weaknesses.

Volume II — Deals with strategy, action plans and assigning responsibilities to key officials of the corporation. The time coverage includes a five year period from 1988 to 1992.

Volume III — Deals with sales plan, production plan, profitability statement and a projected balance sheet for a period of five years from 1988 to 1992.

From the above details it is explicit that the SLTC has used SWOT analysis in preparing its corporate plan. In the process of preparing the corporate plan the SLTC has adopted a participatory approach especially in carrying out the SWOT analysis. Hence the views of all functional heads are incorporated in the corporate plan of the SLTC. As observed in the survey this participatory approach at SLTC has emerged as a result of the following.

1) Interest of the management to prepare a corporate plan for SLTC in mid 1980's.

2) Problems of implementing a corporate plan prepared by an outside consultant.

3) Corporate culture, corporate effort and skills in corporate planning at top level and middle level.

The corporate culture and managers' commitment towards achieving corporate goals of the organization was noticed at SLTC. Planning of operational work and future activities at each functional area is carried out in line with what is stated in the corporate plan. In fact when managers were asked to elaborate on how they plan out their work the immediate response from many of the managers was to refer to the corporate plan and then present a detailed account on operational planning activities at divisional level. This is a clear reflection of managers' involvement in corporate planning processes and its acceptance at operational level.

The existing performance monitoring systems at SLTC were also examined in the present study. The purpose is to study the flow of information within the organization and its effectiveness in solving operational problems. As revealed in the survey most of the matters relating to performance improvement of SLTC are discussed at a

Management Advisory Committee (MAC), Sales & Production Review Committee and Divisional Heads Meeting. The MAC meets twice a month and decides on vital policy matters before it goes to the Board. The Sales & Production review meeting reviews actual performance as against budgeted targets. The Divisional Heads Meeting takes up all types of organizational problems. The net outcome of these practices is a clear understanding of organizational goals among top level and middle level managers of the enterprise. It has also created an environment for open communication and a high level of trust among managers to solve problems efficiently and effectively.

The corporate plan prepared by the NPC has also used the SWOT analysis in diagnosing both external and internal environmental factors that affect its operations. The NPC's corporate plan gives the mission statement, objectives and goals, strategies, indicators, projected profit & loss account and balance sheet, fund flow statement, capital expenditure estimates, key performance indicators and key control factors. It covers a period of three years from 1988 to 1990. However, it does not propose any action programmes, action responsibility and progress reporting systems. In general the corporate plan of the NPC does not seem to indicate a detailed coverage of all the issues relating to peformance improvement of the organization.

The NPC does not seem to have adopted a participatory approach in preparing its corporate plan. It is prepared by the finance division with the assistnce of few other key executives of the organization. The annual budget is not linked with the corporate plan. Hence the operational activities of the corporation is not guided by the corporate plan. It appears that the corporation has prepared this document as an administrative requirement of the supervising ministry. Moreover focus on corporate objectives in planning operational activities at divisional level was also not seen at NPC.

The operational problems and matters relating to performance improvement is taken up at two vital meetings, the progress review meeting and cost control meeting. These two meetings are interconnected and performance related matters are taken up on regular basis at these meetings. In addition, separate progress review meetings are held at factory level to discuss performance related problems on a regular basis.

From the above analysis it is evident that a clear understanding of organizational goals at divisional level does not exist at NPC. Lack of collaboration and team work in promoting corporate objectives were also noticed at NPC. Hence the corporate culture and mutual support among top level and middle level managers stands at a low level.

The CCC has also prepared a corporate plan covering a time span of three years from 1988 to 1990. This was prepared by the accounting unit of the CCC. However, the corporate plan of the CCC does not seem to have followed any of the accepted methodologies in corporate planning. It does not deal with mission, objectives, strategies and action programmes of the organization. This means the CCC has not done a thorough analysis of external and internal environmental factors in designing the corporate plan. It is merely a document to satisfy the requirements of the surpervising ministry. It presents profit and loss account statements for its major divisions (i.e. Earthen ware, Sanitary ware, Insulators, Bricks & Tiles, Raw material — Boralesgamuwa, Raw material — Dediyawala, Raw Material — Meetiyagoda, Raw material — Owela, lime plant at Hungama and Retail outlets) and a consolidated profit and loss statement for the entire organization. This means the CCC has not analyzed business objectives clearly either at corporate level or divisional level. The absence of this dimension makes it exceedingly difficult for corporate management to interact with other divisions of the organization. It is this dimension which enables corporate management to evaluate business plans in terms of risk and to judge the degree of fit among divisional plans. It will be the responsibility of the planning system to facilitate effective incorporation of risk handling through a proper identification of the dimensions of the business plans.

From the above analysis it is clear that the planning systems of CCC are not related to organization purpose, function and environment. The organizational goals are not clear to the management. Open communication and problem solving climate was not observed at CCC. As a result the corporate culture and morale of the organization stands at a low level.

The above analysis is an attempt to explain current practices in corporate planning at enterprise level. The results indicate significant differences among three SOEs in their approach to corporate planning and its influence over operational activities of the enterprise.

This variation could be attributed to the following:

- Low morale of the organization.
- Non-availability of skills in corporate planning at enterprise level.
- Depth and width of the product mix.
- Complexity of the organization.

The differences between SLTC, NPC and CCC in their approach to forward planning could be further elaborated on by using the concept of life-cycle theory.[8] Accordingly any form of SOE's generally go through three phases in its growth pattern over a period of time. The three phases are classified as a sheltered phase, supportive phase and self-propelling phase. These three phases indicate significant differences in the areas of business objectives, strategy formulation, level of analysis, autonomy, mode of finance and performance criteria. More specifically SOEs at the self-propelling stage seem to be more adaptive to both product market and factor market changes and more autonomous in business/government relations. They are more dependent on internal funds and concerned more about effectiveness rather than efficiency in measuring enterprise performance. In contrast the SOEs at the sheltered phase seem to be more influenced by supervising authorities and less dependent on internal funds. They also seem to use public purpose criteria in measuring enterprise performance. The life-cycle concept is further elaborated in Fig. 2.

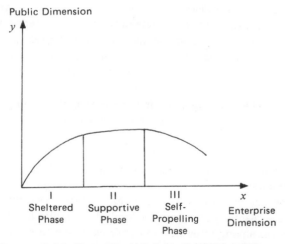

Source: Public Enterprise, Vol. 5, No. 3 (ICPE) p. 269

Fig. 2 —"Growth Cycle" Model of Public Enterprise

In view of the above, the CCC seems to occupy the sheltered phase of the growth-cycle model. This is because of its low morale, low efficiency, high degree of pressure from internal environment, less emphasis on commercial objectives and high cash support from the Government. The NPC seems to be in the early stage of the supportive phase. This observation is made in line with its low profitability, misconception of organizational goals and objectives and lack of forward planning.

The SLTC seems to be in the early stages of the self-propelling phase. This is indicated by its product-market innovativeness, ability to generate internal cash surpluses, clear understanding of corporate objectives and effective forward planning.

Corporate competence and resource availability has been identified as crucial factors in corporate planning. These two aspects were assessed with regard to the three SOEs under study. The assessment is based on value judgements of top level and middle level managers of the three SOEs. The method of semantic differential scale was used for this purpose. The semantic differential scale consisted of seven variables relating to overall performance of SOEs and the assessment is based on a 1 to 7 points scale. The results of the analysis is given in Fig. 3.

Accordingly all the managers at top level are of the view that there is a high degree of government intervention over the activities of SOEs. It also indicates SLTC's high degree of adaptability to changes in technology, product market conditions and factor market conditions. The opinions of managers at middle level were also assessed on the same basis and the results are given in Fig. 4. Accordingly the relative strengths of the three SOEs in the areas of employee motivation, pressure from external environment, corporate effort within the organization and satisfaction towards employee welfare are very low. Their adaptability to changes in product market and factor market conditions are moderate.

The policy maker's opinion about short-term and long-term planning practices in SOEs were also examined in the present study. The results are given in Fig. 5. Accordingly, both short-term and long-term plans prepared by SOEs are not effective. The SOEs are unable to prepare more realistic plans due to non availability of skills and inadequacy of information.

Fig. 3 Top Managers' Value Judgements on Selected Variables Relating to Overall Performance of the Enterprise

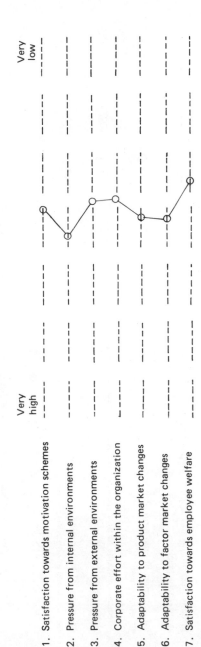

Fig. 4 Middle Level Managers' Value Judgements on Selected Variables Relating to Overall Performance of the Enterprise

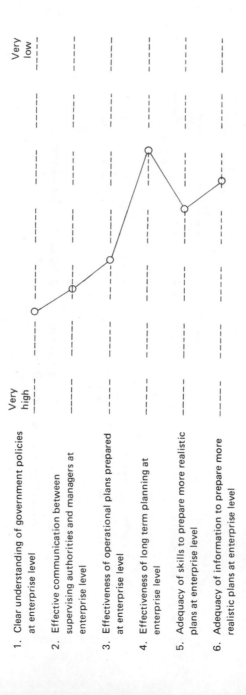

Fig. 5   Policy Makers' Value Judgements on Selected Variables Relating to Overall Performance of Public Enterprises

4.4 Planning with Scenarios

Scenarios could be used very effectively as a planning tool. The success of this tool, however, depends on its ability to link both external and internal environmental events to the unique operating experience of a specific type of organization. The method of scenario planning enables isolation of those sets of economic, political technological, regulatory and market conditions which are most favourable and those which are least favourable for the performance improvement of an organization. The scenario approach explicitly recognises the fact that it is impossible to forecast the future. Instead, it makes an attempt to capture elements of possible developments in the economic, social, political, technological and market spheres.

The exploration of a possible future through the use of scenarios prepares the ground for the evaluation of available options. This is the step where concepts are translated into numbers and the question was asked what if? A reasonable complete evaluation of all possible actions and all possible consequences for even a limited number of futures manages to achieve more flexible and resilient plans.

The three SOEs covered in the present study do not seem to have paid sufficient attention to possible developments in the external environment in preparing their corporate plans. As a result these plans have failed to capture future developments and design sound business strategies to cope with future changes. In exploring future possibilities these enterprises need to pay more attention to changes in the factor market, product market, regulatory system and overall social political economic conditions of the country.

More specifically this should include thorough assessment of changes in technology, consumer lifestyles, regulatory mechanism, macro-economic policies, political climate and price increases in the factor market. To this end a strong and continued commitment of management for planning is an essential tool for coherent, critical managerial thinking in the face of increased social, political and economic uncertainty.

As shown earlier the SLTC has come up to the 3rd phase of the growth cycle of SOEs. This evolutionary process has taken place over a period of 20 years. Clear identification of future scenarios would further enhance the organizational achievements of the SLTC. Many of these scenarios seem to be closely linked with product market and factor market conditions. In other words the SLTC should try to further strengthen its market position by explotting the opportunities available in the changing environment. The other two SOEs have been in business over the last 30 years. But the CCC and NPC are still at the 1st and 2nd phases of the growth-cycle model respectively. This could be mainly attributed to the internal managerial inefficiency of the two SOEs. Especially with the CCC who has failed to adjust itself to the changes in the external environment. The NPC has been very slow in its response to both factor market and product market changes. In addition the organizational efficiency seems to be heavily constrained by external influences. In other words ministerial pressures for achieving the public purpose seem to be more than the market pressures to better economic performance of the enterprise.

Technology management has been identified as an important factor for future growth and development of an enterprise. The total technology management includes development of technological capability of human resources, development of corporate culture and development of organization.[9] The SLTC seems to have made satisfactory progress in these areas. The corporate plan of SLTC further indicates its commitment to develop the organization in the area of technology management. However, the significance of a total technology management concept is not clearly understood by the NPC and CCC.

The significance of R&D work in improving cost effectiveness and market competitiveness has not been identified by any of the SOEs in their corporate plans. This is mainly due to lack of support given by the top management to promote R&D work within the enterprise. Even at the Board level more time is spent on personnel and administrative matters and little time on finance and still less time on R&D work. Hence, the innovative capability of the organization stands at a low level. Lack of staff and other facilities have further aggravated this situation.

Technology development is another important factor that is closely linked with the long-term corporate strategy of an enterprise. This is not so in the case of the three SOEs examined in the present study. Moreover, all three SOEs are using out dated technology. Only the SLTC has made an attempt to introduce new technology through a technical collaboration agreement with M/s. B.F. Goodrich of U.S.A. Still its progress in this area is far behind the technological developments of the industry. The NPC and CCC are also using out dated technology. This aspect has to be improved both at enterprise level and national level in order to improve the performance efficiency of SOEs.

Human resource development has also been identified as an important scenario in forward planning. This is more specific to CCC and NPC. These two organizations should analyze this aspect in detail in order to improve the managerial efficiency of the two enterprises. For example human resource development would lead to high morale, mutual understanding and corporate effort of these two enterprises. As observed earlier none of the SOEs have paid sufficient attention to analyze product market conditions. More specifically this should include study of market size, market growth and competitive conditions. This analysis has to be performed for each product/product group separately. Because effective market strategies and action programmes always result from such detailed exercises. Especially the CCC and NPC should adopt this type of approach in analyzing the product market and classify their product groups according to their strategic value. Hence, effective market strategies could be designed for each product group separately.

5. Conclusion and Recommendations

The emergence and growth of SOEs in Sri Lanka was due to many reasons such as the Second World War, political ideology, emphasis on social welfare, government import substitution policy and self-sustained economic growth. Currently SOEs function in almost all sectors of the economy. Hence the performance of SOEs has a direct influence over the overall economic development of Sri Lanka.

The commercial profitability and value added contribution of SOEs studied in the present study has been unsatisfactory for the period 1982 to 1987. Only the SLTC has registered satisfactory results on return on investment for the years 1985, 1986 and 1987.

The SOE system in Sri Lanka is highly influenced by a wide range of external environmental factors, supervising Ministry, Central Treasury, factor market conditions and product market conditions. They are expected to perform satisfactorily in turbulent times of rapid change.

The operational activities of the three SOEs are guided by their operational (annual) budget. Except SLTC, the other two SOEs have not linked up their annual budget with the corporate plan. It is merely a document prepared in line with supervising ministry requirements. The supervising authorities are of the opinion that planning exercises performed at enterprises level are unrealistic due to non availability of information and inadequacy of managerial skills in planning. Moreover, the three SOEs have not paid sufficient attention to evaluate possible future changes in external environment. There should be a strong and continued commitment of management for planning in order to achieve more flexible and realistic plans.

In view of the above findings the following recommendations could be made to improve the performance efficiency and organizational effectiveness of SOEs.

5.1 Recommended Action at Enterprise Level

1) Top management should define the mission and objectives of the enterprise clearly. Through this long term vision top management should try to provide direction and vision for change and new product development for middle level and shop floor level managers.

2) Top management should also create an appropriate R&D organizational structure within the organization and R&D departments must be managed by the top management. Due recognition should be given to R&D work and importing of new technology.

5.2 Recommended Action at National Level

R&D activities at enterprise level should be adequately supported through grants, subsidies and other support facilities by the supervising ministry and Central Treasury. The Government should also promote and encourage technical collaboration agreements between SOEs and foreign organizations in order to gain access to modern technology.

Conduct organization development workshops for the SOE sector. This has to be arranged for each SOE separately. The target group should include sectional heads of the enterprise and representatives from the supervising ministry and Central Treasury. The subject coverage should include review of policy changes and regulatory mechanism, setting objectives, analysis of future scenarios, setting targets, strategy formulation and designing action programmes. The services of a process consultant are also recommended. The programme should be sponsored by the supervising ministry or Central Treasury.

5.3 Action at the APO Level

A course on planning with scenarios seems to be very essential in improving corporate planning skills at enterprise level. The target group should include top executives of SOEs. The subject coverage should include identification of future scenarios and assessment of their impact over the performance of SOEs. This could be an international training programme for APO member countries.

Develop a training manual on corporate planning for the SOE sector. The purpose is to improve managerial skills on corporate planning at middle level managers through a series of training programmes.

The APO should also function as a coordinator in sharing modern technology among its member countries. This could be achieved by conducting within industry specific training programmes focusing on creativity and technological innovations.

Notes

1. For detailed account on growth and development of SOEs in Sri Lanka see NIBM (1979)
2. See Rees, R (1976)
3. See Amarasinghe, A.R.B. (1971)
4. See NIBM (1979)
5. See NIBM (12/8/1986)
6. Unpublished ILO Report on Survey of Management Practices in Public Sector and Private Sector Manufacturing Enterprises (1985)
7. See MISA (7/10/87)
8. See ICPE (1985)
9. See APO (1986)

References

1. National Institute of Business Management, (NIBM), *Public Enterprises in Economic Development of Sri Lanka,* ed. W.D. Lakshman (1979)
2. Rees, R. *Economics of Public Enterprises*, Morrison & Gibb Ltd. (1976)
3. Amarasinghe A.R.B., *Public Corporations in Ceylon*, Lake House Investments Ltd. (1971)
4. Ministry of Industries & Scientific Affairs (MISA), *Financial Discipline & Cost Control*, Proceedings of the Seminiar (12/8/86)
5. Ministry of Industries & Scientific Affairs, *Work shop on Tender Procedure* (7/10/1987)
6. Ministry of Industries & Scientific Affairs, *Review of Activities*, (1985 and 1986)
7. International Center for Public Enterprises in Developing Countries (ICPE), *Public Enterprise*, Vol. 5, No. 3, pp. 265–282 (1985)
8. Asian Productivity Organization (APO), *Management for Technology Innovation*, Report on APO Top Management Forum 1986

Annex 1   SLTC Organization Chart

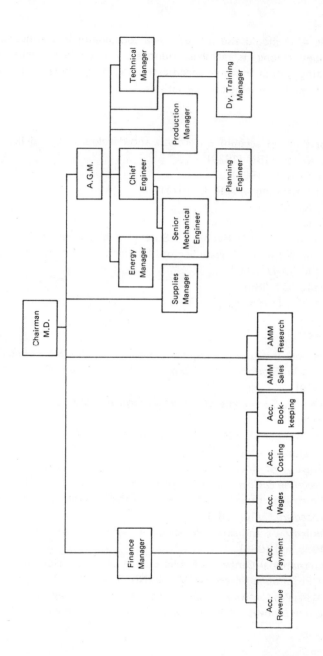

Annex 2   NPC Organization Chart

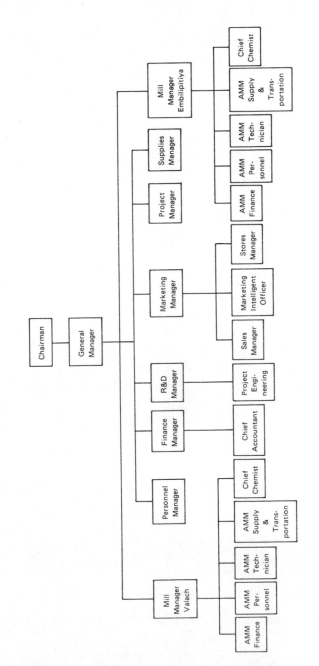

Annex 3   CCC Organization Chart

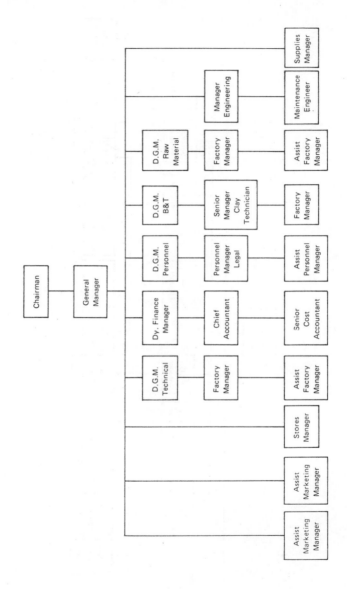

Annex 4 Presentation of SLTC Profit & Loss Statement within an Economic Analytical Format to Derive Value added 1982–'86 (Rs.M)

	1982	1983	1984	1985	1986	1987
Product Flow						
Revenue	+281.6	+309.5	+339.1	+360.2	+410.3	+455.1
Less Business Turnover Tax	−14.0	−23.2	−35.0	−36.0	−40.7	−43.4
Intermediate Payments	−167.6	−225.7	−223.0	−216.9	−236.9	−275.3
Value Added Product Flow	+100.0	+60.6	+81.1	+107.3	+132.7	+136.4
Income Flow						
Employee Compensation	−43.3	−48.9	−55.8	−64.7	−77.3	−80.9
Net Interest	−0.9	−6.2	−3.6	−3.5	−2.1	−2.5
Depreciation	−4.0	−5.2	−5.8	−6.7	−7.0	−7.7
Net Profit	−51.8	−0.3	−15.9	−32.4	−46.3	−45.3
Value Added Income Flow	−100.0	−60.6	−81.1	−107.3	−132.7	−136.4

Source: SLTC Annual Accounts

Annex 5   Presentation of NPC Profit & Loss Statement within an Economic Analytical Format to Derive Value Added 1984 –'86 (Rs.M)

	1984	1985	1986	1987
Product Flow				
Revenue	+481.8	+561.6	+628.6	+674.2
Business Turnover Tax	−44.4	−53.1	−60.3	−64.7
Intermediate Payments	−367.5	−419.3	−450.7	−496.1
Value Added-Product Flow	+69.9	+89.2	+117.6	+113.4
Income Flow				
Employee Compensation	−21.5	−26.7	−26.7	−32.3
Net Interest	−3.9	+0.5	+3.9	−6.6
Depreciation	−33.7	−26.3	−32.1	−31.6
Net Rent	−0.9	−1.0	−1.1	−1.4
Net Profit/Loss	−17.7	−34.7	−56.0	−39.8
Value Added Income Flow	−77.1	−88.2	−112.0	−111.7

Source: NPC Annual Accounts

Annex 6   Presentation of CCC Profit & Loss Statement
within an Economic Analytical Format to
Derive Value Added 1982–'86 (Rs.M)

	1982	1983	1984	1985	1986	1987
Product Flow						
Revenue	+240.5	248.0	+234.1	+263.4	+277.3	+271.5
Less Business Turnover Tax	–9.0	–14.4	–17.1	–18.9	–21.1	–21.6
Intermediate payments	–135.2	–128.8	–114.2	–114.2	–121.1	–113.3
Value Added-Product Flow	+96.3	+104.8	+102.8	+130.3	+135.1	+136.6
Income Flow						
Employee Compensation	–70.7	–85.3	–91.9	–100.0	–113.5	–113.5
Net Interest	–4.3	–12.7	–15.6	–15.3	–13.7	–11.5
Depreciation	–10.8	–5.8	–5.1	–4.9	–4.5	–4.4
Net Rent	–0.5	–0.5	–0.6	–0.7	–0.7	–0.5
Net Profit (Loss)	–10.6	–0.5	+10.6	–9.5	–2.7	–4.9
Value Added Income Flow	–96.9	–104.8	–102.6	–130.3	–135.1	–134.8

Source: CCC Annual Accounts

Annex 7   SLTC Fixed Assets (Rs.M)

	1983	1984	1985	1986	1987
Land & Site Development	2.6	2.6	2.6	2.7	2.7
Building & Installations	21.8	21.1	20.8	19.9	19.4
Plant & Machinery	46.0	49.1	57.5	58.1	61.2
Equipment	1.5	1.5	1.3	1.4	1.9
Motor Vehicles	1.0	0.8	1.5	1.1	2.1
Technological Documentation	0.1	0.1	0.1	—	—
	73.0	75.2	83.8	83.2	87.3

Net Current Assets (Rs.M)

	1983	1984	1985	1986	1987
Stocks at Cost	134.7	146.3	155.0	199.3	192.6
Current Receivables	15.1	19.9	18.3	23.7	31.5
Deferred Revenue Expenditure	0.6	—	—	—	—
Deposits & Payments	6.2	7.2	5.5	6.9	10.1
Advances to Employees	6.3	5.5	7.9	7.6	7.1
Investments	1.3	1.3	7.1	3.5	3.7
Cash & Bank Balance	1.5	(7.3)	0.7	0.3	0.4
	165.7	187.5	194.5	241.3	245.4
Current Liabilities					
Current Payables	18.1	11.2	48.5	62.3	79.6
Income & Tax	16.9	9.3	21.1	23.6	16.2
Tax on Remittance	5.5	18.1	2.5	2.2	2.2
Consolidated Fund	14.0	3.0	7.0	6.0	5.0
Advances Retentions Deposits	0.4	3.2	0.9	2.7	2.5
T.R. Loan	6.5	15.1	—	11.0	—
Bank Overdraft	—	—	0.7	4.2	5.0
	61.4	59.9	80.7	112.0	110.5
Net Current Assets	104.3	127.6	113.8	129.3	134.9

Source: SLTC Annual Accounts

Annex 8   NPC Fixed Assets (Rs.M)

Particulars	1983	1984	1985	1986
Land Buildings	3.5	3.4	3.1	3.1
Land Development	3.4	2.7	2.3	1.7
Building & Structure	61.7	60.2	57.7	54.9
Housing Scheme	10.2	9.7	9.0	8.6
Furniture, Fittings & Equipment	1.1	1.0	0.8	0.8
Building Services	3.0	2.5	2.0	2.7
Process Equipments	158.5	148.3	124.3	109.1
Non Process Equipments	9.9	8.9	7.3	6.0
Process Appurtenances	24.2	20.8	17.6	14.2
Utilities	40.5	36.7	32.7	28.5
Vehicle & Agri-Equipment	2.2	0.6	0.4	3.1
Capital Work in Progress	5.5	175.0	181.4	185.5
Preliminary & Deferred Expenditure	9.7	3.7	1.9	—
Investment in Lanka Chemical Company	168.9	0.2		—
	502.3	473.7	440.5	418.2

NPC Net Current Assets (Rs.M)

Current Assets	1985	1986	1987
Total Stocks	287.1	263.9	268.1
Trade Debtors	117.9	78.8	88.9
Short-term Investments	—	81.9	146.5
Deposits and Payments	136.3	26.6	80.9
Other Current Assets	—	26.1	25.5
Cash Balance and Bank Balance	22.1	128.5	20.6
	563.4	605.8	630.5

Annex 9   CC Fixed Assets (Rs.M)

	1983	1984	1985	1986	1987
Fixed Assets Net Value	376.8	419.7	410.0	401.0	398.9
Capital Work in Progress	0.3	0.5	0.3	1.9	5.6
Investment	213.8	436.8	237.5	241.5	241.5
Long Term Loans	—	—	26.5	27.0	29.2
Fictitious	9.3	—	—		
Total	600.2	857.0	674.3	671.4	675.2

Net Current Assets

Current Assets	1983	1984	1985	1986	1987
Stocks & Stores	138.9	151.9	157.5	130.0	127.7
Debtors	39.5	49.5	26.0	32.2	31.8
Deposits and Payments	17.8	16.6	9.6	20.2	12.5
Advances and Loans to Employees	9.3	10.2	9.9	10.8	11.0
Treasury Deposits	5.5	5.5	5.4	5.5	5.5
Cash and Bank Balance	18.6	18.7	25.6	33.1	20.4
	229.6	252.4	234.0	231.8	208.9
Current Liabilities					
Taxation	28.0	27.7	27.7	28.4	9.6
Creditors	28.5	26.5	8.8	7.3	9.7
Accrued Expenses	11.3	15.8	30.7	41.1	18.8
Advance/Deposits	184.3	439.9	9.5	9.2	8.1
Prov. for Goods Await Inv.	4.7	2.1	2.9	2.9	6.9
Prov. Fixed Assets & Sta. Diff	8.1	8.9	9.9	10.5	8.4
Bank Trust Receipts	15.9	13.3	18.4	20.6	2.9
Bank Overdraft	26.8	27.9	26.7	24.9	5.9
Total	307.6	562.1	134.6	144.9	70.3
Net Current Assets	(78.0)	(309.7)	99.4	86.9	138.6

Source: Ceylon Ceramics Corporation

Annex 10   SLTC — Sales (Nos. '000)

Item	1984	1985	1986	1987
Truck Tyres	88.6	77.8	80.4	81.8
Car & Jeep Tyres	74.5	100.9	80.4	68.8
Light Truck Tyres	43.5	36.8	73.5	101.3
Scooter & Motor Cycle Tyres	5.2	11.4	24.9	36.0
Tractor Tyres	7.8	7.2	10.5	14.3
Radial Tyres	—	—	9.4	18.5
Tubes	170.5	154.9	153.5	175.5
Flaps	33.3	30.0	35.6	41.0
Carpets	0.4	1.8	4.8	4.0

Source: SLTC

NPC Sales

Item	Unit	1984	1985	1986	1987 Jan—Jun
Valachchenai — Paper & Boards	MT	13406	14077	15400	8182
Embilipitiya — Paper	MT	6577	8577	9969	5169
Converted Items	MT	529	331	448	137
Ex. Borks	Nos. Min.	11.8	8.1	4.7	1.9

Source: NPC

CCC Sales

Item	Unit	1984	1985	1986	1987 Jan—Jun
Crockery	MT	3280	2815	2797	1506
Sanitary-ware	MT	725	775	831	358
Insulators	MT	223	88	244	133
Mosaic Tiles	MT	454	250	—	—
Kaolin	MT	7730	6440	4279	2094
Ball Clay (Raw)	MT	11669	12371	16319	6223
Hydrated Lime	MT	369	771	722	330
Bricks & Tiles	Nos. Min.	18.7	20.6	22.0	8.3

Source: CCC

Annex 11 SLTC Capacity Utilization

	Unit	1986	1987 Jan—Jun
Installed Capacity	Std. Tyres	298900	149350
Present Effective Capacity	Std. Tyres	238960	119480
Actual Output	Std. Tyres	183935	96619
Utilization	%	61.6	64.7

Source: SLTC

Capacity Utilization

	Installed Capacity	1986	1987 Jan—Jun
	MT	%	%
Valaichchenai Mill	22500	73	79
Embilipitiya Mill	15000	67	70

Source: NPC

CCC Capacity Utilization

	Unit	Present Effective Capacity	1986	1987 Jan—Jun
Crockery	MT	4075	85%	70%
Sanitary-ware	MT	1000	90%	78%
Insulators	MT	360	66%	84%
Kaolin	MT	8700	72%	69%
Ball Clay (Raw)	MT	15000	136%	140%
Feldspar	MT	—	na	na
Quartz	MT	—	na	na
Hydrated-Lime	MT	5400	16%	4%
Bricks & Tiles	Nos. Min.	30	74%	68%

CASE STUDIES: NEPAL

by Mr. Deepak Thapa
General Manager
Bansbari Leather & Shoe Factory Ltd.,

Introduction

An in-depth survey of the following three enterprises representing successful cases of Nepalese SOEs was undertaken. The information and conclusions drawn from these may be relevant and useful to many SOEs of Nepal.

1) The Agricultural Tools Factory Ltd., an example of the results oriented process of management and technology innovation.

2) New issues in Marketing Management. The Janakpur Cigarette Factory losing monopoly.

3) Tariff policy: Nepal Electricity Authority.

When the right manager, with the appropriate educational background, work experience and aptitude is selected for an enterprise a major part of the internal management problem is over. In the case of ATF, the external environment is not currently an obstacle as in earlier periods. The present management is able to achieve, by building on its inner strength, cooperation and support from the external environment including the controlling agency, the public, i.e. clients, as well as foreign organizations. The achievements are tangible.

In the second case study — The Janakpur Cigarette Factory Losing Monopoly — the conclusion of the author is that even the most able SOE, reputed in terms of its profitability, contribution to Government treasury and employment, may experience a downfall when its monopoly is over. The Janakpur Cigarette Factory although conscious about the probable future challenges which it may have to face, is nontheless a little confused as to what steps it ought to take in the future. The planned establishment of another cigarette factory with its 51% share is a golden opportunity to reallocate its manpower. All it needs to do is pay attention to Marketing and Corporate Planning strategy.

In the third case study — the Nepal Electricity Authority, it was revealed how difficult a merger can be. This, is perhaps because Nepal is experiencing its first merger of this size and scale. Although the merger is a very appreciable and essential step for HMG, its settlement is very difficult. The merger has a great understanding of pricing, but settlements are required more quickly in order to provide timely management input on corporate planning and pricing.

Case Study I — The Agriculture Tools Factory Ltd.

1. Environmental Context

The Agriculture Tools Factory Ltd. was established and began production in 1968 as a limited liability company, with Russian assistance in machines and HMG subsidies amounting to Rs. 10 million initially. It uses results oriented management and technology innovation. Objectives specified in its initial project documents were:

- import substitution
- to manufacture agriculture tools for distribution and demonstration to farmers, at a uniform price throughout the kingdom
- to develop prototypes by comparing the agriculture tools manufactured abroad and in Nepal. Analyzing their cost/price advantages to Nepalese farmer

The context of the establishment of the ATF is indicated by the conicidence of this period with the revolutionary step of Land Reforms Programmes launched by HMG slightly before ATF's establishment, i.e. during the Second Three-Year Plan (1962–65). There was a need to raise agricultural productivity for which the farmers needed improved tools and implements.

Because of its interlinked objectives with agriculture, the ATF has been under the jurisdiction of the Ministry of Agriculture. The Ministry of Agriculture is responsible for directing the company in formulating its plans and programmes, budgets, and to monitor, evaluate, and control its activities. The jurisdiction over planning and budgeting, and financial control, however, is spread to other agencies, particularly the National Planning Commission (NPC), the Ministry of Finance (MOF) and the Auditor General's Office, as in the case of other SOEs.

The majority of the farmers in Nepal have fragmented land-holdings. The Land Reforms Programme (LRP) contributed to this as it set an upper limit to land holdings of 25 bighas (slightly more than 25 acres) in the Terai (plains) and 50 ropanies (about 4 acres) in the hills. This was done in the spirit of distributing land to the landless tenants at more concessional prices with various buying and selling schemes, thereby encouraging intensive farming and agricultural productivity. Because of the small size of holdings, and the further redistribution of land after the LRP, highly mechanized large scale farming was not considered essential. This was due to the comparative high cost to average yield in small holdings. Yet farming needed mechanization, as labour productivity in Nepal is low, and manual farming too troublesome.

This fact was not well understood by the previous managers of the ATF, and so they always concentrated on the traditional items such as spades, scythes, shovels, khukri (Gurkha knife), picks, bullock drawn ordinary ploughs, pedal paddy threshers. As a result the factory was not able to sell much, resulting in excess stock on hand, thereby creating a need to approach HMG for subsidies. It also prohibited expansion.

In 1982, with the appointment by HMG of a new General Manager, this situation changed. After accessing his abilities as General Manager he was later promoted to Executive Chairman. This man, as he himself said, was well aware of what the public expected from his factory. First of all he was an agri-Engineer by profession, who worked as an agri- Loan Officer for 6—7 years in the Agricultural Development Bank of Nepal, and later in the Industrial Services Centre for another 5—6 years as Management Consultant. This background, coupled with personal intelligence enabled him to better manage the ATF after his appointment in 1982.

The changed process after his entry into the ATF in 1982 was a management and technological innovation which is indicated in this study mainly by the organization, management and R and D efforts before and after 1982.

2. Organizational Context

Prior to 1982, the organization of the ATF was simply a dull hierarchical layer of people, everyone doing what they were compelled to do but without much of the required initiatives and team-work to run an organization. The organization had two DGMs under the General Manager, (see Table 1) one responsible for Administration and the other responsible for Technical i.e., production, and engineering aspects. The GM or Chief Executive had all the authority (not delegated) but they (DGMs) were supposed to run the organization with required intiatives.

The R and D activity was a small cell under the Production Division. The R&D Activities were carried out by a separate institution, the

Table 1 Organization Chart of the ATF Prior to 1982

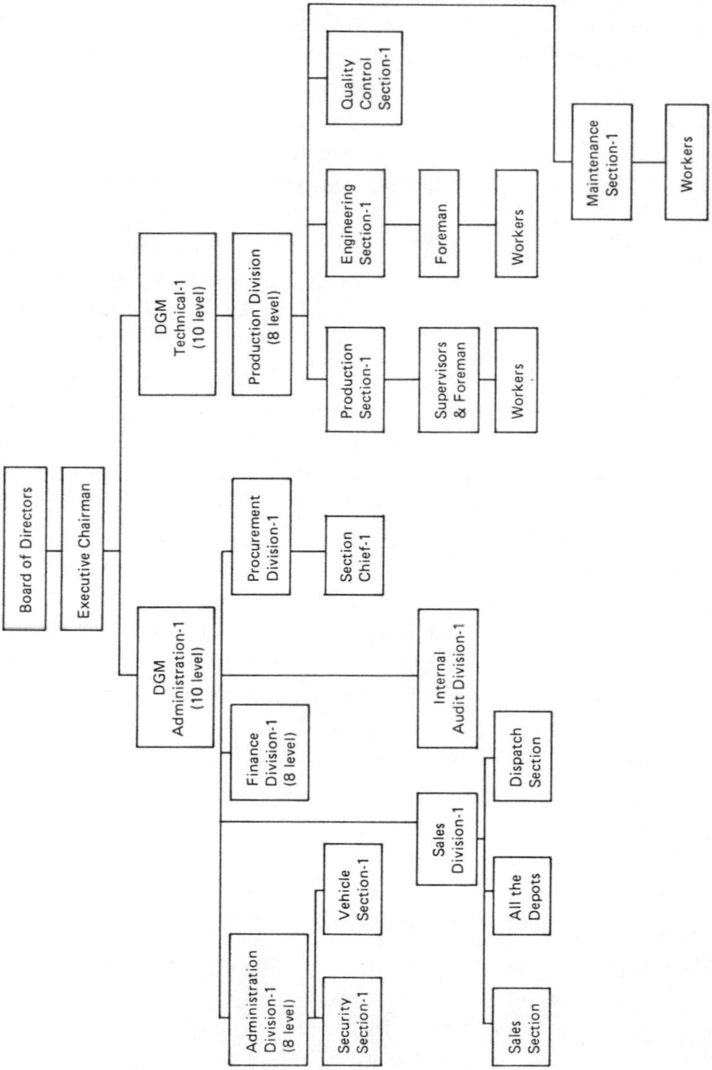

Agriculture Implements Research Centres in Birgunj, but there was no coordination between this institution and ATF. The organization lacked a corporate planning cell. Too much influence was held by the Administration, Finance and Internal Audit Divisions. The Technical Divisions had virtually no say in procurements of raw materials, machines or parts. There was a Sales Division but not a Marketing Division. Mostly, traditional items were manufactured, and quality control was very poor. The only known innovation done at that time was the pedal paddy trasher, apart from this all the items were traditional as will be seen from the functional context.

After 1982, the organization structure was changed. The changes occurred in non technical divisions as well as the technical divisions. A new R&D Branch was created in the initial years, and recently because the Agricultural Implements Research Centre (AIRC) became defunct, the ATF planned for and achieved an important consolidation of the AIRC in the ATF. (Mr. A.B. Karki, Executive Chairman, ATF, ESCAP/Technical Advisory Committee of the Regional Network for Agricultural Machinery Twelfth Session 23–27 Feb., 1988, Islamabad Pakistan, Country Report of Nepal). The R and D Branch was changed to a Divisional level and it is currently made responsible for R&D activities in regard to agricultural tools and implements.

A new Corporate Planning Cell (Divisional level) was recently established. The Sales Division was converted into the Marketing Division with more functions of market research. The Pumpset Division, a newly created division, manned with an 8th level Mechanical Engineer is to manufacture pumpsets in collaboration with the Kirlosker Company of India. The Quality Control Section has been adequately manned and made more alert.

One important purpose for organizational change is to achieve functional inter-relationship, this has been achieved by the new management. First, there are no longer two DGMs in the organization. The technical aspect is being directly supervised by the Executive Chairman. The important divisions, i.e. the Finance Division, the Procurement Division, the Corporate Planning Division, are also under the direct supervision of the Executive Chairman (see Table 2).

In addition to the above mentioned changes in the organization, a new Productivity Improvement Committee (PIC) has been created under the authority of the Executive Chairman (see Table 3). This committee provides organizational commitment and participation of relevant personnel in productivity improvement. All the Divisional and Section Chiefs of the technical divisions including the Production

Table 2   Recent Organization Chart of the ATF
1987

Total Staffs: 267

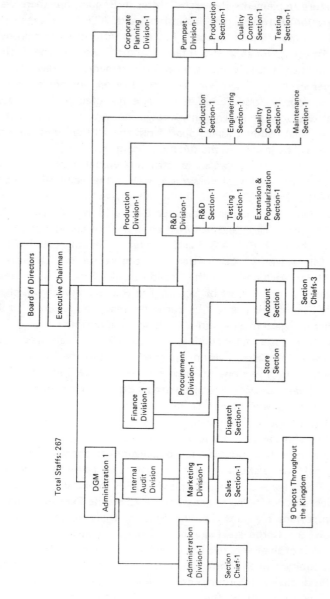

Table 3   Organization of the Productivity Improvement Committee (PIC) 1987

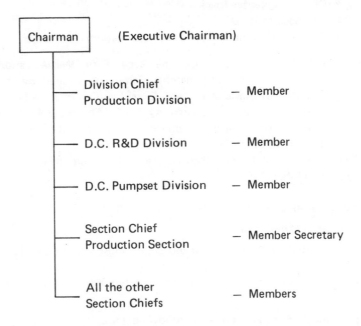

Chairman	(Executive Chairman)
Division Chief Production Division	— Member
D.C. R&D Division	— Member
D.C. Pumpset Division	— Member
Section Chief Production Section	— Member Secretary
All the other Section Chiefs	— Members

Division, R&D Division, Pumpset Division and Marketing Division are members of this committee with the Chief of the Production Division as secretary. The PIC meet, at least, every month to discuss issues in R&D, manufacturing process and to evaluate their impact on marketing and productivity improvements.

The expansion of the R&D Division was done so as to assign additional responsibilities and functions to this division as follows:

- R&D section
  - Research
  - Prototype development
- Testing
  - Testing prototype
  - Collect result
  - Feedback R&D
  - Feedback production
  - Forward to extension & popularization
  - Get feedback on a reverse order

- Extension and popularization
  - Extension of the developed model
  - Obtain market feedback
  - Feedback to R&D
  - Do market promotion (of a technical nature)

The R&D Division also houses the Nepal Farm Mechanization Committee (NFMC) a fourteen member committee chaired by the Secretary, Ministry of Agriculture and Executive Chairman, ATF as Member-secretary recently constituted by HMG. The R&D Division is entrusted with preparing agenda, convening meetings and documenting policy & decisions of NFMC.

The functions of all other divisions are obvious from the organization structure (Tables 2 and 3).

3. Functional Context

3.1 Changes in Manufacturing

Prior to 1982, ATF used to manufacture mostly traditional farm implements such as spades, sythes, picks, shovels, khukri, and bullock drawn ordinary ploughs. The only modern item was a pedal paddy thresher.

Currently the ATF manufactures the following items:

- Power thresher (for wheat or paddy) 5–15 HP range which is 5 times more efficient than hand threshing.
- Hand thresher (wheat or paddy)
- Bullock drawn disc harrow 5 times more efficient than traditional wooden harrow, and comfortable to use.
- Bullock cart wheel rim with pneumatic tyres as a substitute for traditional wooden wheels, advantages being, road preservation, quiet, trouble free.
- Hand operated paddy transplanting M/c (in process of R&D not yet issued to the market).
- Seed-cum-fertilizer drill both hand operated and animal drilled is 3 times more efficient compared to bullock drawn (prototype developed and is in final stage of production).
- Tractor trailer 1–10 tons capacity; marketing has been started, but sales are not yet encouraging.
- Corn sheller for threshing corn (hand operated). It threshes 6 quintals of corn per day and is very comfortable to work.

- Pumping sets (power driven). Power pumps, centrifugal pumps and engines in 5 HP to 8 HP in collaboration with Kirloskar Oil Engines Ltd. (KOEL) of India.

The production Department has six sections and is equipped with a variety of machine tools and equipment. With its emphasis on production of high value-added and higher technology products the ATF has started subcontracting the manufacture of smaller brand tools, and spare parts to village blacksmiths. ATF management reports that this is not only social justice, but also cost effective. Materials, gauges, jigs, fixtures etc. are provided by the ATF to such entrepreneurs to ensure quality of production to uniform standards. Such artisans are trained for about one week before they are subcontracted for the job.

The result of high value production has increased ATF product quantity from 350 M/T in 1980 to 400 MT in 1987.

However in value terms, total production increased from Rs.3.8 million in 1980 to Rs.15 million in 1987. (ATF management). With the initiation of the production of pumpsets in 1988, targeted to produce 2,000 pumpsets annually, total production value can be expected to increase substantially by 1990. For a detailed comparison of products by each category past data was not available in sufficient detail.

Previously, the manufacturing processes were crude but currently wih the development dyes, jigs and fixtures, as well as the addition of some pneumatic and machines, the production process has become more scientific and smooth.

3.2 Changes in Marketing Management

Prior to 1982, marketing was delegated to sales and what severely lacked in this area was contact, communication and feedback from the market place on a continuous basis. The present management, realized that there is free import of agricultural implements, i.e. no protection to ATF because of the government policy of providing cheap inputs to agriculture. The management, during the early 1982s, undertook a study throughout the major agricultural pockets to gain an understanding as to what extent imported machines were used by farmers. The results of this study revealed that it was price-competitiveness, good quality and design and convenience in handling which received the consumer votes of products manufactured. This study was undertaken throughout all their nine depots.

A second important aspect they discovered was that most farmers (consumers), usually importing machines from the India/Nepal border towns, received after sales services from the Indian Manufacturers free of cost. Thirdly, the promotional strategy of the Indian manufacturers was another factor.

After completing the preliminary survey of consumers, the top management immediately prepared a marketing strategy and working plan for the ATF which was approved by the Ministry of Agriculture. Their strategies included:

1) Pragramatic market development schemes by integrating marketing activities with their R&D Divisions as well as the Production Division. First a product idea would come from preliminary market research which is regularly carried out by the Marketing Division together with the section Chief of the Extension and Popularization Section. New products for development by the ATF meant those imported machines that are popular among consumers, are not very sophisticated or costly (because the ATF is not in a position to handle this at the present stage), and are good market prospects.

2) The ATF then procures one such machine from India or abroad. The R&D Division then analyzes every part of the machine in detail to study the manufacturing process. In the case of a machine which they already manufacture but sales are sluggish, a comparative techno-economic study is undertaken with focus on cost and benefits to both consumers and the factory where it is in use, along with the technical attributes of its qualities. At this stage the Quality Control Section is also closely consulted.

3) The R&D Department then produces a report which is presented to the Executive Chairman and the PIC. If the project is feasible then it is formally approved by the PIC for research. The R&D Section then prepares a blue print, based on which, the prototype is developed within an estimated cost and time. The product is then tested and feedback given to the R&D Section. Acceptable products are presented to the PIC and the PIC finally approves it for test marketing at a price fixed by the concerned officials.

4) Finally the products are initially sold based on consumer's orders, and then commercialized. They know in advance, from their consumer survey and correspondence with consumers, whether they are in need or not. Because the Marketing Division is in constant touch with those consumers, it does the follow-up work on receiving their orders.

5) Once the products start selling to consumers necessary arrangements are made for the distribution of the products directly through their depots, the Agricultural Inputs Corporation of HMG, and the Cooperative Societies. Market promotion is done through regular radio programmes, demonstrations, poster displays and individual direct contact with the farmers.

6) There is also an after sales service of roving teams of technicians backed up by a Marketing Engineer who repair and service free of cost. All ATF products are provided with a six month warranty against manufacturing defects with free replacement of the defective parts if any.

3.3 Productivity Changes

As a result of th PIC, the R&D and Quality Control, considerable productivity changes have occurred from product development to the production stages in a number of manufactured items. Data could not be collected for all the items. However, data was collected for two items. For tractor drawn cultivator and power wheat thresher (5 BHP), the labour productivity index increased by 50% and 38% respectively, machine hours decreased by 15% and 18% and price reduced by 10% and 18% as a result. (see Table 4). The Management Reports that many productivity changes occurred also in paddy thresher, corn sheller, and pneumatic tyre/rim manufacturing. However, quantification was not possible in these items.

3.4 Personnel Management

As a small unit personnel management is not so complex. The Administration Division looks after the personnel policies and planning. However, because the Executive Chairman himself is so intimately associated with the staff functionally as a team, he takes lot of initiatives in posting the right man in the right job. One of the most important things which the Executive Chairman did recently was to get quality products. He involved staff from Quality Control and R&D together with the Chief of Procurement Division in procuring necessary raw materials locally or from India. This was done to ensure that the right type of raw material was imported.

Table 4   Product Improvement

(A)   Tractor Drawn Cultivator

No. of Times = 9

Description	Old Design	Improved Design
1. Weight of Material	205 kg	185 kg
2. No. of Component Parts	23	18
3. Production Lead Time (Machine Hours)	34 hrs.	29 hrs.
4. Labour Productivity Index	100	150
5. Price of Equipment (NRs)	9,450	8,500 (−10%)
(B) Power Wheat Thresher (5 BHP)		
1. Weight of Material	225 kg	185 kg
2. No. of Component Parts	33	29
3. Production Lead Time (Machine Hours)	57 hrs.	47 hrs.
4. Labour Productivity Index	100	138
5. Price (NRs)	9,500	7,800 (−18%)

3.5 Financial Performance

The ATF has been operating at a loss each year from 1968/69 to 1986/87. However the loss was reduced from Rs.3 million in 1980/81 to Rs.0.9 million in 1986/87. In the current FY 1987/88 the ATF is expected to make a marginal profit because production volume increased from 400 MT last year to 800 MT during the current FY. By 1990, after the pumpsets in joint collaboration with KOEL are manufactured, the ATF expects that this shall be a major step towards self-sufficiency. For the present, however, the management team reports that part of the reason for not being able to make financial profit is partly because it had to satisfy arrears and dues from the bank.

4.   Conclusions and Recommendations

The Agriculture Tools Factory (ATF), at one time was almost forgotten by the general public, because it had no contact with the public at large nor were its activities pleasing to its controlling agencies. It has today however been able to revive its reputation as a centre for management and technology innovation. With the vision, abilities and concerted efforts of its management, many changes are taking place. It has innovated nine new products, six of which are commercialized, and three are in the process of being commercialized soon. It has built up a very efficient and strong Production Management, Quality Control, and R&D System. It has achieved Organizational Cordination, specifically, by realizing functions of the technical divisions, and a market and consumer oriented approach in production.

As a result of its image, the KOEL of India is willing to participate in joint collaboration with the ATF in manufacturing pumpsets. The total turnover has been increased from Rs.3.8 million in 1980/81 to Rs.15 million in 1986/87, and is expected to increase to Rs.30.4 million by 1987/88. (HMG/MOF, targets and Achievements of SOEs op. cit. p. 2). Capacity utilization of machines has increased from 60% in 1980/81 to 90% in 1986/87.

Major changes have occurred in labour and capital productivity and its efforts in making its products both price and quality competitive is appreciable. With its image and concerted efforts it was announced as a national secretariat of RNAM of which the Executive Chairman ATF is a National Director.

Its policy of product diversification has also restored employment opportunities for the small man, the village blacksmith, whom the ATF trains and sub-contracts the production of petty hand tools from. The ATF itself concentrates on heavy and high value products. Although its total success is yet to be seen in terms of making a profit, the present tempo of managerial improvements if maintained can certainly take it to its destination soon. The following suggestions may, however, be made to provide added dynamics in its management innovation.

1) Currently, the DGM and the Administrative Divisional Chiefs seem to be less involved in the process of organizational decision-making, which is of a technical nature. However they should have a role to play, for example, in personnel planning and policies, financial planning, budgeting and control and even in the PICs. In fact, sometimes the leadership of a technical person in an organization can fail to provide absolute harmony in the organization perhaps because he is too busy building the technical and more important image of the organization. Institutionalization of institution building cannot be achieved unless there is total harmony and functional integration at all levels and departments of an organization. If cost control or profit maximization is the goal or right of technical departments it is also the goal and right of the administrative and financial departments.

Lack of leadership sharing and exchange between the Executive Chairman, the DGM and other functional heads hamper the issue of institution building. Its future becomes uncertain as to what would happen when the present Executive Chairman is transferred and a new man with administrative background is brought in.

2) The corporate planning cell has not been able to develop a long term corporate strategy. In fact, in the absence of a long term corporate strategy, the management does not have any idea as to what it will be doing after 10 years. The corporate planning cell should be strengthened by assigning to them the preparation of a long term corporate strategy and assisting them by providing necessary manpower which they lack at present.

3) The existing depots should not only be engaged in selling the few goods that ATF manufactures. Perhaps it would be worthwhile to give them the necessary jigs, saws, fixtures & other modest equipment to attract local artisans in processing agricultural hand tools through subcontracting in the various depots where it becomes feasible.

4) Staff members are currently getting regrettably low opportunities for training. With the exception of some key staff from the Production Departments most have not received training. To improve the management system, further training seems necessary in the following areas:

- Corporate planning
- Quality control
- Product development
- Personnel planning

Case Study II — Janakpur Cigarette Factory Losing Monopoly

1. Environmental Context

Ever since its establishment in 1964 under Russian Aid, employing Cheez machines, (automatic blending, mixing and processing) with an initial investment of Rs.2.72 crores, (including the machines received as a grant, with land, buildings and working capital made available by HMG) the JCF is probably the only public sector industry in Nepal that shows not only an outstanding record of sales and profit but also leadership qualities and dynamic management traits. This is evident by its rapid expansion, growth, quality and competitiveness over the long term. Starting from an installed capacity of 2,000 million sticks in 1964, the JCF today has been expanded to 5,500 million sticks installed capacity of which 95% is utilized. The years between 1964 and 1968 were its most difficult time when its initial brands of cigarettes Asha and Gaida were not able to penetrate the domestic market.

Government protection was there but the majority of the population had a preference for imported/local bidis (tobacco folded in leaves), imported cigarettes (for high and low income groups), and locally manufactured cigarettes by two local private sector companies:

- The Nepal Cigarette Company at Birganj and Nepal Tobacco Company at Hetauda.
- The then famous brands — Parbat, Sagarmatha were designed to supply low income groups. It took some time for the JCF to take lead in Nepal.

After some time (1968), once consumers realized the taste, JCF brands began to be more and more popular in the domestic market. With Custom Duty on cigarette imports increased up to 350%, the JCF brands are becoming very popular and powerful judged in terms of an average annual growth rate of almost 12 — 15% (ISC Study on Marketing Management of the Janakpur Cigarette Factory, 1984 p. 12) (Note however that its original Asha brand has totally lost ground.) JCF's reputation in terms of growth, self-sustenance, contribution to government treasury, and to social reforms (it offered the highest recorded grant to the Pashupati Trust of Rs.7 lakhs last year) has increased. As is seen in the organizational and functional analysis, JCF is not totally free from managerial limitations. In fact, in recent years, a new company by the name of Surya Tobacco Company (STC) is beginning to give competition to JCF. This competition, at present is mild, but given its missions, and long term strategy one should say that the JCF cannot afford to underestimate STC's likely challenge in the future. The STC was registered with the Department of Industries (DOI) as a private company in 1982, but its production started December 1986. Its feasibility study was done by the Indian Market Research Bureau (IMRB). Initially, it started with a total capital investment of Rs.95 million from the following sources:*

Issued and paid up capital	Rs.15 million
Consortium loans from NABIL, NIDC, NBL, GRINDLEYS and INDOSUEZ Banks	
Fixed Assets	Rs.50 million

---

* Any data/informations obtained from the STC are strictly confidential according to STC Management.

Working Capital   Rs.30 million

Total Investment: Rs.95 million

A comparative study of the objectives of the JCF and the STC indicates that the latter is firmly determined to expand and hopes it can become a competitor of the JCF. When interviewed, the STC's Managing Director wanted to be modest by saying that STC's entry into the market is of a 'supplementary' rather than a 'competitive' nature. His view is not unjustifiable because there is still a large portion of unmet captive demand for cigarettes in Nepal (75% in 1983 according to the I.S.C. study op. cit. p. 20). One should not, however, be misled by simple arithmetic such as this. Actually one cannot deny the fact that STC is going to be a competitor to JCF in the future, although it is difficult at this stage to forecast whether it can be a potential threat or mild competition. This fact can be judged with the benefit of comparative study of the objectives of the two companies. For example, while the STC has an objective of cultivating tobacco in Nepal, the JCF has an objective of only facilitating tobacco development and production locally. In fact, the JCF has not been successful on this accord as will be seen later. Secondly, another objective of the STC is the 'import substitution of a major order'. Thirdly, the STC aims to improve the channels of distribution, meaning to cover a wider network which the JCF seems to have overlooked, at least as part of its objectives. All these factors indicate that the STC enters the market with a firm plan and long term and well designed strategy which can be a challenge to JCF in the long run.

1.1 Comparative Objectives of the JCF and the STC

JCF

- import-substitution of cigarrettes
- to facilitate tobacco development and production locally
- to generate Government revenue
- employment generation

Source: JCF Management

STC

- profit
- cultivation of tobacco in Nepal
- import-substitution of a major order
- improving channels of distribution

- employment
- revenue to HMG

Source: Managing Director, STC

1.2 Controlling Agency

As a general rule applied to all SOEs, the JCF must get approval on its annual/periodic plans/budgets from its Controlling Agency, i.e. the Ministry of Industry. The jurisdiction for planning, budgeting, monitoring, evaluation usually spread over to the Ministry of Industry (MOI), the National Planning Commission (NPC), the Ministry of Finance (MOF). The jurisdiction over financial control is taken over by HMG/ Auditor General's office. In the case of STC there is no controlling agency but its activities are regulated and controlled by the Department of Industries (DOI).

Consumers' Survey undertaken by I.S.C. in 1983 entitled Markeing Management of the Janakpur Cigarette Factory (Op. cit. p. 22) revealed that both rural and urban consumers rated a high score (among qualitative high, medium, low scores) to the JCF brands, i.e. Yak, Gaida, Koselee, Deurali, Dovan (the two brands Sayapatri and Laliguras were not explicitly indicated in the ISC report in terms of brand ratings). Brands were rated in terms of the following:

- fragrance
- taste
- smell
- strength
- flavour
- availability
- indigenous character
- its use till the last puff

Koselee appears to be being driven rapidly out of the market. Partly because it faces competition from the Khukuri brand of the STC (see following para.).

In terms of price, Gaida was considered reasonable by the consumers (N.Rs.4.20 retail price per packet of 20 sticks unfiltered cigarettes), so was Deurali (N.Rs.2.30 retail price per pack of 20 unfiltered cigarettes). However, only 50% of the consumers interviewed under the ISC study indicated the price of Yak (N.Rs.8.50 retail price per packet of 20 filtered cigarettes) to be reasonable.

Laligurans (N.Rs.12.50 retail price per packet of 20 filtered cigarettes) and Sayapatri (N.Rs.13.50 retail price per packet of 20 filtered cigarettes) were generally considered as too expensive.

Besides the positive attributes of JCF Cigarettes, Consumer's opinions regarding the negative attributes were, in general, as follows:

- poor tobacco compactness
- poor packing
- big rough sticks appearing in tobacco

In general the ISC study shows a general acceptance of the JCF products in terms of price and quality attributes, except in the case of Laligurans and Sayapatri. One can access this fact due to increasing consumption of all the JCF brands except Laluguras and Sayapatri (see Section 3).

In the past, the JCF was able to drive its competitors (as mentioned above) from the market, thereby establishing its monopoly. However, it is currently facing its new competitor, the Surya Tobacco Company (STC). In this context, the ISC Study alone would fully explain the buyers' behaviour. In view of this, one dealer of the STC at Kathmandu and 40 retailers at Kathmandu, Janakpur, and Hetauda (selling both JCF and STC products) were interviewed. They indicate that the STC is providing tough competition to the JCF with two of its three brands at present. Khukuri (filtered) which is comparable to JCF's Koselee (also filtered) is preferred by buyers because they like its taste and other attributes (price comparison: Rs.7 Koselee vs. Rs.5.50 Khukuri per pack of 20 sticks). Also the fact is that Koselee was not so popular, in urban areas, even prior to the introduction of new cigarettes by STC. Secondly, retailers report that buyers are also indicating a reasonable preference for Bijuli, STC's second product, over its JCF counterpart Deurali in rural areas but not in urban areas. The third brand of STC, Naulo comparable to Yak of JCF, has not met with any success due to its inferior taste compared to Yak. Thus the buyers' behaviour shows that there is a class of consumers who dislike certain brands of the STC products to some brands of its JCF counterparts on grounds of quality and price. For JCF this should amply indicate what the public expects.

2. Organizational Context

The JCF is almost 5 times bigger than STC in terms of installed capacity and more than 10 times bigger in terms of organizational strength. Naturally this would have major implications on the cost of goods sold between the two companies. This could not be compared as the STC wants to keep its operating costs and P/L Accounts strictly confidential. However, STC being a private sector industry usually offers higher pay-scales and emoluments to its employees compared to that of JCF. Here again comparison was not possible as STC did not disclose anything related to costs and income.

Organizational Strength (Comparison)

STC Simra (1988) Total: 255	JCF Janakpur (1986) Total: 2,700
Direct workers in Factory: 230 (90%)	Direct workers in Factory: 1,000 (38%)
Management Staff: 25 (10%)	Management Staff: 1,700 (62%)

Source for JCF: HMG/Ministry of Finance, Targets and Progress Report of SOEs 1987.

Although organizational cost comparisons were not possible, the organizational strength as well as its distribution between direct factory related workers to white collar jobs (9:1 for STC vs. 3:5 for JCF) places the STC at a highly advantageous position in terms of labour productivity.

2.1 Organizational Structure

Table 1 and 2 show the organization of STC and JCF. The STC Board is comprised of seven shareholding members — one chairman (part time) and six members plus Managing Director (MD) who is an employee and acts as Board Secretary. Under the Managing Directorate there are three Managers one for Finance, Factory Management and Marketing Management. Being a small organization, factory administration at Simra is also taken care of by the Factory Manager. All the Managers report to the MD with his office in Kathmandu which is about 170 kms. north of Simra — the Factory site. The Financial Controller as well as Marketing Manager are also posted to the Kathmandu Office. The Factory Manager, posted to the factory is responsible for day-to-day administration plus the technical jobs — production management, R&D, design, testing, quality control, under him there are 17 Supervisors and many direct workers.

The Financial Manager and the Marketing Manager each have 3 assistants.

The Marketing Manager deals directly with six dealers appointed by the STC to cover the following seven major towns of Nepal and their

Table 1 Organization Chart JCF (Janakpur)

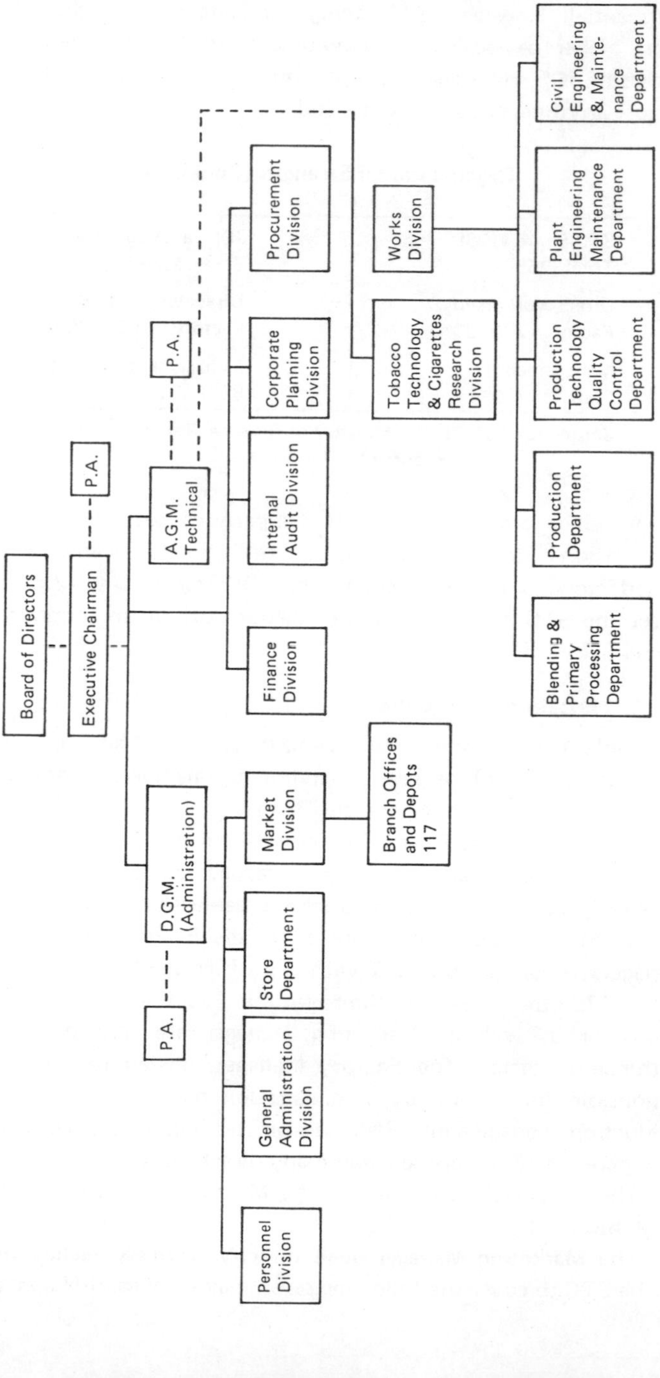

Table 2 Organization Chart STC (Simra)

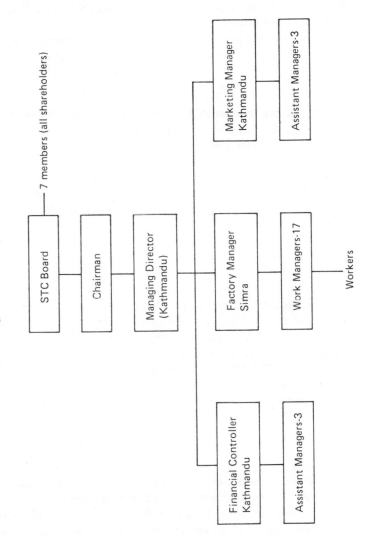

adjoining hill or rural areas:

- Kathmandu, Narayanghat, Hetauda and Briganj
- Bhairahawa and Butwal
- Biratnagar
- Pokhara

- Central Development Region
- Western Development Region
- Eastern Development Region
- Mid-Western Development Region

No dealers are apoointed from the Far Western Development Region but the STC has future plans for this. The dealers appoint wholesalers and the wholesalers distribute cigarettes to retailers. The dealers are given a spread of 1.5 — 1.7% as commission. Credits are also provided as required, but with thorough assessments of risk factors associated with a particular dealer by studying his past records and good will in business. Appointment of dealers is done jointly by the MD and the Marketing Manager.

The Management information system is equipped with direct telephone lines between the factory at Simra, the Branch office at Kathmandu, and all the dealers in different locations. The offices at both Kathmandu and Simra are equipped with intercoms. Regular procurement, dispatch of cigarettes, receipt of sale proceeds, do not need to come to the MD. However, decision for credit to dealers, appointments of dealers, procurements of costly plants, and raw materials, as well as pay/emoluments raise, bonus, need to come to MD with justification. The MD has the authority to sanction, procure or spend any amount within the limit of budgets and plans, with a note to the file. All he needs to do is consult the Chairman and Board Directors by phone call if the amount involved is too big or the issue too important. But there is no defined quantitative limit. Similarly, the other top level or middle level managers do not have defined authority in terms of money.

But the top managers are all formally (or informally) consulted through an Executive Committee of all Senior Managers which meets once a week. Annual or periodic budgets/plans are prepared by the MD with the assistance of his various managers or hired consultant and approved by the Board.

Needless to say, with small and compact organizational strength, capable and qualified executives, tidy office and factory layout, and efficient MIS, the management decisions are prompt and well coordinated. The Kathmandu office with 25 employees is housed within four big rooms in the third storey of the centrally located Blue Star complex.

Compared to a private sector industry, the organization structure of the JCF is naturally departmentalized in the form of a steep organizational complex with layers of administrative and technical levels, typical of Nepalese SOEs in general.

The JCF Board is composed of a Chairman, who is also the Executive Chief of the enterprise appointed by the Cabinet, and four members appointed by their respective organizations, as follows:

- The Ministry of Industry   Under Secretary level
- Ministry of Finance   Director General Department of Excise
- Ministry of Commerce   Under Secretary
- Tobacco Development Company   Genral Manager

The Deputy Director Personnel Division is the Board Secretary. The Board acts mostly as a policy planning and controlling body. More importantly, the matters that come to the Board for approval are annual/periodic plans and budgets, operating rules, promotion of officers, and their appointments, purchase of tobacco/machinery and construction of buildings in amounts above Rs.1 million, and pricing of all brands of cigarette products. Similarly, the dismissal of officer level staff has to meet Board approval. In a conventional way, the JCF Board can be said to be autonomous. But at times they face pressures from their controlling agency, such as in 1981/82, Government pressures on maximum use of locally produced tobacco compelled the Board and the Management to buy too much local tobacco, despite poor quality, and the result was overstocking. (I.S.C., Management Study Report on Janakpur Cigarette Factory Ltd. 1982 p. A4)

Day-to-day management is run by the Executive Chairman with the assistance of a number of immediate subordinates and the various divisions, branches, and sections in the organization. The Executive Chairman is appointed by the cabinet. Under him there is one D.G.M. responsible for administrative affairs of the organization and to act as officiating Chief in his absence. There is an Assistant General Manager (A.G.M.) directly under the Executive Chairman who is responsible for all the technical matters and under whom there is the Works Division (composed of maintenance, blending & primary processing, production, production technology, quality control, civil engineering departments) and the Tobacco Technology and Cigarrette Research Division (composed of Tobacco Technology and R&D Departments).

The Executive Chairman directly supervises the Finance Division, the Internal Audit Division, the newly established Corporate Planning

Division, Procurement Division, and through D.G.M. the Administration and other Divisions. The Marketing Division is supervised by the DGM. Currently there are 400 dealers throughout the kingdom which fall under the jurisdiction of the Marketing Division. There are five Regional Officers at Nepalganj, Kathmandu, Janakpur, Biratnagar, and Butwal, and 117 depots of JCF under the Marketing Division, throughout the kingdom.

Each Depot is usually manned with a depot manager and clerk with the exception of developed towns such as Kathmandu, Birganj, Biratnagar, Nepalganj, Bharharawa, Butwal, Pokhara, Hetauda, Narayanghat where there are more staff. A great distinction between the STC and the JCF is the former does not have any branch offices or depots except in Kathmandu and Simara. Despite this STC has a strategy to improve its distribution channels by choosing the right type of dealer, the JCF has more than 260 employees employed in its depots. Even though, some brands of the STC are penetrating most parts of rural areas (e.g. Bijuli and Khukuri). According to the survey of retailers undertaken in the course of this study, the share of Bijuli vs. Deurali (of JCF) is on an increase in the rural areas. The strange purposes for establishing the depots tend to suggest their little worth (op. cit. p.c. 7):

- to supply stock to the dealers
- to invigorate dealers and cross-invigorate retailers to ensure that no areas are crossed (i.e.; no inter-dealer competition), stocks are well preserved in moth-proof, weather proof, air-heated godowns, no spoilt stocks are forced upon the retailers, and that cigarettes are sold at the right prices (fixed by JCF for dealers and retailers)
- to review their progress every month and report and recommend dealers or new dealers for appointment

Similarly, the conditions of dealership contracts are also unusual as indicated by the facts that:
- JCF can at any time dismiss a dealer without prior notice
- each dealer must report his performance to the depot or JCF (whichever is closer) every month
- each dealer is compelled to clear at least 90% of annual stock within a year, failing which, he may forfeit his security deposits or even have his dealership cancelled
- those dealers who choose to lift their stock periodically from their depots, must place their specific demand a month in advance at his depot

This combined with the excess staff at the Centre and Branch offices, as shown by layers, sub-layers, and large administrative staff (1,700 administrative staffers vs. 1,000 technical staffers in 1986/87) undoubtedly suggests that labour-productivity of the JCF should be in contrast with that of STC as can be indicated by sticks per employee of 166,666 for JCF vs. 235,300 for the STC.

A proportionate number of dealers must be appointed to the numerous depots. About a 30% reduction in JCF's operating costs is possible with proper personnel planning. Those funds can be reallocated to improving quality or reducing the price of cigarettes, which would make JCF products more competitive especially with STC products.

Gaida of JCF are currently in need of quality improvements to combat their negative attributes (explained above). Such negative attributes (rough tobacco sticks, non-compact tobacco in cigarettes and packing deficiencies) are virtually non-existent in the STC products particularly in Naulo which is currently sluggish in penetrating the market as a competitor to Yak of JCF. The retailer's opinon is that Naulo is deficient in terms of its taste and fragrance, which STC, as efficiently as they are run, can certainly improve in the future.

At present it appears that the JCF would benefit in terms of proper resource allocation by cutting at least 10% of its total staff (excluding the technical staff). Ironically, the top management is in no position to do this unless it is decided at the political level, as hiring is common but firing painfully difficult in Nepal. (see Survey Report Phase I, ref: Suv/III/86 2326 p. 18). Solutions should be found to resolve the staffing issue which is not merely a problem of the JCF but a common problem of all SOEs.

3. Functional Context

3.1 Top Management and the Board of Directors

Currently, the Board of Directors, including top management do not seem to have given enough attention to JCF's corporate planning and strategy formulation, or trying to clarify objectives, and operating norms. The BOD have simply not endeavoured to fix targets for JCF in terms of: financial rate of return, cigarette prices, spreads and commissions for dealers and between dealers and retailers, policies regarding appointment of optimum no. of dealers, depots, labour and capital productivity. The Corporate Plans are not prepared for mid-long terms. As a result, the JCF's objectives and strategies are not so evident (see also ISC, Management Study Report on JCF, op. cit. p. A3–A5). Everyone seems pleased with JCF's profit and its contribution to the state treasury, as well as employment generation. No one has bothered to ask what if the JCF begins to falter in the future with the loss of its monopoly?

3.2 Production Management

The Works Division is expected to use a high percentage of Nepalese tobacco in cigarettes. Therefore, as per notice of HMG and Top Management, the Procurement Division is supposed to procure tobacco from the Nepal Tobacco Company a parallel running SOE that encourages local farmers, particularly in the Terai plains, to grow and process their own tobacco. In the early 1980's JCF procured large quantities of tobacco from NTC, 30—35% of its tobacco, and discovered that due to low nicotine content, the quality of cigarettes, especially Asha, was poor. The consequence was the continued drop in sales of the Asha brand. (op. cit p. 16). Additional consequences were that in 1981/82 the JCF had 5,600 M/T of tobacco, worth about Rs.80 million, in stock for more than a year plus the extra cost of storage in godowns (working capital tied up).

After that experience, the JCF demanded its own choice of procurement, which was granted by HMG and the Board. Currently it procures almost 80% of its tobacco from India and abroad and 20% locally (Interview with the JCF Management). In the case of STC, currently it meets almost all its requirements from imports. The use of imported tobacco by the major cirgarette factories of Nepal have greatly affected the output of the NTC from 3,000 M/T in 1981/82 to 500 MT/ in 1985/87. However, until the NTC is in a position to improve its supply bottlenecks (including lack of motivation to farmers and quality and production costs of local tobacco) there is no point in forcing the JCF to procure local tobacco. Another fact is that the current price of local tobacco and imported tobacco (the cif border prices) adding internal transport & handling costs, are the same i.e.; fluctuating between NRs. 15—20 per kg. (JCF Management Information). However, the Indian and foreign tobacco procured by JCF has a slightly higher nicotine content.* This situation could see improvement if the NTC were consolidated into JCF under the vigilance of the Works Division.

The ISC study (op. cit. p. A10) indicated that the tobacco wastage and material losses were very high for JCF. This is because the process

---

* The desirable nicotine content is 1% while the Nepalese tobacco has a nicotine content variation from 0.3% to 0.8% (op. cit. p. 48)

of sorting tobacco stems, which ought to take place prior to blending, is currently taking place after blending. Secondly, there are problems in proper filling, tipping and dust and moisture control in tobacco. Thirdly, maintenance aspects are not being given due attention, machines are kept running to maximize production. As a result machines breakdown and protective maintenance becomes necessary.

Another problem of the Production Department is the frequent jamming of hoppers due to non-uniform processing of cigarettes. The efficiency of the making and packing machines are as follows:

	Making M/C	Packing M/C
Efficiency	80.9%	61.8%
	(97% in JTS)*	(98% in JTS)*
Tobacco wastage ratio	7.7%	1.5%

* JTS: Japan Tobacco and Salt Public Corporation

Other problems include cigarette breakage during production, and a lack of proper quality control prior to blending. At present, the JCF has achieved a 95% capacity utilization on its machines. This indicates very high productivity on its capital investment, which should be tested in terms of consumer preference, in the course of time. But before analyzing sales performance, and future sales prospects, the above analysis sufficiently indicates that there is a considerable need to improve the quality of JCF products.

3.3 Marketing Management

3.3.1   Size of Domestic Market

JCF started cigarette production by F/Y 1965/66 and until 1983/84 it had a market share of about 25%, according to the Marketing Management Study undertaken by ISC. Rupee-wise share of JCF was estimated to be 21.38% in the same year. The base of the cigarette smoking population in estimations done by the above ISC study also included smokers of Bidi and Kakad. These were included because with changes in the conditions of accessibility, as well as consumer incomes there would be a tendency to switch over to cigarette smoking. The JCF believes that it covers an 80% share of the market for cigarettes only (imported and local production). The STC Management, on the other hand, believes that it now has at least 40 — 50% (educated guess) of the domestic market for cigarettes, Bidis, Kakads. The MD reports that Nepal is the world's highest per capita consumer of cigarettes, 8.6

sticks per person per day, followed by the People's Republic of China, at 8 sticks.

In any case, the market for cigarettes is large. The production and sale by both JCF and STC cannot fulfill total demand at present. This fact is acknowledged by both the JCF Management and the STC Management.

3.3.2 Proliferation of Supply

Prior to JCF almost all cigarettes had to be imported into Nepal with a very small proportion of domestic demand being met by the two companies mentioned. Today, except for a few high priced sophisticated brands, Nepal is becoming self-sufficient in cigarette production.

In its earliest years, JCF produced 2 brands — Asha and Jwala. In 1966/67 it manufactured Singha, Chuchura, Janaki and Gaida (Rhinoceres). In the course of time none of the brands stood the test of the market except Gaida. Jwala, Singha, Chuchura and Janaki ceased production after 1969/70. Yak was introduced in 1972/73 at a retail price of Rs.3.60. Despite its rise in price Yak is gaining popularity and remains one of the most preferred cigarettes in urban and rural areas. Koselee, introduced in 1967/68, priced at Rs.2.60, was popular in its early years. Due to its irritating taste its popularity was gradually lost.

Later on in 1980/81 three other brands were introduced by the JCF, the Laliguras (king size filter) and Sayapatri, designed to supply upper income groups, and Deurali, for lower income groups. Laliguras and Sayapatri failed in the market due to unpleasant taste and high price. Deurali succeeded in the market.

Consumer's Survey by brand preference undertaken by ISC in 1984 indicates that Yak has the highest share of the market in urban and rural areas. Its success is due to its quality attributes and price. Yak is followed in the market by Gaida and Deurali, as indicated by consumer preference. See Table 3.

The Consumers' survey confirms the increasing sales of Yak, Gaida and Deurali cigarettes both in M. sticks as well as in Rupee terms while those of Koselee, Laliguras and Sayapatri show declining trends. See Table 4.

Compared to JCF products, currently the STC produces 60 million sticks on a monthly average. In the beginning it produced 10 — 20 million sticks every month. Total capacity of STC is 100 million sticks per month. If we assume that it shall continue to produce 60 million sticks per month, then its annual production shall be 720 million. This implies a 60% capacity utilization of its 1,200 million sticks annual

Table 3 Consumer Brand Preference

Brands Presently Smoked

JCF Region	Smoker Respondent Sample %	Sayapatri	Laliguras	Yak	Koselee	Gaida	Deurali	Others
Biratnagar Urban	270	8	5	191	9	47 (17.40)	6 (2.22)	4 (1.48)
Rural	358 (20.32)	1 (0.28)	9 (2.51)	250 (69.83)	3 (0.84)	83 (23.18)	10 (2.74)	2 (0.56)
Kathmandu Urban	38 (4.56)	– (0.00)	– (0.00)	24 (53.15)	1 (2.63)	11 (28.45)	2 (5.26)	– (0.00)
Rural	421 (23.9)	1 (0.24)	– (0.00)	129 (30.64)	2 (0.48)	134 (31.83)	109 (25.89)	46 (10.93)
Butwal Urban	165 (19.81)	1 (0.60)	– (0.00)	50 (30.30)	– (0.00)	62 (37.58)	49 (29.70)	3 (1.82)
Rural	460 (26.12)	– (0.00)	5 (1.09)	122 (26.52)	3 (0.65)	131 (28.48)	194 (42.17)	5 (1.09)
Nepalganj Urban	138 (16.57)	– (0.00)	1 (0.70)	72 (52.17)	2 (1.44)	55 (39.86)	8 (5.80)	– (0.00)
Rural	280 (15.9)	3 (1.07)	4 (1.43)	136 (48.57)	2 (2.86)	96 (34.28)	30 (10.71)	3 (1.07)
Janakpur Urban	222 (26.65)	– (0.00)	3 (1.35)	107 (48.20)	4 (1.80)	82 (36.44)	25 (11.26)	1 (0.45)
Rural	242 (13.76)	– (0.00)	6 (2.48)	135 (55.78)	3 (1.24)	65 (26.86)	33 (13.64)	0 (0.00)

(Figures in parenthesis are percentages)

Source: ISC, Marketing Management of the JCF, 1984 p. 120 and 121.

Table 4   Trends of JCF Sales by Brands

Year	JCF Sales in '000 Sticks					JCF Sales in M. Rupees				
	Deurali	Gaida	Yak	Koselee	Laliguras	Deurali	Gaida	Yak	Koselee	Laliguras
1977		407,607	70,006	8,642	7,079		58,083,998	21,001,800	1,901,240	2,831,600
1978		525,117	126,853	6,348	5,787		74,829,173	38,055,900	1,396,560	23,148,000
1979		625,158	166,834	6,027	3,469		89,085,015	50,050,200	1,325,940	1,387,600
1980		659,930	197,490	6,266	3,516		98,989,500	64,184,250	845,910	1,511,880
1981	817,946	530,284	327,801	10,688	1,292	59,301,085	79,542,600	106,535,325	1,442,880	555,560
1982	1,401,182	650,226	477,559	9,258	2,833	101,585,695	97,533,900	155,206,675	1,248,930	1,218,190
1983*	1,357,685	611,933	391,344	11,042	5,542	112,009,013	100,968,945	136,970,400	2,760,500	2,493,900

* Only ten month sales totals

Source: ISC. Marketing Management of JCF, op. cit. p. 60

capacity, which is at present only 21% of the JCF capacity. The MD of the STC reports that they have a monthly running average stock of 1 — 2 million sticks. In the case of JCF, stock is also not a problem for Yak, Deurali and Gaida.

3.3.3 Market Planning and Strategy Formulation

Both JCF and STC indicate that their future cigarette production and sales growth shall be in the order of 10 — 15% per annum. But in the case of JCF the growth rate shall be greater due to a plan to establish the Seti Cigarette Factory in the Far Western Development Region with an installed capacity of 650 million sticks per annum. The factory is going to be set up with 51% JCF share from its surplus capital and 49% private share, total authorized capital being Rs.6 crores as shown by the pre-feasibility studies. A detailed feasibility study has yet to be done. In view of this, the JCF needs to prepare a long term corporate plan and marketing strategy including a programme for R&D of its existing brands and new brands that it would want to introduce in the market. It should examine through such studies the following aspects:

- whether it should continue to manufacture the unpopular brands or if it decides to stop production of those brands, then what new brands it should introduce in the market. In doing this it can take advantage of the existing studies as well as initiate new research geared to discover what consumers want in terms of quality and price.
- among the existing brands it should have a strategy to improve some of the negative attributes of the preferred brands. (Yak, Gaida, Deurali).

Unfortunately, these steps have not yet been initiated by the JCF. The JCF is aware of the entry of STC into the market. But they are not currently thinking about its effects in terms of a corporate strategy. The JCF can take great advantage of a new marketing strategy which should be emphasized on three aspects:

- a strategy to improve quality of cigarettes by increasing its positive attributes based on consumer preference.
- an appropriate pricing strategy so as to be able to fare well in competition.
- better distribution channels and better dealership conditions that can motivate the dealers.

Currently adopted marketing strategy include:
- a costly approach of increasing depots and dealers.
- promotional tools such as advertisements, through local news media and coupons/sponsorship of foreign tours, luxurious equipments and other rewards.
- tours to various regions for inspecting the performance of dealers and retailers.

A marketing strategy must be very closely linked to production management, financial management and the whole organizational context including the difficult issue of personnel. Actually, by establishing the new Seti Cigarette Factory, the JCF shall have an un-solicited opportunity for transferring some of its surplus personnel to the new company. It requires a serious Marketing Strategy which should not merely be a forecast of production and sales, but should be a comprehensive study or action plan for both JCF as well as the Seti Cigarette Company (SCC). It should sufficiently touch upon the issues of:
- quality
- pricing strategy
- organization structure
- personnel policy
- production management (blending, making, packing and the whole issue of tobacco use and processing):

In doing this the JCF should give due regard to possible competition.

3.4 Financial Management

Earlier studies on the Financial Management of JCF have indicated that there was inadequate staff especially in the Accounting Department. (I.S.C. study, op. cit. p. D3). The cost finding system uses controlling accounts on general ledger, but not with separate subsidiary records based on costing forms. Procedures in use in the process of the costing system are not well defined. The costing information is formulated so as to know total product cost. However, it does not include the standard budget cost, labour time utilization, idle or spoiled time, M/c time utilization, spoiled or defective materials, fixed and variable expenses (not classified), direct and indirect labour. Needless to say, the lack of a management accounting system makes the time pressed management understanding of the productivity of capital and labour difficult.

Lack of written procedures/manuals on budgeting for both capital and operating budgets are hampering the process of budget formulation. It appears that there is a need for training the financial managers and accountants. (For financial indicators see Table 5).

3.5 Personnel

The personnel issue is mostly dealt with in section 2 (organizational context). The Personnel Division needs to be made more responsible for personnel planning.

**Table 5   STC and JCF — Financial Indicators
1987/88**

In Percentage

	J.C.F.	S.T.C.
1. Return on Sales	5.23	na
2. Return on Investment	13.4	na
3. Return on Equity	25	na
4. Net Worth (Rs. million)	10	na
5. Labour Productivity ('000 sticks per employee)	167	235

4. Conclusions and Recommendations

The JCF must be congratulated for being one of the most profitable SOEs which last year made a total profit (before income tax) of Rs.70 million and paid various taxes (excise, sales, income tax etc.) to HMH of Rs.460 million. It is a fast and steadily growing organization which initially started with a capital investment of Rs.20.67 million but is worth more than Rs.1,000 million today in terms of capital accumulation and net worth (Deurali, 1987 p. 10). Despite this, it is beginning to lose its monopoly and some brands of its cigarettes are losing their market. The STC, a new private sector company is giving competition to the JCF products. In this context the present study highlights the following summary of problems and recommendations.

4.1 Problems

1) JCF's Koselee, Laliguras, and Sayapatri brands of cigarettes are rapidly losing their share in the market. The former (Koselee) is partly losing its market share because it faces competition from its counterpart Khukuri manufactured by the STC, a private sector company, as a result of price and quality. The remaining two brands of

cigarettes are losing their share in the market because they are both expensive as well as distasteful to the consumer.

The JCF Management has so far taken no action on the issues of these unpopular brands. Neither their quality has been improved, nor have they been removed or replaced by other brands.

2)   Some brands of the JCF including Yak, Deurali and Gaida are very popular brands, as indicated by their rising trend in sales, and confirmed from consumers' opinion. Their positive attributes according to consumers' opinion are price, fragrance, taste, smell, strength, flavour, availability and indigenous character. However, these brands are not free from some negative attributes such as big rough tobacco stems in cigarettes, non-compact tobacco. About 50% of the Yak's consumers point out these defects.

3)   The products of the newly established Surya Tobacco Company (STC) — particularly Khukuri, Bijuli and Naulo are beginning to penetrate the domestic market. The Bijuli and Khukuri with all their positive attributes as well as price advantages, vis-a-vis their JCF counterparts Deurali and Koselee, have begun to outstrip them in the domestic market. Retailers' opinon is that Koselee has almost been replaced by Khukuri in the urban areas and Deurali is gradually being routed by Bijuli in the rural areas because both Khukuri and Bijuli are totally without any negative attributes, and price-wise they are cheaper. Naulo of STC designed to give competition to Yak at exactly the same price, has been unable to stand the test of the market so far. In fact the retailers' view is that Naulo is becoming unpopular, a fact acknowledged by its Managing Director.

The JCF is planning to establish yet another cigarette factory in Seti Zone (Far Western Development Region) with a capacity of 650 million sticks per annum and an initial authorized capital of Rs.6 crores, in which the JCF shall have a 51% share and 49% private sector participation.

4)   The JCF lacks a Corporate Plan with focus on more rational objectives, financial targets, pricing and marketing strategy, production planning and management to combat its low profile. The competition from STC which is approaching its bay at the moment should be seriously watched before it causes JCF irreparable damage. Looking at the objectives of the STC, e.g. to cultivate tobacco in Nepal, to improve distribution system and to substitute import of a major order, it appears that the STC has come up with firm grounding and strategy. Currently it has only six dealers, and no sales depots, but it is able to

give stiff competition to the JCF in Bijuli and Khukuri.

If we compare JCF and STC from the point of view of resource allocation, the STC with a smaller organization, high labour productivity (235,000 sticks per employee), and a technical to administrative manpower ratio of 9:1, it is a more flexible organization and far superior to JCF with its heavy/rigid organization, low technical to administrative staff ratio (3:7), and low labour productivity (167,000 sticks per employee).

The JCF needs to pay attention to all the above aspects both in formulating corporate plan strategy, and in the establishing of Seti Cigarette Company (SCC).

5)   The Works Division of the JCF needs to be studied in greater detail to ensure lower wastage rates in packing/making, and improving the production and blending quality of cigarettes. The STC did not permit the team a factory visit. So not much could be compared. However, they have a combination of Indian and German machines and highly qualified engineers. Also there is a need for training foremen and supervisors in areas such as plant engineering, blending, and maintenance.

6)   The Finance Division lacks manpower, a management accounting system, and proper budgeting procedures. Training is needed in managerial accounting and budgeting.

4.2 Recommendations

1)   The JCF should immediately prepare its corporate strategy covering at least a ten year period from 1988 — 1998. It should try to make its objectives more rational, keeping in its objectives only those things which it can fulfill (e.g.; its objective of facilitating Nepalese tobacco production). In addition to the objectives the JCF needs to make its strategies clear. For example, how it is going to achieve the policy of facilitating Nepalese tobacco production and use by taking over the operation from the present Nepal Tobacco Company, or other means.

The corporate plan thus prepared should be devised in the context of a more pragmatic marketing strategy with focus on how to combat its low consumer image in certain brands, or how to still exonerate the image on the existing popular brands by eliminating their negative attributes, particularly stem in cigarettes, and non-compact filling. For this purpose, the JCF should immediately mount a study of its corporate strategy. The study should be geared to resolving all the problems mentioned above. It should embrace the activities of the SCC also.

2)   JCF needs to immediately decide on a plan of action for Koselee, Laliguras and Sayapatri brands. It may be recommended that all these brands be discontinued. Instead of Sayapatri and Laliguras, a new brand being developed, catering to the high income groups and comparable in quality to the State Express 555 or Marlboro, feasibility study involving technical assistance of a tobacco technologist of high calibre, should be undertaken. In the case of Koselee, R&D work is necessary to come up with the best solution. The R&D should focus on both price-competitive options as well as quality improvements. However, the brand name should be changed.

3)   The JCF Management should make efforts to eliminate the negative attributes of the existing popular brands — Yak, Gaida and Deurali. The existing study by ISC has much in the way of suggestions, and there is no need for further consumer surveys. The JCF should involve the tobacco technologists and Work Division personnel in preparing a quick report on improving these negative attributes.

4)   The best strategy on dealership is to find the best dealer, who has a combination of network, public contacts, goodwill, and experience in distributing goods to the accessible and remote areas of the nation. At present, the good thing about STC's strategy is that the STC awards contracts to dealers, at a spread of 1.5 — 1.7% of the ex-factory price, who in turn sub-contract the award to wholesalers at more than this rate (the dealers did not want to disclose their spread rates), the wholesalers sub-contract the retailers at a still higher spread. The STC has only 6 reliable dealers and its does not incur any administrative costs. All it receives from its dealer is a quarterly progress report. The JCF may adopt a similar system, and like STC, can give credit facilities to the dealers. By doing this, the JCF can save the costs of operating depots. With this strategy we would argue that roughly 90% of the Depots can be eliminated with that personnel transferred to the SCC in the near future.

5)   In addition to reducing Depot staff, the JCF administrative staff needs to be reduced. At present technical to administrative staff ratio is 3:7 which is very low by any standard. Part of the administrative staff may be transferred to the upcoming SCC.

    Part of the problem can be resolved by transferring some of the administrative staff to the Finance Division where there is need for additional staff.

For the remaining staff, the JCF cannot immediately do anything to deploy them properly.

6) To ensure better coordination of work, the Production Department, the Plant Engineering and Maintenance as well as Quality Control Departments should be converted into one big Department under the Works Division.

7) A productivity profile of the JCF at various efficiency levels needs to be prepared.

8) Training of JCF staff is necessary in the following fields:
   - Corporate planning
   - Productivity concepts, measurement tools, methods of analysis etc.
   - Quality control and waste minimizing (technical)
   - Tobacco technology, with focus on blending, sorting etc.
   - Study tour of selected cigarette factories in Asian countries.

The above suggested training programmes are regularly provided by the APO. APO can make some special arrangements to make these available for the JCF staff and other SOEs of Nepal. It should also be mentioned here that such training facilities should be provided in Nepal because there appears to be a need for the staff of many other SOEs to obtain similar training. A study should be mounted by the APO to assess training needs of SOEs in Nepal. Such training needs assessments, and the providing of such training to employees should be limited to those SOEs who are in a position to take advantage of it. That is, those SOEs who show some managerial dynamism, and that the management is willing to achieve something.

Appendix 1: Production Targets of the Janakpur Cigarette Factory

Unit in 'M' (1M = 1,000 sticks)

FY	Target (M)	Achievement (M)	Value in Rs.'000
1982/83	2,124,400	3,039,727	431,614
1983/84	2,336,840	3,600,224	519,504
1984/85	2,700,000	4,213,559	650,935
1985/86	3,051,000	4,722,005	720,528
1986/87	3,356,100	5,261,835	877,418

Source: Deurali, 1987, A Publication of JCF.

Appendix 2: JCF Cigarette Sales Target and Achievement

Unit in M (1M = 1,000 sticks)

FY	Target	Achievement	Value in Rs.'000
1982/83	2,124,400	3,007,766	425,889
1983/84	2,336,840	3,572,621	515,450
1984/85	2,700,000	4,120,411	637,536
1985/86	3,051,000	4,775,004	728,922
1986/87	3,356,100	5,079,151	842,783

Source: Deurali, A Publication of JCF.

Appendix 3: JCF Taxes Paid to HMG

(Unit: Rs. '000)

FY	Excise	Sales Tax	Income Tax	Total
1982/83	173,544	60,443	15,862	249,849
1983/84	206,773	74,619	18,793	300,185
1984/85	240,082	92,531	23,732	356,326
1985/86	270,330	104,131	29,500	403,961
1986/87	304,264	126,794	29,242	360,300

Source: Deurali op. cit.

Appendix 4: CF Profit/Loss

(Unit: Rs. '000)

FY	Profit/Loss	
1982/83	28,796	Profit before Income Tax
1983/84	31,163	"
1984/85	57,668	"
1985/86	41,275	"
1986/87	70,000 (Estimated)	"

Op. cit.

Appendix 5: JCF Consumption of Tobacco

(Unit: kg)

FY	Nepali	Indian	Overseas	Total
1982/83	1,543,479	1,880,470	49,019	3,472,968
1983/84	1,163,663	2,628,084	122,303	3,914,050
1984/85	1,349,433	3,164,587	23,580	4,537,600
1985/86	1,658,466	3,422,034	–	5,080,500
1986/87	1,488,045	4,424,955	–	5,913,000

Source: Deurali op. cit.

Appendix 6: 1988 Retail Price of JCF and STC Products

JCF	No. of cigarettes in a package	Retail Price (W. Rs.)
1. Yak (filtered)	20	8.75
2. Sayapatri (filtered)	20	13.50
3. Laliguras (filtered)	20	12.50
4. Gaida (unfiltered)	20	4.20
5. Deurali (unfiltered)	20	2.30
6. Dovan (unfiltered)	20	2.10
7. Koselee (filtered)	10	3.50
STC		
1. Naulo (filtered)	20	8.75
2. Khukuri (filtered)	20	5.50
3. Bijuli (unfiltered)	20	2.25

Case Study III — Management of the Nepal Electricity Authority (NEA) with Reference to Tariff Policy

1. Environmental Context

1.1 Framework

1.1.1 Establishment

Nepal Electricity Authority (NEA) was established in August 1985 under the NEA Act 1984 (Special Charter), by amalgamating the various power subsector organizations, into a single corporate body to plan, construct and operate public power facilities in Nepal. The context of NEA's establishment and its Special Charter status, reveals that there was a need to improve corporate performance of the power subsector organizations by consolidating their objectives, functions, and authorities instead of scattering them in diverse directions, making coordination difficult, and the sum total of their output trivial. More importantly, through the creation of NEA, its new organization design, as well as its long term corporate strategy HMG hopes to:

- improve institutional superstructure (see Appendix 1) and through it address the immense future challenges facing the power subsector, chiefly the need to manage a $1.3 billion (in current terms) investment programme over the next 10 years (1986/87 — 1995/96) which is the largest ever undertaken;

- pursue a hydro — power — led export strategy of growth (see Appendix 2);
- fulfill socio-economic objectives pertaining to the power and energy policy of HMG (see Appendix 3).

1.1.2 Mission

NEA was set up with the following mission as defined in its Acts: "The development and maintenance of an economic reliable and safe supply of electricity to consumers in accordance with sound commercial principles and HMG's policies for national development."

NEA is still in a formative stage, due to delays in the transfer of assets and liabilities from previous power subsector organizations, although a detailed working procedure, valuations of assets/liabilities and organization design were long recommended by consultants (Coopers and Lybrand Associates) hired under ADB assistance. To date NEA has developed an organization structure and outlines for preparing a corporate plan which emphasizes the need for an appropriate pricing strategy based on Least Cost Generation and Expansion Programme (LCGEP) and Long Run Marginal Cost (LRMC). Needless to say, the long-run success or failure of the NEA greatly depends on its tariff policy, which is based on efficient resource allocation as well as equity considerations. This is underscored by its Missions and Objectives.

1.1.3 NEA's Corporate Objectives (as formulated by the NEA Act 1984)

- efficient resource allocation by adopting commercial principles (chiefly reduction of system losses, least cost generation and transmission, appropriate tariff policy).
- to ensure consumer's satisfaction from its services.
- making widespread use of electric power by expanding the hydro-electric network and the national grid.
- making electricity tariffs competitive vis-a-vis the traditional fuel wood, modern fuels (kerosene) and border tariff rates.

As a corollary to these objectives there are some specific conditions laid by the donor agencies (IDA/ADB) in the form of financial agreements required for obtaining international soft loan assistance. These are:

- that the NEA should achieve a minimum rate of return on investments (net assets) of 5.5% every year up to 1986/87 and 6% after 1986/87.

- that NEA should generate surplus equivalent to 1.3 times the debt service requirements.
- that NEA should maintain a debt: equity ratio of 3:2.

1.1.4 Financial Arrangements and Capital Structures

All the assets and liabilities of the liquidated Nepal Electricity Corporation (NEC), Small Hydro Development Board (SHDB), the Electricity Department (ED), and the Kulekhani Hydro Development Board (KHDB) were transferred to the NEA on the vesting date, 17 August 1985. Due to delays in verification, and revaluation of assets and liabilities, the actual capital structures and the consolidated balance-sheet of the NEA have not yet been prepared. The NEA intends to complete the process of valuation of all the on-going capital investment projects by F/Y 1988/89. However, to have some idea as to the probable capital structure of the NEA, we have a schedule of the HMG Fund for NEA prepared and recommended by Coopers and Lybrand Associates (ADB/HMG Consultant) as follows in Table 1.

In this regard some guidelines of the NEA Act are:

- Valuations of assets so transferred would be made at replacement cost.
- Ten percent of NEA's share capital shall be raised from the general public and the rest to be inherited from previous power subsector organizations.
- General meetings shall be held after 10 percent of NEA's shares are sold to the general public.
- Once the shares are sold to the genereal public and the General Meetings are held the Board of Directors, consisting of eight members, will be elected. Until the General Meeting is held, the BOD shall be as nominated by HMG.
- Also until General Meeting is held NEA's accounts shall be audited by the Auditor General's office (HMG). The auditor shall be as appointed at the General Meeting.

1.1.5 Responsibilities/Functions

- to recommend HMG on the formulation of short and long term power policies.
- to prepare plans for generation, transmission and distribution projects of Nepal's power subsector and to construct, operate and maintain the various generation stations, substations, distribution centres, and all the facilities related to distribution lines.
- formulate electric power tariffs (for approval by HMG).

Table 1 Nepal Electricity Authority Schedule of HMG Fund
(Disclosed in individual balance sheet as of 16 July 1983)

(Unit: Rs. '000)

Organization	Share Capital	Share* Allotment Suspense	Capital Reserve	Profit/Loss (Loss)	Grant-in-Aid	HMG Fund	Total
NEC	398,109	57,048	1,580,331	(15,558)	–	–	2,019,930
ED	–	–	–	–	691,344	189,201	850,545
KHDB	–	–	–	–	60,385	330,102	390,487
SHDB	–	–	–	–	16,727	42,634	58,361
	398,109	57,048	1,580,331	(15,558)	768,456	560,937	3,349,323

* i.e.:   Share allocated for HMG for value received transferred for a number of hydroelectric projects.

Source: C & L Associates, Final Report Design for The Nepal Electricity Authority January 1984, Figure 1, Schedule 9.

Note that due to the shift in vesting date from 1983 to 1985 the above capital structure had to be updated.

- import and export electric power with the approval of HMG.
- to sell electric power and to correct tariffs.
- to undertake necessary research and development work in relation to electric power generation, transmission and distribution.
- to make necessary arrangements for more sophisiticated training in related fields for preparing a cadre of skilled manpower.

1.1.6 Authorities

NEA enjoys full autonomy in the execution of its annual programmes including:

- power to raise loans from inside Nepal;
- to raise loans outside Nepal with the prior approval of HMG;
- to buy or sell power internationally with the prior approval of HMG;
- to formulate electric power tariff rates with the prior approval of HMG;
- full executing power to carry out such works as are necessary to fulfill its functions and duties.

Reference to HMG is only officially required on matters involving either national policies (e.g. uneconomic extensions of electricity supplies to be subsidized by HMG). HMG's finances (e.g. loans to be on-lent from the ILAs), export/import of power and tariff policies.

1.2 Controlling Agency

The major line Ministry with energy responsibility, the Ministry of Water Resources (MWR), acts as the controlling agency. It has general responsibility for all public sector activities related to electricity supply, with jurisdiction over the NEA. The Minister of Water Resources is also Chairman of NEA Board and Chairman of the Water and Energy Commission (WEC). The WEC secretariat (see Appendix 4 for organization) works closely with NEA in load forecasting, system planning, tariff design, and hydro-electric project preparation.

The NEA Act requires NEA to provide the MWR with certain information as to its performance and plans each year, more importantly:

- a report on audited financial statements, performance statistics, progress reports on the capital projects, manpower, and training programmes.
- plan for long term system development.
- tariff proposals.

Institutional responsibilities, for planning, monitoring/review or control on policy levels, are usually divided among the Ministry of Water Resources (MWR), Ministry of Finance (MOF), and the National Planning Commission (NPC), with the former recommending plans and budgets for approval jointly. The controlling Agency, the MWR, reserves the right through the NEA Act 1984 to approve plans/programmes involving foreign borrowing, the tariff rates proposed by NEA as well as the import/export of electricity.

1.3 Public Expectations

Interviews with the President of Nepal Consumers Association and various industrial undertakings inside and outside the Industrial Estate (Chiefly the Patan Industrial Estate with some problems of electricity supply), indicate a general unacceptance and resentment over the rapid increase in electricity tariffs between 1978 and 1985. They were disappointed that each time the rates were revised the consumers were neither consulted nor pre-notified. The rates were revised by 35% in 1978/79, about 56% in 1983, about 35% in March 1985 and 22% in August 1985. During the period between 1974/75 — 1984/85, the average tariff rate increased by 14% a year in current terms and 3% a year in constant terms. The main cause of resentment is the sudden and sharp spurt in the later years.

The President and General Secretary of the Federation of Nepal Chamber of Commerce and industry, (FNCCI) when interviewed, indicated that it did not matter whether the rise in tariff rates were geared towards improving the financial position of NEA, or making it self-sufficient as a condition for international borrowing. The crucial question that one should examine is to what extent their tariff revisions reflect internal efficiency or increased productivity of their own labour and capital employed. Their assessment is that capital and manpower in the NEA are not efficiently employed. This, they feel, is indicated by their overcrowded manpower resources, most of which are not properly utilized. The employment of capital is not based on least cost alternatives, as indicated by excess costly equipment, and a large number of costly expatriate advisors.

By consumer category, the households as represented by the Nepal Consumers' Association (NCA), indicate that significant unfavourable impacts face the middle class, who consume between 25 kWh and 300 kWh per month, for which they pay Rs.1.10 per kWh. The lower class, who consume up to 25 kWh per month are largely subsidized. They pay a flat rate of Rs.11 per month for the whole quantity consumed.

The upper class consuming above 300 kWh per month are well to do people with greater income levels. The gross assessment of the NEA is that, on an average, the lower-middle and middle-class would be spending between 5 and 15% of their household budget on electricity.

Interviews with industries and management within the Patan Industrial Estate with 85 industires, having 1,500 kW of installed capacity under two low voltages (one 11 kV and 440 Volt), indicate that the electricity bills of power intensive industries (Annapurna Chappel Industries, NECOENCO, Shanghai Plastics, Pasupati Rubber, J.S. Plastics, Bira Furniture etc.) comprise approximately 10 − 20% of their annual operating expenses. Even a modest rise in electricity tariffs would greatly jeopardize their operation. At preset the PIE makes a bulk purchase of electricity from the NEA at a rate of Rs.75 per kVA. It sells to industries at rates of, Rs.25/kW for small industries using electric power up to 80 kW installed capacity, and Rs75/kW to those with installed capacity above 80 kW.

The PIE Management makes running charges of:
- N. Rs.0.85 per kWh for industries above 80 kW
- N. Rs.0.90 per kWh for industries below 80 kW
- In addition it imposes a 10% service charge.

Since there are only two large industries the PIE mostly runs at a loss, last year's loss amounted to Rs.2 lakhs (approximately). Despite this, the PIE Management receives frequent complaints from client industries to reduce electricity charges. In addition, frequent break-downs caused by transformer explosion due to overloaded transmissions, and PIE's lack of funds to repair or replace transformers is causing problems.

All the repair and maintenance work is the responsibility of the industrial estates and they feel that the NEA should either reduce their rates or extend their services to cover repair and maintenance.

The Hetauda Industrial District (outside Kathmandu Valley) and the Balaju Industrial District (at Kathmandu) do not seem to have as severe problems as the PIE. This is due to the large number of large scale industries they accommodate. These large industries can afford to have their own electricians for servicing and repair of facilities on their premises. However, they too feel that the present rates are too high. In the case of Hetauda Textile Industries the electricity bill amounted to Rs.3 lakhs.

Industries outside the Industrial Districts, particularly Krishna Loaf and Biswo Furniture (both at Kathmandu) indicated that they pay 12 and 18% respectively, of their operating expenses on electricity.

They feel that any further rise in electricity tariffs would be most unwelcome.

2. Organizational Context

2.1 The Board of Directors (BOD)

NEA's Act specifies that the composition of its Board is eight members who will be elected at the annual general meeting. The general meeting shall take place once HMG has sold 10% of the NEA's shares to the general public, private shareholders could then be elected as Board Members. However, until this process is constituted, the Act specifies that the Board will consist of:

1) Honourable Minister of Water Resources   Chairman
2) Member, National Planning Commission   Member
3) Secretary, Ministry of Water Resources   Member
4) Secretary, Ministry of Finance   Member
5) Secretary, Ministry of Law and Justice   Member
6) Secretary, Ministry of Industry   Member
7) An Official designated by HMG   Member
8) A Representative of a Financial Institution   Member
     designated by HMG
9) Two non-governmental persons nominated by   Member
     HMG
10) The Managing Director of NEA   Member
                                              Secretary

     (appointed by HMG as Chief Executives of NEA)

2.2 Organization Structure

The current organization structure of the NEA as approved by the Board, is shown in Appendix 5. There are six directorates under the overall management/supervision of a Managing Director. Brief overview of their key functions, are presented below. Each Directorate, except Finance and Administration, is headed by a Director-in-Chief (DIC) responsible for a number of Departments under him, each managed by a Director. The Finance and Administration Directorate are presently being administered by the DIC Planning. Internal audit is a staff function reporting directly to the Managing Director.

2.2.1 Planning Directorate

- to advise the Board and Managing Director on Corporate Planning, System Planning, and other Corporate matters, and

policies.
- to prepare corporate plans, system plans, tariff structures, for approval by the Board as well as HMG.
- to carry out organization-wide monitoring and evaluation.

The Planning Directorate and the Finance/Administration Directorate are looked after by the DIC Planning, which is what was suggested by Coopers and Lybrand Associates, in their Design for NEA, Jan. 1984. One can see from the above functions/responsibilities of the Planning Directorate that it is given great importance. Tariff policy, and formulation of electric tariffs is an important function of the Planning Directorate.

2.2.2 Engineering Directorate

- to identify, and prepare detailed engineering designs for the generation and transmission projects for both the interconnected (grid) systems as well as the isolated systems. (Transmission is defined as all lines with voltage exceeding 33 kV).
- to maintain a pipeline of projects for decision of execution by higher authorities.
- to set NEA's engineering standards.

The Engineering Directorate works closely with the Water and Energy Commission Secretariat (WECS) and Water and Energy Resources Development Project (WERDP) currently assisted by Canadian Consultants from CIDA, from where it receives technical assistance.

2.2.3 Construction Directorate

- Construct, or make necessary arrangements to construct all large and small generation, transmission projects within NEA.
- Receive and review design documents from the Engineering Directorate.

The Construction Directorate's responsibility for a project is finished on the date after commissioning agreed with the Operation and Maintenance Directorate. But power sources with an installed capacity of less than 5 MW are directly handed over to the Distribution and Consumer Services Directorate (DCS).

2.2.4 Operation and Maintenance (O&M) Directorate

- operating and maintaining the generation and transmission

system of the Authority with the exception of isolated diesel generation of less than 5 MW capacity (directly operated by DCS)

- power system operation and control
- supply of electricity to the D&Cs Directorate
- maintenance of the Authority's heavy equipments
- operation and maintenance of all small hydro-plants and associated distribution

2.2.5 Distribution and Consumer Services (DCS) Directorate

- supplying consumers with electric power they require and collecting the revenue due from them
- to plan, design and implement the distribution system up to 33 kV distribution lines and substations whose incoming voltage is equal to or less than 35 kV
- to operate and maintain
  - i) the distribution network; and
  - ii) isolated diesel generation of less than 5 MW and associated distribution
- to establish procedures for and to execute all household connections, meter reading, billing, revenue collection and banking of money received
- to record system losses, rectify and take necessary action for its reduction
- consumer services
- collecting data for load forecasting

2.3 Finance and Administration

2.3.1 Finance and Accounts

- define, install and set to work all financial systems for NEA
- to produce adequate and timely financial information for the management and others in need (including the preparation of the Authority's consolidated annual accounts)
- to define, install and put into use the procurement and store systems, and process bills and payments
- to manage cash resources, working capital of the Authority
- to interpret the financial performance targets for the Authority

2.3.2 Personnel

- short-term manpower planning

- installation of personnel systems including levels of pay and grading, recruitment, promotion, retirement and discipline
- to begin the installation of a comprehensive personnel planning system by FY 1988/89

Problems of the existing organization structure with some implications to Annual Operating Cost:

1) First, the creation of too many Directorates in the NEA is not functionally advantageous. Four Directorates would suffice according to the following recommendations of the ADB Consultants:

   - Generation and Transmission (G&J) Directorate which would be responsible for project preparation, engineering works, construction and operation and maintenance. The advantage of integrating these functions is obviously the same as "the rationale" for consolidating the previous power sub-sector institutions into NEA, to integrate the engineering, construction and O&M responsibilities.
   - Distribution and Consumer Services Directorate (DCS) to carry out all the functions presently carried out by this Directorate (mentioned above) except generation of the projects up to 5 MW.
   - Rural Electrification (RE) Directorate which would be responsible for all rural electrification and small hydro-projects.
   - Planning, Evaluation and Finance (PEF) Directorate, essentially a Corporate Planning and Resource allocation unit acting as advisor to the Managing Director and the Board, other additional functions to include financial management as well as Personnel/Manpower management/planning.

Carefully viewed, it appears that functional structures of all the other Directorates except the PEF are correct. In the case of PEF, we disagree with the recommendations of ADB consultants to overload this Corporate Planning Directorate with Finance as well as Manpower/Personnel Planning. In essence, the Finance and Administration Directorate currently created by the NEA are correct and they should look into a manpower planning aspect also. This view is supported by the World Bank study (op. cit. p. 18). So altogether there should be five directorates. It should also be emphasized that the Finance and Administration Directorate look into the training aspect of personnel. However, this Directorate is not currently manned with a Director-in-Chief, and this, it is felt, is very urgently required.

2)   The present position classification of the NEA is too hierarchical as evidenced by several administrative layers of Director-in-Chiefs, Directors, Assistant Directors etc. Instead, each Directorate could be manned with a Director as a chief and under him directly placing functional engineers, supervisors, officers, and clerks as required. Again each Directorate has one technical support cell, one Account and Administration cell, as well as P.A. for both Director-in-Chief and Director. Needless to say each Director should be given one secretarial assistant depending on his/her work-load. All the administrative and accounting work should be performed by the Director with the help of functional support staff for each function within a Directorate. The same structure of administrative and accounting Cell, P.A. etc. in Branch Offices, Power Houses, Substations indicates a most hierarchical and extravagant organization structure with great wastage and inefficiency. Needless to say, reform on this line would save a good deal in annual operating expenses of the NEA, which ultimately would have its implications on labour productivity, resource allocation and tariff policy.

3)   On the vesting date the NEA inherited 6,677 personnel. At the end of December 1986, there was additional recruitment making the total number of personnel approximately 7,000. This easily gives the NEA the lowest annual sales and generation per employee in any Asian Country for which data is available (43 and 61 MWh respectively compaared to 93 and 153 MWh for Bangladesh, which is the next lowest) (World Bank, Nepal Power Subsector Review Aug. 7, 1987 p. 17).

Available data on consumer/employee ratio for NEA as compared to the utilities of other Asian nations indicates the following differences (Arun Adhikary, Study on Power Subsector Organization, Ministry of Water Resource p. 6).

Utilities/Nations	Consumers/Employee Ratio
NEA Nepal	25:1
CEB Sri Lanka	30:1
PLN Indonesia	90:1
NEB Malaysia	69:1
PUB Singapore	179:1

Salaries and allowances as a proportion of total operating expenses also increased from 53% in 1985/86 to 59% in 1986/87. (see Appendix 6). Salaries and allowances per 1,000 kWh increased from N.Rs.260 in 1985/86 to N.Rs.300 in 1986/87.

Secondly, there is a lack of Organizational cohesiveness in NEA. The NEA staff having come from the previous power sub-sector organizations e.g., the Electricity Department (E.D.) which was a Government Department, and the Nepal Electricity Corporation (NEC), have not been formally confirmed in post although they have been working there for nearly two years. The root of the trouble appears to be that for ED staff, as civil servants, promotion was much slower than for the NEC staff. As a result, former ED staff face the chance of being junior in salary and rank to former NEC employees with the same or fewer years' experience. The fact is also that many ED staff did not want to be transferred from the Government service with its higher prestige.

At present there is room for improving the organization structure and to make manpower planning effective in the NEA. NEA has not even implemented the short-term manpower planning system proposed by its consultant Coopers & Lybrand. One reason is that the Administration Department is not yet manned with a Director whose job description calls for an organization-wide manpower planning and training programme.

The World Bank (op. cit. p. 18) recommends that the job of Administrative Director should be:

- hiring and/or retraining staff to fill identified gaps.
- deploying surplus (and redundant) staff, that could include loaning them on a "pay back" basis to other Government entities.
- plan for enhancing sales and generation to employee ratio.

3. Functional Context (with particular reference to tariff policy)

3.1 Institutional Framework for Tariff Formulation

Tariff formulation is part of NEA's requirements for an Integrated Institutional Development Plan (IIDP). This arises from the stipulation in the NEA Act that NEA should submit, along with its audited accounts, an annual report to the Government providing:

- details of NEA's plans for future electricity supply.
- a detailed progress report on NEA projects.
- projected financial statements for the next five years including tariff policies, and projections.
- details of actions taken to implement government directives.
- any other information that NEA deems necessary.

The NEA is given power to formulate tariffs for electricity sales by virtue of Article 20 of the NEA Act. In substance, the Act does not define specific methods of tariff formulation but it has some implicit guidelines (based on a synthesis of the various clauses of the Act) that the NEA should have regard to:

- the present and future costs of continuing to supply additional power and energy to consumers at particular voltage levels at particular times of the day/year.
- the revenue required to meet loan covenants entered into with international lending agencies or other bodies.
- the social and distributional policies of HMG.

Within NEA, the Director Corporate Planning prepares recommendations on tariffs, in close consultation with the Director of Systems Planning and the Distribution and Consumer Services (DCS) Directorate as well as Finance and Administration Directorate. The proposed tariff is then reviewed by the NEA Board, after which the proposals are submitted to the Ministry of Water Resources (MWR), after which they proceed to the Ministry of Finance (MOF), the Cabinet and finally to H.M. the king for Royal approval.

3.2 Actions Taken by the Top Management Team in IIDP and Pricing

The top management team which includes the Board, the Managing Director as well as the Directors-in-Chiefs have not, to date, been able to submit to HMG the IIDP which includes a corporate plan, audited balancesheet and a revision of the electric tariffs as required under the new objectives/conditions stipulated by the NEA Act.

To provide a basis for discussion of the tariff issue, the World Bank/IDA Mission estimated the economic cost of supply of electricity. They were based on NEA's 'base case' load forecast, or zero option (i.e. without thermal generation except during peak) according to which total sales within Nepal are projected to increase at 12.4% a year during the period 1985/86 — 1995/96 and 5.7% a year during 1995/96 — 2005/06, (World Bank op. cit. p. 38) (Also see Appendix 7). The industrial and residential sectors would continue to be the largest consumers in the expansion of the Nepal interconnected system, projecting a combined 76% of sales in 2005/06. The industrial sector alone would account for 42%, the household sector 34%. The rest would be accounted for by the commercial sectors.

3.3 Major Assumptions of the "Zero Option"

1) Units generated are projected to increase at an average annual rate of 10.4% during 1985/86 — 1995/96 and at 5.7% during 1995/96 — 2005/06.

2) Load factor (ratio of average to peak demand) would show little change from the present 50.4% to 51% by 2005/06 without demand management and to 54% with demand management i.e.; time of the day metering and separate tariffs for separate times. The slow growth projection of load factor is due to projected increase in rural residential electrification with a projected load factor of only 25%.

3) In terms of the number of households, NEA projects an annual increment of 20,000 households every year through 1995/96 and then a progressive 60,000 h.h. per annum up to 2005/06. But because future connections are expected to cover a large part of rural areas this appears to be a very ambitions programme.

4) Besides the domestic supply, the base case projection focuses on the most likely export option, the 25 MW arrangement currently concluded between India and Nepal.

5) The System Loss Reduction Programme (SLRP) is projected to decline from the present level of 30% to 20% over the ten years period 1985 — 1995.

6) Management of demand as well as the differing tariffs for various times of day may lead to the rejection of the Thermal generation option as it would be very expensive. Then the demand would be mostly met by hydro-generation. (For details see Appendix 8). The analysis showed that the long run marginal cost (LRMC) was lower for the zero option sequence without thermal generation (1.25 Rs./kWh) compared to the Gas Turbine or other thermal sequence in which 10 — 15% generation would be made by thermal energy. (Rs.1.33/kWh).

7) Costs are estimated based on expansion plans and represent future costs rather than 'sunk costs'.

8) Standard cost estimates are based on the preparation for Arun 3, Phases I and II, although there are eight candidate hydro-electric projects to be considered each of which were studied to either the prefeasibility or feasibility levels. But the Arun 3 Phase I with 201 MW capacity 1986/87 — 1995/96 as well as Phase II, 201 MW up to the 2005/06 time horizon appeared to be sufficient from the zero option point of view.

9) Cost estimates were based on he present value of the capital and operating costs.

Finally it appears that the IDA estimates on the least cost generation and expansion sequence represents ideal cost per kWh: as it significantly undermines the operating expenses usually represented by the energy cost. Available reports did not make this point clear. To clarify this, the Director of the Corporate Planning Directorate was interviewed, and indicated that this includes the administrative and other running costs only for the Arun 3 projects selected. The total operating costs per kWh generated of the NEA as a whole are not reflected in the long run marginal costs. The Director of Corporate Planning, also indicates that there is a future Corporate Development Plan to estimate the actual cost of generation per kWh. However, the long run marginal cost (1 rmc) is a guideline which indicates ideal economic costs and economic tariff justified. It does not include the unnecessary overheads and running costs, except those pertaining to the specific projects undertaken.

Table 2   Average Revenue from Electricity Sales

1975 — 1985 N.Rs./kWh

FY	Current Price	Cost of Living Index*	Constant 1975 Prices	Index
1975	0.229	100	0.229	100
1976	0.262	105	0.250	109
1977	0.390	106	0.368	161
1978	0.387	117	0.331	145
1979	0.391	121	0.323	141
1980	0.435	136	0.320	140
1981	0.520	156	0.333	145
1982	0.522	178	0.293	128
1983	0.550	192	0.286	125
1984	0.795	204	0.390	170
1985	0.840	212	0.396	173

* Kathmandu Cost of Living Index
Source: World Bank op. cit. p. 55.

Table 3   Structure of NEA Costs of Supply*

	Net Generation (N.Rs./kWh)	High Voltage (N.Rs./kWh)	Medium Voltage (N.Rs./kWh)	Low Voltage (N.Rs./kWh)
LRMC	1.25	1.68	2.41	3.53
Medium Term				
Capacity costs	1.22	1.66	2.38	3.50
Energy costs				
Whole year				
Peak	0.16	0.17	0.19	0.21
Off peak	0.00	0.00	0.00	
Dry season				
Peak	0.27	0.29	0.32	0.36
Off peak	0.00	0.00	0.00	0.00
West season				
Peak	0.05	0.06	0.06	0.07
Off peak	0.00	0.00	0.00	0.00

Source: World Bank, op. cit. p. 56
* Allowing for, Seasonality 25 MW Exports; 'zero option', Arun 3 Phase I
Commissioned in 1995/96

3.4 NEA Tariffs and LRMC

Table 4 indicates the relationship between long run marginal cost (LRMC) of supply for the three major customer categories. As can be seen from the Table, the LRMC vary by voltage levels, increasing as the voltage levels drop. It shows that the existing tariff rates, as a proportion of LRMC, vary from a low of 15% for the "life line" rate to a high of 69% for hotels served at 11 kV. All consumers are paying substantially less than the LRMC.

3.5 NEA Tariffs and the Average Cost

Based on NEA's profit and loss account, NEA's ratio of gross revenue (i.e. before deduction of income tax) to operation and maintenance costs were 74% in 1985/86 and 87% in 1986/87. Thus indicating loss from operations, although these losses (NEA, Revenue and Expenditures Estimates for FY 1987/88) were substantially reduced compared to the previous years, after tariff rates were revised and raised in four major spurts in the past. However, the net revenue (after deduction of interest and taxes) to net operating expenses would be substantially low.

Table 4   Comparison between 1987 Tariff Levels and LRMC

Tariff Category	kWh/kW/month load factor (%)		Av.cost/kWh			LRMC per kWh
			200 (27)	400 (55)	600 (82)	
Industrial						
Large	H.V.	N.Rs.	1.01	0.86	0.75	1.68
Medium	11 kV	N.Rs.	0.98	0.91	0.89	2.41
Small	LV	N.Rs.	1.03	0.96	0.94	3.53
Commercial						
Hotels	11 kV	N.Rs.	1.66	1.46	1.39	2.41
Hotels	LV	N.Rs.	1.66	1.46	1.39	3.53
Others	11 kV	N.Rs.	1.43	1.27	1.21	2.41
Others	LV	N.Rs.	1.43	1.27	1.21	3.53

		Av.cost/kWh				LRMC per kWh
	kWh/month	25	75	200	400	
	Load factor	(3)	(10)	(27)	(55)	
Residential (LV)	N.Rs.	0.52	0.91	1.03	1.13	3.53

Source: World Bank op. cit. p. 89

3.6 Electricity Tariffs — Current Situation

In the absence of any latest revision of tariffs and/or endorsement of the proposed LRMC, the NEA applies the tariffs dating from August 1985 which includes seven consumer categories as follows:

3.6.1   Residential Consumers

● "Life-line" rates upto 25 kWh/month — Rs.13.
● Middle class consumers (25 — 300 kWh/month — Rs.1.10 per kWh)
● Upper class consumers (300 kWh-above) — Rs.1.35 per kWh.

3.6.2   Industrial

● Smaller up to 80 kW installed capacity
   — Rs.0.85/kWh + Rs.75/kW of installed capacity
● Larger above 80 kW installed capacity
   — Rs.0.90/kWh + 75/kW of installed capacity

3.6.3 Commercial

- Hotels   Rs.0.95/kWh
- Others   Rs.0.90/kWh

Historically, the NEA and its predecessor NEC, increased tariffs on four occasions on the recommendations of the IDA/ADB. In 1978/79, the average tariff rate was increased by about 35%, in 1983, by about 56%, in March of 1985 by about 35%, and in August 1985 by 22%. As a result of these rapid increments in the tariff rates the NEA has been able to achieve a more satisfactory rate of return on historically valued average net fixed assets which increased from 0.1% in 1981/82 to 2.5% in 1983/84, while in 1984/85 it deteriorated to −0.6% but following a tariff rise it went up to 5.4%. As recommended by the IDA/World Bank authorities, the NEA is going to further raise tariffs to meet 6% rate of return under the tariff covenants of the World Bank.

3.7 Tariff Formulation and Management the Key Issue

Thus it becomes obvious from the foregoing analysis that "tariff" is the most crucial issue of the NEA Management. Its proper formulation and application can boost the given objectives of the NEA, where as lack of it (i.e. uneconomic or unjustifiable tariffs) defeats the very purpose of its establishment. Despite the four major spurts in the tariff rates in the past, the O&M expenses of the NEA are still so high which are hardly accentuated by the amount of revenues collected. But ironically, the past increases in electric tariffs were not easily accepted by user groups.

Given the objectives and operating principles of NEA as stipulated in the NEA Act, the Management of NEA first need to understand the rationale and logic for raising tariffs in the future. If tariffs are to be raised for meeting the "covenanted rate of returns" then they ought to consider the fact that the objective can also be fulfilled by the adoption of optimum resource allocation with heavy emphasis on the reduction of O&M Cost where possible. This could be achieved, for example by a flatter organization with direct one to one relationship between the supervisor and the technically inevitable functional staff. The excess staff could be loaned to other new or old institutions where required. Before HMG takes any initiative on this, primary intiative must come from the NEA Management itself. Another area in which NEA management needs to focus on is the rapid system losses (although at present it has been achieving approximately 1% system loss reduction every year), through more aggressive steps in disconnecting lines of the delinquent consumers, by giving investment priorities on transmission and distribution lines which due to excess load are also contributing to system losses (World Bank op. cit.).

Medium to long term cost reduction could also be achieved by more pragmatic and thorough manpower planning. For example, interviews, with the various Directors of the NEA, indicates that about 20 – 25% of the annual operating costs (unaccounted directly in the P/L account) are allocated for the expatriate consultants. Along with a proper manpower development programme, a phasing needs to be developed to replace costly expatriate consultants with local manpower.

Costs could also be reduced by local fabrications of plants/machines from the existing 400 engineering and allied workshops existing in the kingdom, instead of importing all the machines, plants equipments at costly prices. A recently established transformer manufacturing company (wishes not to be quoted) complains that the NEA is not ready to buy its products, although it is competitive in price to the foreign products. Similarly there are a number of cable industries (e.g. Swodeshi Cable and Himalayan Cable) who produce and can supply large quantitites of electric cables locally. There are a number of engineering workshops (e.g. Team Yon, Structo Nepal, Balaju Yantra Shala) who can supply poles, turbines, discs etc. to meet NEA's requirements. One problem with the NEA Management is that its contracts are usually very large, requiring bidding on a global level. However, the donor agencies would certainly not disagree if NEA proposes, as a condition of contract, that local contractors and fabrication materials be used through subcontracting as far as standard materials and workmanship are provided.

Cost over-runs are also caused by delays in project execution due to inefficiency, lack of total awareness about procedures, and a lack of delegation of authority (World Bank, op. cit.). Needless to say, there are many ways of minimizing the opearing costs of NEA. However, the NEA Management has not done much to resolve these issues.

The next step in tariff formulation is that tariffs should be raised only when the cost reduction approach alone would not be sufficient. Even when there is a need to raise tariffs, the management should understand that fast and sharp rises in tariffs, as in the past, may bring public resentment. This can sometimes also be against social justice. For example, the rate of Rs.1.10 per kWh charged to the lower middle class consumers, say consuming between 25 – 100 kWh per month costs them very heavily and is not socially desirable. Perhaps, the management can make four tiers instead of three. This is also prescribed by the IDA study.

Thirdly, the Management also needs to raise revenue not just by raising tariffs per se, but also by employing a demand management concept. The Management could consider the time of day metering system, and apply differential tariff rates for differing time, whereby it could reduce capacity cost through a high load factor.

The Top Management of NEA faces a serious challenge in the future, 5 —10 years to come, and the major source of this challenge is to determine and implement approximate tariff rates which fulfills all its given objectives.

4. Conclusions and Recommendations

4.1 Problems

The top management of the NEA faces a serious challenge in adopting an appropriate tariff structure for electricity sales. All the user groups (consumers) except the low income category customers, are unhappy about the abrupt hike in electricity charges in the past. The current structure of electricity tariffs are neither socially justifiable nor economically efficient from the point of view of resource allocation.

The management does not seem to have indicated any action towards realizing revenue from tariffs by adopting the long run marginal cost curves so arduously designed by the World Bank.

Current efforts of the NEA to approach tariff strategy with least cost method is constrained by the overwhelming proportion of operating costs in the form of:

- very costly organization structure.
- lack of a coherent strategy of loss reduction.
- too much involvement of foreign expatriates.
- low productivity of capital and labour.
- lack of management concepts, and tools among the various managers of NEA.
- lack of a policy for utilizing local fabrication, local latent and materials.

NEA Management consider that there are new users of electricity, and there is demand, so any tariffs they raise would be acceptable to the public. But the public expects social justice. HMG expects NEA to embody the principles of social justice and make electricity charges competitive vis-a-vis fuel wood (environmental protection) kerosene (import substitution objective) and to make it competitive with border prices of electricity (export promotion objective).

The current average tariff rate of Rs.1.76 (Coopers & Lybrand op. cit. Section 7.7) is well above the rate of Rs.1.01 at which HMG has agreed to sell electricity to India under the Indo-Nepal Power Exchange Agreement. The current electric tariff is not competitive with fuel wood (see Appendix 9) or kerosene. Although with proper demand management it can be expected to compete with kerosene (Nepal Electricity Corporation Tariff Study Aug. 31, 1982, p. 37).

Electricity cannot be a substitute for fuel wood or kerosene in cooking. It can only be a substitute for kerosene in lighting. The top management of the NEA should immediately make this point clear and accordingly revise their objectives.

There have been considerable delays in the preparation of necessary reports by NEA for submission to HMG. The delayed reports include: the audited balance sheet, valuation of assets, future corporate development plans, and tariff proposals, they expect to complete and submit these reports by 1990. This delay in the preparation of the corporate development plan is hampering the process of tariff formulation and management action on cost reduction programmes.

Public resentment about tariff hikes are widespread. The public wishes to be consulted or informed prior to raising tariff rates.

Management of electricity supply by the Industrial Estates is causing many difficulties and hardships for the IES, they have neither equipment nor experience in its management. If NEA undertakes the management of electricity supply within IES then only it can justify the charges it is currently making.

If adopted a system of demand management for the electricity supplied/sold to the various user groups would improve the present load factor substantially.

Preference in electricity sales are currently given, by the NEA, to household buyers, the industries or commercial organizations are not receiving a greater priority. If priorities were given to industries and commercial entities there would be a greater chance of improving load factor.

Manpower planning is very poor, with a large administrative staff (36%), and low skill levels in both the technical and administrative areas. Staff productivity and performance are poor, and staff training has not been effectively pursued. Lack of a Director-in-Chief in the Administration, and Finance Directorate, also hamper the issue of manpower management.

The organization structure is steep, i.e. with too many layers of administrative staff, P.As., and clerks. Conversely, there is a lack of necessary technical personnel. Also, lacking is organizational cohesiveness, and job mobility.

The Coopers & Lybrand Associates (Consultants hired under ADB assistance) have recommended that a "twinning management" for staff training with a suitable utility be immediately launched. But management has been very slow to take action in this matter. This view is also endorsed by the World Bank.

The staff from the Electricity Department (ED) have not been formally confirmed in their posts. This involves the issue of seniority. NEA staff, being junior in terms of number of years in service, are senior in position to ED staff. This is due to slow promotions for ED staff while under the government. Additionally, many of the former ED staff had little desire to be transferred to the NEA. As of yet, management has not taken any steps to tackle this issue, which is one of the causes of poor staff motivation and work morale.

Poor work conditions and low pay, result in efficient NEA staff seeking part-time work elsewhere.

4.2 Recommendations

Top management of the NEA should immediately begin to revise the tariff structure with an approach, as close as possible to the long run marginal cost, proposed by the World Bank/IDA. Prior to this, the NEA (if necessary with the assistance of foreign consultants) should look into the options and possibilities of cost reduction. The NEA should examine whether it is possible to have:

1) A flatter organization, smaller administrative staff, and consider options for hiring, retraining, or loaning the staffs to other agencies as required.

2) The present rate of system loss reduction is appreciable. But it can be sped up with vigorous efforts at reequipping, and repairing the distribution and transmission stations.

3) The management should devise a plan for training local staff, as future replacements for expatriates.

4) Major areas in which training is necessary include:
   - the operation and maintenance system
   - distribution and consumer services
   - corporate and management planning methods

5)　Training programmes should be designed for all levels of management upper, middle and lower.

In each field, each level of training provided should be suitably interlinked with the concept of productivity and innovative tools. The training programmes could be arranged in many ways, but more importantly it would be useful to have training programmes launched as follows:

- training programmes should be launched either in Nepal or in other Asian countries.
- "Twining Arrangements" be developed on a reciprocal basis, the utility preferably from a south east Asian Nation (because the SAARC Regions aren't as experienced as the S.E. Nations in utility management). Done in such a way that the personnel of the foreign utility come to train NEA staff in key areas (as explained above). At the same time there should be an arrangement to send some of the prominent staff of NEA abroad and gain from learning there (i.e. in other utilities).
- training programmes should first be developed.
- we recommend that the Asian Productivity Organization (APO) or similar productivity organizations, should become a partner in both the productivity related training programme and twinning arrangements.

6)　The NEA Management should without delay start the deployment of excess manpower to other organizations where they would be necessary. The NEA Board should first bring this issue with a proposal to the line Ministry (i.e. the MWR).

7)　The NEA Chairman and the Management take an approach to make the representative of the Ministry of Industry in NEA Board responsible for identifying the key industries that could cater to the equipments needs of the NEA from time to time. Similarly, the NEA Management should perhaps, develop a roaster of local contractors, study their performance records, pre-qualify them and use them in generation, transmission and maintenance works with or without foreign contractors.

The present tariff structure should revised at least to make four user categories for the residential consumers instead of only three, as follows:

- those consuming up to 25 kWh/month.
- those consuming between 25 and 100 kWh/month.
- those consuming between 100 and 300 kWh/month.

- those consuming above 300 kWh/month.

Priorities in providing new connection lines be given to industrial and commercial purposes, as these are the ones that contribute to improved load factor.

A study be immediately launched to examine the feasibility of introducing time of day metering, i.e. demand management, through which load factor can improve.

It should be recommended that tariff rates be carefully examined vis-a-vis border prices. Thereby, determining whether it is economically feasible to provide electricity to India at a rate of N.Rs.1.01 in the long run. If NEA cannot reduce the cost of supply, the result will be a loss from export, which means imposing the cost to domestic consumers, even at the current average rate of Rs.1.76/kWh.

Further negotiation with India be initiated for time of the day, supply to India, which would be an alternative to option F, above, if NEA/HMG fails to renegotiate rates with India.

NEA should carefully examine whether the objectives and roles assigned to it by the NEA Act are at all compatible. We doubt that the supply of electricity can be any substitute for fuel wood in lighting, and cooking. The HMG's Seventh Plan envisages to achieve environmental protection through the use of electricity, but this does not appear as a sound alternative.

All the staff of the former ED, as well as NEC be immediately confirmed or rejected by properly assessing their demands.

Conditions for services for the NEA staff be revised as recommended by the NEA/ADB consultants Coopers & Lybrand (see Appendix 4).

5. Selected References

1. World Bank, Nepal Power Sub-Sector Review August 7, 1987.
2. HMG/Nepal Electricity Corporation, Tariff Study August 31, 1982.
3. HMG/Ministry of Water Resources, Water & Energy Commission, Commercial Energy Cost & Pricing Study Nepal.
4. Nepal Electricity Authority Electricity Load Forecast, 1986.
5. Coopers & Lybrand Associates, Final Report, Design for the Nepal Electricity Authority.
6. HMG/Ministry of Water Resources, WEC, Nepal Rural Electrification Task Force Interim Report.
7. NEA, The Role of NEA in the Development of the Nepal Power Sub-sector 23 January, 1988.

8. NEA Act 1984.
9. NEA, Profit and Loss Account 1987/88.
10. Corazon Morales Siddayao, Ed, Criteria for Energy Pricing Policy Graham & Trotman 1985.
11. Ralph Turvey and Dennis Anderson, Electricity Economics. A World Bank Research Publication 1977.
12. HMG/National Planning Commission, Seventh Plan (1985 − 90).
13. APO, Report of the Coordination Meeting of the APO Survey on Management of state-owned Enterprises (SOEs) 15th − 18th September 1987, Bangkok, Thailand.
14. APO, Management for Technology Innovation, Report on APO Top Management Forum 1986.

Appendix 1

Brief History of the Power Sub-Sector Institutions in Nepal

Prior to the government control of public electricity supply through the creation of the Electricity Department (ED) in 1950, electricity supply in the early part of the century was from small privately owned plants with expatriate management. But the supply was negligible.

In 1962, the Nepal Electricity Corporation (NEC) was created in accordance with the Government policy to transfer to public enterprises functions previously carried out by Government Departments. But in practice the ED retained control over the planning, preparation and implementation of the generation and transmission projects, handing over completed projects to NEC for operation.

In 1974 a separate Eastern Electricity Corporation (EEC) was created for the Eastern Region. The 1970s saw a new departure of hydro-power management through various boards such as the Kulekhani I, Marsyangdi, the small Hydro Development Board (SHDP) for hydro-power projects up to 5 MW.

By the late seventies the fragmentation of responsibilities, and lack of coordination in the power subsector were seriously affecting its efficiency. NEC had little contact or influence over the ED, or development boards in the planning and construction of new generation and transmission facilities. The diffusion of responsiblity also led to inefficient staff deployment, confusion in decision-making and poor financial performance. Following studies financed by the ADB, HMG agreed in 1982 to establish a single public sector enterprise, the Nepal

Electricity Authority (NEA), with responsibility for the planning, construction and operation of all public power facilities in Nepal. NEC took over the EEC in the same year. But NEA could not be established until 1985. There is still private sector involvement in the power subsector in Nepal, but these are negligible and not dealt with in this report.

Appendix 2

Opportunities and Prospects for Power Supply Nepal

A base case domestic load forecast projected to increase at a rate of 12.4% a year during 1985/86 — 1995/96 and 5.7% a year during 1995/96 — 2005/06 (World Bank, Nepal Power Sub-Sector Review August 7 1987 p. 38) which means a peak demand of 286 MW by 1996 and 501 MW by 2006.

The hydro-power-led export strategy is particularly good as the Government of India (GOI) estimates India's load growth call to the extent of additional 5000 MW capacity (i.e. the potential power shortage in India) per annum in the years to come. (op. cit. p. 75). Note that this is consistent with the stated desire of the GOI "to import any available quantities of power (from Nepal) over the medium term." (Extract from Official Protocol of visit of the Minister of Finance of HMG/N to India December 1986).

Export up to 25 MW is stipulated under the present Indo-Nepal Power Exchange Agreement at a price of I.Rs.0.60 (N.Rs.1.01 or US$ 0.045)/kWh, as agreed to by the relevant power utilities of both countries, but still subject to Government approval.

Foreign technical and financial assistance are being constantly obtained and do not appear to be too much of a problem for Nepal. Under the technical assistance programmes, multi-lateral assistance were being provided by the ADB, World Bank and the IDA for investigation approximately 20,000 MW at varying length and depth long-term power generation prospects (e.g. Chisapani, Burhi Gandaki, Kali Gandaki, Arun-3, Marsyangdi, Sapta Gandaki etc.). As far as financing is concerned, the long-term foreign exchange loans covered NEC/ NEA's (or Power Sector's) 49% of the capital requirements, foreign exchange grants provided 34%, and Government equity constitutes 13%, while net internal cash generation (of the NEA) only covered 4% of its capital investment.

Appendix 3

Overview of Government Policies

Nepal has an estimated hydro-power potential of 83000 MW but her present installed capacity of 180 MW and a per capital power consumption of 22 kWh is one of the lowest in the World (World Bank op. cit.). The present consumption of power satisfies about 2.2% of the total energy requirements, 5.5% being met by other commercial sources (petroleum, coal) and the remaining 92.3% from traditional sources (fuel-wood, dung, and agricultural wastes). This contrast between the actual and potential hydro-power generation, coupled with the massive depletion of forest resources at an alarming rate, which by 2000 A.D. is estimated to completely perish at the present scale of deforestation/afforestation, and the need to pay increasing amount of foreign exchange for importing petroleum products and coal — all represent a formidable challenge to Nepal in development (see Appendix 3). Correctly, therefore, HMG/N considers an efficient exploitation of this enormous resource as one of Nepal's most important economic priorities which can be judged from the stated policies of the Seventh Five Year (1985—90) as follows (HMG/NPC Seventh Plan 1985—90 p. 161).

Promoting common use of electric power in the domestic economy to enable substitution of fuel wood (environment protection), petroleum products/coal (import substitution) and to earn foreign exchange (improving b.o.p.) through exports of power (to India).

Development of large, cost-effective hydro-power projects on a mid-term and long-term perspectives to meet domestic consumption and export market requirements.

Pursuing tariff policies that encourage more consumption in general, making electricity tariff rates, particularly to the productive sectors, more attractive, also making it more competitive in the export market.

To ensure an efficient generation, transmission, distribution and O&M system through operating efficiencies as well as by minimizing system losses (optimum resource allocation).

Institutional reforms.

Consolidating/extending national power grid network, and promoting public and private rural electrification programmes in rural areas where connection to the national grid system is not possible.

Seeking bilateral/multi-lateral assistance in the development of power projects.

Longer-term Development Objectives Covering (1986/87—2005/06)

Identify and construct low cost, large and small scale hydro-power plants in order to increase hydro-generated production capacity in Nepal for domestic and export consumption.

Extend and develop the transmission system into a national grid.

Expand the distribution network, particularly in rural areas.

Reduce systems losses and establish efficient and effective power management systems.

Short-term Development Objectives (1986/87—1990/91)

Institutional consolidation and strengthening to manage the business, and hence support HMG's efforts and activities in the power subsector more effectively.

Improvements in operation and maintenance procedures and distribution and consumer services.

Appendix 4

Nepal Electricity Authority
Organization Chart

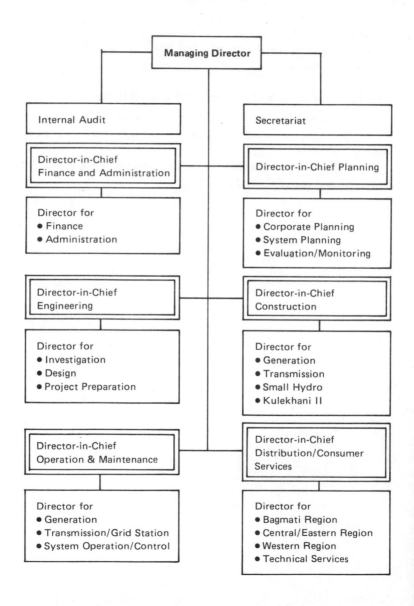

NEA Salaries

Salaries

1. The current salary scales of NEA employees are shown in the following table:

NEA Salary Scale Effective December 16, 1986

Salary Level	Categories of Staff	Salary Scale, N.Rs./month*
Special	Managing Director	4100 — 4550 (3 x 150)
12	Director-in-Chief	3175 — 4095 (8 x 115)
11	Director	2775 — 3603 (9 x 92)
10	Joint Director, Manager	2420 — 3230 (10 x 81)
9	Deputy Director, Deputy Manager	1925 — 2389 (8 x 58)
8	Assistant Director, Assistant Manager, Senior Engineer	1725 — 2189 (8 x 58) EB-2639 (6 x 75)**
7	Assistant Engineer, Administration Officer, Senior Surveyor Senior Draftsman	1530 — 1944 (9 x 46) EB-2432 (8 x 61)
6	Assistant Administration Officer, Assistant Accounts Officer	1400 — 1814 (9 x 46) EB-2302 (8 x 61)
5	Supervisor, Overseer, Head Mechanic, Surveyor, Draftsman, Office Assistant, Accountant, Security Officer, Meter-Reading Inspector, Cashier, Crane Operator	1195 — 1420 (9 x 25) EB-1720 (10 x 30)
4	Foreman, Sub-Overseer, Mechanic, Senior Electrician, Foreman-Driver, Driver-Mechanic, Driver, Junior Accountant, Office Assistant, Junior Accountant, Senior Meter Reader, Meter-Reading Supervisor, Security Guard-Commander	975 — 1155 (9 x 20) EB-1395 (10 x 24)
3	Electrician, Linesman, Junior Mechanic, Blacksmith, Operator, Mason, Carpenter, Welder, Fitter, Plumber, Security Guard, Clerk, Meter Reader, Telephone Operator, Silt Analyser, Work Sarkar (Head Worker)	700 — 826 (9 x 14) EB-996 (10 x 17) EB-1196 (10 x 20)
2	Junior Electrician, Assistant Switchboard Operator, Assistant Linesman, Cook, Guard	620 — 728 (9 x 12) EB-858 (10 x 13) EB-1008 (10 x 15)
1	Cook, Peon, Sweeper, Gardener, Watchman	510 — 582 (9 x 8) EB-682 (10 x 10) EB-826 (12 x 12)

* Figures in parentheses indicate number and amount of annual increments to reach top of scale.
** EB = Efficiency bar

Allowances

2. NEA employees are eligible for various allowances that may add 10% or more to their monthly salaries.

Appendix 5

NEA Profit and Loss Account (Fiscal Year)

Rs. '000

Revenue Cost	1985/86 Actual	1986/87 Revised Estimates	1987/88 Estimates
(A) Revenues	364078	472591	549667
Electricity sales (Domestic)	341099	449027	526443
Export to India	4532	4877	2224
Miscellaneous incomes*	18447	18687	21000
(B) Less operating and maintenance expenses	308834	351117	425983
Operation and administration	124039	171356	221244
Electricity import	10531	5928	10340
Fuel (for production)	6264	3576	7200
Interest on long-term loan	100000	98700	97686
Depreciation on fixed assets	68000	71617	89513
Gross profit (A − B)	55244	121474	123684
(C) Income tax provision	30338	48566	49921
(D) Net profit	24906	72908	73763

Appendix 6

Alternative Cost of Cooking

The main source of fuel for cooking in Nepal is fuel wood. Purchased from the National Fuel wood Corporation in Kathmandu, wood costs Rs.30.5/50 kg. Assuming the heat content of wood to be 3,500 kcal/kg and 20 percent efficiency in cooking, the cost per 1,000 kcal in end use is in the order of Rs.0.9. By comparison, the average annual cost of electricity for 1,000 kcal at end use is about Rs3.7 assuming 860 kcal/kWh, 70 percent efficiency in end use and a marginal cost of Rs.2.2/kWh (annual). Based on the marginal costs of producing electricity in the wet season, the cost per 1,000 kcal would be in the order of Rs.1.8/kWh (assuming 860 kcal/kWh and 70 percent efficiency).

Kerosene is also used for cooking in Kathmandu. At Rs.4.9/L and assuming a calorific value of 9,800 kcal/L, and 70 percent efficiency in end use, the cost per 1,000 kcal in end use is about Rs.0.75 to Rs.1.0.

This suggests that at the marginal cost, electricity is not competitive with alternative sources of energy for cooking. To be competitive, the price should not be more than about Rs.1.00/kWh. Moreover, to be competitive for cooking, the supply of electricity must be reliable and nominal voltage levels must be maintained.

Alternative to Autogeneration

In general, autogeneration is not a very attractive alternative to electricity supply from an electricity grid provided the supply is reliable. In recent years, this has not been the situation in Nepal and with regular load shedding, many commercial and industrial outlets have had to provide their own back-up generation.

The cost of autogeneration in Nepal is estimated at Rs.2.4/kWh, as shown in Table 1. This compares to marginal cost of producing electricity at 11 kV of Rs.2.2/kWh.

Table 1

Assume load of 1.0 kW at 0.42 load factor		
Assume installation of 1.5 kW per kW of load		
Capital cost @ $700/kW = $1,050		
Uniform annual payment at 12% for 10 years	=	$185/yr/kW
Fixed operation and maintenance at 2% of capital	=	21
Fuel at 11.2 US¢/kWh (Reference 3)	=	412
Variable operation and maintenance at 1.5¢/kWh	=	55
Total	=	$673/yr/kW
or	=	1.8 ¢/kWh
or	=	2.4 Rs./kWh

This suggests that commercial and industrial consumers would be willing to pay the marginal cost of electricity, if the supply is reliable.

Appendix 7

Nepal Power Subsector Review

Typical Daily Load Curves for NEA Interconnected System

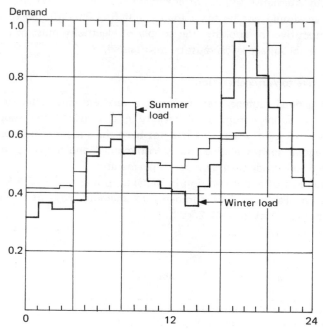

Source: NEA

Appendix 8

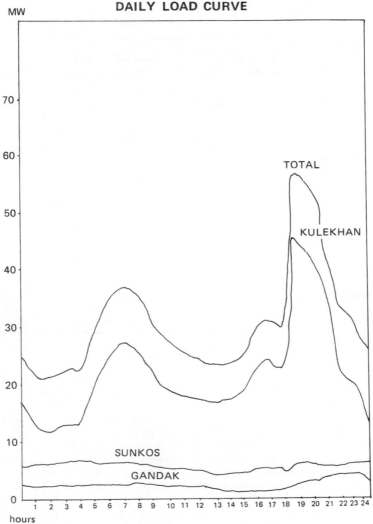

**NEPAL ELECTRICITY CORPORATION
CENTRAL NEPAL POWER SYSTEM
DAILY LOAD CURVE**

Nepal
Power Subsector Review

Existing Generating Plants on the Interconnected System

Name	Date in Service	Number of Units and Size MW	Installed Capacity MW	Firm Capacity MW	Firm Energy GWh/yr
Hydro-electric:					
Trisuli	1962	7 x 3.0	21.0	18.0 *1	114.6
Sunkosi	1973	3 x 3.35	10.1	5.8 *2	56.7
Gandak	1979	3 x 5.0	15.0	9.4 *3	43.8
Kulekhani I	1982	2 x 30.0	60.0	60.0 *1	154.7
Devighat	1983	3 x 4.7	14.1	14.1 *1	89.7
Kulekhani II	1986	2 x 16.0	32.0	32.0 *1	95.0
Subtotal — Hydro			152.2	139.3	554.5
Misc. Small Hydro			6.0	6.0	23.2
Total Hydro — Interconnected System			158.2	145.3	577.7
Diesel: *4					
Hetauda		4 x 2.5	10.0	10.0	21.9
Misc. Diesel			15.0	7.0	15.3
Subtotal — Diesel			25.0	17.0	37.2
Total Plant Installed			183.3	162.3	614.9

*1   Kulekhani I and II share a common hydraulic system and can only be operated in "tandem" as (30 + 6) = 46 MW units. Similarly, unit outages at Trisuli require reductions at Devighat. The flow limitation at Trisuli applies during all months of the year, because it is designed to have only six units operating at any one time, resulting in some spillage of water.

*2   Seasonal variation in hydrology reduces firm capacity to 5.8 MW.

*3   Gandak system has no spillway, consequently only a maximum of 2 units may be operated safely to avoid danger of flooding the power house.

*4   Diesel firm capacity reflects the operating state of existing units.

Appendix 9

Nepal Power Subsector Review
Electricity Supply and Consumption, 1976 – 1985
(Public Supply Only) MWH

	1976	1977	1978	1979	1980	1981	1982	1983	1984	1985
Total Generation (Gross) of which:	150,226	165,380	186,379	211,901	228,578	231,443	267,776	345,021	372,078	410,479
Hydropower Stations	128,814	139,019	153,454	170,319	176,678	175,943	208,296	286,019	313,674	334,870
Diesel Power Stations	1,980	3,336	6,169	7,116	18,124	14,195	10,153	4,633	2,924	4,041
+ Imports — From India	25,372	29,141	32,726	40,626	38,972	45,070	56,759	63,291	65,793	82,143
- Exports — To India	5,940	6,116	6,970	6,160	5,196	3,765	7,432	8,922	10,313	10,575
Total Internal Consumption	42,965	45,789	54,724	62,988	66,639	68,229	83,884	114,405	125,567	122,651
(Power Station Use, Transmission and Distribution Losses)										
Consumption										
Residential*	61,787	65,679	71,348	77,221	74,823	78,570	9,066	119,005	129,613	154,928
Industrial	32,128	39,036	42,751	47,827	52,089	50,202	61,280	81,953	88,748	100,137
Commercial*	9,173	10,405	13,068	18,020	25,244	23,203	17,834	21,342	19,465	21,204
Transportation and Agriculture										
Others	4,173	4,471	4,488	5,845	9,813	11,239	14,112	8,316	8,685	11,559
Total	107,261	119,591	131,655	148,913	161,969	163,214	183,892	230,616	246,511	287,828

* To facilitate comparison, NEA has adopted for reporting purposes the same tariff classification that existed prior to April 1983. Since April 1983, the Commercial sector consists of (1) starred hotels (called (commercial)) and (2) schools, hospitals, offices etc., that previously came under "Residential". According to the present tariff classification, the consumption by sector for 1984 and 1985 was as follows:

	1984	1985
Residential	101,411	125,345
Industrial	78,342	92,517
Commercial	48,140	49,798
Agriculture, Transportation and Water Supply	10,885	11,631
Others	7,733	8,537
Total	246,511	287,828

Appendix 10

NEA 1986 Load Forecast for the Nepal Interconnected System *1, *2, *3, *4, *5

Sales (GWh)

Sector	1985	1986	1987	1988	1989	1990	1991	1996	2006	Annual Growth Rate (%) 1986–1996	1986–2006
Domestic	103.6	133.9	155.0	175.7	195.8	223.9	245.2	335.5	529.1	9.6	4.7
Industrial	59.9	92.7	123.1	143.7	169.3	193.2	218.1	356.4	652.6	14.4	6.2
Commercial	20.4	21.5	23.0	25.0	25.9	26.8	27.6	36.8	72.4	5.5	6.8
Non-commercial	29.6	33.7	43.5	53.5	56.2	52.0	48.3	67.7	133.2	7.2	7.0
Street Lighting	3.4	3.8	3.8	3.8	3.8	4.3	4.4	4.9	6.0	2.6	2.0
Drinking Water	5.3	5.6	6.0	6.3	6.8	7.2	7.8	11.2	23.0	7.2	7.5
Transportation	1.8	1.8	1.8	1.9	1.9	2.0	2.0	2.2	2.7	2.0	2.1
Irrigation	4.4	17.6	21.8	21.8	22.9	26.2	39.0	60.0	103.9	13.0	5.6
Self-Consumption/Temporary Supply	4.2	6.2	7.6	8.6	9.7	10.7	11.8	17.5	30.5	10.9	5.7
Subtotal	232.6	316.8	385.6	440.2	492.2	546.3	604.3	892.3	1,553.4	10.9	5.7
Loss Reduction Sales	—	—	5.5	12.6	21.1	31.2	43.2	127.5	221.9	na *6	na
Total Sales	232.6	316.8	391.0	452.8	513.3	577.5	647.5	1,019.8	1,775.3	12.4	5.7
Losses	108.7	135.8	159.8	176.1	189.8	202.9	215.8	254.9	443.8	6.5	5.7
Bulk Sales	10.6	20.7	6.6	6.6	6.6	6.6	6.6	6.6	6.6 *7	na	na
Total Generation	351.9	473.3	557.5	635.5	709.7	787.0	869.9	1,281.3	2,225.7	10.4	5.7
Peak Demand (MW)	79.7	107.1	124.0	141.1	157.7	177.4	196.3	286.5	501.3	10.3	5.8
Load Factor (%)	50.4	50.4	51.3	51.4	51.4	50.6	60.5	51.1	50.7		

*1   1985 Data are actual; 1986 data are estimated.

*2   HMG/N plans to extend the Nepal interconnected system to include Mechi & Rapti-Bheri (1990), Sagarmatha (1991) and Seti-Mahakali (1993). Koshi & Janakpur were connected in 1986.

*3   Some numbers may not add up due to rounding.

*4   Because the sectoral sources of non-technical losses have not been identified, the loss reduction savings have been put in a separate category.

*5   Year refers to fiscal year.

*6   na = not applicable.

*7   Bulk sales will increase to 109.5 GWh, once the Arun-3 project is commissioned.

Source: NEA

Appendix 11

Per Capital Energy Consumption

		1965	1985
1.	Bangladesh	—	43
2.	Bhutan	—	—
3.	Nepal	6	17
4.	Burma	39	74
5.	India	100	201
6.	China	178	515
7.	Pakistan	136	218
8.	Sri Lanka	107	139
9.	Thailand	80	343
10.	Malaysia	312	826
11.	Republic of Korea	237	1241
12.	Hong Kong	424	1264

Source: Report on Commercial World Energy Development
— Table 9, p. 218

STUDY ON SOEs: REPUBLIC OF KOREA

by   Mr. Jong Soo Lim
Assistant Section Chief
Korea Federation of Small Business

1. Introduction

Korean state-owned enterprises played a very important role in the national economy in that they contributed 9.7% of gross domestic products (GDP) in 1984. At the end of 1985 their operating assets amounted to 69.8% of the industry total and they owned 25.9% of total national foreign debt. Its business activities had great effect on the industries nationwide.

Despite the important role that the state-owned enterprises (SOEs) played in the national economy, their management efficiency was considerably lower than that of the private sector. For instance, normal profit to total assets and operating profit to business capital of SOEs in 1982 (prior to implementation of the new strategy) remained at barely one third of the industry average.

Until 1983, the operation of SOEs had been governed by the Congressional Act for Incorporation of State-Owned Enterprises, the SOE Budgeting and Accounting Act, and the SOE Management Act, etc. which accounted for excessive intervention by the government authorities in SOE operations and presented great difficulties in exercising independent management of SOE operations. As a result, the objective evaluation of SOE business achievements was not possible and the line of responsibility for success or failure became obscured. The government authorities complained about the management decisions of the SOE officials and the SOEs claimed excessive intervention by the government authorities in delineating responsibilities for any SOE business outcome. Neither was it possible to conduct a systematic or objective evaluation of merits and/or demerits of the outcome of an SOE enterprise.

In December 1983, the government decided to drastically eliminate pluralistic and miscellaneous preliminary control measures and to convert to a control system that gives prime consideration to the post evaluation reports. Thus, the State-Owned Enterprise Management Standards Act was enacted to develop independent and responsible management systems in the state-owned enterprises. It provides for independent budgeting, personnel management, procurement, etc., as well as for an incentive programme that awards bonuses in different scales according to the level of achievement of the business operation. Provision is made for the dismissal of a president from his position when the business outcome proves to be unsatisfactory. This Act has been enforced since 1984.

Section 2 of this report describes the role of SOEs in the national economy, the problems faced by SOEs and their causes.

In Section 3, the fundamental concept which paved the approach to the development of the New State-Owned Enterprise Management Policy is discussed and followed by a brief treatment of the general framework of the New Management Policy.

In Section 4, the report treats the new management evaluation method that constitutes the nucleus of the new SOE managing policy, focusing on the indices of evaluation. What are the targets for evaluation in the state-owned enterprises? As a barometer of efficient SOE management, what are the attributes that the evaluation indices should possess? Of what elements should the indices be comprised in order to be valid? These questions are discussed in detail and then the evaluation indices currently applied in Korea are presented in this chapter.

Section 5 discusses the extent of contributions made for the improvement of SOE management efficiency. It introduces the new policy which was preceeded by efforts to minimize administrative requirements and was characterized by improved management autonomy and by the new approach to post-evaluation of SOE business outcome.

Finally, in Section 6, the subjects discussed in this report are summarized and followed by a brief discussion on the indicators derived from the report and on the tasks to be worked out in the future.

2. Current Status of the State-Owned Enterprises in Korea

2.1 Definition of State-Owned Enterprises (SOE)

The SOE may be defined in several ways depending on the theoretical approach. In this report, the SOE is defined as an enterprise which is possessed by a government organization, i.e., a central government agency or a local administrative body. This means that the ultimate responsibility for managing its business lies with the government body. This definition is a formalistic approach to the question of "What is the state-owned enterprise?"

We often find that an objective approach is sought in defining SOEs. When we question the purpose of the SOE, we often consider the SOE in light of its public service or public interest. The definition derived from such an objective approach bears significant meaning and becomes a requisite concept in developing efficient management strategy of SOEs.

In this report, SOEs are further defined as enterprises in which 50% or more shares of the issued stocks are held by government organizations. As of end of 1986, there were 25 state-owned enterprises in operation.

2.2 Roles of State-Owned Enterprises in the National Economy

In 1984, the magnitude of SOE budgets amounted to a total of US$29.442 million which represented 1.8 times the amount of the budget of the central government for the same year. In terms of the value added, the SOEs produced a total of US$8,107 million which comprised about 9.7% of gross domestic products (GDP) and represented the value added mainly in the sectors of indirect social capital and manufacturing industries.

In the formation of fixed assets, SOEs contributed almost 30% of the total fixed assets accrued domestically during the past 20 years. During 1984, the fixed assets accrued by 24 SOEs amounted to US$ 3,388 million representing 13.5% of the domestic total of US$25,133 million. The fixed assets gained by SOEs in machinery reflected 67.5% of the SOE total and signified the capital intensive nature of the SOE industry. The magnitude of the SOE's relative effect to the overall industry is such that 60 to 70% of the SOE products were used by other industries as intermediaries. In other words, the quality of SOE products substantially influences the product quality of other industries which use the SOE products.

The significance of SOE industry in the national economy is further reviewed in terms of its contribution to added values, relative effect to other industries, and the scale of accrued fixed assets:

2.2.1 Contribution to Added Value

The value added by SOEs in the gross domestic products, as shown in Table 1, had increased from 9.2% in 1970 to 9.7% in 1984. This reflects that the Korean economy is oriented by private enterprises but the SOEs are gaining influence in the national economy.

Table 1　Value-Added by SOE Sector in GDP

(Unit: %)

	1970	1975	1980	1984
Value added by SOE in Gross Domestic Products	9.2	8.3	9.1	9.7
Value added by SOE in GDP less agriculture and forestry	13.0	11.3	10.7	11.2

Note:　SOE sector includes government operated agencies (National Railways, Post Telephone and Telegraph), SOEs having more than 50% of stocks owned by government authority (Korea Electric Power Corp., Korea Development Bank, etc.), government invested enterprises (Korea Exim Bank, Pohang Steel, etc.), and SOE affiliated companies (Wonjin Rayon, Kyun-ju Development, etc.)

Source:　Financial statements of SOEs
　　　　　Annual Statistics of Korean Economy published by Bank of Korea.

Table 2 shows a comparison of values added by SOEs vs. overall industry by elements comprising the added values. It shows that the labour cost was 52.5% in overall industry against 29.6% in SOEs and the depreciation cost which reflects the magnitude of fixed assets was 17.3% in overall industry against 33.9% in the SOE sector. This substantiates the previous statement of SOEs being capital intensive management structures.

Table 2　Comparison of Value-Added by SOEs vs. Overall Industry (1984)

(Unit: %)

	SOE	Overall Industry
Labour cost	29.6	52.2
Depreciation cost	33.9	17.3
Net profit before tax	23.1	8.9
Financing cost	11.8	16.3
Taxes and public imposts	0.6	2.2
Rental cost	1.0	3.1
Total	100.0	100.0

Source:　Financial statements of SOEs
　　　　　Annual Statistics of Korean Economy, 1984, published by
　　　　　Bank of Korea

2.2.2 Relative Effect on Overall Industry

Table 3 shows that the average backward leakage effect of the SOE sector was somewhat lower than that of the overall industry while the average forward leakage effect of the SOE sector indicated higher ratings over those of the overall industry. A notable achievement was made in the forward leakage effect of the SOE sector: The rating of 0.6202 for 1980 was raised to 0.6708 for 1984. It is believed that the improvement in management efficiency and production quality of the SOE sector, whose forward leakage effect is rated high, will eventually contribute to the quality level of overall industry.

Table 3 Industrial Leakage Effect of the SOE Sector

	Forward Leakage Effect		Backward Leakage Effect	
	SOE Sector	Overall Industry	SOE Sector	Overall Industry
1980	.6202	.5144	.5579	.6622
1984	.6708	.5122	.5471	.6508

Source: Tables of leakage effect, 1981 and 1985, by Bank of Korea

2.2.3 Contribution in Accrued Fixed Assets

During 1984, the accrued fixed assets of the 24 SOEs (excluding Korea Gas Corp.) amounted to a total of US$3.388 million and amounted to 13.5% of the total of domestic accrued fixed assets. Details of these assets are broken down by type in Table 4. In domestic total, buildings occupied the largest part at 38.4% followed by machinery at 28.8% and so on. On the other hand, the SOE total was comprised of 67.5% for machinery, 21.8% for structures, 10.4% for buildings, etc. The fact that the fixed assets of the SOEs occupied 13.5% of the total of domestic fixed assets accrued, coupled with the fact that the SOE assets were amassed by machinery, again substantiates the leading roles of SOEs in the capital intensive strategic industrial sectors.

Table 4 Breakdown of Fixed Assets Accrued in SOEs (1984)

(Unit: %)

Fixed Assets	Building	Structure	Machinery	Transport	Total
Domestic total	38.4	22.1	28.8	10.7	100.0
SOE total	10.4	21.8	67.5	0.3	100.0

Source: Financial statements of SOEs
Annual Statistics of Korean Economy, 1985, by the Bank of Korea

2.3 Problems of SOE

As discussed previously, the SOEs were categorized into the industry sector of high forward leakage effects, and, thus, their efficiency in management significantly influenced the national economy. Inefficiency by an SOE would have cost the efficiency of other industries who used the inefficient SOE's products as inter-mediaries in their manufacturing process. As such is the case, the efficiency of the SOE management was a significant factor not only in the growth of SOEs themselves but also in the growth of the national economy.

2.3.1   Inefficiency of SOE

Despite the importance of SOEs as described above, the SOEs in the past had been operated by relatively poor management systems compared to those of the private enterprises. Table 5 depicts the normal profit to total assets and the operating profit to business capital attained by the SOEs and the overall industry. The normal profit to total assets is an index which is used to determine the efficiency or productivity of available capital by showing the ratio of value added by an enterprise in one fiscal year to the total assets of the enterprise. Included in the total assets, there is both operating capital, which was provided during the course of manufacturing, and non-operating capital such as invested assets, capital account for construction in progress, etc. which was not directly committed to the manufacturing activities during the period.

(Normal profit to total assets = Value added ÷ total assets x 100). For the year 1982, the average NPTA of SOEs was 7.8%, less than one third of the 27.5% attained by overall industry.)

Table 5   Rate of Return on Capital (1982)

(Unit: %)

Normal Profit to Total Assets		Operating Profit to Business Capital	
Overall Industry	SOE Sector	Overall Industry	SOE Sector
27.5	7.8	10.1	3.7

Source: SOE financial statements for 1982
          Analysis of Business Management, 1983, by the Bank of Korea

The operating profit to business capital is the ratio of operating profit to the operating capital which was used for business operation out of total assets. The operating profit represents that portion of the total revenue deducted by the cost of revenue and the marketing and administrative expenses which include interest paid, extraordinary losses corporate tax, etc. The operating capital represents that portion of total assets excluding the account for construction in progress, invested and other assets and assets in surplus and including fixed and current assets.

(Operating Profit to Business Capital = Operating profit ÷ Operating Capital x 100). For the year 1982, the average operating profit to business capital of the 24 SOEs was 3.7%, far below the overall industry level of 10.1%.

2.3.2   Causes of SOE Inefficiency

Business is operated under the fundamentals of capitalism, namely, the freedom of choice, the principle of competition, the principle of incentive, and the principle of private ownership.

In the business environment where pricing mechanisms of free enterprise are inadvertently manipulated by invisible hands, inefficient business enterprises are bound to be weeded out by natural selection. In a competitive market, there exists a system of an automatic evaluation in which efficient enterprises and inefficient enterprises are clearly distinguished by the act of the pricing function, and it is generally true that such principles of market functions apply and act upon most of the private enterprises.

However, when it came to the SOEs, the market function, namely, the automatic evaluation system did not apply well for two reasons. First, most of the SOEs were engaged in monopolized industry and were immune to the acts of invisible hands. Secondly, the goods produced by SOEs were designed for the realization of public interests and therefore, the results earned from the production of goods had no direct bearing on the efficiency or productivity of the SOEs. Also, since the prices of goods were determined arbitrarily the automatic evaluation system was hardly expected to act upon the SOE enterprises.

The monopolistic nature of the SOEs and the pursuance of public interests allowed artificial pricing practice while depriving the SOE's of autonomy in business management. The intervention of government authority in management had caused a semi-bureaucratic type of operation to form. The principles of economy were invalid for application in such a business environment. After all, to the SOEs, which were immune to the functions of the market, signals for prompting any management decision were diminished and the necessity of striving for improvement in management as a means of survival was weakened. These were the main causes that brought forth inefficiency in SOE business management.

The causes of inefficiency may as well be interpreted from the following two aspects. First, the government control exercised over the operation of SOE operations, and second, insufficient provisions in the schematic system for evaluating management efficiency of SOEs.

The government control which was exercised over SOE operations in the past prevailed in the broad range of SOE's management functions. In other words, the government authorities concerned made important management decisions in advance leaving the operating officers of the SOEs with no other choice but to concentrate on the execution of government directives instead of pursuing rationalization of SOE business operation. Creative and self-controlled long term management effort was set aside and short sighted efforts for fraudulence prevention preceeded the management concern.

As for the second aspect, in executing corporate budget and procurement tasks, strict compliance with governing regulations was emphasized and any attempt to exercise flexibility to cope with fluctuation that developed from external conditions was discouraged. To make matters worse, outsiders were frequently appointed or employed, weakening professional comradeship among management staff and lowering morale in the working level. The organizational structure was also under government control and lacked the flexibility of private enterprise in meeting with changing situations. In addition, the SOEs were subject to duplication in auditing and controlling channels by government authorities causing another factor of inefficiency and conservatism in their operation.

Another factor that caused the inefficiency of SOEs may be found in the absence of versatility of evaluation measures. As a matter of fact, there were some evaluation systems that existed before the introduction of the new evaluation system. Although they failed to achieve their purposes, they remained as procedural formalities.

In the review of failures of previous evaluations, we found an absence of prerequisite conditions which would enable reasonable evaluation. As reviewed earlier, the SOEs were subject to numerous controls by government authorities concerned, denied appropriate incentives commensurate with the evaluated ratings, and were confronted with technically questionable indices for evaluating their operational achievements, instead of provisions for the autonomy that would assure their authority and responsibility in operating enterprises.

In essence, the SOEs, whose nature may not allow application of the principles of the free market, should be introduced to sufficient capitalistic concepts in order to assure them of an autonomous business operation, to provide them with competitive edges in market places, and to enhance their entrepreneurship as business enterprises. For state-owned enterprises, we must have a sound system of properly evaluating operational achievements.

3. New SOE Management Policy

In consideration of the inefficiency of SOEs, brought about by old management strategy that failed to define a clear line of responsibility between the government imposed controls and the SOE management actions, the government decided to abolish the old policy and enacted the State-Owned Enterprise Management Fundamental Act providing the basis of new policy for managing the SOE businesses.

In the new policy, provisions were made to ensure autonomous operation of SOEs (Article 3 of Act), to establish SOE management goals in advance and conduct evaluations based on the preset goals by the SOE Evaluation Board, a body newly organized by the Act (Article 4 of Act).

3.1 Autonomy in Business Operation

The autonomy assured in the new strategy covers budgeting, procurement and personnel functions which constitute the nuclei of business management. First of all, the Fundamental Act delegated the authority of organizing and adjusting the budget to the SOEs. Previously, this authority was exercised in the following manner: The Economic Planning Board (EPB) drew up budgeting guidelines for SOEs to follow in preparing fiscal budgets. The budgets so prepared were forwarded to the ministries concerned for review and to EPB for another review at the ministerial level. The budget proposals were then submitted to the Cabinet for deliberation and resolution and to the President for final approval.

Secondly, the Fundamental Act delegated the authority of executing procurement and construction contracts to SOEs. This authority was previously vested to the Office of Supply which acted as the central procurement agent for all government organizations including SOEs in accordance with the Procurement and Contracting

Fundamental Act. This practice hampered SOEs' operation in making timely and technically professional procurement actions.

Finally, and significantly, the Fundamental Act provided SOEs with autonomy in personnel functions. The authority for appointing SOE officials and directors which was previously held by the concerned Minister was transferred back to the president or the chief executive officer of the SOEs. It also limited the directorship to the insiders of SOE organizations and, thus, curtailed inexperienced outsiders from entering into the SOE business. In August 1983, prior to the new Act, outsiders made up 53% of the incumbent directors of SOEs.

3.2 Evaluation of Achievements

As early as 1968 an evaluation programme was first introduced into SOEs. Then, the ministers concerned assigned the fiscal goals and SOEs made annual performance reports by January 31 of the following year. The ministers reviewed the reports for presentation at the Cabinet Meeting by February 28. The fiscal goals established during earlier days merely presented budgetary figures and had no yardsticks to measure any improvements made vs. previous performance. The absence of incentive provisions was another factor that caused the programme to be run as a formality. In early 1972, EPB initiated a study for an incentive programme and came up with the SOE Management Act and the SOE Accounting Act for implimentation in 1973 which introduced a new SOE evaluation programme. This programme failed to prove its effectiveness because the evaluation indices used financial ratios only and the incentive awards were not based on the degree of merits obtained but were granted mostly in fixed rate compensation.

In 1984, the SOE Management Fundamental Act was enacted and introduced a new evaluation programme which reflected a remarkable difference in every aspect from the previous one.

First, the indices used for evaluation were based on measuring the efficiency of business performance in light of the SOE's business purposes in favour of measurements by numerical achievements indicated in terms of financial ratios. In addition to the quantitative indices, qualitative indices have emerged.

Secondly, a professional SOE Evaluation Group was organized to improve the professionalism and objectivity of the SOE evaluation activities. In contrast to the previous practice of employing personnel from civil service in the evaluation work, the new evaluation programme formed a group represented by certified public accountants having over five years of practical experience, doctoral members of the government subsidized research institutes, and university professors to draw up evaluation indices and to conduct evaluations of SOE business performance. Table 6 shows the number of professionals that composed the SOE Evaluation Group each year. As you can see, university professors and CPAs constituted the majority with some representation from the research institutes. Particularly noteworthy was the participation of professional managers of private enterprises who were appointed to the Group by the recommendation of concerned ministries.

Thirdly, the incentive awards were made in steps depending on the ratings of the evaluation appraisal and induced the keen interest of SOE top management. Table 7 shows the ratings of evaluation conducted each year and the incentive awards made commensurate with the ratings. it is notable that, since 1986, incentive steps were further segmented within each ratings.

Table 6   Composition of SOE Management Evaluation Group

(Unit: In number of person)

	1983	1984	1985	1986
University professors	8	8	8	19
Public accountants (CPA)	12	13	13	18
Institute researchers	1	4	6	4
Professional managers	5	2	5	2
Total	26	27	32	43

Table 7   SOE Evaluation Ratings and Incentive Bonus Awarded in Steps

(Unit: %)

Rating	1985		1986		1987	
	SOE	Bonus	SOE	Bonus	SOE	Bonus
A	—	300	—	300 and above	—	300 and above
B	18	250	15	250 – 299	20	250 – 299
C	5	200	9	200 – 249	4	200 – 249
D	2	150	1	150 – 199	1	150 – 199
E	—	100	—	100 – 149	—	100 – 149

3.3 Organization and Specialization for Evaluation

The new SOE Management Fundamental Act provided for, the establishment of the SOE Evaluation Board within EPB in order to augment the existing organizational functions of deliberation and resolution concerning SOE management matters. It also set up the SOE Evaluation Group with efficient and competent professionals in order to specialize in drawing up the evaluation indices and to conduct the evaluation works.

3.3.1 SOE Evaluation Board

The evaluation programme aims to attain rational management of businesses and the proper evaluation of business performance will support the exercising of responsible management functions. In order to ensure the objectivity of evaluation works and to continue developing rational evaluation methods, it is considered necessary to have an independent body that has autonomous authority to resolve its findings instead of leaving the evaluation authority with the individual ministries concerned. Because of the difference of business involved by each SOE, the management goals of SOEs must be assigned with due consideration paid to the difference in their attainability. Therefore, it is also considered necessary to have an independent body, the SOE Evaluation Board, where drafts of management goals are presented by SOEs, adjusted by the ministries concerned, and deliberated in all respects by the board members for final resolution.

For these reasons, the SOE Evaluation Board is presided by the Minister of EPB and seated by the Ministers of Finance and the ministries concerned with SOEs and by up to five non-standing members of knowledgeable and experienced professionals. The Board is vested with the authority to deliberate and resolve matters concerning guidelines for the adoption of evaluation indices, management goals, guidelines common to organizing budgets, business evaluation reports including their evaluation methods, incentive bonus rates to be applied within an evaluation rating, and dismissal of SOE directorship.

3.3.2 SOE Evaluation Group

This Group was organized to provide technical and professional advice to the SOE Evaluation Board on matters concerning business evaluation. The Group prepares a manual of business evaluation for use as criteria for evaluating business performance and conducts the evaluation work based on the criteria established in advance.

In order to make fair and accurate appraisal of any business performance, we need to have professionals who are thoroughly experienced and knowledgeable in the theory and practice of the field of evaluation. The SOE Management Fundamental Act and its Enforcement Order stipulate that the Minister of EPB entrust the Group members with university professors who have professional knowledge in the operation and management of SOE business, members of government subsidized research institutes who hold doctors' degrees or equivalent qualifications, certified public accountants having over five years of practical experience, and the professionals who have sufficient knowledge and experience in the field of SOE operations and are recommended for the membership by the ministries concerned. The Group members are entrusted at the time of working on the evaluation indices for a particular SOE and for conducting the evaluation work until such time that the work is completed.

The group does an analysis of major business activities of the relevant SOE based on its business purpose, identifies main areas of control to attain the goals established for each activity, and adopts appropriate indices for evaluating such control areas as considered controllable and improvable so as to induce main efforts of SOE Management in these areas. These works which are defined as the works for establishing evaluation indices and the work involved in conducting evaluations based on the indices pre-established comprise the two main activities of the Group.

4. Indices for Evaluating State-Owned Enterprise Performance

The wholly competitive market functions are the most effective system of economy because, under this system, the inefficient enterprises are combed out by invisible hands. The free market functions not only distinguish between efficient and inefficient enterprises, but also brings growth and profit to the efficient enterprises and bankruptcy to those which are inefficient. Under this market system, a perfect business evaluation cycle takes place automatically.

However, most of the SOEs operate in exclusive industries such as railways, electric power generation, telecommunications, and monopolized products. Their utilitarian nature necessitates controls by government authorities. SOEs are free from the invisible hands which function as automatic devices of evaluation. In other words, SOEs are never bankrupted because of inefficient operations and SOE management is insensitive to the success or failure of SOE operations. Improvement efforts in SOE operations can hardly be expected. This is why we must have artificial means of evaluating the state-owned business operations. Without the means of finding the rights and wrongs of SOE business performance, SOE operations will wind up in confusion and in the absence of a valid evaluation system SOEs will find no way for improvements.

Then, what should the artificial means of evaluation be? They should be the means that will allow SOE management to enhance the efficiency of SOE operations with confidence and creativity. They must be applied periodically, systematically and reasonably by evaluators based on correct and rational criteria and with complete fairness and accuracy. And above all, unbiased rewards and punishments commensurate with the evaluated ratings which are essential in order to have a valid and workable evaluation system.

Here, we must note that the criteria of evaluation must be given due consideration before other factors in the system. Since it is difficult to evaluate SOE operations with the methods used for private enterprises, it is necessary to thoroughly research and analyze the nature of SOE businesses. We must understand the typical characteristics of the SOEs in order for the ensuing evaluation to clearly and objectively define the details and the limits of efficiency or inefficiency of the SOE operations. Therefore, we must have a valid system of evaluating the SOE operation and the criteria of evaluation as the nuclei of measurement of SOEs' operational efficiency. In short, the nuclei of SOE evaluation rest on the indices which enable us to measure the efficiency of SOE business operations.

4.1 Establishing Evaluation Indices

In establishing evaluation indices, we must ask:
- What are the subjects to be evaluated in the SOE operation?
- What are the attributes that the indices must retain as signals for SOE operations which are free from the functions of invisible hands?
- Of what elements should the individual indices consist?

4.1.1 Scope of Evaluation

There are three points to be considered in evaluating the SOE operations:

First, we have to evaluate the management efforts that were actually exerted in the operations. The evaluation of a business operation can be divided into the evaluation of business management and the evaluation of the business enterprise itself. The former evaluates the efficiency on the part of management staff which is demonstrated in a given environment. Even if a business shows a deficit, the management effort which contributed to reducing the deficit must be rated positively. Conversely, a negative rating must be given to the management effort if it caused the profits to shrink because of its laxity. In short, the evaluation of a management staff must focus on the efficiency of management efforts, whether it was best or not under a given operational environment, in order to be a valid and fair evaluation.

Superficial figures may appear that indicate good performance of the SOE business which did not actually result from any management effort. As an example, it is possible that the operational profit or loss of the SOE business may be directly attributable to the escalation of utility charges and fluctuation of the prices of raw materials that cause variations in input and output values. In such cases, evaluation must be based on substantial value of profit or loss which are computed on the basis of constant prices.

Second, we have to evaluate a business in light of both long-term and short-term operation concurrently. The most important point to consider in evaluating SOE business performance during a set period of time is the numerical expressions from the financial statements covering the period. These financial statements express short-term business performance in terms of profitability, growth rate, stability, etc. of the business. On the other hand, even though it may not show up during the period covered, there are considerable management efforts exerted during the period in anticipation of achievements to show up in the future. For instance, the management effort of SOEs exerted in such areas as long-range planning, improvement of administration, or customer services would pay off gradually after the period of evaluation. Therefore, we must have indices for evaluating long-term management effort to prevent SOEs management from sticking to short sighted and short-term oriented practices and to ensure healthy growth of the state-owned enterprises.

Third, we have to direct our evaluation effort to the performance and achievements of SOE business. We must induce the management and employees of SOEs to choose the right course of operation to reach certain management goals. If we set out a typical model of the course and method of operation and conduct evaluations based on the application of these models, the enterprises will lose their initiative and creativity and will look at business management simply as a means of following the tracks laid before them by the evaluators. If the essence of SOE business management is to obediently follow the instructions and orders from the government authorities and the evaluators, there are absolutely no reasons to conduct evaluations of business performance nor are there any incentives to become involved in evaluations that may take place.

If the evaluation is focused on the resultants of the SOE business performance, our evaluation must not depend solely on the measurement of total output. We must evaluate the output in comparison to the costs involved in making the output possible. In other words, in conducting such types of evaluation, we must base our evaluation on the value of output per unit cost of input.

4.1.2 Attributes of Evaluation Indices

In order for the SOE management to strive for efficiency in SOE business performance with confidence and creativity, the evaluation criteria, which are designed to function as signals of the free market functions, must be objective and rational. However, it may be practically impossible to define and establish universally applicable criteria or attributes of indices for evaluating the SOE business achievements. This is true because we must consider not only the typical nature of the SOE businesses but also the factors unique to each individual SOE business. In this paper, we will briefly discuss the main attributes which must be considered in defining and establishing the indices for evaluating SOE business performance.

1) Measurability

The subjects of evaluation must be measurable in order to ensure the objectivity of evaluation. In general, in order to eliminate any prejudice from evaluation, the indices must be so defined to enable quantitative measurement. In cases where qualitative evaluation is required, non-quantitative indices must be developed. Whether it be quantitative or non-quantitative, each index must be analyzed in depth in light of the applicability of available measuring methods.

2) Improvability

In view of the purpose of evaluating business performance, the indices must be established in consideration of the improvability of the relevant area of operation. No matter how good an index might be, if it is designed for an area that has no room for improvement, it does not serve any purpose. An index must be established so as to stimulate the area of operation where there is a great potential for improvement.

3) Controllability

The indices must be oriented to the management effort which can exercise control over the business operations. The factors that are not controllable by the SOE management, in particular pricing of utility charges and changes in government policies, should be screened out as much as possible or adjusted to a form that bears some controllability. And again, the indices should be defined so that they are comprehensible and helpful to SOE management in determining their position and performance under the established indices.

4) Relative materiality

There are a variety of main business activities, management goals, etc., depending on the type of SOE businesses that are the subjects of evaluation. Indices for the variety of these subjects must be defined and established in accordance with their relative materiality. The adequacy of the type and number of these indices may be different depending on the purpose and subject of evaluation but, it is desirous to keep the types and numbers of indices to the minimum possible.

5) Sufficiency

The evaluation indices should be comprehensive in their descriptions and be clearly definable among the indice items, sufficient enough to evaluate the business achievements attained by SOE operations. It is desirous to eliminate the possibility of making dual evaluations of the same achievement using different indices. It is also desirous to define and establish the indices so as to avoid a counteraction of the same element of a subject because it may invite confusion in the strategy of a business operation.

6) Comparability

In principle, the evaluation indices must maintain continuity in order to insure the stability of evaluation and business operations, and to enable comparison of the business achievements made and the extent of improvement attained each year. Except in cases where certain changes in government policy and an unexpected change in operating environment may adversely affect efforts to improve the operations, it is considered most important to maintain the continuity of evaluation indices.

4.1.3 Elements of the Evaluation Indices

The elements of evaluation indices consist of formula, standard, weight, and gradation.

First, the evaluation formula describes the substance of the indices and determines the factors to represent the renumerator and the denominator. The evaluation formula is determined according to the subjects selected for evaluation. In the case of quantitative indices, the substance of the formula is generally described by quantity (or value), percentage, etc., and the definitions of the quantity and value will become the most important factors in developing the indices. The evaluation formula details the operational achievements of the subject to be evaluated and is divided into quantitative and non-quantitative types of evaluation formulas.

Second, the evaluation standard functions as the basis for determining the performance and achievements of the business operation in connection with the intended evaluation indices. In other words, a standard value must be established for the value to be calculated by the evaluation formula. If this standard value is not properly established, the result obtained from its application becomes meaningless. In establishing the standard value, several methods are used as yardsticks, such as the average performance value of similar business for the same period, the trend of past performance values obtained by the same business, technical characteristics demonstrated by certain activities, and the business plans.

Third, the ratings of an evaluation should be graded in accordance with the degree of achievement attained. Once the formula and standard value are established, a performance is rated by calculating the values of performance based on the formula, and compared with the standard value established to find the level of achievement above or below the expected level. There will be performances rated higher or lower and we cannot agree to treat them all the same. This necessitates a gradation in the rating of performances and defining the range of each grade becomes as important as determining the standard value of evaluation.

Fourth, with the elements established as described above, we can come up with the values of ratings under each evaluation index. However, in order to make an overall evaluation of a business entity, we need to give certain weight to each index according to the relative materiality it occupies in the business. More weight is distributed to each index if it has higher relative materiality or priority, higher improvability, lesser susceptibility to outside influences, or higher objectivity in measuring the performance.

4.2 Evaluation Indices Currently in Use

4.2.1 Type of Indices

1) General index for overall business efficiency

The current indices being used for evaluating 25 state-owned business enterprises (SOEs) include the index for rating overall business efficiency (non-quantitative index with relative weight of 3). This index is established to minimize the possibility of inducing rigid management practices such as concentrating on the activities related to evaluation indices only.

The substance of this index is oriented mainly to creativity, adaptability to changing environment, morale of employees, stimulation of motivation, the subjects not measurable by other indices yet bearing significantly on SOE's management effort, and the adjustment of problems encountered in control of indices as a result of unexpected changes in management environment.

2) Management goal index

The management goal index is established to evaluate the subject of goals which is set forth in accordance with Article 5 (Establishment of Management Goals) of the SOE Management Fundamental Act. The subjects of evaluation by this index are:

- The purpose of incorporation and the production, revenue, and progress achieved with respect to the major functions assigned.
- The business goals as a prerequisite to budget organization.
- The typical research and development project and the customer service improvement programme which are considered important in SOE business operations.
- The project earmarked by the SOE's president for main effort during the fiscal year.

The majority of current management goal index uses quantitative type index that measures performance against goal but, where it is difficult to quantify the subject or it is necessary to measure a qualitative level, non-qualitative type index is also established. The relative weight distributed to this index is variable depending on the year and the characteristics of the SOE involved but, in general, it is kept within the range of 10 to 15 and distributed to each index depending on its importance and attainability. In the event that the management goal is changed due to changes in government policies or management environment, the substance of the index is adjusted accordingly and the performance is evaluated based on the revised index. As an example, the management goal index, 1986, used for four SOEs are presented in

Table 8 below.

Table 8   1986 Management Goal Index (Illustrated)

SOEs	Index Titles	Evaluation Methods	Relative Weights
CNB	Net increase in total deposits received	Obj. vs. perf.	4
	Total credits granted	''	4
	Citizen's passbook, its popularity	''	1
	Increase in amount of credit cards used	''	1
	Effective control of branches	Non-quan.	4
			(14)
KTA	No. of subscribers	Obj. vs. perf.	3
	LD carrier service	''	1
	Digitalizing carrier networks	''	4
	Rate of automatic telephone troubles	''	2
	Development of high-technology	Non-quan.	3
			(13)
ISDWRDC	Construction of multi-purpose dams	Obj. vs. perf.	5
	Control of water reservoirs	''	12
	Construction of new cities	''	2
	Major project controls	Non-quan.	6
			(25)
KTPC	Assisting trades in general	Obj. vs. perf.	2
	Assisting political trades	''	1
	Assisting import tradings	''	1
	Collection of trade information	''	2
	Participation in exhibitions	''	1
	Export contracts	''	1
	Sponsoring domestic trade fares	''	1
	Sponsoring Seoul International Exhibition	''	1
	Operating general consulting office	''	1
	Usage of general exhibition hall	''	2
			(13)

3)   Quantitative type index

The quantitative type index presents objective and numerical values of the performance measured and the standard value established for the evaluation. The quantitative type index which uses the evaluation method of trend value, Beta (β) distribution value, value of performance vs. goals (mainly management goals), etc., are mostly established for measuring short-term performances, such as profitability, marketability, progress, etc., of the SOE operations concerned. This index currently gives adequate consideration to the purpose of incorporation, major business activities, future trends, main areas of control, improvability, etc. The quantitative type index which focuses on the operational results and the efficiency of operation should receive greater attention in index development efforts in view of their controllability and objectivity in the method of measurement. The quantitative type index used for the four SOEs illustrated earlier are presented in Table 9 below (excludes the index of performance vs. goal).

Table 9   1986 Quantitative Type (Illustrated)

SOEs	Index Titles	Evaluating Standards	Evaluation Methods	Relative Weights
CNB	Control of operating profits	Operating profit=f (operating capital)	Value of 5 year trend	8
	Control of Operating expenses	Operating expenses=f (operating capital)	''	12
	Funding from internal sources	Funding=f (Currency circulated)	''	8
	Funding per employee	Funding=f (No. of employees)	5 year β distribution	4
	Credit write offs	Total deferred total paid on behalf=f (Total credits payment guarantees + Paid in behalf)	5 year trend	7
	Popular lending	Lent amount=f (Total credits granted)	''	5
	Administrative expenses	Expenses=f (Operating capital)	''	6 (50)
KTA	Productivity of operating fixed capital	Operating profit=f (Operating fixed capital)	7 year trend	18
	Service utilization	No. of calls=f (No. of sub-scribers)	''	3
	Telephone trouble time	Total trouble time=f (No. of subscribers)	''	3
	Local procurement of plant equipment	Local purchase/ Total purchase	3 year β distribution	3
	Administrative expenses	Expenses=f (Sales)	7 yr. trend	5

SOEs	Inded Titles	Evaluatin Standards	Evaluation Methods	Relative Weights
Savings in labour costs		Labour cost=f (Sales)	7 year trend	2
	Cost per plant equipment	Total cost=f (No. of plant)	''	2
	Repayment capability of loans	(Net profit before tax + depreciation + interests paid)/(Repayment of principal + interest paid)	3 year β distribution	3
	Inventory control			
	— Capital items (specific)	Value used/ average inventory value	4 year trend	3
	— Operational items	Average inventory=f (Value used)	7 year trend	2
	Control of manpower level	Subscribers/ employees	4 year trend	3 (47)

4) Non-quantitative type index

The non-quantitative type index, which employs five rating groups in its evaluation method, is designed to evaluate qualitative aspects of the management system and the business operation. It emphasizes long-term achievement instead of short-term.

Among the current non-quantitative indices, there are, as shown in Table 10, the indices commonly applicable to all 25 SOEs such as long-term business management, improvement of management systems, in-house evaluation programmes, service improvement, research and development, etc., and some typical index items that are applicable to individual SOEs. As an example, the index items for the customer service improvement programme are illustrated in Table 11.

Table 10 Non-Quantitative Indices

	CNB		KTA		ISWRDC	
	Index	Weight	Index	Weight	Index	Weight
Common indices	– Efficiency of comprehensive management	3	– Efficiency of comprehensive management	3	– Efficiency of comprehensive management	3
	– Long-term management	3	– Long-term management	4	– Long-term management	3
	– Improvement of management system	10	– Improvement of management system	8	– Improvement of management system	10
	– In-house evaluation programme	7	– In-house evaluation programme	7	– In-house evaluation programme	7
	– Improvement of service	5	– Improvement of service	2	– Improvement of service	3
		(28)	– R&D	2 (26)	– R&D	4 (30)
Special indices	– Supply of fund . Judgement . Management of credit granted	4	– Satisfaction degree of telecommunication service	3	– Management of water resources	4
	– Effective management of bank shops	4	– Quality promotion of telecommunication	3	– Managment of major project	6
		(12) 40	– Development of telecommunication technology	9		
			– Effective management system	2 (17) 43		(10) (40)

Table 11   Improvement of Customer Services (Citizens National Bank)

Items Evaluated	Descriptions
1. Service for deposit accounts	• Effort to shorten time at counter • Variety of marketing effort for inducing deposits by customer • Employees attitude in handling cases and positive responses to customer grievances
2. Service for credit accounts	• Screening against excess credit and simplification of credit documentation • Adequate credit counseling and providing information service • Treatment of credit customers' opinions and grievances

4.2.2   Weight Distribution

The relative weights are determined by giving due consideration to the relative materiality, improvability, controllability, etc., of the activities being evaluated with respect to the subject of evaluation. The relative weights for the quantitative index is assigned within the range of 60 to 40 points taking into consideration the typical characteristics of the SOEs concerned.

In general, the relative weights assigned to quantitative and non-quantitative type indices for similar SOEs are kept as close as possible. The distribution of relative weights made in 1986 for individual SOEs by type and nature of the index are shown in Table 12.

4.2.3   Evaluation methods

The methods of evaluation are applied differently depending on the types of index used, i.e., quantitative index, performance vs. goal index, and non-quantitative index.

1) Quantitative type index-establishing the standards of value

Except for the progress evaluation type index, most quantitative indexes use regressive analysis method or Beta (β) distribution method as the method for establishing standards of evaluated values. Only in special cases, is the method of a simple arithmetic mean value used. In this report, we will discuss the methods of regressive analysis and Beta (β) distribution.

Table 12 Distribution of Relative Weights (1986)

SOEs	General Index Quanti-tative	General Index Non-quanti-tative	General Index Sub-total	Business Purpose Index Quanti-tative	Business Purpose Index Non-quanti-tative	Business Purpose Index Sub-total	Management Control Index Quanti-tative	Management Control Index Non-quanti-tative	Management Control Index Sub-total	Total Quanti-tative	Total Non-quanti-tative	Total Sub-total
KDB	20	3	23	40	12	52	—	25	25	60	40	100
IBK	20	3	23	40	12	52	—	25	25	60	40	100
CNB	20	3	23	40	12	52	—	25	25	60	40	100
KHB	20	3	23	40	12	52	—	25	25	60	40	100
KSE	25	3	28	15	27	42	—	30	30	40	60	100
KSPMC	14	3	17	46	12	58	—	25	25	60	40	100
KEPC	27	3	30	38	9	47	—	23	23	65	35	100
DCC	15	3	18	45	15	60	—	22	22	60	40	100
KMPC	—	3	3	60	13	73	—	24	24	60	40	100
KPDC	—	3	3	45	20	65	—	32	32	45	55	100
KGCIC	—	3	3	45	21	66	—	31	31	45	55	100
KTPC	—	3	3	55	20	75	—	22	22	55	45	100
KHC	25	3	28	35	10	45	—	27	27	60	40	100
KNHC	20	3	23	40	10	50	—	27	27	60	40	100
ISWRDC	25	3	28	35	10	45	—	27	27	60	40	100
KLDC	22	3	25	38	10	48	—	27	27	60	40	100
APC	10	3	13	50	12	62	—	25	25	60	40	100
AFMC	10	3	13	43	18	61	7	19	26	60	40	100
KTA	21	3	24	36	17	53	—	23	23	57	43	100
KNTC	—	3	3	52	22	74	3	20	23	55	45	100
KBS	—	3	3	44	33	77	—	20	20	44	56	100
NTC	20	3	23	40	15	55	—	22	22	60	40	100
KODC	4	3	7	46	32	78	—	15	15	50	50	100
KLWC	12	3	15	43	15	58	—	27	27	55	45	100
KGC	—	3	3	40	30	70	—	27	27	40	60	100
Total	330	75	405	1,051	419	1,470	10	615	625	1,391	1,109	2,500
Average	13.2	3.0	16.2	42.0	16.8	58.8	0.4	24.6	25.0	55.6	44.4	100.0

i) Regressive analysis method

For trend values, a linear regression model is used in principle. In cases where there is a significance in time (year) and statistics, the time is taken as an independent variable (i.e., productivity of operating fixed capital: public interest/operating fixed capital=f(t), and in cases where there is a variable which is inter-dependent on a dependent variable other than the time, that variable is taken as the independent variable (i.e., administrative costs=f(revenue)).

The value of trend computes the standard deviation registered for previous performance during the past 3 to 7 years to determine its standard value and gradation of ratings. The following is the formula for computing the standard value and the standard deviation:

Standard Value: $Y = a + bx_p$

Standard Deviation:
$$\sqrt{\frac{\sum\limits_{i=1}^{n}(Y_i-a-bx_i)^2}{n-2} \times \left\{1 + \frac{1}{n} + \frac{(X_p-X)^2}{\sum\limits_{i=1}^{n}(X_i-X)^2}\right\}}$$

X = independent variable,
X_i = X value in i year,
X_p = X value in the year of evaluation
Y = dependent variable,
Y_i = Y value in i year
a, b = parameter derived from regressive analysis
n = duration of regressive analysis

ii) Beta (β) analysis method

This method is used when there is less significance in analysing value of trends, and when used, bases its analysis on 3 to 5 years of performance depending on the type of SOEs. The standard value and the standard deviation are computed as follows:

Standard Value: $Y = \dfrac{a + 4m + b}{6 - 1}$

Standard Deviation: $S = \sqrt{\dfrac{(b - a)^2}{36}}$

a: The least performance value attained during the period
b: The best performance value attained during the period
m: The performance value of the previous year

Gradation was done in five rating groups and rating points. Since we found the standard deviations, the next step is to determine the range of probability of the performance values relative to the standard value or norm, to determine the gradation of evaluated ratings.

The gradations or rating groups are divided into five groups, namely, A, B, C, D, and E group and their distribution of probability is the upper most 10% for A group, the upper 20% for B group, the middle 40% for C group, the lower middle 20% for D group, and the lower most 10% for E group as depicted in Figure 1.

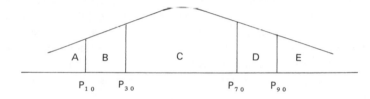

Fig. 1   Distribution of Probability of Rating Groups

The P_{10}, P_{30}, P_{70}, and P_{90} in the Fig. 1 represent the points that distinguish each rating group. To these points are added P_{95} and P_5 each of which represents the midpoints of rating group A and E respectively. The dividing points of rating groups are calculated by adding the standard deviation to the quotient obtained by multiplying the standard deviation by the norms of each individual probability factor as shown in Table 13.

Table 13   The Values of Standard Norms of Distribution Factors

Dividing points	P_5	P_{10}	P_{30}	P_{70}	P_{90}	P_{95}
Regular distribution	−1.645	−1.282	−0.526	0.526	1.282	1.645

In assigning rating points, the performance value is measured first to determine the rating group followed by a computation of the rating points within the rating group according to the formulae given in Table 14.

Table 14   Formulae for Computing Rating Points

Rating Groups	Formulae
A	$95 + 2.5 \times \dfrac{(\text{Performance value} - P_{90})}{(P_{95} - P_{90})}$
B	$90 + 5 \times (Pv - P_{70})/(P_{90} - P_{70})$
C	$75 + 5 \times (Pv - P_{30})/(P_{70} - P_{30})$
D	$80 + 5 \times (Pv - P_{10})/(P_{30} - P_{12})$
E	$77.5 + 2.5 \times (Pv - P_{5})/(P_{10} - P_{5})$

The upper and lower limits of the rating points, set to 100 and 75 points respectively, do not allow for going above or below these points.

2)   Performance vs. goal type indices

The progress rating indices evaluate the progress made against the goal established in terms of the percentage of progress made against the established goal. Except in cases where there are no other methods of evaluation presented in the relevant indices of the SOEs concerned, and where there are certain variable goals and the goal assigning indices are specifically established for the SOEs concerned, the performance vs. goal type indices generally compute the progress made towards the goal based on the following formula:

$$\text{Progress Achieved (\%)} = \frac{\text{Performance}}{\text{goal}} \times 100$$

Depending on the nature of goals established, there are indices that rate the performance high for greater progress made (upward goal) and those that rate the performance low for less progress made (downward goal). The rating points for individual cases are computed on the following formulae:

* Upward goals: $75 \text{ points} + \dfrac{X_i - 85}{15} \times 25 \text{ points}$

* Downward goals: $75 \text{ points} + \dfrac{X_i - 100}{15} \times 25 \text{ points}$

Note: X_i = Progress achieved in the year evaluated

3)   Non-quantitative type indices

The non-quantitative type indices, which cannot measure performance in quantity, also use the five rating groups of A, B, C, D, and E. To ensure better objectivity of the evaluation, detailed rating criteria and rating points are developed and assigned to each group of ratings.

4) Overall rating points

The overall rating points are calculated by adding up the sums obtained by multiplying the points given to each of the quantitative indices (including the performance vs. goal indices) and the non-quantitative indices by the relative weight assigned to each of the indices. The meanings of the overall rating points are defined in Table 15.

Table 15   Overall Rating Points

Points	Group	Standard
95 – 100	A	The SOEs which showed marked improvement in business achievement over the previous year
90 – 95	B	The SOEs whose business achievement improved over the previous year
85 – 90	C	The SOEs which showed business achievement similar to the previous year
80 – 85	D	The SOEs whose business achievement showed no progress over the previous year
75 – 80	E	The SOEs whose business achievement decreased from the previous year

4.2.4   Incentive Programme

As discussed earlier, a business evaluation system must be tied in with an appropriate incentive system in order for the evaluation system to be readily accepted as a means of motivation for business improvement. In this regard, the current SOE business evaluation system provides adequate incentives for achievement by SOEs in their business operations.

Presently, the rate of incentive awards is set in steps from a maximum of 300% to a minimum of 100% providing a range of 200% for gradation in steps.

During 1983 and 1984, at the inception of the evaluation system, a uniform rate of incentive awards was adopted for each rating group. Since 1985, each rating group has been further classified by introducing an overall rating point system and the rate of incentive award has been differentiated within each rating group, except for the A group of 300%. In the previous system, a difference of one rating point at an upper or lower margin of a rating group could cost 50% in the rate of incentive award. This gap was reduced to 10% by the application of the new rating system. A comparison of the incentive rates in 1984 and

1985 is shown in Table 16.

Table 16   A Comparison of the Incentive Rates by Groups

(Unit: %)

Points	Group	Rate of incentive award	
		1984	1985
95 – 100	A	300	300
90 – 95	B	250	250 – 290
95 – 90	C	200	200 – 240
80 – 85	D	150	150 – 190
75 – 80	E	100	100 – 140

5. Effectiveness of the New Policy

The New SOE Management Policy was introduced in 1984 with the purpose of improving SOE business operations which play a vital role in the national economy of Korea. What are the effects of the New Policy?

A survey was conducted to assess the influence of the New Policy, on the improvement of SOE business operations. The questionnaires responses from 750 directors and employees in SOE businesses revealed that the business operations of all twenty-five SOEs are changing their styles remarkably.

As shown in Table 17, the area that received the most positive response was the determination of top management for business improvement. Of the total respondents, 79.1% felt increased determination of the top level management for improvement of the business operations. In the area of mental attitude of the employees towards business improvement, 71.5% responded positively. Of the respondents, 76.8% felt the impetus of the evaluation system introduced by the new policy. It also revealed that there was a remarkable leap in the improvements made in the area of customer services. On the other hand, we found negative responses in over 10% of the total respondents in the areas that included personnel programmes, effectiveness of long-range planning and its policy, mental attitudes of employees towards business improvement. These areas indicate the need for further improvement efforts.

Another notable effect was seen in the positive responses on the effect of the new policy from middle management which overwhelmed those of the lower level employees. This apparently reflected the approval of middle management regarding the provisions of the New

Policy which banned outsiders from executive positions (including vice presidents) and drastically reduced the number of incumbent outsiders to 5% of the total number of incumbent directors by the end of 1986 from 53% in 1983.

As described above, the determination for improving SOE business operations is prevailing throughout the organizations from top management down to low level employees and from workers in managing and controlling positions to those in the fields of operation.

Table 17   Analysis of Responses to Questionnaires

(Unit: %)

Questionnaire	Responses		
	Positive	Negative	Neutral
1. Progress in overall improvements	64.4	7.3	28.3
2. Determination of top management and its influence in daily operations	79.1	6.5	14.4
3. Improvement in personnel programmes	29.3	15.2	55.5
4. Efficiency of budget and property control	55.3	6.3	38.4
5. R&D activities	61.4	5.9	32.7
6. Improvement in customer service	70.6	2.3	27.1
7. Effectiveness of long-range planning and its strategy	57.4	11.2	31.4
8. Change in mental attitude of employees towards improvement of business operation	71.5	13.2	15.3
9. Impetus of evaluation system in daily operation	76.8	5.0	18.2

Note: Positive responses include very positive and somewhat positive, and negative responses include very and somewhat negative.

Source: The Korea Development Research Essays, KDI 1987 Summer Edition pp. 93 to 100.

Next, we will discuss the effect of the new policy in terms of improvements in the business operations. According to the quantitative regressive analysis made on the cost of production by comparing projected cost of sales against actual cost of sales, the productive efficiency of SOEs in performing their business operations improved considerably.

During the three years from 1984 to 1986, total net savings in production costs were projected at US$346 million. During the first three years after the inception of the New policy, the average rate of the cost of sales of all SOEs was 69.9%, which is 4.1% less than the 74.0% cost before 1984. The savings expressed in monetary value would correspond to an amount of US$1,309 million. However, the analysis reported the estimated net savings of US$70 million in 1984, US$99 million in 1985 and US$182 million in 1986. This takes into consideration the difference of over 1.86 times the standard deviation of the accuracy of projected costs of sales from the actual costs of sales.

As evidenced above, since the inception of the New SOE Management Policy, the mental attitudes of SOE employees are changing positively and the SOE business operations are changing their styles, along with remarkable improvements being made in the efficiency of

Table 18   Comparison of Actual and Projected Cost of Sale Rate of SOEs

(Unit: %)

	1984	1985	1986
Finance			
● Actual cost of sale rate	80.5	76.8	76.9
● Projected cost of sale	82.3	83.1	84.0
● Difference rate	1.8	6.3	7.1
Construction			
● Actual cost of sale	80.3	76.2	76.3
● Projected cost of sale rate	81.7	82.0	82.6
● Difference rate	1.4	5.8	6.3
Manufacturing			
● Actual cost of sale rate	73.4	79.0	74.5
● Projected cost of sale rate	77.7	81.1	79.0
● Difference rate	4.3	2.1	4.5
Service			
● Actual cost of sale rate	54.1	59.9	64.7
● Projected cost of sale rate	70.1	70.0	70.3
● Difference rate	16.0	10.8	5.6
Energy & telecommunications			
● Actual cost of sale rate	68.2	67.0	62.0
● Projected cost of sale rate	70.9	69.4	66.5
● Difference rate	2.7	2.4	4.5
Total			
● Actual cost of sale rate	71.7	70.2	67.7
● Projected cost of sale	74.7	74.3	73.1
● Difference rate	3.0	4.1	5.3

Table 19 Projected Cost Difference and Net Savings in Production Costs by SOEs and by Year

(Unit: US$ thousand)

	1984			1985			1986		
	Cost Difference	Standard Deviation	Cost Saved	Cost Difference	Standard Deviation	Cost Saved	Cost Difference	Standard Deviation	Cost Saved
KDB	△26.290	–	–	△2.779	–	–	17.141	–	–
CNB	26.796	11.752	4.936	75.738	11.690	53.993	97.750	12.830	73.886
IBK	19.620	8.979	2.920	22.935	9.024	6.151	25.064	10.676	5.207
KHB	17.183	7.364	3.486	40.759	6.927	27.783	39.129	7.492	25.194
KSE	0.330	0.115	0.116	0.883	0.124	0.653	4.292	0.212	3.897
Subtotal	–	–	(11.458)	–	–	(88.580)	–	–	(108.183)
KSPMC	0.489	–	–	1.470	–	–	3.913	1.375	1.357
NTC	3.420	1.291	1.020	0.189	–	–	△0.319	–	–
Subtotal	–	–	(1.020)	–	–	(0)	–	–	(1.357)
KEPC	161.163	69.270	32.788	130.827	65.413	9.157	177.925	63.545	59.731
KTA	△3.355	–	–	△10.882	–	–	93.938	–	–
DCC	△1.259	–	–	23.321	–	–	26.849	13.652	1.456
KMPC	0.445	–	–	0.887	0.330	0.273	1.420	0.349	0.770
Subtotal	–	–	(32.788)	–	–	(9.430)	–	–	(61.956)
KNHC	△1.780	12.288	–	△11.785	10.607	–	25.111	15.288	0
KHC	2.296	–	–	5.829	–	–	20.086	–	–
ISWRDC	9.270	4.890	0.190	16.730	8.665	0.612	27.335	9.567	9.540
KLDC	6.536	31.061	0	71.460	49.357	0	32.790	45.296	0
Subtotal	–	–	(0.157)	–	–	(0.612)	–	–	(9.540)

	1984			1985			1986		
	Cost Difference	Standard Deviation	Cost Saved	Cost Difference	Standard Deviation	Cost Saved	Cost Difference	Standard Deviation	Cost Saved
AFMC	3.275	0.803	1.783	1.076	0.933	0	△3.031	1.264	0
KNTC	0.572	—	—	2.447	1.174	0.263	3.855	1.705	0.684
KBS	60.888	23.169	17.794	36.664	21.038	0	21.453	21.248	0
KODC	△0.144	—	—	△0.139	—	—	0.275	—	—
KLWC	1.740	—	—	2.817	—	—	1.932	—	—
Subtotal	—	—	(19.577)	—	—	(0.263)	—	—	(0.684)
Total	—	—	65.000	—	—	98.886	—	—	181.720

Notes: 1. Standard deviation:
2. Costs saved: (Cost difference) − (1.86) · (Standard deviation)
* tolerance of 5%

the SOE business operations.

In other words, the New SOE Management Policy is playing its role successfully acting in place of the "invisible hand" to the SOE businesses where the functions of free market principles are not apt to apply. The New SOE Management Policy reduced government controls drastically, granted autonomous authority to SOE management and provided SOEs with the evaluation indices aiding in management decisions. It also provided the means for stringent post-evaluation of business performance and follow-up action. The New Policy is now functioning in place of the free market system.

5.1 Achievements Made by SOE

The amount of value added by SOEs in 1986 reached US$5,576 million which was an increase of 19.8% from the previous year and exceeded the GDP rate of increase by 5.2%. From the amount of value added, US$792 million (28.3%) was expended for labour costs and US$792 million (14.2%) for financing costs.

Table 20   Value Added by SOE Businesses

(Unit: US$ millions)

	1985	1986	Increase (%)
Value added by SOE	4,503	5,576	19.8
GDP	84,824	100,429	14.6
Share of V.A. (%)	(5.3)	(5.6)	—

Source: National Economy, 1986, Bank of Korea

Table 21   Composition of Value Added by SOEs

(Unit: US$ millions)

	Labour Cost	Depreciation	Profit	Pretax Financing Taxes			Total
				Cost	Duties	Loans	
1985	1,360	1,295	931	672	198	49	4,505
(%)	(30.2)	(28.7)	(20.7)	(14.9)	(4.4)	(1.1)	(100)
1986	1,579	1,618	1,275	792	256	55	5,575
(%)	(28.3)	(29.0)	(22.9)	(14.2)	(4.6)	(1.0)	(100)

Source: Economic Planning Board, 1987

Next, we will look into the revenue or sales of SOE businesses. The total sales of SOE businesses registered US$11,723 million in 1986 and reflected an increase of 11.4% from the previous year owing to the business upturn. It closely compared to the 12.4% increase in sales registered by the business posted in the stock market. On the other hand, the stability in prices of energy and raw materials helped keep operating expenses to an increase of only 8.8%. Thus, the operating profit was US$2.735 million, an increase of 20.9% which was slightly above the level achieved in the previous year. As a result, the SOE businesses were able to produce a remarkable leap in the growth of net profit (30.3%) to US$922 million in 1986.

Table 22 Profit and Loss of SOE Businesses

(Unit: US$ millions)

	1984	1985	1986	Business on S/E (1986)
Sales	9,628	10,186 (13.8)	11,723 (11.4)	(12.4)
Oper. expenses	7,675	7,997 (12.1)	8,988 (8.8)	(12.9)
Oper. profit	1,953	2,197 (20.6)	2,735 (20.9)	(4.8)
Net profit	740	684 (−0.5)	922 (30.3)	(34.6)

Note: Figures in (   ) represent % of increase from the previous year.

Source: Economic Planning Board

In 1986, SOEs' total assets increased to US$57,687 million by 9% from the previous year. This increase was proportionally lower than the increase of 11.4% made in sales in the same year. Consequently, the return on total assets turnover showed a slight increase from 17.7% in 1985 to 18.0% in 1986. The total liabilities also increased by 8% to US$50,364 million while a greater increase was made in the capital investment that Debt of ratio to capital decreased from 358.9% in 1985 to 344.7% in 1986 resulting in a slight improvement in SOEs' financial positions.

Table 23 Financial Position of SOE Businesses

(Unit: US$ millions)

	1985	1986	Increase (%)
Assets	57,687	64,975	9.0
Liabilities	45,117	50,364	8.0
Capital	12,570	14,611	12.5
Total assets turnover (%)	17.7	18.0	−
Debt ratio (%)	358.9	344.7	−
Net worth ratio (%)	21.8	22.5	

Source: Economic Planning Board

As discussed in the above reviews, there are indications that the efficiency of SOE business operations is improving gradually since the inception of the New SOE Management Policy. Still, the SOE businesses would need sustained effort to resolve their problems, particularly in the areas where the problems are pinpointed in the course of implementing the evaluation programme.

5.2 Evaluation Sample of a Typical Enterprise (KTA)

5.2.1 General

The Korea Telecommunications Authority which is responsible for performing as the backbone of the telecommunications industry of Korea succeeded in resolving the chronic problem it faced with long accumulated subscription applications and began responding to new subscriptions spontaneously in 1986 except in certain remote areas. It provided adequate telecommunications support for the 1986 Asian Games and is now endeavoring to expand its services throughout the nation. In spite of lowering the service charges for long distance and overseas telephone calls, it has attained a 139% increase in net profits for the year 1986. This and other achievements in its operations helped it rate "the business performed in a manner superior to previous years or "B" in the rating groups."

5.2.2 Quantitative Evaluation

The KTA's productivity of operating fixed assets reflected an increase of 30.6% in 1986 over the operating profit attained during the previous year and the usage of telephone service was increased by 19.8%. The telephone service was extended to 1,572,000 subscribers and 42 regional areas were linked with automatic digital networks. The long distance carrier routings have accommodated 33,048 lines to mark a 16.6% increase against the planned goal. The digitalization of carrier networks was also effected in 47.9% of cases in metropolitan area and in 51.4% in local areas meeting the target established for the year. The rate of automatic telephone trouble was kept to 1.49% which satisfied the trouble rate established for the target year.

The average number of telephone subscribers increased by 19.8% in 1986 while the total trouble time was reduced by 3.8%. The capital investment for plant equipment was controlled while increasing domestic procurements, and the overall expenses including labour costs are being reduced. In 1986, the revenue from sales increased by 14.5% based on current prices while the operating expenses increased by 29.9% and presented the need for saving effort in the area of operational expenses.

5.2.3   Non-Quantitative Evaluation

The accumulation of technical skill satisfies the need for exapnsion in plant facilities. There is an untiring effort to enhance the efficiency of plant equipment invested, through the optimum telecommunication services rendered to customers throughout the country.

The quality of customer service is generally considered adequate and the level far exceeded the service rendered in the previous year. However, it is necessary to continue to improve the quality in light of the ever-increasing demand for better communications services.

In the area of technical development, notable efforts were made in the field of high technology, such as the development of TDX, but additional efforts in developing coordinated inter-ministerial measures will be needed in order to provide for the mass information era. It was also noted that more effective measures will be required to commer-cialize newly developed technology and to speed up the growth of the telecommunications industry.

In the area of procurement, there was some laxity found in resource saving attitudes in the course of planning and implementing the procurement budget and material control. It will require additional effort to improve budgeting and organizational control. Utilization of in-house evaluation programmes, TQC activities and suggestion pro-grammes may help to improve this critical problem area.

On the other hand, KTA was successful in laying groundwork for a reasonable manpower programme by completing a thorough and systematic job analysis. Its manpower control was excellent and was in line with the personnel requirements generated by the development of technology. KTA was able to present its long range objectives by making unbiased analysis of its own weaknesses. It deserved the high appraisal received by the group which conducted the evaluation works.

5.2.4   Rating Points Given by Indices

Table 24   Rating Points Obtained Per Index

Index Title	Evaluation Standard	Evaluation Method	Weight	Rating Group	Rating Points
1. General index			(24)		(23.78)
a. Productivity of operating fixed capital	Operating profit = f (Operating fixed capital)	Value of 7 year trends	18	. A	18.00
b. Use of telecom. service	No. of auto. telephone calls = Total subscribes	"	3	A	2.78
c. Overall operational efficiency		5 rating groups	3	A	3.00
2. Business objective index			(53)		(50.28)
a. Response to service demand			7		6.76
o Subscriptions	o Installed: 1.558 lines	Obj. vs. Perf.	(1)	A	(1.00)
	o Automatic: 42 areas	"	(2)	A	(2.00)
1 LD carriers	o 28.332 lines completed	"	(1)	A	(1.00)
o Improvement effort		5 rating groups			
	o Adequacy of demand vs. supply		(1)	C	(0.88)
	o Effectiveness of plant expansion & invest- ment in equipment		(1)	B	(0.94)
	o Adequacy of plan for Olympiad		(1)	B	(0.94)
b. Quality of service			12		11.45
o Digital carrier system	o City: 47.8%	Obj. vs. Perf.	(2)	A	(2.00)
	o Local: 51.1%	"	(2)	A	(2.00)
o Trouble rate, auto telephone	1.5%	"	(2)	A	(2.00)
o Trouble time	o Annual trouble time/ subscribers	Value of 7 year trends	(3)	B	(2.71)
o Improvement effort		5 rating groups			
	o Quality		(1)	C	(0.87)
	o Utilization		(1)	C	(0.87)
	o Security		(1)	A	(1.00)
c. Technical development			12		11.38
o Local purchase	o Value/Total 3 year β distribution purchases	3 year β distribution	(3)	A	(3.00)
o Improvement effort		5 rating groups			
	o High-tech development		(3)	A	(3.00)
	o Quality insurance		(2)	B	(1.38)
	o Commercializing new technology		(2)	C	(1.75)
	o Support of growth		(2)	C	(1.75)
d. Effectiveness of management			22		20.69
o Admin. cost	Admin. cost = f (Sales)	7 year trends	(5)	E	(3.90)

Index Title	Evaluation Standard	Evaluation Method	Weight	Rating Group	Rating Points
○ Savings in labour costs	Labour cost = f (Sales)	7 year trends	(2)	A	(2.00)
○ Control of cost per plant	Total cost = f (Plants)	,,	(2)	A	(2.00)
○ Repayment of loans	(Prof. before tax + depreciation interest)/ principal repaid + interest paid	5 year β distribution	(3)	A	(3.00)
○ Inventory operation					
— Investments	Value used/average inventory	4 year trends	(3)	A	(2.87)
— Operational	Average inventory = f (Value used)	7 ear trends	(2)	A	(1.92)
○ Manpower control	Subscribers/employees	4 year trends	(3)	A	(3.00)
○ Improvement effort	Control of manpower management	5 rating groups	(2)	A	(2.00)
3. Management index			(23)		(20.37)
a. Long range management		5 rating groups	4		3.81
	○ Adjustment of business plant to fit with changes in business environment		(1)	A	(1.00)
	○ Rationality in long range planning and relationship with short range plans		(1)	B	(0.94)
	○ Reasonableness of investment plan and adequacy of its implementation		(2)	B	(1.37)
b. Improvement in management		5 rating groups	8		7.31
	○ Operation of board of directors		(2)	B	(1.87)
	○ Control of personnel and organization		(1)	C	(0.88)
	○ Operation of budget		(3)	C	(2.62)
	○ Efficiency of management information		(1)	B	(0.94)
	○ Control of energy		(1)	A	(1.00)
c. In-house evaluation system		5 rating groups	7		5.63
	○ Internal goals and their reasonableness		(2)	D	(1.63)
	○ Adequacy of measuring method		(1)	C	(0.87)
	○ Effectiveness of incentive programme		(2)	E	(1.50)
	○ Action for improvement through evaluation		(2)	D	(1.63)
d. Service improvements		5 rating groups	2		1.81
	○ Control of existing service		(1)	C	(0.87)

Index Title	Evaluation Standard	Evaluation Method	Weight	Rating Group	Rating Points
	o Development of new service and their commercialization		(1)	B	(0.94)
e. Research and development		5 rating groups	2		1.81
	o Performance and contribution of its findings		(1)	C	(0.87)
	o Securing technical manpower and cooperation of concerned industries		(1)	B	(0.94)
Quantitative total			57		55.18
Non-quantitative total			43		39.25
Grand total			100		94.43

6. Conclusion and Recommendations

The state-owned enterprises of Korea contribute highly in adding values, share foreign debt, have a high ratio of operating assets, and have high leakage effects. They truly occupy a very important position in the national economy. Nevertheless, it is also true that their operating efficiency is low. Their monopolistic business nature curtails the free market functions which would normally act upon them so that an efficient business is difficult to distinguish from an inefficient one. Adequate compensation for achievement is neglected in these business operations. Therefore, there must be certain stringent artificial signals provided for SOE management in order for them to improve the efficiency of their business operations. It was because of the controls and intervention of the government authorities and the absence of such artificial signals that inefficiency prevailed in SOEs.

For these reasons, the government withdrew its conventional SOE management policy, which had only obscured the line of responsibility between the government control and the SOE management. It then enacted the SOE management Fundamental Act and advocated the New SOE Management Policy. The framework of the New SOE Management Policy consisted of ensuring autonomous authority in business operations, limiting the exercise of government controls, and conducting post-operation evaluations. It provided the SOE management with the autonomous authority to manage its own business operations, instituted the means to accurately evaluate SOE business performance with pre-established indices of evaluation, and required fair reward and penalty following the evaluations.

Thus, designed to function as an artificial signal for SOE management decisions in place of the free market functions, the New Policy's focal point was the pre-establishment of evaluation standards. In our earlier discussions, we have enumerated and reviewed the subjects of evaluation, the attributes and elements of evaluation standards along with the current evaluation indices being used for SOE businesses, and the effectiveness of the New SOE Management Policy. A survey of SOE operations covering the 3-year period (1984—1986) at the inception of the New Policy reported obvious indications of determination for improvement emerging from the SOE management. It also recognized a change in mental attitudes of SOE employees towards the improvement of their business operations. The employees were feeling the impetus of the New Policy in their daily operations. Appointment of outsiders to the executive positions were drastically curtailed. It was particularly noteworthy that the survey reported the New Policy was accepted more positively by the executives and the middle management than the lower level employees. In other words, since the inception of the New Policy, the determination for operational improvement is prevailing in the SOE business at large, and the style of SOE business operation is changing remarkably.

According to the analysis made by quantitative regressive approach, the productivity of SOE business operation was also greatly improved. During the three-year period from 1984 to 1986, the net savings in the production cost of SOEs were projected at a total of 346 million. This project alone may very well serve as proof of the effectiveness of the New Policy in the overall SOE business operation.

By now we know that because the SOEs are monopolistic in nature and operate in the public interest, the prices of the products and services of the SOEs are established artificially. The SOE business operation is deprived of autonomy by government controls and interventions. Functions of free market principles are not apt to act on SOEs. It was possible to improve the economy of SOEs by introducing the concept of capitalism into the SOE business, releasing their operations from government controls, and improving their competitiveness. We also found that, for SOEs which are immune to evolutionary evaluation devices ("invisible hands"), the injection of an artificial evaluation device and a fair and stringent evaluation effort prompted by such device will serve as nuclei to the management policy. By subjecting the SOE business to the principles of capitalism, we may expect to see the SOEs making better contributions in the national economy.

Finally, we will conclude this paper with the following statements as recommendations to the government authorities with a view to sustain or improve the strategic effectiveness of the SOE business performance evaluation system now in its implementation stage.

First, the current evaluation indices consist of quantitative and non-quantitative type indices and most of them are commonly applicable to all SOEs, namely, general index, performance vs. goal index, and management index. It is desirous that this index structure be revised to include SOE common index, specific business index (common to types of business such as banking, manufacturing, construction, service, policy implementing, etc.), and SOE unique index, etc., in order to increase the effectiveness of the evaluation system and to conform to the type of business to be evaluated.

Secondly, the evaluation is presently conducted during the period from March to June. This period of time does not coincide with the time that professors may leave the school campus, and the actual time spent for evaluation work was found to be limited to approximately two months. Therefore, it is recommended that the actual evaluation time be extended to four or five months. In order to improve the professionalism in the evaluation works, it is particularly recommended that the members of the evaluation group be appointed in September or October of the previous year to allow them a period of familiarization with the specific SOE to be evaluated.

Thirdly, the evaluation teams are organized for each different index and each member of a team is assigned to a certain number of SOEs to conduct the evaluation work according to the current practice. This method may have advantages in terms of professionalism and specialization but may also be susceptible to a subjective approach by the team members. Therefore, it is recommended that each member of the team be assigned to evaluate all twenty-five SOEs concurrently. This method is considered more substantial even though it may be more time consuming.

Fourthly, current incentive is limited to 300% of bonus awards. In general, this amount of incentive bonus is regarded as only a portion of the bonus level being paid to the employees of private enterprises and may cause a negative effect on the SOE incentive system. Therefore, it is recommended that the 300% incentive bonuses be converted to normal or ordinary bonuses and a separate incentive programme for the evaluation system be introduced. A multiple type incentive programme including pay raises, cash awards, citations, etc., and closely tied-in with the appraisals resulting from the evaluation should improve the effectiveness of the evaluation system. A recommendation for dismissal of directors, if deemed necessary, should be given due consideration. A careful and sufficient review must carried out if incentive awards are to be differentiated depending on the positions held.

Name of SOEs

AFMC	Agricultural & Fisheries Marketing Corp.
APC	Agricultural Promotion Corp.
CNB	Citizens National Bank
DCC	Daihan Coal Corp.
IBK	Industrial Bank of Korea
ISWRDC	Industrial Sites & Water Res. Development Corp.
KBS	Korea Broadcasting System
KDB	Korea Development Bank
KEPC	Korea Electric Power Corp.
KGC	Korea Gas Corp.
KGCIC	Korea General Chemical Industry Corp.
KHB	Korea Housing Bank
KHC	Korea Highway Corp.
KLDC	Korea Land Development Corp.
KLWC	Korea Labour Welfare Corp.
KMPC	Korea Mining Promotion Corp.
KNHC	Korea National Housing Corp.
KNTC	Korea National Tourism Corp.
KODC	Korea Overseas Development Corp.
KPDC	Korea Petroleum Development Corp.
KSE	Korea Stock Exchange
KSPMC	Korea Security Printing & Minting Corp.
KTA	Korea Telecommunications Authority
NTC	National Textbook Co., Ltd.
KTPC	Korea Trade Promotion Corp.

Part III.

Resource Papers Presented
at the Follow-up Symposium

MANAGERIAL EFFECTIVENESS
— ONGC'S CASE STUDY

by   *Col. S.P. Wahi*
      Chairman
      Oil & Natural Gas Commission (ONGC),
      India

1. Introduction

The performance of any enterprise whether in the public or private sector, depends primarily on the efficiency and productivity of Management which is the function of leadership.

In India, we have a large number of public sector enterprises which are being managed very effectively but there are also many which are not doing so well. One common factor leading to effective management is the quality of the leadership. Many sick companies have been turned around by effective leadership.

2. Oil and Natural Gas Commission

The Oil & Natural Gas Commission (ONGC) is responsible for exploration and exploitation of hydrocarbon resources. The refining and marketing of petroleum products is handled by other companies.

The Commission has shown a growth of over three-and-a-half times in the last six-and-a-half years with stability and continuous improvement in productivity — Figures 1—12 reflect the growth and productivity improvement. This has been achieved, through emphasis on the following aspects:

- Scientific management (managerial)
- Human resource management (leadership)
- Management of environment

The scientific part of management deals with planning, organization structure, layouts, systems and procedures, technology forecasting, upgrading, modernization, research & development, materials management and all other aspects which could be handled with the help of outside consultants.

It is needless for me to mention that it is the man behind the machine who is more important than the machine and technology itself. There are ample examples to prove that one man at the top can make or mar an organization through management or mis-management of human resources. No outside consultant can help in the management of human resources. It is related to the quality of leadership.

Inspite of the best scientific management, desired results may not be obtained if the outside environment is not managed effectively i.e. management of bureaucracy, politicians, local pressure groups and people around the areas of operations of the enterprise.

3. Situation Audit

In 1981–82, a SWOT analysis was conducted with a view to identify areas which needed strengthening. This analysis was conducted with the participation of a large number of people within the organization by focussing attention on the following:

- Growth
- Generation of surpluses profit
- Optimization of resources – human, material and financial
- Technology
- Research and development
- Information technology
- Innovation and creativity
- International norms of productivity
- Socio-economic activities
- Morale and motivation
- Quality of life

4. New Initiatives

As a result of this SWOT Analysis, the following initiatives were taken:

4.1 Long Term Plan

A Long Term Plan up to the year 2004-5 was formulated which gave direction for growth and generated the desired enthusiasm among the people who could then perceive their own growth with the goal of the organization. This one factor alone contributed considerably towards the motivation and better morale of the people, some of whom were stagnating in their positions for years. The Government could appreciate the future potential for economic development through the growth of the oil sector and the industry could plan their investments to meet the future needs of the oil sector. The 10-year operative plans were drawn on the basis of the long term conceptual plan and the five-year plans were derived out of the 10-year plans. This strategy ensured that the investments were incremental and not cyclical which is so vital for continuous growth. Figure 6 indicates the growth in investments over the years.

4.2 Defined Mission and Objectives

The following Mission and Objectives were identified to make sure everyone works to a common objective:

Mission:

To stimulate, continue and accelerate efforts to develop and maximize the contribution of the energy sector to the economy of the country.

Objectives:
- Self-reliance in oil
- Self-reliance in technology
- Promoting indigenous effort in oil related equipment and services.
- Assist in conservation of oil, more efficient use of energy and development of alternate sources of energy.
- Environmental protection.

4.3 Re-organization

The Commission was earlier organized on a territorial basis, i.e. offshore and onshore which resulted in compartmentalization and technological blockage and between the two groups, consequently technological upgradation, modernization, and growth of the people suffered. Further, from the exploration angle, the territorial structure resulted in certain leads being missed in the basins which extended from onshore to offshore as interpretation work was undertaken at different places. The Commission was reorganized on a business group basis i.e. exploration, drilling, operations and technical services supported by finance and personnel. These groups are now being further sub-divided, as an alternative to subsidiary companies, for better focus on finance, productivity and cost effectiveness. To get separate subsidiary companies established is a very difficult task due to bureaucratic control and lack of autonomy with the public sector enterprises. Additional powers have also been delegated down the line so that each business group is accountable and has the desired autonomy for implementing the plans. The basic philosophy of management is centralized policy making and decentralized administration. The exploration activities are now based on a common basin approach.

4.4 Research and Development

The long term plan also gave an indication of future technological challenges. As a result, the planned expenditure on R&D in the seventh plan (1985—86 to 1989—90) has been increased to Rs.248 crores as compared to Rs.38 crores in the sixth plan. The following four R&D institutes have been or are being established:

- Institute of Production Technology
- Institute of Engineering & Ocean Technology
- Institute of Petroleum Safety & Environmental Management
- Institute of Bio-technology and Geo-tectonics Studies.

The above institutes are in addition to the three institutes already in existence:

- KDM Institute of Petroleum Exploration
- Institute of Drilling Technology
- Institute of Reservoir Studies

4.5 Research and Development Profit Centers

As a result of brain-storming with scientists, a concept of profit centers was introduced in the working of R&D institutes to create time, quality and cost consciousness among the scientists. Eighty percent of the work in the institutes is sponsored by the operating regions. The basic research is being farmed out to the universities and other scientific organizations.

4.6 Information Technology and Logistics

The operations of ONGC are spread all over the country. Communications and logistics were the weakest links in the system. ONGC has spent Rs.47 crores on communication and Rs.50 Crores on computerization in the last five to six years. For logistics, support helicopters have been provided, and a company-owned fixed-wing plane is available for quick transport to operations by the Senior Executives. Now live data is received in the Headquarters and live support is given to operations, instead of historical data which was received in the past, the post-mortems showed lost efforts, inefficient operations and low productivity.

4.7 Optimization Measures — Task Force Concept

Management audits, different from internal and statutory audits, are conducted by composite teams from different disciplines including finance, have created cost consciousness and optimization of resources resulting in reduced costs and higher productivity. Task forces are created for specific assignments to bring about quick results. The price for crude being paid to ONGC since 1981 to date has remained the same, but profits have been increasing due to increased activity, improvement in productivity and cost consciousness.

4.8 Continuous Review of Organizational Structure

To keep the organization dynamic and to improve operations, constant review of the organization is done to identify changes required. Management of change is a difficult task, particularly in a large organization, but has to be ensured through deliberate strategies. The strategy followed in ONGC is through task forces constituted for the purpose.

4.9 Divestment through Cooperatives

During SWOT analysis, it was noted that ONGC was operating with the lowest to the highest technologies. This had resulted in uncontrolled growth of manpower in the low technology areas such as transportation, shot-hole drilling, maintenance and cleaning of buildings, etc. The tail to teeth ratio was alarmingly high. It was, therefore, decided to divest certain activities to the cooperative sector, industry and to other organizations both in the public and the private sector. Some of the employees were motivated to seek premature retirement and form cooperatives by taking away low technology equipment and working back for the ONGC as contractors. This strategy has shown excellent results in productivity and the growth of manpower particularly in the low technology areas has been controlled. The cooperative movement has become popular as the members of the cooperatives have generated tremendous surpluses for themselves. This strategy is also helping us to resist pressures for employment in non-operational areas.

4.10 Ventures Abroad

As a deliberate strategy it has been decided to invest at least 10—20% of resources for exploration in the basins abroad. This has created the desired enthusiasm among employees as they would get an opportunity to work in the international arena.

5. Human Resource Management (Leadership)

The following philosophies were identified for improving management of human resources:

1) Personal matters have to be treated 'personally' and not impersonally.

2) Anybody who ceases to improve, ceases to be valuable.

3) Everyone has an innovative mind, but needs different treatment for getting the best.

4) Motivation and morale are good ingredients for better performance and improvement in pruductivity for which the following are essential:
   - Growth
   - Recognition and reward
   - Quality of life — medical, housing, sports, cultural activities.
   - Organizational culture — participative, culture of excellence (zero-defect philosophy) and aggressive commercial culture.
   - Success

ONGC believes in mutual love, respect and confidence. This is its philosophy of dealing with people, the unions and associations. A constant search is made to find out the attitudes of the people, for which two Industrial Psychologists are on the job. In addition to the normal grievances procedure, an informal group outside the Commission has been created to examine the grievences with an open mind. A long term welfare plan has been formulated, so that expectations and aspirations of people are anticipated well in time to avoid confrontations.

5.1 Human Resources Development

A climate for self-development has been created to motivate people to update their professional and management knowledge. To cultivate the habit of reading, the executives are asked to indicate in their self-appraisal the books they have read in the previous year. During the formal interviews for upgradation, through the process of interaction people are made to understand the necessity for self-development.

An Institute of Management Development has also been set up at ONGC headquarters in Dehradun. In addition, full use is being made of other Management Institutes in the country for training and development of our executives. The training needs are being identified for each individual from the lowest to the highest level. Three staff training institutes have been set up for the training of supervisors and workers. The expenditure on training and development today is Rs.5.5 crores as compared to only Rs.25 lakhs in 1980—81. Special emphasis is laid on leadership training. The leadership style is to set personal example and ensure participation as a matter of culture. The senior executives have been motivated to adopt the style of control through management by wandering. The philosophy is that the soldier in the front should not have to look over his shoulders for anything. The people responsible for quantifiable results should be provided all assistance at the place and at the time they need. Their time under no circumstances will be given low priority. This is the only way to get maximum productivity.

5.2 Creative Thinking

Apart from formal suggestion schemes, a continuous drive is launched to touch the innovative minds of people through formal and informal channels by motivation and incentives. A special magazine called 'Pace Setter' has been introduced to project the image of people who come out with innovative suggestions for the improvement of any aspect of the Commission's work. The people are awarded and rewarded through many schemes including projection of individuals as Managers of the Year, Technicians of the Year, Scientists of the Year, etc. This has electrified the minds of the people for better productivity performance. Creative Thinking Groups have been formed where lowest to the highest paid employee could interact to give suggestions for the betterment of the Commission.

5.3 Welfare of Families of Retired/Deceased Employees

The wards of the deceased employees, retired employees and their wards get assistance from the organization. Ladies clubs have been started to take care of the socio-economic needs of the areas in which we operate and to provide assistance to the wards of the retired/deceased employees by training in the Vocational Centres and in the Polytechnics being run by the ladies clubs. This has also helped in improving the morale of the employees.

5.4 Quality of Life

A long term welfare plan, referred to above, has taken into account improvement in the quality of life. A major emphasis is being given to sports and cultural activities. Assistance is also provided to the local youths for sports. This has helped us in the creation of esprit de corps and a culture of mutual trust and team spirit.

A very high standard of motivation and morale has been achieved through a culture of participation. The Management demands a high standard of performance and is tolerant to the genuine mistakes of the employees.

6. Management of Environment

Special emphasis is given to taking care of the environment around the areas in which we operate. Through proper budgets, assistance is given to the villages to meet educational, medical and other infrastructural needs of society. The hospitals, sports complexes and other facilities created within the organization are also allowed to be used by society thus earning their goodwill for assistance and support to further the objectives of the Commission.

6.1 Advisory Councils

A number of advisory councils have been constituted with eminent professionals, retired bureaucrats, journalists, management experts and ONGC's retired employees, to meet periodically and review the performance and future strategies of the Commission. This has given the public an insight into the working of a major organization so vital for the economy. The Commission is able to benefit from such combined wisdom of experienced and eminent people. This system of participation is a model for the young executives of the 'open mindedness of the Top Management'.

6.2 Corporate Communication — Projecting an Image

The Corporate Communication Public Relations department has been placed under the charge of Director Incharge of Management Services, with the responsibility of communication within and outside the organization. Through innovative strategies, this department has also made effective use of the media/TV for communication within the organization, thus enabling quick information flow to the remotest places. This helps in creating a sense of belonging, so essential for morale. Through balanced information flow outside the ONGC, the correct corporate image has been built. This organizational change has given excellent results.

7. Conclusion

ONGC has achieved growth the stability and continuous improvement in productivity. Its potential for growth is still higher. Its
objective is perfection but it has still to go a long way to achieve that.
We are aware of the areas needing attention and the challenges ahead,
which have to be faced and overcome keeping the mission and objectives of the Commission in view.

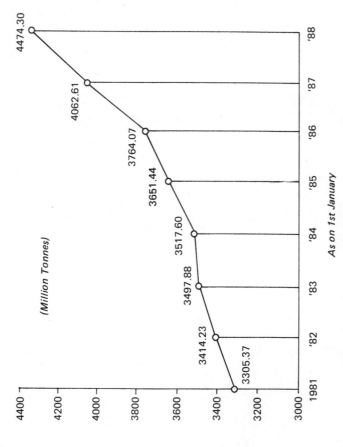

Fig. 1   Hydrocarbon Reserves (in place)

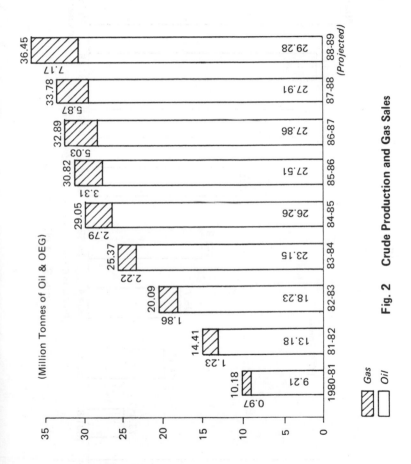

Fig. 2   Crude Production and Gas Sales

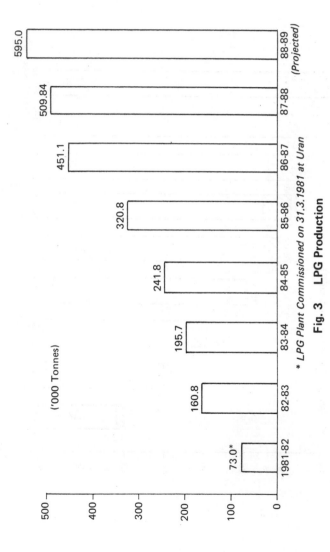

Fig. 3   LPG Production

* LPG Plant Commissioned on 31.3.1981 at Uran

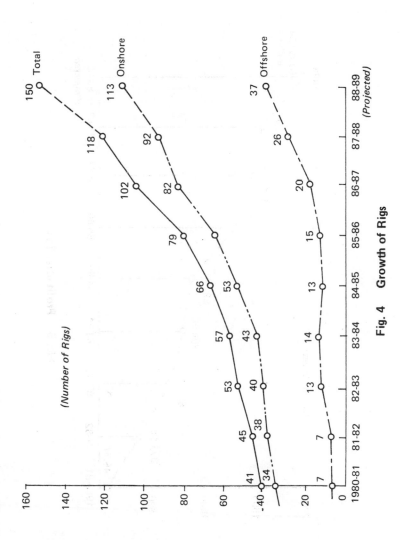

(Number of Rigs)

Fig. 4   Growth of Rigs

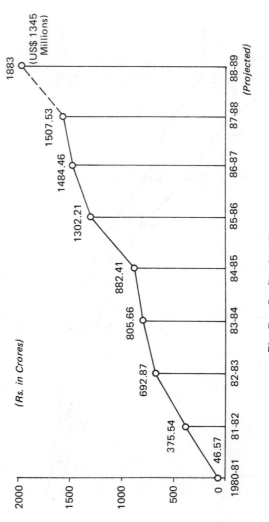

Fig. 5   Profit after Tax

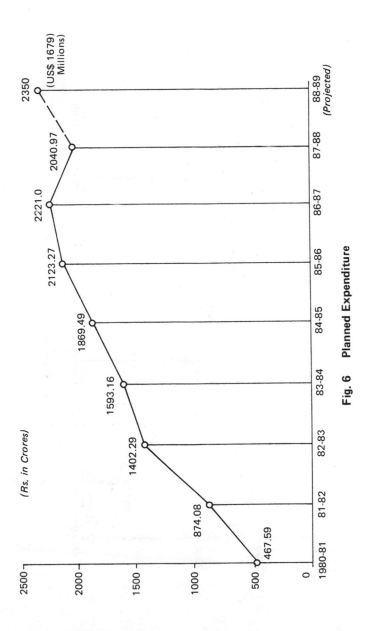

Fig. 6   Planned Expenditure

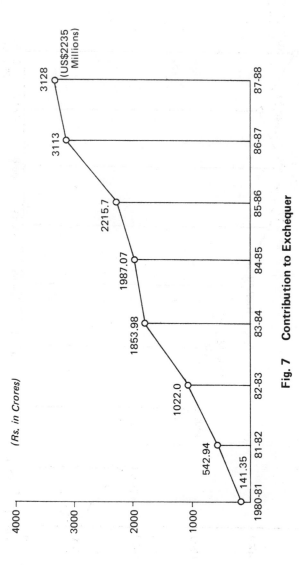

Fig. 7 Contribution to Exchequer

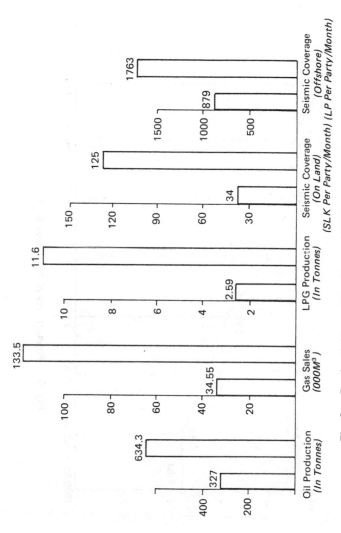

Fig. 8 Productivity per Employee *(1980-81 to 1987-88)*

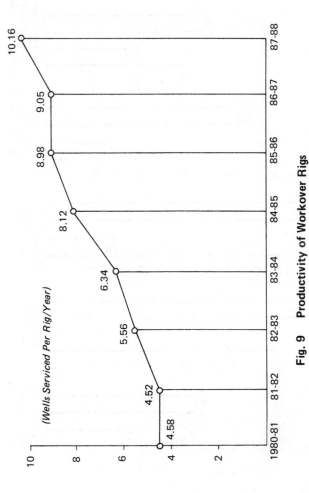

Fig. 9   Productivity of Workover Rigs

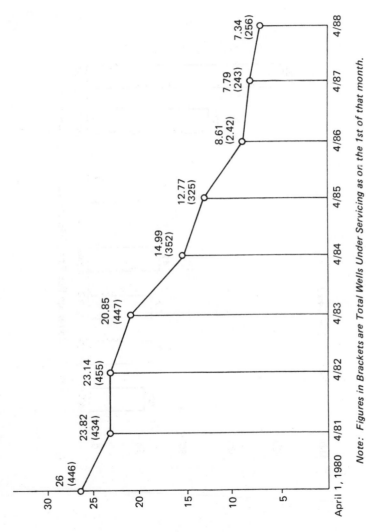

Note: Figures in Brackets are Total Wells Under Servicing as on the 1st of that month.

Fig. 10   Percentage of Wells Under Servicing

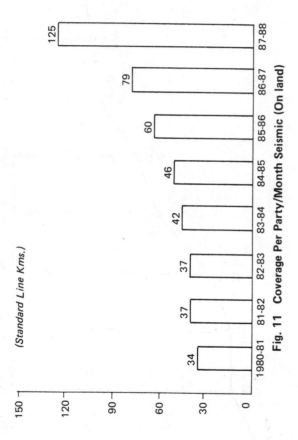

Fig. 11 Coverage Per Party/Month Seismic (On land)

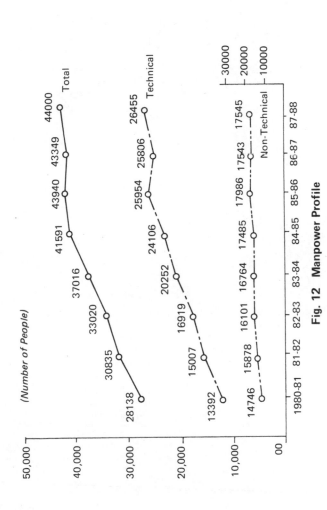

Fig. 12 Manpower Profile

THE DYNAMICS OF CHANGE IN
THE PRIVATIZATION OF BRITISH TELECOM

by   Mr. Roger Antell
Director
British Telecom Overseas Division

It is important to put privatization in perspective. Privatization as such is not well understood by many people and it is a relatively recent phenomenon. But governments in many countries do understand very well what they want of their state industries; they are looking for greater efficiency, profitability, better customer service, financing for much needed investments, more commercial standards and practices, and the availability of modern technology. Sadly, for a mixture of reasons, these objectives have not been met in many cases, and therefore a more radical approach has now developed to make state industries more like private companies in the hope that the discipline of the private sector will force these changes to take place.

But privatization is not as simple as that. It is not a once-and-for-all-time thing, but the combination of many activities. Like a journey along a road, there is a goal, an end in view. But the journey's end is reached after a number of milestones have been passed. So it is with privatization. It comes as the climax of a number of changes which must all come beforehand. In the example of British Telecom (see Fig. 1), up to 1969 the post office in the UK was responsible for posts and telecommunications as a government department. The prevailing attitude of the post office at that time, was like our English religious prayer book when we speak of God: "As it was in the beginning, is now and ever shall be." In fact, change was beginning to happen. In 1969, the post office was made into a national corporation (a state company). Management was restructured and Post and Telecoms began to be run as businesses. However, government control and involvement remained strong; and as the need for expansion and investment grew, so also did frustration within the corporation at government restrictions. In 1981 came the most important change so far: posts and telecoms were separated and became separate businesses under their own Boards of Management. At the same time some telecommunications markets were opened to competition and British Telecom, as it was called, was required to develop new financial and fair trading

MOOD

	MOOD
• PRIOR TO, 1969 GOVERNMENT DEPARTMENT POST OFFICE (POSTS & TELECOMS)	"As it was in the beginning is now and ever shall be."
• 1969–81 NATIONAL CORPORATION POST OFFICE (POSTS & TELECOMS)	Growing dissatisfaction and frustration at Government restrictions.
• 1981 SEPARATION OF POSTS AND TELECOMMUNICATIONS PUBLIC CORPORATION BRITISH TELECOM	Anticipation, apprehension, resistance to change.

• 1981–84
COMMERCIALIZATION
OPENING OF MARKETS:
    CUSTOMER APPARATUS
    VALUE ADDED SERVICES
	Growing enthusiasm, confusion.

• 1984 PRIVATIZATION FLOTATION BRITISH TELECOMMUNICATIONS PLC	Excitement
• 1984–89 LICENSED TELECOMMUNICATIONS OPERATORS REGULATED COMPETITION FOR NETWORKS	Reflection, realism.

Fig. 1 Recent History of British Telecom

policies. This was a time of great change within the corporation as managers had to adapt to a new environment; naturally there was apprehension about the future and some resistance, especially by the unions. However, there was also a feeling among managers that the reduction of government control would enable British Telecom to take proper commercial decisions and concentrate on serving its customers better. In 1984, British Telecom was made a private company, with all the share equity owned by the Government; within a few months 51% of the company was sold by the Government to private investors. This was a time of excitement, of new things happening. It was the first major privatization by the UK Government and it attracted 2.3 million shareholders. With privatization came competition, and a regulator was appointed to make sure that British Telecom competed fairly and that new competitors were able to enter the market.

Whatever one may think of the underlying philosophy or the rights and wrongs of certain stages, the important thing to observe is that it took from 1969 to 1984 — 15 years — to change British Telecom from a government department to a private company. And that was in a developed economy with strong and active financial markets. Investors will not invest in losses and therefore, if privatization is the final objective, the organization must be in a sound commercial position — and that can take a number of years to achieve. It is important, therefore, to recognize that the most crucial decision to implement in state enterprises is to introduce commercial disciplines. These will include responsibility to reach a certain level of output or service, control of prices, decisions on investment and allocation of revenue, proper financial accounting and so on. Privatization of itself does not necessarily bring efficiency but relates more to transfer of ownership; it is the introduction of "commercialization" that brings greater efficiency and responsibility.

And even after privatization, judging by the experience of British Telecom, it is not the end. A new road appears, and the journey continues. For the new private company now has to come to terms with its new environment and the raised expectations of its customers. This can be a difficult time, as in British Telecom found. Customers now recognize that they have increasing choice not to use British Telecom, even for telephone calls. They are louder in their criticism, because they know that British Telecom will have to improve; when British Telecom was a government department many did not bother to complain because they believed nothing would change. The necessity of continually raising our standards of service in order to stay in the market place is recognized are devoted large sums of money — $3.5 billion each year — in major investment programmes to increase our quality.

Organization of British Telecom

Figures 2 and 3 compare what British Telecom was like in 1978 and what it is like in 1988, to give some idea of the changes that have occurred from before commercialization to after privatization.

British Telecom is the main telecommunications operator in the UK with 23 million telephone connections in the UK and 230,000 staff worldwide. In global terms, it is among the five largest telecom operators in the world. It runs the full range of telecom services from speaking over the telephone to advanced and high speed data transmission techniques. $350 million was spent on research and development in 1987 and 3,000 staffers work in that area at a research centre. Through an extensive international network, all customers in the UK can dial directly for themselves to over 180 countries around the world. Total turnover last year was $17 billion and profits amounted to $3.5 billion. Assets are worth over $20 billion — a large company by any measurement.

From Post Office to Thriving Business

Let us turn the clock back, and look at how this thriving business in 1988 compares with the Post Office of 1978.

Post Office Mission: 1978 (as defined by Government)

"The Public Corporation Will:

- be responsible for developing the most efficient services possible at the lowest charges consistent with sound financial policies;
- carry on in a worthly manner the Post Office tradition of service to the public;
- develop relations with its staff in a forward-looking and progressive way

I don't think anyone could disagree with these statements. The problem in implementing them was twofold, however. Firstly, the statements are too general to be translated into effective policies. For example, what was "the Post Office tradition of service to the public"? At the risk of being unkind, I could remark that the tradition of service was "take it (as we supply it) or leave it (because you have no choice)."

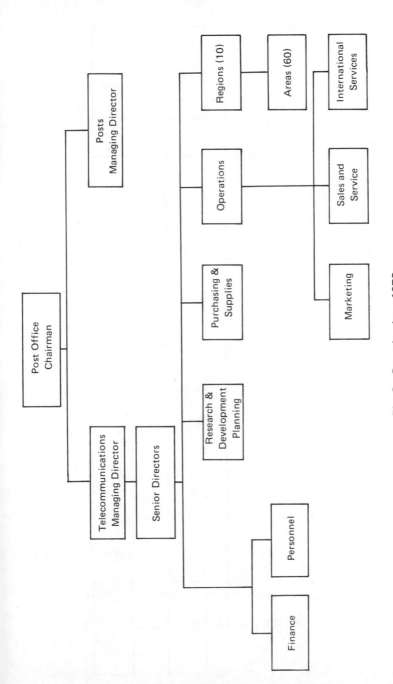

Fig. 2 Organization: 1978

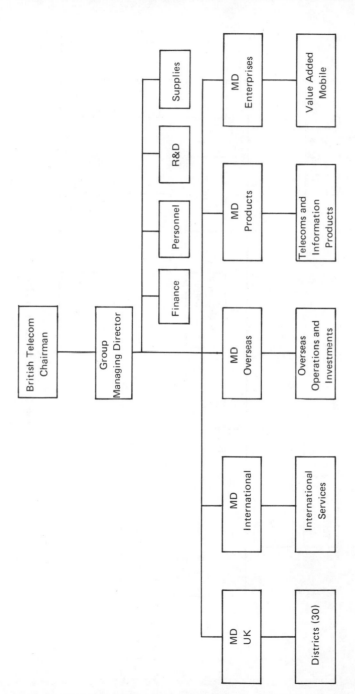

Fig. 3 Organization: 1988

Secondly, even if the statements could be defind better, the Post Office management had only very restricted power to implement these policies, since they could be, and often were, overruled by the politicians. Unfortunately, therefore, the mission statement did not have much meaning in practice.

British Telecom Mission: 1988

"British Telecom's Mission, Our Central Purpose, Is:

— to provide world-class telecommunications and information products and services; and
— to develop and exploit our networks at home and overseas;

so that we can:

— meet the requirements of our customers;
— sustain growth in the earnings of the group on behalf of our shareholders; and
— make a fitting contribution to the community in which we conduct our business."

Some generalities remain. But it seems to be a more focused statement about the businesses British Telecom intends to be in, the international dimension to its activities, the priorities it sets for itself, and its responsibilities to its customers, shareholders and the wider community. What is more, the Directors of British Telecom now have it within their power to make these statements of intent work in practice. As a manager this mission statement gives positive direction to my activities, which was lacking in 1978.

Organization and Staff Structure

There have been major changes in which British Telecom has organized itself, responding in large part to the need for the organization to get closer to its customers and be market-led in the development of its services.

In 1978, the organization had already changed from a civil service structure to reflect the demands of new products and services and a rapidly moving technological environment. (see Figs. 4 — 7) Telecommunications was run as a separate business with its own accounts and policies. But there remained the classic civil service hierarchical bureaucracy, with staff finding a place within vertical bands of functionality, for example engineering, administration, sales, personnel etc. There was little movement horizontally across the organization and the culture of 'closed communities' of interest was prevalent. As an

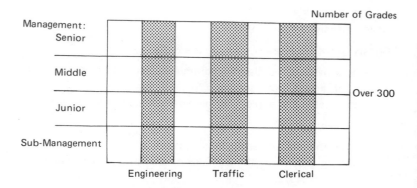

Fig. 4   Staff Structures: 1968

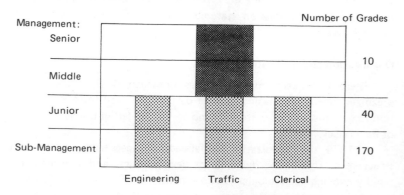

Fig. 5   Staff Structures: 1978

Management:		Number of Grades
Senior	Senior Management Group	1
Middle		10
Junior		
Sub-Management		95

Fig. 6   Staff Structure: 1988

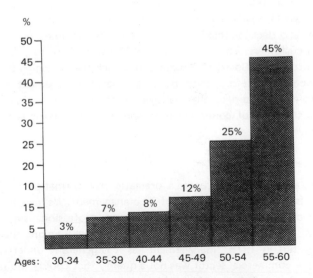

Fig. 7   Senior Managers: 1978

example, a personnel manager was present in each one of the 60 operational areas in the UK, but he was there to implement policies decided at the central Personnel group which even the Area General Manager was subject to and had little power to influence. As another example, "Marketing" was the responsibility of a Head Office group and was largely concerned with the development of new products. The Marketing approach as an ethos throughout the company was not understood.

However, the hierarchical structures were breaking down. Already in 1978, a single career structure for middle and senior managers was in place, enabling managers at this level to cross hierarchical boundaries. At junior management level 40 different grades of staff existed, and below management there were 170 grades. In 1988, the staff structure has changed dramatically. There are now only 10 levels of junior and middle management, and a single structure for senior managers. Grades below management have been reduced to less than 100. The organization has become flatter and much more integrated, bringing managers closer to their staff and closer to the customers.

There are now 3 major operating divisions, constructed so as to address British Telecom's markets at home and overseas. Each division has its own Managing Director who has under his control all of the resources and decision-making powers he needs to run his business and serve his customers. Through the Group Managing Director, each Division reports to the Board of Directors (of which the Managing Directors are members). Therefore, there is a clear line of management responsibility from the Board to the managers of the separate business units, enabling the flow of communication and decision-making within the company.

Management

One area which has been a dramatic transformation in British Telecom is the style and quality of its management. We have for many years prided ourselves on the quality and professionalism of our engineers — our research and development has been among the world leaders — but in 1978 "management" as it is generally understood in the private commercial sector was not a quality that could genuinely be applied to British Telecom. As could be expected for an ex-Government department, civil service traditions were strong. Rather than management, a more appropriate word would be "administration". The telephone service was administered, sharing the resource impartially among the subscribers according to a set of rules that governed almost all eventualities. Managers worked by the rule book, which ran into many volumes and thousands of pages. The Area General Manager had little initiative in dealing with his subscribers as his scope of action was already laid down.

In the same way, jobs were filled by a system of seniority succession, or as we call it "dead men's shoes." It was almost impossible for anyone to lose their job, however indolent they were. Rewards were fixed in terms of rigid pay scales, and there were no incentives to recognize effort and skill. Recruitment was at the lower levels, and therefore there was a predominance of older people at middle and senior administrative levels. As shown in Figs. 7 and 8.

A significant obstacle to consistent "management of a business' arose through the accountability of managers to politicians. Priorities were political and often were at variance with what would be regarded as good business practice. For example the level and changing of prices was always a political decision, depending on how the Government wanted to run the national economy.

One also has to take account of the role of the trades unions who exercised a major (some would say dominant) role in decision-making. Unions were consulted on every change in working practice, and the negotiations could be drawn out over years, slowing down considerably the responsiveness of the organization to changes in the environment.

In 1988, it is possible to speak of a transformation from ten years prevoius. (see Figs. 9 and 10) The company is managed according to completely different criteria and standards. Since it is owned by shareholders who have invested their own money in the company's future, the managers now are accountable to the shareholders for continuing and improving profits and earnings. But it is accountable in another way. Customers now have a choice for their products and services and British Telecom must take account of its customers' preferences and wishes if it is to continue as a successful company.

Of course, there are rules in the company in the sense that there are company policies which apply to all employees. But the style of management is different. Initiative is encouraged and managers are required to take responsibility for their actions. Objectives are agreed upon and incentives provided for being successful in achieving these targets. Rewards are more flexible in recognizing achievement and the value of particular skills and expertise to the company. Recruitment takes place at all levels in the company, ensuring that jobs are filled by the people most qualified for them. Internally, employees can apply for any job for which they believe themselves to be suited, thus pro-

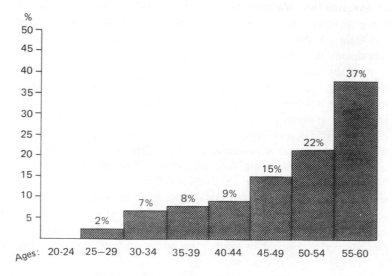

Fig. 8   Middle/Junior Managers: 1978

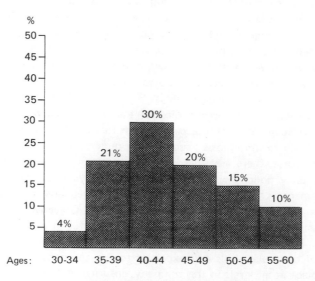

Fig. 9   Senior Managers: 1988

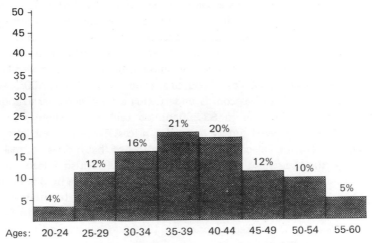

Fig. 10   Middle/Junior Managers: 1988

viding movement within the company from one unit to another. This results in the development of a keen and lively spirit which brings health to the organization. The average age of middle managers is 40 years and for senior managers 45 years, which is 10 years younger for both groups than 10 years previously.

Many employees also have shares in the company, which gives them a greater interest in its success.

The Unions have recognized that the future welfare of the staff lies with the company being successful and meeting the requirements of its customers.

Finances

Such is the demand for telecommunications services everywhere that it is potentially a very profitable business. However, when there is political responsibility for telecommunications, decisions can be taken on other grounds. The need to provide telephone service to everyone, the wish to keep prices low, a requirement to provide jobs; these can result in losses, low profits and lack of investment. In 1978, British Telecom was subject to government restrictions on the prices it could charge, the pay of its staff and the amount of investment it could make. Decisions could be arbitrary; agreement for an investment plan could be reversed the following year.

The change into a private company has meant that British Telecom can now take full control for all its financial and operating decisions. We can determine the appropriate level of operating costs, dispose of our income as we wish, make investment plans and stick to them. During the time of running a commercial business, while turnover has increased by over 220% since 1980, profits have increased by 400%. At the same time British Telecom is undertaking a massive modernization programme ammounting to $3,500 billion each year. These results have not been achieved simply by raising prices. There are restrictions on how far British Telecom can raise its prices so that it does not make profits at the expense of its customers. Since 1984, British Telecom has only been able to raise its prices at a rate below inflation by 3%. From 1989, prices can only be raised 4.5% below inflation. If inflation is less than 4.5%, British Telecom will have to reduce its prices. In fact British Telecom last raised its prices in 1986 and will not do so again until 1989 at the earliest, as a voluntary decision. So in relation to inflation, customers are getting cheaper and cheaper telephone services.

Research and Development

As I mentioned earlier, we in British Telecom have always been proud of our technical skills. However, there is always the danger that in a technological company, it is the technologists who will lead, and insufficient attention will be paid to the actual needs and requirements of the customer. In recognizing this danger, we are trying to bring closer together the technology push (which is very important) and the market pull from which researchers and technologists are often distanced. To prevent what we call the "ivory tower" approach, where pure engineering solutions are unaffected by any regard for the market, British Telecom now has a research sponsorship scheme. Any research project has to be sponsored by one of the operating divisions which provides customer services and products. In this way we are developing a culture of customer solutions rather than engineering priorities.

Suppliers

Since 1978, British Telecom's relationship with its suppliers has also changed. At that time, the UK telecoms market was a monopoly for the post office. Suppliers could expect to get a regular round of equipment orders at high prices, which in the end the customer had to pay for. One could even say that the post office was dependent on its suppliers and lacked much of the expertise needed to manage its supplier relationships properly.

There are a number of differences in 1988. The most important of these is the openness of the UK telecoms market. Many suppliers have sprung up to meet the challenges of competition and the traditional suppliers of British Telecom now find that they have to win the order from us rather than take it for granted. There is aggressive, competitive tendering from world suppliers on world prices, bringing the advantages of lower costs and cheaper products to the customers. In the UK, British Telecom is seeking to drive the pace of change so that suppliers are always being required to develop the latest techniques to meet higher quality standards.

A brief comparison of major changes between 1978 and 1988 is as follows:

1978	1988
100% Government owned	51% Privately owned
Bureaucratic	Commercial
Monopoly	Competition
Regulator	Regulated
Under-invested	Investing $3.5 billion each year
Union dominance	Management control

It is an impressive change, although it has been painful. But what of the future? Although privatization is on a road of changes, there is still much to do.

Firstly, we must improve our quality of service and our aim is to be the best telecommunications operator in the world for quality of service and customer satisfaction. That is why we are investing such huge sums of money.

Next, we have to develop a 'customer culture'; a sense throughout the company that the customer is the most important person. Our advertizing has a message to our customers: "It's you we answer to." It is easy for managers to say that, but immensely difficult in an organization of over 200,000 people to make sure that the telephone operators, and the engineers who call at the customer's house, all present the right, positive attitude of putting the customer first, in big and little ways. We have therefore undertaken an internal company improvement programme in which eventually all staff will participate. The secret is to involve the staff themselves in analysing difficulties and finding solutions, because then they are committed to make them work.

Thirdly, we have to live with competition and regulation of our activities for the coming 5 years at least. Our management controls must be thorough and our marketing imaginative so that we rise to the challenge.

Another new area for British Telecom is expansion overseas. As the Post Office we were unable to work outside the UK except for a small amount of consultancy and training. Indeed, there was no need to do anything overseas. Now, with competition at home and the immense opportunities developing internationally, we are working on the enlargement of our business base through overseas sales and investments.

Lastly, now that telecommunications has become a high technology business, we have to make sure that we are one of the technology leaders. This will involve new products and techniques and the definition and implementation of new standards and specifications.

At the conclusion of this, you may well ask me the question; is this applicable to the developing countries? After all, what you have described for British Telecom took place in a developed economy.

To answer that, I would ask a question in return. Where is your country on the road of change? Don't forget that it took 15 years for the Post Office to turn from a government department into British Telecom, public limited company. There is no need to imagine that it can all be done quickly, and in fact it will probably take twice as long as anyone thinks. But there is something that any government can do now, and that is to introduce commercial practices into its state industries whether it wants to privatise them or not.

The discipline of having to take responsible decisions, to have control of costs and revenues, to take decisions on business, not political criteria; these are some of the things I mean. Improved efficiency will lead to better service for the customer and will attract sources of finance for investment to improve service, revenue and profits still further. The industry becomes less of a drain of government money and attention and brings political credit to the government for its handling of its industrial and economic affairs.

Thank you for attending to my presentation. It has been a most interesting and sometimes exciting period to live through, and I hope that I have helped you to feel part of that change for a short time.

ORGANIZATION INNOVATION AT IRI

by   Dr. Umberto Del Canuto
Economic Research Department
IRI's Headquarters
Instituto Per La Ricostruzione Industriale (IRI),
Italy

1. Government Intervention in the Economy and the Italian State Shareholdings System

State intervention in economic policy can be run through a diversified bunch of measures, which in principle vary among countries according to social, political and cultural features.

Each instrument adopted, per se, aims at a particular goal.

To adhere to a general scheme, we can refer to three groups of intervention:

- social aid, in the form of employment allowances, social benefits and pension schemes, normally funded by an earmarked tax on salaries, aimed at the re-conversion of mature industries and at a countercyclical approach in declining regions;

- grants, reduced interest rates and tax allowances, that private corporations can obtain to finance investment or R&D programmes in developing sectors or areas;

- direct economic activity in infrastructure, utilities and manufacturing, run by the State itself through a nationalized industry, a public corporation or a mixed venture with private capital, in the form — typical in Italy and increasingly in France, United Kingdom, Spain, Austria — of a State Shareholdings System.

The most important feature of this last instrument is the fact that companies are run by professional managers (not by politicians appointed by the Government) with the same technicalities employed in competing private groups on a worldwide scale.

Which are then the essential features of the Italian State Shareholdings System?

1) Companies are incorporated, and then subjected to the same common law rules, which all private companies must comply with.

2) They form a group by the same rules applied by international regulations: operating companies are generally controlled in the form of 51% or more majority, or even through a lower share, if a "public company" listed in the Stock Exchange is involved.

3) The public holding (IRI) — and not the State itself — is the owner of the shares. The Holding is a public corporation ruled by a special law, which states the holding's goals and powers, and defines the ruling bodies and the way in which the holding's officials are appointed by the Government: the appointments are not subject to the spoil system and last a definite time span. IRI's status is that of a long term finance institution which is empowered to rule (directly or indirectly) the dependant corporations both financially and industrially. As the only owner, IRI can sell the shares of the controlled companies, create new companies, purchase the shares of private companies, both domestic and international, under the same rules applying to private corporation.

4) The State Shareholdings System (four holding companies, with the same characters as IRI, do actually now exist in Italy) is vetted by a Government Minister (Minister for the State Shareholdings) who has the right to be informed of the activities of the Holdings in matters concerning
    * movements in shares
    * appointments
    * long term planning

and to approve of them and give directives to the Holdings on the same matters. The Minister relates the Government and Parliament on the activities of the State Shareholdings System, along a set of rules stated by different laws; in particular he makes proposals to the Government for appointing members of the Boards of the Holding and the CEOs. He also submits to the approval of the Parliament, in the yearly budget law, the required increases of owner's capital proposed by the Holdings as a share for financing their investment long term programmes without prejudice for their existing debt-equity ratios. The Parliament itself decides on those needs in the discussion of the yearly budget.

It is worthwhile considering the striking effects of the actual features of the Italian system of state shareholdings in the economic and strategic performance of the companies operating in it.

1) Each company, being ruled under the common law, must be profitable and can go bankrupt in case of permanent loss.

2) Personnel are not public servants, and the Trade Unions sign contracts for them according to the general regulations.

3) Strategic planning, programming and budgeting and controlling are acted on from a central basis: this allows each Group to be competitive as whole.

4) In particular the Group structure allows for strategies of diversification from mature sectors (for instance steel, shipyards, basic chemicals, aluminium, textiles) into emerging ones (telecommunications, new materials, biotechnology, computer hardware and software) without major problems for existing local or sectoral occupations.

It is most important to note this last (point 4) relevant feature of the Italian system, which is not present in other countries where sectoral vetting on the state enterprises is done by sectoral ministries (for instance in France or in India).

Sectoral structures do not allow diversification, which is an important strategic feature in the struggle for profitability of modern corporations. The Italian system is more like the conglomerate groups operating in Japan, and can allow important changes in the structure of the state industries over a period of time, according to the actual needs of the changing economic structure of the country.

Enlarged structures, in the system of state shareholdings provide also for a mobile boundary between public economy and private initiatives allowing state companies privatization, purchasing private corporations or running joint ventures, along with the strategic goals of the state industrial holding, without any direct parliamentary or governmental intervention in the form of new laws or rulings.

2. IRI's History and Strategic Performance

The history and structure of IRI are carefully explained in Dr. Veniero Ajmone Marsan's study on the "Instituto per la Ricostruzione Industriale."*

2.1 The Gestation Period

Italy was a late-comer among European countries which in the nineteenth century followed the lead of England in industrialization. The first great industrial upswing, during which growth was especially

---

* Published in the volume Public Enterprise — studies on Organizational structure by professor V.V. Ramanadham.

rapid in the producer goods sectors and in power production, started only in 1896, co-inciding with the turning point of an international cycle and the ensuing upsurge in economic activity both in Europe and in the United States. The subsequent period of rapid industrial expansion lasted for a good decade and saw the creation from virtually nil to important new industrial branches requiring very large investments. Given the lack of capital accumulation within industry itself or from other sources, a crucial role in the financing of this development fell upon the banks, who took equity stakes in new firms and offered bridging finance until such time as market conditions became suitable for the placing of the companies' shares with the public. The banks therefore became heavily dependent on the behaviour of the stock exchange and were obliged to support operations on the stock market: inevitably the banks' commitment with client firms tended to reach the point where a retreat could no longer be envisaged, thus transforming de facto the banks' position into that of holding companies.

The postwar crisis of the 1920's was marked by severe economic difficulties and a banking crisis which led to new rescues of commercial banks by the Bank of Italy and the consequent transfer to it of controlling interests in important industrial firms, which were included in the portfolio assets of the Banks. The final blow to the system came with the onset of the worldwide depression of the early thirties. In 1933 the Instituto per la Ricostruzione Industriale (IRI) was created as a statutory agency, at first of a temporary nature.

The IRI took all the industrial stock and related credits together with the inherent losses from the mixed banks, which prepared the ground for the banking reform of 1936 and put an end of mixed banking in Italy.

The management of the industrial enterprises by the State was institutionalized in 1937 when IRI was established as a permanent agency. Since then the system has continued to expand as a result both of internal growth and of new rescues and acquisitions. Although this was not because of any deliberate nationalization policy by the Italian state, but essentially to compensate for the inertia or the unwillingness of private entrepreneurship in the historical context in which the country's industrial development had to proceed.

2.2 Four Decades of Development

The first four years 1933—36 of IRI's existence was devoted, on one hand, to the sale of most holdings in small scale firms and, in terms of sectors, in the electrical industry, textiles, agriculture and real estate;

also, IRI started the reorganization and financial consolidation of its larger enterprises. As early as 1983 the agency grouped its three telephone subsidiaries under a sectoral sub-holding company (STET) which was followed in 1936 by a second specialized subholding (FINMARE) for the management of the shipping companies. In both cases new long term strategies and investment plans were laid down and the necessary finance secured through the issue of convertible bonds. These were the first steps towards an organizational structure which was to be extended to other sectors and become an important instrument of decentralized management of the large and diversified group IRI had to govern. The sub-holdings, which are ordinary joint-stock companies, play a useful role for suppliers of finance to their subsidiaries with resources derived from borrowing and share issues on the capital market.

In 1937 a third sub-holding (FINSIDER) was set up along with the launching of a large-scale investment programme for the steel sector, including the construction of an integrated shore-based plant in the Genoa area.

As a result of these actions, by 1939 the value of IRI's interests in the five major sectors (steel, engineering, telecommunication, shipping and electric power) accounted for 90 percent of the total, against 57 percent in 1934. In national terms, the group were of a dominant position in the following lines of manufacturing: pig iron (77 percent), steel (45 percent), shipbuilding (80 percent), arms and ammunition(50 percent), heavy electrical machinery (39 percent); it was fairly important (ranking between fourth and fifth) in other engineering lines; as for services, it controlled the telephone network of the northern and west-central regions and about 90 percent of Italian passenger liner shipping. Altogether about 170,000 were employed in the IRI group in 1939, three quarters of which belonged to the steel and engineering sector.

The outbreak of the war led to a rapid expansion of IRI's war production (in the engineering and shipbuilding firms employment rose from 70,000 to 100,000), at the same time severe damage was inflicted on the steel and shipping sectors. Both these circumstances were bound to cause serious difficulties when the fighting ended.

The post-war period is best analyzed by distinguishing three phases.

The first came to a close in 1953 and was dominated by the post-war re-conversion problems of IRI's engineering and shipbuilding sectors, which were further aggravated by the fact that IRI was called upon to rescue five private engineering plants in northern Italy. Conversion plans were entrusted to a newly created sectoral sub-holding (FINMECCANICA) and had to be carried out without adding to the unemployement. From 1948 onwards IRI embarked upon long range investment programmes among which the reconstruction of the coastal steel centre, interrupted by the war, was of major importance. This decision was based on the view that, although Italy had no indigenous sources of most raw materials, it was possible to establish a competitive steel industry based on imported coal and ore. The successful implementation of this strategy was the precondition for the great expansion of the Italian engineering industry in subsequent years. The growing steel requirements of the country could hardly have been met cheaply in a stable way through imports of finished steel nor could steel producers have relied on regular imports of scrap to be used in non integrated plants. The early adoption of this policy later enabled Italy to face the European integration process which started with the Coal and Steel Community in 1953. In addition it became possible through time to locate important extensions of the steel sector in southern Italy.

A new field of activity was added to the group in the immediate post-war period, when IRI started two airlines, one in partnership with the British (ATI), the other with the American (Alitalia).

After 1953, as Italy joined the European Coal and Steel Community, a second phase may be said to have begun, lasting until 1963, when the rapid expansion of the Italian economy was halted for the first time. In this decade IRI's steel sector had to face the challenge of competition in the new tariff-free European market. The group's major decision was the building of a new integrated steel plant in the South (Taranto): with a capacity of about 3 million tonnes, it ranked then among the largest in Europe. With the completion of this project in 1964 southern Italy was endowed with the most important and modern segment of this basic industry. A further initiative of these years was linked with the rapid growth of motoring in Italy. In 1959 the construction of the "Autostrada del Sole" running from Milan to Naples (Km. 755) was initiated marking the entry of IRI in the toll-motorway field, on a concession basis. In 1961 Parliament approved the first ten-years of the Motorway Plan and the IRI was entrusted with the construction and management of about two thirds (the rest was assigned to private concessionaries) of the Km. 3,200 national network. The large capital resources required were raised — apart from a small contribution from the State — through bond issues guaranteed by the IRI. In the shipbuilding sector a major rationalization programme was launched which was accompanied by the establishment of a new sectoral sub-holding (FINCANTIERI) to which all shipyards were transferred from FINMECCANICA in 1959.

In 1957 the IRI acquired control of the two remaining private telephone companies, operating in central and southern Italy, and was thus assigned the entire telephone network under concession, including all the urban and most of the domestic trunk system (the rest being run by a state agency).

The years after 1963 and up to the mid-seventies were marked by a growing instability of the Italian economy and, after 1973, by the structural imbalances created by the oil crisis. This new phase started for IRI with the withdrawal from the electricity sector following its nationalization in 1962. The problem of how to use the compensation which was paid to the former electricity companies was resolved by investing, in part, in the group's telephone and steel sectors and, in part, in the development of the South. This was put into effect by transforming SME, one of the major electricity firms of the group, into a holding company which used a large part of the compensations for the entry into new sectors, mainly food and confectionery.

A new group was thus formed in a relatively short time on a sufficient scale to be able to start new ventures in the South.

During these years a great impetus was given to the electronics sector: IRI's electronic interests were placed under the control of STET, in order to exploit the important link with telecommunications, also controlled by STET, which could secure a growing outlet for electronics and stimulate innovation. In this period the IRI also took over SGS, the largest Italian enterprise in its field (electronic components) which had entered a crisis after the withdrawal of the America group that first promoted it.

In sum, the intervention of the IRI enabled Italy to share in the worldwide expansion of a strategic sector for a modern economy. In this context the setting up in 1969 of a software company (ITALSIEL) must also be noted. This company, in which other state holding agencies as well as major private industrial groups and large banks were associated, now has as staff of which four fifths are technicians; it is carrying out a considerable amount of work both for public administration and enterprises to which it offers an alternative to the traditional dependence in this field from the suppliers of hardware.

In 1966 all enterprises of the steel and engineering sectors working in the area of plant design and construction were grouped in a new company (ITALIMPIANTI) which has become an importnt supplier at home and abroad of engineering know-how and a vehicle for increased exports of machinery and components by the group as well as by private Italian industries.

In the area of infrastructural activities, where the group first entered the field of toll-motorways, a large private construction firm was purchased from the private sector and new units created, among which one was for the building of an urban motorway for the Naples conurbation and one for the operation of Rome airports. All these enterprises were grouped in 1968 under a special sub-holding (ITALSTAT). Among he objectives of this reorganization was that of placing at the disposal of the state and local authorities a technical unit capable of acting as main contractor for the carrying out (normally with private participation) of large infrastructural and residential building programmes. This role has proved important for its export potential, as the group has been bidding successfully for some of the world's largest construction projects, especially in the developing countries.

2.3 Most Recent Strategies

After the first shock of the world oil crisis, the dominant objectives of IRI's action in the highly unstable world setting of the eighties period have been: the rationalization and conversion of its industrial structure; the promotion of innovation and of high technology sectors and the strengthening of the international position of the group. In pursuing these objectives, the IRI faced major problems in two areas: labour relations and finance.

A great deal has been done by way of joint ventures or technical and marketing agreements with both domestic and foreign companies.

A few examples worth quoting are:

- the agreement between Alfa Romeo and Nissan Motor Co. to jointly produce a car in a new plant near Naples;
- the agreement between Italtel and GTE (USA) to join forces in developing a range of digital telephone exchanges;
- the joint ventures between Aeritalia, IRI's aerospace manufacturer and a number of foreign companies (Aérospatiale, Boing, Embraer of Brazil, etc.)
- the merging of activities in electronic components run by SGS with the French group Thomson, in a new European venture coordinating the worldwide production of the two companies and holding a high stake of the market in Europe in this strategic sector.

Another sign of the group's ability to react to the adverse trend has been the increase in foreign sales by IRI's manufacturing companies. To a growing extent this was the result of the setting up, within the group, of firms specialising in supplying complete plants with the associated engineering and manufacturing know-how (based on the varied in-group experience) as well as manpower training before start-up.

Not surprisingly IRI's most difficult task in these years of crisis was that of carrying through the reorganization and streamlining of the group's industrial structure. This required injecting capital and management in those ailing subsidiaries which appeared once restructured and relieved of their surplus labour to have long term potential; but it implied selling off those which, because of their field of activity or small size, could not serve the long term objectives of the group; finally there was the problem of closing down companies which clearly offered no hope of recovery.

Given the cut-back in the rate of growth and the constraints thus imposed on employement, especially in the South of Italy, one should not under-rate the relatively slow pace of progress achieved, until recently, in the restructuring process. In a few cases the entire programme of adaptation was carried through.

In addition, during the seventies and eighties the IRI dismissed some thirty controlled companies which were considered unnecessary for the fulfilment of the core strategic goals to be reached by the Group by the end of the century: the most notable case relates to the company Alfa Romeo, which was acquired by the FIAT group in 1986.

Most recently an internal restructuring moved manufacturing in electronics out of the telecommunications holding company (STET) to the engineering (FINMECCANICA), in order to strengthen internal synergism to enter new advanced technology sectors.

3. Institutional and Organizational Arrangements

The present section reviews the main aspect of the relations between IRI and the political authority as well as the international organization and management procedures of the group.

The problems and solutions devised in both these areas can only be understood against the historical background of the purposes leading up to the establishment of the IRI as a permanent institution in 1937. From the brief description given in the previous sections, it is clear that historical necessity brought about the decision by the Italian State to accept the role of an enterpreneur.

The fundamental issue was that in certain fields (where the risks were too great for private enterprises or the capital requirements exceeded what the private sector was able to supply from sources other than deposit-taking banks) there was need for State economic initiative.

This, however, did not mean giving up the essentials of a market economy. On the contrary, State-held firms and private firms would continue to co-exist in most sectors and compete under the common rules. Indeed the assumption by the State of directly productive functions was not conceived as an end in itself, but as an instrument which would eventually promote a larger amount of private enterprises investment than would otherwise come forth.

Another significant aspect to be stressed is that once the Italian State decided to take up its new role, this was entrusted to an ad hoc agency, accountable to the Government but separated from the bureaucratic framework and not subject to civil service procedures. In fact IRI was conceived as a holding concern and endowed with the degree of autonomy needed for the task of managing enterprises which maintained the status of joint-stock companies, regulated by private commercial law, requiring them to behave as a business. The reform of the industrial system thus went hand in hand with that of the State.

3.1 The Gradual Development of a Formal Framework

As an instrument of public policy, the new agency clearly had to serve the strategic ends of the Government, but at the same time preserve the conditions for an enterprising managment, which was the first requirement for the pursuing of those ends.

These have been the circumstances in which the priorities of public policy were met by the group's initiative without any additional cost which current market prices could not cover. However, in many other cases public policy aims are at odds with market profitability at company level. In these situations the objectives of the public sphere turn into specific constraints in the sphere of enterprises decisions and it was obviously of crucial importance for the IRI to establish rigorous criteria for meeting both its social and its commercial obligations.

The line of conduct initially followed by IRI was that of striving to keep the burden of low or non earning investments within the limits of its revenues from earning investments and profits on the sales of assets.

The reasoning behind the above-mentioned criterion evolved in those early years, within the IRI itself, by Professor Saraceno, then a senior staff member of the Institute. The essence of Saraceno's position was that (a) the State could not refuse to take upon itself the burden of extra costs (or lower revenues), if any, caused to IRI by the pursuit of policy objectives and (b) the required compensation could be obtained through the State's contributions to IRI's capital by allowing the extra costs to absorb a part of, or all, the returns which the State would otherwise have derived from the endowment fund.

The year 1956 saw the emergence of a new formal structure: the direction and control of the system was entrusted to an Interministerial Committee and to a new Ministry of the State Shareholdings which has the task of ensuring that the Government guidelines are pursued by Autonomous Management Agencies like the IRI, which must operate according to the criteria of "economic viability".

The creation of a sponsor Ministry and its inclusion together with the technical or sectoral Ministries and the Treasury in economic planning Cabinet appropriately reflects the decision making process which will be covered by the sums allocated by Parliament. CIPI ex- the State-held system. Government policy in the various fields in which IRI operates (industry, telecommunications, transport, etc.) or which have direct relevance for the group (Southern Italy, Research, Labour, etc.) remains the responsibility of the non-sponsor Ministries which lay down the policy goals and related strategies for the different areas falling within their purview. The coordination of sectoral goals and strategies is achieved within the Planning Cabinet in which the Treasury ensures the necessary compatibility with the budgetary policy.

In this context the Ministry of the State Shareholding receives specific requests relating to the possible contribution of State-held enterprises to the policy objectives of the various non-sponsor Ministries. These requests form the basis of the policy framework for the Ministry of State Holdings, whose essential role at this stage is to ascertain whether and on what terms and conditions the State-held system may respond to Government policies without impairing the survival of enterprises operating within the discipline of a market environment.

This in turn necessarily implies the cooperation of the Holding agencies with the sponsor Ministry in order to: investigate all possible opportunities for entrepreneurial initiative which may promote the Government goals; make sure that the constraints due to social or political priorities remain within limits which will allow efficient management to gradually eliminate the ensuring extra costs or lower revenues; evaluate such costs and submit to the Government the problem of their funding as all other classes of public expenditure.

3.2 IRI and the Government

The formal structure and systems of the Government control over the IRI are at present the following.

1) On the top level are the two Interministerial Committees for Economic Planning (CIPE) and for Industrial Policy (CIPI). CIPE issues general guidelines and verifies their observance on the basis of the annual Planning Report which the Ministry of State Shareholding must submit to, based on IRI's rolling multi-year programmes. CIPI formulates the criteria for evaluating the extra costs of political origin which will be covered by the sums allocated by Parliament. CIPI expresses its opinion on the proposal which the Ministry of State Holding makes concerning the awards to IRI's endowment fund.

2) The Ministry of State Shareholding, as a member of both CIPE and CIPI, participates in the formulation of the general guidelines and thereafter supervises their implementation. Therefore the Ministry has extensive day-to-day contacts with the IRI and has the right to prior information on important matters such as the acquisition or sale of controlling holdings, the creation of new companies, capital increases or write-offs of subsidiary companies, etc.

The Ministry's views are communicated to IRI but are not binding. IRI's Annual Report and Accounts are transmitted to the Ministry (as well as to the Treasury) for review and subsequent submission to Parliament together with the Ministry's yearly Planning Report and Estimate of Expenditure.

The Ministry, moreover, is involved in the informative stage of the IRI's medium-term planning, providing the political inputs and expressing its reactions to the Institute's proposals, valuations and requests. Here again the Minister formulates views and directives but cannot issue an injunction. IRI's compliance with the Ministry's guidelines must indeed be the result of an autonomous decision, having regard to the Institute's incumbent duty to safeguard the value of the capital (endowment fund) which it has been awarded by the State; moreover, it is the IRI, not the Ministry, that has the responsibility of the overall funding of the group's programmes, which it has undertaken to carry out on the basis of the capital made available by the State and the resources that both IRI and its constituent companies must secure from the market.

IRI's rolling multi-year programmes are submitted yearly to CIPI by the Ministry of State Shareholdings together with a detailed report on the implementation of the programmes already approved.

3) Parliament exercises its scrutiny and guidance on the basis of the formal information which flows from CIPI (investment programmes), the Ministry of State Shareholdings (IRI's Annual Report and Accounts) and the State Court of Accounts (reporting on the observance by IRI and the Government of the respective statutory and legal duties). Besides, Parliament holds hearings and carries out special investigations. IRI's Chairman and General Manager as well as the Chief Executives of the Group's companies are regularly called upon to answer questions when the Group's programmes and operations are scrutinized once a year. Parliament exercises its function through a Joint Standing Committee which is the counterpart of CIPI for the strategic direction and overview of the National Industrial Policy and is composed of fifteen Senators and fifteen Representatives. The Government must obtain the opinion of this Committee on: IRI's medium-term programmes and the proposed awards to its endowment fund; the criteria for ascertaining and measuring the extra costs of political origin; the reports by the Ministry of State Shareholdings on the implementation of IRI's programmes; Government proposals for the appointment of IRI's Chairman and Vice-Chairman.

4) Finally, the allocation by law to IRI's endowment fund is made through the standing Budget Committees of the Senate and of the Chamber of Deputies, and a full House vote on the bill proposed by the Ministry of State Shareholdings.

3.3 Internal Organization and Control Systems

As a statutory agency, the IRI is endowed with a legal identity and its own capital awarded by the Treasury; it exercises stockholder's rights according to the provisions of ordinary company law; it raises funds on the market through all available forms of short and long-term borrowing, which it uses, together with its own capital, for meeting the funding needs of the group's companies and maintaining its cotrolling (or equal partnership) shake in the same; its financial accounting and reporting conform to the standard principles followed by private companies; its staff are hired under private law and are regulated by the collective agreements applied in the banking sectors.

In functional terms IRI is the central holding company of the group and its relations with its subsidiaries correspond to those of large private groups. So do the main areas of IRI's decision and control activity in respect of the formulation of guidelines for the investment and production programmes of group companies; the provisions and allocation of the necessary sources of financing; the selection of the companies' top management and the adoption of efficient organizational structure and management systems.

The IRI's administrative components consist of a Board of Directors with a Chairman and a Vice-Chairman, an Executive Committee and a Board of Auditors.

The Chairman (full-time) and Vice-Chairman (part-time) are appointed by decree of the Head of State with the advice of the Cabinet and of the earlier mentioned Joint Parliamentary Committee, upon the recommendation of the Minister of State Shareholdings; their term of office is three years (renewable no more than twice). The Board includes twelve Directors (part-time), nine of which are senior civil servants (two from the Treasury, and one from each of seven other Ministries, including the Ministry of State Shareholdings) and three are outside experts appointed by the Minister of State Shareholdings for a three-year term, renewable without limit.

The three "experts", together with the Chairman and Vice-Chairman, form the Executive Committee, to which the Board of Directors delegates all decisions regarding the management of the IRI and its relations with subsidiary companies, except for such matters as the purchase and sale of holdings and other assets, the issue of bonds, capital increases or write-offs, etc.

The IRI's statute provides that a General Manager be appointed by the Minister of State Shareholdings on the proposal of the Chairman after consultation with the Board. As a rule, General Managers have been drawn from the cadre of senior executives of the group.

The Board of Auditors consists of five members appointed by the Minister of State Shareholdings; its functions are analogous to those of the corresponding private company auditing boards.

All meetings of the administrative components of IRI are attended by a Magistrate of the State Court of Accounts (which is entrusted with the control of all agencies permanently financed by the State). The role of the Court is of special importance, as it must ensure that the capital awarded to IRI by the State is safeguarded, a condition which implies the constant observance, by Government and the IRI alike, of the "economic viability" criterion which the 1956 Law prescribes for the management of State holdings. In this context the Court is not concerned with the merit of managerial decisions, but with the correct application of the decision-making rules which are a precondition of "economic viability"; this refers in particular to the requirement that any extra costs of political origin be accurately evaluated and fully compensated and that adequate financing will be forthcoming from the Treasury once IRI's programmes have been approved.

The Court's findings are included in a yearly report which is presented to Parliament. In recent years the Court has repeatedly called the attention of the political authorities to the deviations from the above-mentioned rules which have seriously affected the IRI's financial result and prevented a meaningful assessment of managerial performance.

A fundamental feature of the IRI's management system is the grouping of subsidiary companies operating in the same sector in interrelated lines of activity (for instance: telecommunications and electronics) under a parent company which takes over from the IRI the shareholdings of the relevant operating companies. These sectoral sub-holdings can be viewed, in part, as an extension of the IRI, improving the guidance and control functions of the Institute and supplementing its financing capacity; but in part they are a vehicle of greater synergism for their subsidiaries in various areas (marketing abroad; research and development; joint-venture negotiations; EDP systems, etc.).

The management systems and practices within the group are not suject to any statutory or other outside regulations and correspond to current good practice in large private groups.

Appointments of board members and top level executives, to be proposed to the shareholders' meetings of subsidiaries in which IRI has a direct stake, (essentially sectoral sub-holdings and other parent companies) are based on general guidelines established by IRI's Board of Directors. Both executive and part-time members of boards are selected by IRI's Chairman and submitted to the Executive Committee whose role is to check that the candidates meet the qualifications specified in the guidelines.

Boards of subsidiaries include outside members consisting mainly of people drawn from the Italian public and business life, representative of sizable minority shareholders, credit institutions, etc. appointed on a part-time basis. In addition the Heads of Departments at the IRI's headquarters who are responsible for planning and liaison functions with subsidiary companies sit on the Board of Directors and sometimes on the Executive Committees of the first-level subsidiaries; for second-level subsidiaries similar arrangements are made with junior staff from IRI departments.

All other appointments within first and second-tier subsidiaries are delegated to the top executives of the same; for major companies IRI's Executive Committee is informed of the appointments of full-time board members and of General Managers (who are normally also members of company Boards). It should be stressed that, as in most other countries, the primary role of the Board in Italy is in practice that of providing legitimacy and authority for management's actions. This justifies the inclusion on the Boards of non-executive appointees which often are de facto proposed to IRI by the sponsor Minister. Civil servants of the Ministry of State Shareholdings are normally members of the Board of Auditors of the major companies of the group; the Audit Boards of nearly all subsidiaries include IRI's comptroller or one of his senior staff, together with outside members drawn as a rule from the accounting profession.

The internal organization of the Institute is based on Departments, whose heads serve under the General Manager and are in charge of the Headquarters general services and of the liaison with, and supervision of, the management of the subsidiaries.

There is a continuous and close relationship between IRI and its major subsidiaries, which is maintained in a variety of ways. The two most important procedures consist of the annual review of multi-year programmes and discussion and approval of the draught Report and Accounts of IRI's direct subsidiaries.

Investment programmes with a rolling multi-year horizon are now a standard practice in all subsidiaries. The planning cycle starts in the spring with the formulation by the IRI of general and specific guidelines and the fixing of basic external perimeters to be used by all companies for their projections. The plans are submitted to IRI head-quarters in October by sectoral sub-holdings and other parent companies which have the task of consolidating the operating companies' plans in a global sector perspectives.

Each plan is submitted to the IRI's Executive Committee together with comments by the Planning Department and are discussed at a meeting attended by the top management of the relevant sub-holding or parent subsidiary. By the end of the year these deliberations are completed. The overall funding requirements of the programmes are naturally of overriding importance and represent crucial issues for the IRI and the Government's consideration. The consolidation of all programmes at IRI closes the cycle with the submission of the group's multiyear programme at each year-end to the Executive Committee. Subsequently, when endorsed by the Board of Directors, the programme is submitted to the Ministry of State Shareholding.

The draught report and accounts of the most important sub-sidiaries are discussed at two meetings of the Executive Committee: the first to debate a report by the Comptroller on the criteria which the company proposes to follow in drawing up its yearly accounts; the second to review the resulting financial statement with the comments of the Comptroller based on the trend over recent years and into the immediate future. These meetings are held in the spring and attended by chief executives of the company concerned. The Report and Accounts are subsequently submitted to meetings of shareholders for formal approval.

Important contacts are held between the Heads of Departments at Headquarter and their counterparts in the major subsidiaries (especially for coordinating, and assisting in, the raising of funds in the domestic and international markets).

Negotiations with labour unions on wage agreements, redundancies etc. are handled by Intersind, in consultation with the company concerned. Intersind is an employer's association to which, since 1957, IRI companies belong after their departure from the thereafter solely private employers' association (Confindustria).

4. Present IRI Structure in the State Share-Holdings System

The present structure of the IRI group is axled around four large areas: manufacturing, service activities (telecommunication and transports), infrastructures, banking.

In manufacturing, a large stake of the IRI's activities are in mature technology sectors, notably in steel and shipyards, where a strategy of personnel reductions, productivity and re-conversion is under way.

This is in fact counterbalanced by the presence of high technology activities (such as power plants, railway systems, computerized manufacturing, radar systems, aircraft industry, semiconductors, telecommunication appliances) where employement and R&D are developing.

In the services the most important area is telecommunications: an IRI company runs the whole Italian TLC system and all the international links.

Sea and air transport companies, software, broadcasting and television are other service activities controlled by the IRI.

In the infrastructures IRI runs the Italian toll highways system and controls engineering companies operating worldwide.

Three large Italian banks are also controlled by the IRI; they hold a considerable stake in the most important Italian merchant bank, Mediobanca.

The Italian State Shareholdings System includes, besides the IRI, other holdings: ENI, EFIM, Ente Cinema.

ENI operates in oil and gas, as well as in basic chemicals, deep sea engineering and textiles.

EFIM is a minor holding, with activities in aluminium, motor-car windows, bus and train body manufacturing and helicopters.

Ente Cinema runs the production of films in its owned "Cinecittà" plant.

Total production of the Italian State Shareholdings System is about seven percent of GNP, with a wide range of stakes according to the current sector total employment of the State Shareholdings System is about 700,000 employees, some 5% of dependent labour in Italy.

Part IV.

Symposium Report

SYMPOSIUM REPORT

1. Background

The performance and management of State-Owned Enterprises (SOEs) are inviting increasing attention in the world. In many developing countries, in particular, SOEs have a great impact on national economies by controlling some of the largest revenue-earning activities and generating a large number of employment opportunities. Despite these features, more often than not SOEs have not been very successful in terms of corporate performance per se and in turn they make increasing claims on the national budgets. Major factors behind their poor performance are attributed to inadequate autonomy, rigidity, deterioration of commitment, inadequate competition and the like. In contrast to these, the private sector under a competitive environment has to continuously improve its performance and produce better quality goods and services. There is growing pressure on SOEs to meet similar demands of excellence. Some countries are also trying to induce private sector vitality into their SOEs through privatization. The coming age of change, kindled by rapid technological breakthroughs, is bringing forth significant improvements in the management of industries and services. The SOEs cannot afford to remain a mere observer of these changes. In short, SOEs have to significantly improve their efficiency and effectiveness, as public institutions fulfilling social objectives.

Keeping the above in view, the Asian Productivity Organization (APO) undertook a two-year intensive Survey on Management of State-Owned Enterprises from 1987 to 1988 with Dr. Vudhichai Chamnong, Professor of Organizational Behaviour, School of Business Administration, National Institute of Development Administration, Thailand, as Chief Expert. This study, shedding light on the dynamic process of management improvement of SOEs at the enterprise level, is being participated in by National Experts drawn from nine member countries, namely, the Republic of China, India, Japan, Republic of Korea, Malaysia, Nepal, Singapore, Sri Lanka and Thailand.

Following the above survey, five-day Symposium on Management of State-Owned Enterprises was organized by the APO in collaboration with the Asian Development Bank as well as National Institute of Business Management, Sri Lanka, from the 17th to 21st October 1988 in Colombo Sri Lanka. The meeting was meant to deliberate on innovative management practices of outstanding SOEs and to share some corporate experiences in this field from within as well as outside the region. The meeting had 20 participants from 12 APO member countries and three observers from the Asian Development Bank, Industrial Development Board (Sri Lanka), United Nations Development Programme (Sri Lanka). Dr. Vudhichai Chamnong, Col. S.P. Wahi of the Oil & Natural Gas Commission, India, Mr. Roger Antell of British Telecom, the U.K., Dr. Umberto Del Canuto of IRI, Italy and Mr. H.D.S.A. Gunawardena, Sri Lanka acted as resource speakers. A list of participants and resource persons and the programme and schedule are attached in Appendices 3 and 4.

2. Inauguration

Following the Sri Lankan traditional lighting of a lamp and opening remarks by Prof. B.L. Panditharatna, Director General of National Institute of Business Management and Alternate Director for Sri Lanka, the symposium was inaugurated by Honourable Denzil Fernando, Minister of Industries and Scientific Affairs, Government of the Republic of Sri Lanka. Citing the revival of Chrysler corporation in the U.S., the minister underlined the importance of identifying the defects and appropriate remedies and applying the remedies with a will. Further, Mr. Fernando underlined the differences between Manager of a State-Owned Enterprise and Civil Servant and the need for the former to know functions of the enterprise, and to be guided by the noblest motive for public good. He ended his address by urging an increasing need to apply Science in Management.

The inaugural address was followed by an address by Mr. Nagao Yoshida, Secretary General of the APO, which traced the preceding APO Survey on Management of SOEs, organization of the current symposium with support from the Asian Development Bank (ADB) and the intention of the APO to organize a follow-up seminar for Senior Managers from SOEs.

Mr. Justin Dias, Secretary, Ministry of Industries and Scientific Affairs and APO Director for Sri Lanka then presented an address on the objectives, and special features of SOEs and their management. In particular, he cited the Swedish experience in forming a holding company of State-Owned Enterprises and separating management of SOEs from political considerations.

3. Keynote Address

Integrating the outcome of the preceding survey, Dr. Vudhichai Chamnong delivered the keynote address. In order to study the whole picture of SOEs, he highlighted an approach through the following 3 contexts:

1) SOE's environmental context, covering
   - Establishment aspect, defining the "path" of SOE performance. Strategies, such as, privatization, merger, diversification, modification and or improvement of functions could be conceived from this point of view.
   - Controlling agencies ... which might be helpful hands or obstacles.
   - Public expectation ... favourable/unfavourable to SOEs.

2) SOE's organizational contents
   - Technological Aspect ... development of own hightech., transfer, collaboration, adoption of hardware, etc.
   - Social relationship aspects
     - Organizational Culture ... usually brought in and built-up by top executives, will determine effectiveness and efficiency.
     - Management and leadership style of the CEO ... is the most important determinant of culture and performance behaviour.
     - Organizational members ought to understand the four levels of ideas:
       - Philosophical level
       - Conceptional level
       - Strategic level
       - Operational level
     Board of Directors Members and Executive should concentrate on, in particular, the philosophical level and conceptual levels. They should not be "operational executives".
   - Procedal structure aspect
     - Communication structure, formal/personal
     - Participation, more/less
     - Difficulty in applying agricultural civilization in an industrial and/or information society
     - Manager is not only a problem solver (fire fighter) but should also take creative preventive and promotive measures.

3) Functional contexts
    ● Financial Performance is expected to be just providing services
      to the public and/or a source of government income.
    ● Marketing Managing – to be strategically implemented. It tends
      to be spoiled by monopolistic operation of SOEs.
    ● Production Management – closely related to the degree of
      technological development.
    ● Human resource management – key for efficiency and effective-
      ness improvement.
      Development of entrepreneurism, sense of quality and establish-
      ment of management credibility are vital to productivity en-
      hancement, in addition to motivational and skill development.

Along with the above analytical view, Dr. Vudhichai stressed that
SOEs' executives play the most significant roles in the performance and
development of SOEs, and a comprehensive executive development
programme, with emphasize on the developmental concept, i.e. continuous and long term, rather than just training programme.

It was suggested that the syllabus of the programme cover at least
three main aspects:
    ● Conceptually dynamic frame for management of organization.
    ● Illustrative cases of both successful and unsuccessful SOEs.
    ● Emphasize TAKE HOME VALUES for executives, i.e. im-
      mediate implementation of practical concepts learned helping
      hands in the follow-up process, and developmental evaluation of
      resolutions.

4. Resource Presentations

Based on the experience of the Oil and Natural Gas Commission
(ONGC) of India over the last several years, Col. S.P. Wahi analyzed
crucial factors behind managerial effectiveness in SOEs. The commission had grown over three and a half times in the last six and a half
years with stability and continuous improvement in productivity.
This was achieved by an emphasis on the following three aspects:

1) Scientific or managerial aspects of Management i.e. (organization
    structure, systems and procedures, financial and material manage-
    ment, professional expertise, R&D, information technology,
    modernization etc.)

2) Human resources management and leadership aspects of manage-
    ment.

3) Management of governmental environment. Politicians, media and people around that area of operation. (this calls for both good managerial and leadership ability or talents.)

Col. Wahi stressed, in particular, the importance of the man behind the machine, his motivation and morale and creation of the right culture and climate for excellence in performance. Keeping the above in view, ONGC has succeeded in altering over the last seven years more than 80% of bureaucratic approaches and culture. As for management of the environment, it was argued that SOEs' power usually rests with the bureaucracy and accountability rests with management.

Thus, it is necessary to bring power to the Board and under such a set-up, involvement of bureaucrats could be a strength, as they would bring in their wisdom.

"The presentation by Mr. Roger Antell on the "Privatization Experience" of British Telecom (one of the five largest telecommunications operation worldwide) dealt with the comprehensive organizational and commercial innovation brought forth in the company over the last 10 years. He stressed the objectives that privatization was aimed to achieve. In the UK, the government of Mrs. Margaret Thatcher was committed from the beginning to the extension of competition throughout the British economy and undertook a programme of returning state industries to the private sector and subjecting them as much as possible to competition. The intention was to bring greater productivity of operation, better customer service through the adoption of commercial standards and appropriate technology, and to make available finances from the private sector to meet the operating and investment plans of these industries.

Mr. Antell commented that privatization was the final point on the road to change: turning a state organization into a private company. In developing economies, full privatization might not yet be the appropriate solution. There were, however, other actions that could and should be made to make state organizations more efficient, in particular introducing commercial practices, better financial accountability and some element of competition or regulation. The history of British Telecom gave an illustration of this. Up to 1969, telecommunications was run as a Government Department as part of the Post Office and the mood prevailed "as it was in the beginning, is now and ever shall be." The first step towards commercialization was taken in 1969 when a national corporation was set up to run Posts and Telecoms. In 1981 Posts and Telecoms were separated into different businesses and markets opened to competition for customer equipment and value added services. Then in 1984 British Telecom was turned into a private company and the Government sold 51% of the equity to the general public. The sale was hugely successful with over 2 million shareholders and even in 1988 there are still 1.3 million shareholders of British Telecom.

Following privatization, a number of changes have happened by comparison with what was usual beforehand. British Telecom is now fully in control of its costs and the allocation of its revenues, whereas beforehand many of these decisions were controlled by Government decisions. Investments are made according to commercial rates of return and British Telecom has flexibility over how it raises investment funds, together with control over the timing and implementation of its investment decisions.

When British Telecom was privatized, the Government allowed competition for all telecommunications services. However, because British Telecom controlled the market, and it was difficult for competitors to become established, a rule was introduced that British Telecom could not raise its prices by as much as it wanted. From 1984 to 1989, price rises have kept below UK inflation by 3%, and from 1989, below inflation by 4.5%. This regulation has forced British Telecom to increase its productivity and reduce its costs. Another rule says that British Telecom cannot use its profits to charge prices below costs to stop competitors being successful and this gives the opportunity for competitors to come in for many services, even to offer customers telephone calls on a different network system.

This has resulted in British Telecom becoming more customer oriented. Its organization is different from a Government Department and takes account of the various markets it serves. Restructuring into a flatter organization and reduction of the number of grades has made the company more efficient, and management functions are easier with closer access to the customers. R&D is managed with reference to end-markets and a combination of technology push/pull markets leads to "customer solutions" rather than just technical problem-solving. British Telecom's suppliers have to be competitive to win contracts so that British Telecom can be competitive in supplying its customers.

The success of British Telecom in responding to these challenges can be seen in the latest financial figures. Between 1980 and 1988 profits increased by 400% which was nearly twice the increase in turnover the the same period. The Government also saw a better financial return with an increase in revenue receipts from British Telecom of over 300% as a result of corporate taxes and dividends, something which would not have been possible before privatization.

Dr. Umbert Del Canuto's presentation on the "Italian State Share-holdings System" dealt with state intervention of SOEs, as well as the most recent strategy of an Italian state shareholding company, IRI (Instituto per la Reconstruczione Industriale) under the control of IRI, about 600 companies including the finance, manufacturing and service sectors are grouped together. They are legally free to diversify overall as per specific strategies internally decided by the IRI. While French and British SOEs are connected to different ministries, thus hindering a strategic management orientation at a holding company level, in Italy the Ministry for State Shareholdings has political unitary super-vision over the state industrial holdings like IRI but is not directly operating in strategic decisions. Accordingly, the content of the strategic role of IRI could be decided on its own according to market rules.

The Parliament approves IRI programmes submitted each year by the Ministry of State Shareholdings. Strategic management decision — to enter new sectors, to divest mature industries, to go public on the stock exchange — are submitted to the IRI Board by the "Committee for Strategic Issues" with the contributions of sector holdings under IRI, and operating companies. Through its drastic strategic manage-ment, IRI has successfully restructured the business activities of the group, and 250 companies (or 41%) among the group account for 95% of the group's turnover and employment. Group turnover amounts to US$40 billion and more than 400 thousand people are employed by the IRI group.

So, IRI is now coping with the strategic issue of uppermost im-portance, i.e., the opening up of the European market in 1992. IRI's commitment is crucial for system innovation in Italy through the achievement of large networks in telecommunications, multimodal transport, banking and R&D connections. For instance, in telecommu-nications huge investments have been planned to catch up with the pace of digital networks introduced by the United Kingdom, France and West Germany. Organizational restructuring of all the sectors in the group is envisaged through joint ventures at the international level to manufacture new digital equipment.

The presentation by Mr. H.D.S.A. Gunawardena on "Rationali-zation of the Institutional Framework in the Telecommunication Sector of Sri Lanka" dealt with his experience in a privatization scheme of telecommunication business; as well as difficulty in applying the scheme in his country.

The structural pattern of the telecommunication sector in Sri Lanka follows closely that of other countries. The telecommunication sector as a government department is not result-oriented, with revenue collection about six months behind. The organizational structure was the main hindrance to achieving maximum results operationally and financially.

The first step towards rationalizing the telecommunications sector in Sri Lanka was to separate it from the postal services. Then a presidential committee was set up to study the reorganization of the Telecommunication Department. The study discovered that the demand for telecommunication lines is more than what the Telecommunication Department can supply.

Telecommunication engineering in government service was not highly paid. Many engineers left the Telecommunication Department. This affected the quality of telecommunication services.

The presidential committee recommended that the Telecommunication Department be handled by an entity which is free from governmental rules. And an independent commission be established for regulating the entity and ensuring fairplay between the government, the entity, telephone customers and the general public. The entity should function under a licence and aspects such as tariffs should be controlled by the independent commission. To materialize the recommendation the Telecommunication Board of Sri Lanka was set up to draw up the necessary legislation.

But implementation of the rationalization process was hampered because of a lack of private management experience and possibly, a baseless fear of losing existing benefits by some of the staff. A need to educate and change the thinking of politicians, bureaucrats and public sector managers in order to create a private sector mentality and transformational leadership existed.

5. Sailient Points

Sailient points of the various presentations and ensuring discussions were as follows:

5.1 Specialities of SOEs

SOEs seem to have corporate growth cycles like that in the private sector. It is featured with three life stages, i.e., a sheltered phase, supportive phase and self-propelling phase. Because of this the development phase, strategy formulation, autonomy, mode of finance and criteria have to be different. More specifically SOEs at the self-propelling stage seem to be more adaptive to changes in the market and autonomoty in business/government relations. They are also more dependent on internal funds and concerned more about effectiveness, rather than efficiency in ensuing enterprise performance.

The roles and/or functions of particular SOEs are also determined directly by environmental contexts such as the establishment of the SOE, its controlling agencies and the public expectation. The different scope and reasons for the establishment of SOEs in each country would determine the concentration of their operations. Their development through the history of each SOE seems to follow its establishing objectives.

However, it seems that, to a certain extent, the government establishes SOEs in order for them to perform "official functions business like". But once they are set up it turns out to be that SOEs are performing "business functions official-like". The case study in Malaysia indicated four main reasons to which SOEs failure could be attributed, incompetent management, corruption, political interference and lack of effective central coordination and monitoring mechanism.

The case study in Japan on the other hand indicated constraints at the macro level, for instance, contradiction among direct interest groups, i.e., the government and labour unions; lack of proper corporate strategies, limited marketing activities, finance not based on cost consciousness, lack of research and development, and a tall and strict structure.

Controlling agencies of SOEs are often blamed for creating unfavourable rules that lead to ineffectiveness, inefficiency, low productivity, or even the failure of SOEs. As per the strict regulation, quite a number of SOEs practice routine management functions in order to satisfy controlling agencies. However, in the successful case of the ROK, where evaluation of SOEs is based on financial ratios and wide ranging autonomy is provided to SOEs, the controlling agencies can be big boosters for ailing SOEs. It is expected that the controlling agencies be catalysts but not world police.

5.2 Institutional Restructuring Strategies

It could be observed that entrepreneurial and flexible organization in the private sector tends to change into a bureaucratic and centralized one as the organization grows up. Against this, the on-going trend in privatization represents the restructuring of enlarged bureaucratic state owned enterprises into delegated and risk-taking organizations.

With the above in view, the concept of "privatization" might be beneficial to both sectors.

Privatization is not a goal in itself. It is rather a tool leading to greater efficiency. The mission of SOEs needs to be carefully evaluated vis-a-vis the required efficiency of these enterprises. A mission, in any case, would be incomplete without efficiency. Standard precise rules/ regulations of a commercial nature leading to greater efficiency are necessary. The company rules should give decisions on finance, personnel, technology, innovation and budget control. When SOEs cannot satisfy the governing conditions of efficiency, the issue of privatization should crop up.

The objective of privatization is to improve the management of SOEs. The privatization should not be discussed with respect to ownership criteria alone. Privatization can lead to added dynamism of an SOE. In other words, the major emphasis behind privatization should be on introducing competition because monopolies are often found inefficient. BT indicated that privatization can be achieved in different stages, depending on local political and economic conditions. Share flotation is the final stage, and the introduction of commercial practices can be made at an earlier state. In fact, a commercial approach is necessary before a state organization is ready to be privatized.

Instances of the case studies from the developing countries suggest that there needs to be a pre-condition as well as methods/procedures for privatization. While some countries have succeeded in vitalizing SOEs through privatization, countries like India here succeeded in transfering privately owned poorly managed businesses to the state for better management. Success of organizations may rest heavily with management competence and commitment rather than ownership.

In examining whether it is a private industry or SOE, the most important issue is to clearly define how much social, commercial and economic efficiency (i.e. by world market standards) an enterprise possesses.

Privitization is not related to ownership but related to how an SOE behaves. This concept hence could be warranted for any SOEs in several ways.

1) An institutional framework for management should be provided and protected by law in order that an SOE is able to resist political elements in its decision making.

2) A long-term appointment of CEO would help him behave more independently and shape the corporate management style like a private entity.

3) Profit seeking and market orientation are the ultimate action guidelines, government involvement must be limited to long-range
planning, long-run funding, and the appointment of top management.

Merger among SOEs can sometimes be a key to solving SOEs
operational problems. Merger can create such benefits as economy of
scale, synergy and management betterments, in various functional areas
like Production, Personnel, Marketing, R&D etc. In addition, mergers
among SOEs might be a good step prior to privatization. If merger
could improve financial performance of an SOE, it could also enhance
the total value of the company. A successful merger will help government make more money when it sells stock to the public in the process
of privatization. This will lead to wider distribution of private ownership after the privatization.

Diversification could be regarded as another strategy to enhance
efficiency of SOEs as the Keppel Corporation of Singapore has tried.
It could be eventually called "A National Company". Other SOEs in
Sri Lanka, India, and Nepal for example, take a straight forward
approach to improving their own management through the modification and/or development of business functions like Production,
Marketing and technology transfer.

Pakistan's approach, which led to the establishment of a state
owned holding company was practical and unique in the Asian context.
The present approach in Pakistan is to convert SOEs to joint stock companies with an autonomous Board of Directors. The supervisory role of
the Ministry was seen as positive in the "smooth management of inter-
linkages" between the economy and government. The importance of
political leadership was emphasized.

5.3 Internal Efforts for Management Innovation

Organizational Culture will induce effective performance since it
reflects the way people do things in the organization. Keppel Corporation in Singapore obviously maintains mutually supportive relations.
That kind of organizational culture helps facilitate growth and
effectiveness of SOEs to a large extent. NTT of Japan has also changed
after privatization from a conservative culture to a challenging and
aggressive culture.

ONGC launched a continuous drive to touch the innovative minds
of people through formal and informal channels by motivation and
incentives. A special magazine has been introduced to project the image
of people who come out with innovative suggestions for the improve-

ment of any aspect of the Commission's work. The people are awarded and rewarded through many schemes including promotion (exhibition) of individuals. This has electrified the minds of the people for better productivity performance. Creative thinking groups have been formed in which the lowest to the highest paid employees can interact and give suggestions for the betterment of the Commission.

It is currently realized that high productivity and advancement of enterprises depend largely on high technology and qualified human resources.

For the concentration of limited resources on high technology, it is effective to disinvest certain activities to the cooperative sector, to industry and to other organizations both in the public and the private sector. Some of ONGC employees have been motivated to seek premature retirement and form cooperatives by taking away low technology equipment and working again for the company as contractors. This strategy has shown excellent results in productivity and the growth of manpower, particularly in the low technology areas, has been controlled. This strategy is helping ONGC to resist pressures for employment in non-operative areas.

In the coming Information Age, Telecommunication Authority of Singapore (TELECOMS) was seen to be the key institution to lead the way. Nippon Telegraph and Telephone Corporation of Japan (NTT) is committed to developing the new generation of telecommunications equipment and services called ISDN (Integrated Systems Digital Network).

Most SOEs however, seem to gradually develop software technology based on foreign technology and know-how. Sri Lanka Tyre Corporation(SLTC) for instance has recently entered into a technical collaboration agreement with B.F. Goodrich of the U.S. to harness advanced technology to produce a tyre up to an internationally accepted standard.

The Oil Natural Gas Commission of India (ONGC) takes another route of continuous search for excellence. Within a span of 30 years, ONGC has assimilated the world's best petroleum expertise developed in the last 100 years. It has emerged as a multidisciplinary organization with complete in-house expertize and is becoming increasingly self reliant in the well advanced and sophisticated oil exploration and production technology.

A concept of profit centers could be introduced in the working of R&D institutes to create quality use of time and cost consciousness among the scientists. This scheme might not be successful without the full consent of the scientists.

Another measure, as introduced by British Telecom, is a requirement for all research programmes to be sponsored internally within
the organization or by external agencies, leading to better-focused
management of the development activity.

SOEs selected in the current survey are more or less successful
cases in which most of them are enjoying making their financial ratios
look good. As in the case of CPDC of China, it is reported that the
merger resulted in satisfactory financial performance. Some Thai SOEs
and Keppel Corporation in Singapore have issued bonds.

Cost saving is another aspect many SOEs have taken. Nepal
Electricity Authority (NEA), for example, has implemented a cost
reduction scheme to a successful extent. ONGC of India demonstrates
very good cost consciousness. Due to improvement in productivity and
strong cost consciousness, profits have been increasing, while the price
for crude oil being paid to ONGC since 1981 till date has remained the
same.

Most SOEs originally enjoyed their monopolistic operation to the
extent that they tended to ignore the significance of the marketing
function. However, it is noticeable that the influence of private
business's marketing aggressiveness has recently aroused SOEs to pay
more attention to their marketing aspect of enterprise.

In managing SOEs, their effort might be uniquely featured in the
management of environment. They put special emphasis on
management of bureaucracy, politicians and local pressure groups.
Earning their goodwill, assistance and support is instrumental in
furthering the objectives of SOEs.

5.4 Leadership Management Style

What is crucial behind success is not the ownership of an organization — whether it is publicly or privately owned —, but the quality of
leadership.

Labour productivity is essentially a reflection of managerial productivity, which in turn is a function of quality of leadership.

While a "manager" could bring his ability into full play under a
well organized "system", a good system could also be created through
quality leadership. Good leadership style is to set a personal example
and ensure participation as a cultural norm. Senior executives have been
motivated to adopt a style of control through 'Management by Wandering'. The philosophy is that the soldier in the front should not have to
look over his shoulders for anything.

Keppel Corporation in Singapore is said to have a managing director who is "a man of — vision." This is backed up by the cooperative network of Singapore's SOE leadership team.

What makes NTT of Japan so successful? It could be its management style. Initially, working groups of middle management were set up to survey problems for privatization. It is also observed that people from the bottom to the top gather regularly, not just two every weeks as was done in the former hierarchical chain. Likewise, MUL of India has established good a communication system or, it may be called, an informal, and personal system. They have practiced open office policy, including regular meetings, printed documents, displays, etc. And through the device of proper communication, SLTC of Sri Lanka could reach information to make efficient effective decisions.

For developing positive management style and leadership, the concept of ownership (making top management possess some shares of his SOE while in his tenure) might be useful.

To get separate subsidiary companies established is a very difficult task for an SOE due to bureaucratic control and the lack of autonomy with the Public Sector Enterprises. Hence additional powers have been delegated down the line in ONGCs so that each business group is accountable and has the desired autonomy for implementing plans. The basic philosophy of Management of ONGC is Centralized Policy Making and Decentralized Administration.

Practical human resource management depends to a large extent upon SOEs' management and leadership styles. ONGC and MUL of India have taken very appropriate human resource strategies to improve their productivity and efficiency.

These companies mainly stress human resource strategies as follows:

- entrepreneurial development;
- limited but competent work-force
- convey a sense of equality; and
- establish credibility of management etc.

6. Industrial Visit

On the fifth day of the Symposium, the participants visited Ceylon Ceramic Corporation whose case study was covered earlier under the precedent survey project. The visit gave a first hand understanding of management practices by sharing experiences with managers of the corporation.

7. Syndicate Discussions

Towards the end of the symposium, the participants, resource persons and observers were formed into two syndicate groups to conduct in-depth discussions on the major findings of the meetings and identify strategic directions to be proceeded in by SOEs for their further development. They also considered syllabuses of training programmes for senior/middle managers of SOEs, as possible follow-up actions by APO in this field.

8. Conclusions and Recommendations

The outcome of the group discussions was presented to the symposium on the concluding day by the representatives of the two groups, namely Col. (Dr.) S.P. Wahi, a resource person from India, and Dr. Umberto Del Canuto, a resource person from Italy. Ensuing discussions led to unanimous adoption of the following conclusions and recommendations.

8.1 Nature of SOEs

There appear to be conceptually "two models" in defining SOEs, i.e. type A and type B.

Type A: Those SOEs that must retained their SOE status, since they are "natural monopolies" and their objectives are stipulated by "policy missions".

Type B: Those SOEs that could be privatized in the future, since they are no longer monopolies and the significance of their "policy mission" is less than that of type A.

These two types of SOEs should be discussed on different grounds, in terms of their objectives, evaluation criteria, personnel and incentive policies, and legal systems to be controlled.

Type A SOEs might cover public utilities, transportation, rural development, and the like. Type As in less developed countries covers even manufacturers of basic consumer goods. Profitability might not be an appropriate measurement of performance. Instead,

1) The degree of policy mission attainment or

2) The efficiency of operation(to provide the goods or services at the lowest cost) might be the primary criteria for evaluating business performance.

Type B SOEs are enterprises which are in a relatively competitive market rather than in a monopolistic market. The market mechanism therein dictates optimum resource allocation, entrepreneurship and innovation in management as well as which technology they are in dire need of A type B SOE must be run as per commercial objectives, i.e. profit seeking. Social objectives to be fullfilled, must be quantified and recorded separately, and further they may have to be fulfilled by a mutual and formal agreement between the SOE and the government.

Political assignment might be necessary for type A SOEs to fulfill their policy mission while type B SOEs might transform themselves into "holding companies" to keep themselves away from political influence and enable them to practice their business activities on the most appropriate commercial basis.

8.2 Management Thrusts

In the above light, the emphasis of management of Type A SOEs might be placed on improvement in efficiency (or cost reduction). Hence, certain productivity indices or standards (developed for international comparison) would be helpful in improving the efficiency of the operations.

Type B SOEs might be more keen in innovation or effective at the strategic and operational levels of their changing market context. Empahsis of their management has to be placed on:

1) Environmental management — Covering the management activities concerned with external relationships, such as Government, opinion leaders, economic factors, market and social conditions.

2) Scientific management — Covering the business management activities required for running a profitable business. This includes the preparation of a corporate plan, with a situational audit, and the definition of long term objectives and mission. From this a plan for implementation is devised, dealing with such things as organization, search, research and development, training, marketing and financial performance. The focus should be on productivity improvements and cost reduction. The "profit centre" concepts should be implemented throughout the organization to provide incentives, give measurable objectives, and promote internal competition.

3) Human resource management — Covering the specific issue of leading and motivating staff. It is characterized by a concern for people, and their motivation and morale.

These two types of SOEs indicate both extreme of SOE models. The realities of SOEs could be deemed to be rather widely dispersed between the two models, being subject to public needs, market conditions, technology innovation, government policy and the like. In other words, where individual SOEs should be positioned rests with management views on change in the business environment and resources/possessions to be developed. It also heavily depends on management's philosophy of change. With the above in view, the significance of leadership to be taken by SOE top managers as well as farsighted catalytic roles of controlling agencies have to be stressed again. They have to keep their eyes on the transitional timing and preconditions for possible privatization of SOEs.

8.3 Syllabus of Training Programmes

In light of the significance in developing positive management style and leadership, syllabuses of training programmes for senior/middle managers of SOEs were formulated as per the SOE models mentioned above, i.e. Type A SOE (policy, mission oriented) and type B SOE (market oriented). The above two syllabuses were designed to be used for a three week training programme.

For Type A (Policy Mission Oriented) SOEs
Senior/Middle Management Training Programme

1. Modern Management and the Firm Theory

1) The core business
2) Innovation in the product cycle
3) Marketing
4) Manufacturing
5) Going Global
6) The value chain

2. Running Staff Functions

1)	Strategic management:	New business and diversification
2)	Budgeting:	Fixing objectives and analyzing the results
3)	Finance:	Internal funds
		Commercial borrowing
		Long term loans
		Risk capital
		International borrowing
		Foreign exchange management
4)	Personnel:	Recruiting
		Internal turnover
		T.U. bargaining
		Market compensation and management by objective
		Fringe benefits
		Training and retraining
5)	R&D activities:	Make or buy an organization for R&D
		Venturing with technologically able companies

6) Organizational and upper management styles:

         Decentralization — line staff

         Central Decision making and strategic control at Board level

3. Management of Modern SOEs

1) Optimal government rules: The Controlling bodies vs. holding
   prices
   Information
   Authorization
   Control
2) Public goals vs. efficiency: Defining the mission of finance
   Defining managers' responsibility
   for:
   Competition at market prices
   Monopoly and tariff fixing
   Non-profit mission
   — investment grants
   — state subsidies
3) Emerging losses: Accounting rules and certification
   of balance sheets
   Budget control
   Fixing by management
   Financing the losses

Notes:

1. This course should contain information about
   — Modern management and the firm theory
   — Managing of staff
   — Finance
   — Defining the rules valid for A type SOEs.
2. The course should emphasize also attitudes and behaviour of management in SOEs, define worldwide scenarios and future expectations in the developing economies along with global vision on macro-economic evolution, define in a more precise way the methods of evaluation of SOEs.
3. Favour the exchange of SOE managers among different countries so that they can benefit from experiences relating to diverse policies and economic contexts. These exchanges should take into account similarities of industrial sectors and different performances in type A and type B SOEs.

For Type B (Market Oriented) SOEs
Senior/Middle Management Training Progrmme

1. Conceptual — Organization Level

1) Economic Situation of the Country
2) International Economic Situation
3) International Finance

2. SWOT Analysis or Situational Audit

1) Corporate Plan
2) Commercial Orientation: Finance
Marketing
Productivity
Cost reduction
Technology/analysis of state of the
  art technology
Research & Development
Information technology
Preparation of strategic business
  plan
Study of organizational structures

3. Skill Development

1) Management of Change   Through case studies and
2) Management of Crises   participation of international
3) Development of Aggressive   experts
4) Commercial Culture
5) Public Speaking
6) Communication and Corporate Image
7) Profit Centres Concept to improve internal competitiveness
    and bring about cost consciousness — task force strategies to
    bring about management of change

4. Human Relations

1) Human psychology
2) Behavioural science
3) Attitude studies
4) Rewards and other motivational matter to improve morale
5) Through group discussions bring about styles of participative
    management and an ownership concept sense of belonging.

6) Concern for people, mutual respect and confidence even with the lowest level of employees

7) General study — study of biographies and autobiographies of great leaders

Appendices

Appendix 1

List of Contributors

Participants

Republic of China	Mr. Chen-Cheng Huang	Chief of Corporate Strategy Commission of National Corp. Ministry of Economic Affairs 109 Hankow St. Sec. 1. Taipei, Taiwan
	Dr. Dah-Hsian Seetoo	Dean & Professor Graduate School of Business Adm. National Chengchi Univ. 187-1, Ching-Hwa St., Taipei, Taiwan
India	Mr. Suraj Bhan Jain	Adviser Standing Conference Public Enterprises (SCOPE) 7 Lodi Road, New Delhi-110 003
Indonesia	Mr. Manullang Gison	Head of Personnel Guiden/ Development & Adm. Department State Electricity Corp. Jln. M.R.R. No. 1, Jakart — Pusat
	Mr. Djoehana Manaf	Jakarta Branch Manager P.T. Pantja Niaga (Ltd.) Kramat Raya 94 — 96
Iran	Mr. Mohammad Ali O.E. Vesaghi	General Manager & Representative of Bonyad Mostazafan Fundation in Iran Air Filter, Boulevard Keshavarz/N. Dr. Mofateh Ave. No. 346 Teheran
Japan	Prof. Makoto Kanda	Associate Professor Meiji-Gakuin University 2-37, 1-chome, Shiroganedai Minato-ku, Tokyo 108
Republic of Korea	Mr. Jong Soo Lim	Assistance Section Chief Korea Federation of Small Business #16-2, Yoido-dong, Youngdeungpo-ku, Seoul

Malaysia	Mrs. Musalmiah Asli	Director Work Systems Div. Malaysian Administrative Modernization & Management Planning Unit (MAMPU) Prime Minister's Dept. 11th F1., Bangunan Kuwasa, Jalan Raja Laut, Kuala Lumpur
Nepal	Mr. Deepak Thapa	General Manager Bansbari Leather & Shoe Factory Ltd. Bansbari, Kathmandu, Nepal P.O. Box 227
Pakistan	Mr. Mohammad Aslam	Joint Secretary Ministry of Industries Gov't of Pakistan, Secretariat Block A, Islamabad
	Mr. Abdul Malik	Managing Director, Fazal Vegetable Mills, Sector I/9, Industrial Area, Islamabad
	Mr. Saiyid Zafar Ali Naqvi	Joint Secretary Ministry of Production Gov't of Pakistan 822165 Islamabad
Philippines	Mrs. Carmen Perez Reyes	Chief, Personnel Management Dept. & OIC, General Adm. Sugar Regulatory Adm. (SRA) North Avenue, Diliman, Quezon City
Singapore	Dr. Douglas Joel Sikorski	Senior Lecturer Schoool of Management National University of Singapore Singapore 0511
Sri Lanka	Mr. K.S. Chandrasiri	Senior Consultant National Institute of Business Management 120/5, Wijerama Mawatha, Colombo 7
	Mr. V. Kanagasabapathy	Deputy Director General Treasury Ministry of Finance & Planning Colombo 1

	Mrs. Manique N. Mendis	Deputy Director Public Enterprises Div. General Treasury Secretary Building, Colombo 1
Thailand	Mr. Phiphat Thaiarry	Director Public Enterprise Institute Chulalongkorn Univ. Bangkok 10500
	Mr. Chamnan Thamnathikom	Training & Development Div. Chief, Metropolitan Electricity Authority (MEA) 121 Chakpet Road, Bangkok 10100

Resource Persons

Dr. Vudhichai Chamnong	Professor of Organization Behaviour School of Business Administration National Institute of Development Administration (NIDA) Klong Chan, Bangkapi Bangkok 10240, Tahiland
Col. S.P. Wahi	Chairman Oil & Natural Gas Commission 7th Floor, Bank of Baroda Building 16, Sansa Marg, New Delhi-110001 India
Mr. Roger Antell	Director British Telecom Overseas Division Aeradio House, Hayes Road Southall, Middlesex UB2 5NJ U.K.
Dr. Umberto Del Canuto	Economic Research Department IRI's Headquarters Veneto, 89 — 00187 Roma, Italy
Mr. H.D.S.A. Gunawardena	Senior Consultant/Project Coordinator Telecommunications Board of Sri Lanka
Mr. Peter C. Brinkmann	Project Economist Industry & Minerals Division Asian Development Bank P.O. Box 789, Manila Philippines

Mr. Nanda Senanayake

Representative of Technet Asia
General Manager
Industrial Development Board (IDB)
615 Galle Road, Katubedde
Moratuwa, Sri Lanka

Mr. Bhekh Bahadur Thapa, RR

UNDP
P.O. Box 1505
Colombo, Sri Lanka

APO Secretariat

Dr. S.K. Subramanian

Technical Consultant and Head of
Research and Planning Division
Asian Productivity Organization

Mr. Shuji Aoyama

Research and Planning Officer
Asian Productivity Organization

Appendix 2

Programme & Schedule

17th Oct. 1988 (Mon)

Morning Session:

08:00 — 08:20	Registration
09:30 — 09:45	Inaugural Function
10:15 — 11:45	Keynote Speech by Prof. Vudhichai Chamnong, Chief Exert

Afternoon Session: [Mr. Chandrasiri]

13:00 — 14:30	Resource Presentation by Col. S.P. Wahi, Chairman of ONGC, India
15:00 — 17:15	Country Case Study by National Experts (ROC, Singapore, Japan)
17:15 — 17:30	Review by Resource Persons

18th Oct. (Tue)

Morning Session: [Mr. Jain]

09:00 — 10:30	Resource Presentation by Mr. Roger Antell, Director, British Telecom Overseas Division, U.K.
11:00 — 11:45	Country Case Study Presentation by National Experts (Malaysia)

Afternoon Session: [Dr. Seetoo]

13:00 — 14:30	Presentation by Dr. Umberto Del Canuto, economic Research Dept., IRI
15:00 — 17:15	Country Case Presentation by National Experts (India, ROK, Nepal)
17:15 — 17:30	Review by Resource Speakers

19th Oct. (Wed)

Morning Session: [Mrs. Asli]

09:00 — 10:30	Presentation by a Local Resource Speaker from Sri Lanka
11:00 — 11:45	Country Case Study Presentation by National Expert (Thailand)

Afternoon Session: [Dr. Sikorski]

    13:00 – 13:45   Country Paper Presentation by
                         National Experts (Sri Lanka)
    14:00 – 17:00   Selected Country Paper
                         Presentation by Non-Survey
                         Participants

20th Oct. (Thu)

    09:00 – 12:00
    13:00 – 15:00   Syndicate Session

21st Oct. (Fri)

    09:00 – 12:00   Industrial Visit
    14:00 – 15:30   Discussion and Concluding Session:
                         Chairman – Closing Ceremony

Asian Productivity Organization

4-14, AKASAKA 8-CHOME
MINATO-KU, TOKYO
107 JAPAN
TEL.: (03) 408-7221
TELEFAX: (03) 408-7220
CABLE: APOFFICE TOKYO
TELEX: APOFFICE J26477

(700.11.1989)